1998

THINKING ABOUT THE HOLOCAUST

Jewish Literature and Culture

Series Editor, Alvin H. Rosenfeld

Thinking about the Holocaust

After Half a Century

EDITED BY

ALVIN H. ROSENFELD

Indiana University Press

BLOOMINGTON AND INDIANAPOLIS

The paper used in this publication meets
the minimum requirements of American
National Standard for Information
Sciences—Permanence of Paper for Printed
Library Materials, ANSI Z39.48-1984.

Manufactured in the United States of
America

Library of Congress Cataloging-in-Publication Data

Thinking about the Holocaust : after half a
  century / edited by Alvin H. Rosenfeld.
      p.   cm. — (Jewish literature and
  culture)
    Includes bibliographical references and index.
    ISBN 0-253-33331-8 (cloth : alk. paper)
    ISBN 0-253-21137-9 (pbk. : alk. paper)
    1. Holocaust, Jewish (1939-1945)
  —Historiography. 2. Holocaust, Jewish
  (1939-1945), in literature. 3. Holocaust,
  Jewish (1939-1945)—Influence.
  I. Rosenfeld, Alvin H. (Alvin Hirsch), date. II. Series.
  D804.348.T55 1997
  940.53'18—dc21   97-3086

  1 2 3 4 5 02 01 00 99 98 97   r97

For Robert A. & Sandra S. Borns

CONTENTS

PART ONE

The Holocaust in Historical Writings, Literature, and Cinema

PART TWO

The Holocaust, the Zionist Movement, and the State of Israel

PART THREE

The Impact of the Holocaust on American Jewish Life and Thought

PART FOUR

European Jewry in the Postwar Period

ACKNOWLEDGMENTS

A book of this kind is a collaborative effort of many minds, chief among them those of the thirteen scholars whose work is represented here. My first thanks, therefore, go to my colleagues in this country and abroad who gathered on the Bloomington campus of Indiana University in May 1995 for several days of intense deliberation on World War II and the Nazi Holocaust of European Jewry. Carolyn Lipson-Walker and Patricia Ek were of invaluable assistance in helping to organize those meetings, and they have my sincere appreciation for all of their fine efforts then and since.

I am also grateful to my colleagues John Efron, Derek Penslar, and Dina Spechler for carefully reading the articles that resulted from those meetings and giving me the benefit of their critical judgments. I also wish to thank Randi Blank for her editorial assistance in the preparation of the manuscript.

It is a special pleasure to acknowledge the generous support of Robert and Sandra Borns, without whom it would not have been possible to launch the project whose final fruits are represented by the scholarly work collected here. The vision, dedication, and commitment of these two friends are invaluable to much of the most creative work carried on through the Jewish Studies Program at Indiana University, and I am happy to dedicate this book to them.

INTRODUCTION

YOU THINK THAT JUST BECAUSE IT'S HAPPENED,
THE PAST IS FINISHED AND UNCHANGEABLE?

—MILAN KUNDERA

Fifty years after the end of World War II, how do we look back upon and understand the nature and consequences of that catastrophic event? In particular, what kind of historical consciousness has developed over the past half century with respect to the Nazi destruction of European Jewry? These questions go to the heart of the issues that are explored by the contributors to *Thinking about the Holocaust: After Half a Century.* They are issues whose explication is as demanding and important as any that scholarship on the twentieth century faces right now, and while in many cases we may still be far from reaching conclusive answers, the questions have a significance all their own and need to be continually raised.

The subject is daunting, as anyone who seriously reflects upon it comes to see. For instance, the author of a recent book on American war fiction begins his chapter on World War II literature on the following note: "Fifty million people were killed in World War II. If that is the first sentence, what could possibly be the second?"[1] The sense of cognitive impasse that registers in this simple yet stunning question (not so much a question, really, as an expression of disbelief) is understandable given the devastation wrought by the war. And yet, for all of its immense and destructive horror, we have been able to assimilate the major lines of the history of World War II within the normative categories of Western historical consciousness. The real problems for understanding arise when we turn attention to that dimension of World War II that, more than any other, lingers on as a pressing but almost imponderable urgency—the Nazi "Final Solution of the Jewish Question." It is in attempting to face *this,* the unprecedented character of Hitler's genocidal war against the Jews, that one experiences the paralyzing sensation of having nowhere to go, of coming up against the limits of the sayable.

For all of its strangeness, this experience is, in fact, a familiar one. As far back as 1948, in looking at some pictures of the liberated Nazi camps, Lionel Trilling registered a sense of the uncanny that must have rung true for many of his generation and is hardly foreign to those who have come after: "The great psychological fact of our time which we all observe with baffled wonder and shame is that there is no possible way of responding to Belsen and Buchenwald. The activity of mind fails before the incommunicability of man's suffering."[2] Others have written similarly, both in the immediate postwar period and since. Indeed, a sense of cognitive arrest—as Trilling put it, "before what we now know the mind stops"—is an identifying characteristic of much of the most thoughtful writing about the Nazi crimes against the Jews.

This sense of of being dumbfounded by events and doomed to speechlessness, however, is by no means the only response. Far from it. In the five decades and more that have passed since the end of World War II, a large body of historical writing, testimonial literature, documentary and imaginative poetry, prose, and drama, essayistic reflection, and more has accumulated and continues to grow apace. Whatever the challenges to understanding and intelligent articulation—and they are many and formidable—the mind has not ceased to be drawn back to the period of Nazi terror and to produce a literature and other forms of representation that have taken us well beyond the stunned silence that Trilling and others seemed to predict would be the inevitable legacy of the Nazi crimes.

The contributors to the present volume have taken it as their task to examine this corpus as it has developed over the past half a century within a variety of national settings (Austria, France, Germany, Israel, the United States) and generic forms (history writing, film, literature, commemorative monuments and memorials, painting, theological reflection, etc.). Their aim throughout has been to assess the impact of the Holocaust on postwar consciousness as well as to analyze the impact of contemporary modes of scholarship on our understanding of the Holocaust itself. Attention to the interplay between what is being described and the disciplinary mode within which it is being interpreted varies from selection to selection, but the net result of these scholarly articles, as the reader will discover, is to put on display a variety of responses that the Holocaust has elicited and continues to elicit across the disciplines of scholarship. A great deal still needs to be discovered and said about the origins, character, and legacy of the Nazi crimes, but, as the contributions to this volume clearly indicate, thinking has not been arrested at the point of incommunicability. On the contrary, in ways that are both serious and trivial, clarifying and banal, the past fifty years have brought forth a broad and variegated body of responses to the Nazi war against the Jews. These responses and our reactions to them are some of the key markers of Western culture's historical and moral development in the postwar period; as such, they can help us understand the extent to which we are intellectually equipped to contend with the catastrophes that for millions of people have come to define the nature of living and dying in the twentieth century and that threaten to destroy the very notion of culture itself.

These deaths—not just the numbers of the dead but the manner of their dying—have produced a specialized nomenclature of their own. And by now "Holocaust," or "the Holocaust," has become accepted as the term of choice to designate the Nazi campaign of genocide against the Jews and is today in wide circulation. Indeed, the language of "Holocaust," in its manifold verbal and visual forms, has become part of common cultural parlance, even, one might say, of common cultural inheritance. In North America, Western Europe, Israel, and, increasingly, in some of the countries of Eastern Europe, public attention to the anti-Jewish crimes of the Nazi era has become pervasive. That has not always been the case, as some of the essays in this book show; nor, as others show, has a broader exposure to Holocaust words and images necessarily resulted in new levels of historical awareness or deeper ethical insights. To this day, Nazism fascinates, and no doubt will continue to fascinate, but the forms that this fascination assumes are various, and the cultural yield is decidedly a mixed one: There have been gains in knowledge, to be sure, but there has also been a good deal of vulgarization. We remain transfixed by a resonant terror associated with Hitler and the worst atrocities of his regime, but we are still far from understanding all that we feel the need to understand about the history that produced the Nazi horror or what it truly means to live in its aftermath. As the critic Geoffrey Hartman has accurately described our situation, we may be "after" Auschwitz, but we are certainly not "beyond" it.[3]

It is clear that this is not a past that will go away soon. It is also evident that its forms and meanings are far from fixed. Consequently, we cannot predict what shapes "the Holocaust" will assume fifty years from now. What we can know—and the present book is devoted to helping us attain such knowledge in clear and specific ways—is that over the past fifty years thinking about this subject has changed considerably. One finds little emphasis in recent scholarship, for instance, on "fascism" and "totalitarianism," categories that in the past prominently guided serious discussion of the Nazi era. Accompanying some notable conceptual shifts in our efforts to understand the nature and enormity of the Holocaust, memory itself has changed—deepening for some, dwindling into kitsch forms and even forms of denial for others. For all of its variable character, however, this is a history that not only persists but demands attention. Although we do not live in anything remotely like a traditional memory culture, the past— and *this* past in particular—is constantly being represented to us by a multiplicity of sources. Documentation is certainly not lacking, nor, after five decades, are innumerable attempts by historians, memoirists, novelists, poets, playwrights, filmmakers, religious thinkers, and others to probe the dreadful history that these documents convey. As the writer Cynthia Ozick recently put it, however, while "there is no paucity of the means to remember, there may be a paucity of the will to remember."[4] The editor and contributors to *Thinking about the Holocaust: After Half a Century* hope that readers will find in these pages a strengthening of both the means and the will to remember.

NOTES

1. John Limon, *Writing after War: American War Fiction from Realism to Postmodernism* (New York: Oxford University Press, 1994) 128.

2. Lionel Trilling, "Art and Fortune," in *The Liberal Imagination* (New York: Viking, 1950) 265.

3. Geoffrey Hartman, *The Longest Shadow: In the Aftermath of the Holocaust* (Bloomington: Indiana University Press, 1996) 11.

4. Cynthia Ozick, *Fame and Folly: Essays* (New York: Alfred A. Knopf, 1996) 200.

PART ONE

The Holocaust in Historical Writings, Literature, and Cinema

ONE

The Extermination of the European Jews in Historiography

Fifty Years Later

SAUL FRIEDLANDER

IN CONTRAST TO THE FORTIETH anniversary of the end of World War II, no "historians' debate," no *Historikerstreit* marked the semicentennial commemoration of the Allied victory over Nazi Germany in 1995.[1] This may be only a temporary respite. The debates about memory and the Nazi epoch, the Holocaust, and particularly about adequate forms of commemoration of the victims seem to be more intense than ever.[2]

In what follows I will concentrate on some aspects of the present state of the historiography of Nazism, particularly that of the Holocaust. I will attempt to show that notwithstanding the existence of clearly contending interpretations, a historiographical synthesis is possible and that despite all unresolved differences, we presently have at our disposal a body of knowledge and frameworks of interpretation sufficiently interrelated to serve as the basis for further significant historical elaboration. Yet, as I shall indicate at the end of this text, some aspects of the contending interpretations that are muted for now may carry the potential for major new historiographical confrontations.

Contending Interpretations

What distinguishes recent approaches, which have become part and parcel of present-day historiography of Nazism and of the "Final Solution," from the challenges of some fifteen years ago is the apparent totality of the reinterpretation. We are seemingly faced with a basic reconsideration of the historical categories used in our most general understanding of this aspect of German and European history. In order to describe the contending positions I shall successively refer to a "traditional" and to a "new" interpretation; these terms are used without any value connotation.

Let us consider the historical background of Nazism and of the aspects of it generally linked to the "Final Solution." The traditional position defines this historical background as the conjunction of a secular anti-Semitic tradition, of a crisis of German national identity, and of the growth of a radical *völkisch* ideology as part of this special historical course (*Sonderweg*).[3] The new interpretation—and here I am essentially following Detlev Peukert's work—defines the same historical background in terms of a general crisis of modernity, the rise of racial science (mainly eugenics), and a belief in a social engineering of sorts; all of this is considered to be an offshoot of the social crisis of the turn of the century and later of the German crisis of the 1920s and early 1930s.[4] Both positions describe the twenties as a period of reinforcement of these trends; but whereas the first (or traditional) position concentrates upon an exacerbation of *völkisch* views, and of anti-Semitism in particular, the new position puts the emphasis on the growth of "negative eugenics" as a result of the increasing disenchantment with the possibility of a positive social therapy and the impact of theories of biological selection fostered by the war.[5]

In terms of the characteristics of the Nazi system, the first position stresses its irrational dimension, its antimodernism, and the special role of Hitler's charismatic impact as a major source of the radicalization of the entire system.[6] The second position focuses on the inherent rationality of the system, its partaking of the most basic aspects of modernity and modernization, as well as on its essentially technocratic features.[7]

Finally, with regard to the "Final Solution" as such, the contrary positions regarding the historical background and the years most immediately preceding the onset of extermination are compounded by a further dichotomy. On the one hand, the traditional view points to anti-Semitism as the direct cause of the exterminations—stressing their counterrational, noninstrumental dimensions—as well as to the irrational aspect of Nazi policies.[8] More recent views, on the other hand, either underline a wider trend—that of an overall policy of extermination of which the "Final Solution" was merely a part—or they accentuate the instrumental rationality of the extermination of the Jews as planned by Nazi technocrats.[9] Obviously, the approach that I define as traditional has always stressed the modernity of the means used by the Nazis to achieve their antimodern and irrational aims. The new position, picking up a thread spun by Max Horkheimer and Theodor W. Adorno in their *Dialectic of Enlightenment,* does not concentrate on the unquestionable modernity of the means but does present the aims of Nazism as the expression of an all-pervasive modern instrumental rationality.[10]

Both approaches, but particularly the latter, have undergone some significant changes in recent years. For example, ongoing historical research again stresses the centrality of Hitler's charismatic impulse within the overall system, a centrality which now emphasizes constant interaction between the Führer and surrounding society.[11] Other recent studies have once more underlined the decisive role of ideology as the central framework for decisions. Most recent historical work in these domains also seems to represent the search for a coherent synthesis between positions which, although divergent in many respects, are not totally exclusive of each other.[12] In my own attempt to present such a synthesis, I will exclude some extreme or marginal interpretations while retaining the two main approaches referred to here as major leitmotifs.

The Elements of a Synthesis

Modernity and Myth

With regard to the general historical background of the Nazi phenomenon and its anti-Jewish impetus, we are apparently faced with the meeting of the logic, the goals, and the instruments of modernity as well as the representations and impulses of myth or, in other terms, with the aims of instrumental rationality *and* the phantasms of irrational thinking. But the two interpretive trends previously mentioned need not be considered as entirely separate positions; they are, in fact, dealing with two *contrary but coexisting aspects* of Nazism.

The dichotomy between modernity and myth does not imply that myth itself cannot be suffused with "scientific" thinking. The Nazi image of the Jew, for example, presented two different aspects of mythic thinking. The first aspect, steeped in *völkisch*-racist theories and imagery, focused on the danger inherent in the biological nature of the Jew, in the racial characteristics carried by Jewish blood. This mythical view partook nonetheless of the "modern" and "scientific" discourse of nineteenth-century racial thinking. The presence in the midst of the *Volk* of any group partaking of "racially foreign" (*artfremd*) blood was deemed mortally dangerous. Here, myth and scientific discourse were one. There was, however, another aspect of the myth that did not rely on scientific categories and which was directed solely at the Jews.

According to this second aspect, the Jews were not only dangerous as a result of their innate racial nature, they also represented an active and deadly force in history, one that was bent on world domination and possibly world destruction. This view transformed the struggle against the Jews into one of life or death, the outcome of which would decide the perdition or the salvation of Aryan humankind. As mentioned, racial anti-Semitism of the first kind was an integral part of the modern racist discourse; the other face of myth, one that could be defined as "redemptive anti-Semitism," had deeper historical roots.[13] In other words, contrary to Detlev Peukert's formulation, the "Jewish bacillus" *did not replace* the "Eternal Jew" under the impact of modern "scientific" racial thinking.[14] These were two separate aspects of the overall Nazi representation of the Jew.

Redemptive anti-Semitism, nurtured by the deep soil of Christian religious tradition, resurfaced in late nineteenth century Germany as one of several ideologies of salvation brought forth by the forebodings of decline and catastrophe which had seeped into the imagination of the epoch. Paul Rose has linked the new radical wave of anti-Judaism to the revolutionary movements of the nineteenth century.[15] In my view, the structure of these radical views exhibits all the religious, eschatological aspects of the millenarian anti-Judaism of the late Middle Ages so powerfully described by Norman Cohn.[16] In its new form, this representation of evil was not merely religious, not merely racial, not merely political. It was a stage-by-stage aggregation of these successive waves of anti-Jewish hatred, of the successive layers of a tale of Jewish conspiracy against Aryan humanity. The religious-eschatological core of redemptive anti-Semitism was reinforced at the turn of the century by the racial dimension.[17] Both the religious and the racial visions of redemption through the elimination of the Jew found their final and most extreme justification in the nationalist belief that the Jews had plotted Germany's defeat in the war and that Bolshevism was an instrument of world Jewry. In other words, redemptive anti-Semitism led from Christian millenarianism to the nineteenth-century ideologies of salvation and, by way of the Bayreuth circle and Houston Stewart Chamberlain's reworking of "the role of the Jew in history," to postrevolution and postwar frenzy, to the German adoption of *The Protocols of the Elders of Zion*, to Dietrich Eckart, and finally, in part simultaneously, to Adolf Hitler.[18] Let me restate this first point: with regard to the Nazi myth of the Jew, archaic religious themes and so-called modern scientific theories were interwoven in a multifaceted representation of the archenemy of the Volk.

I shall now indicate, though in a most schematic way, how the historiography of these two trends could converge in an integrated interpretation of the impact of the charismatic impulse on the dual system of party and state, of the internal dynamics of the system itself, of the relation between system and society at large and, finally, of the immediate background to the "Final Solution."

Charisma and Bureaucracy

I shall not return here to the historiographical debates about Hitler's centrality and role in the unfolding of Nazism and its policies. Suffice it to recall that the analytic social history of the seventies played down this centrality for theoretical reasons and also because in the fifties, the notion of Hitler's centrality had sometimes fulfilled an apologetic function. This being said, Hans Mommsen's projection of a "weak dictator" never took hold within historical thinking, and various conceptual compromises were applied in defining Hitler's role.[19]

In a recent and strange twist, the identification of Nazism and modernity, which usually dwells on the evolution of long-term factors and on social-structural characteristics, has presented Hitler as the ideologist and promoter of the Nazi modernizing drive. This unabashedly apologetic tendency, which systematically downplays Hitler's involvement in the policies of mass extermination, tentatively follows David Irving's trail, and is mainly represented by Rainer Zitelmann and his various coauthors; it now seems to have lost most of its credibility in mainstream historiography.[20] This extreme trend aside, there is nowadays a clear return to the notion of Hitler's decisive role, but in terms of a constant interaction among "Führer," system, and society. There is little doubt that with regard to the anti-Jewish ideology and policies of the movement and the regime, Hitler's impact was decisive, as was well perceived by Eberhard Jäckel and also by Martin Broszat.[21]

The Nazi leader understood how to adapt the fanatical course dictated by total belief to the ad hoc demands of political circumstances. In other words, in relation to the Jews, as in other domains, Hitler radicalized to the utmost the ultimate significance of the myth, but often, during the first years of the regime at least, he pragmatized its immediate corollaries. Hitler embodied the violence and the fanaticism of mythical thinking without losing awareness of the imperatives of modern bureaucratic policies.[22]

The "Führer's" mediation between the ideological-mythical impulse and the dynamics of the system does not by itself explain the inner workings of the system, that consummate expression of the modern bureaucratic state. Here, too, we must consider several different levels: the interaction between various agencies and political fiefdoms within the overall structure; the interaction between the dual system which included party and state and wider reaches of the population; and, finally, the evolution of that overall structure as such. The central question at each level remains that of the nature of the radicalizing process.

As far as the interaction between various agencies is concerned, the *Führerstaat* was indeed "organized chaos," as shown again in the recent work of Dieter Rebentisch.[23] But, in regard to anti-Jewish policies as in other domains, the guidelines expressing the Führer's will led to a constant effort to overcome the chaos by an ongoing alignment of the system. Agencies and individuals were, according to a 1934 formula adopted by Ian Kershaw, "working towards the Führer."[24] Party and state bureaucracies, as well as related economic units or cultural and religious institutions, coordinated their efforts as a consequence of their passive or active acceptance of the main goals of the regime. Coordination, as understood here, did not eliminate bitter infighting; but such infighting was caused by internal power struggles, never by questions as to the legitimacy or validity of the general goals defined by the Führer.

Thus, if "working towards the Führer" is taken as a fundamental impetus of the system, the bureaucratic apparatus involved in the persecution of the Jews was not an autonomous machinery that required only an initial triggering impetus, as suggested by Hilberg, nor merely a chaotic network of rival agencies whose very rivalry propelled the system to ever more radical measures, as outlined by Mommsen.[25] The apparatus, as chaotic as it was, was constantly aligning itself according to *ongoing* orders, notwithstanding delays and internal confrontations. It sometimes anticipated the concrete steps that could be surmised from the general guidelines; it faithfully ensured the most thorough fulfillment of its tasks in the face of all common obstacles. In other words, the standardized practices of a highly modern industrial-bureaucratic state were attuned on an ongoing basis to the ideological goals of the regime as expressed by its leader. When, on an issue of any significance, the order from above was not forthcoming, state and party agencies had to wait.[26]

Such an approach does not reject the inherent "logic" of bureaucratic organizations or the possibility of some sort of cumulative radicalization of the system as the result of the infighting between its constitutive units. Rather, this radicalizing impulse was both controlled and accelerated by Hitler's constant input, and the infighting itself never transgressed the limits of common cooperation within the framework set by Hitler's guidelines for the fulfillment of his goals. In other words, the radicalization process was fed by initiatives taken at various levels of the party hierarchy, but no major decision could be taken without Hitler's assent. More often than not the Führer himself initiated the new and more radical steps, and all agencies aligned themselves accordingly. Finally, initiatives stemming from party agencies often received Hitler's general agreement; their implementation, however, was left to the decisions of the initiators, as was the case, for example, with the genesis and the evolution of the "Final Solution" in the Warthegau.[27]

"Ordinary Men" or "Ordinary Germans"?

One of the crucial yet unclear aspects of this overall process of radicalization is the role played in it by German society at large. We know of the mobilizing impact of the "myth of the Führer," but we are less certain about the measure of penetration of Nazi ideology into various strata of the population and the support given to the goals of Nazism as a result of the widespread participation of the most diverse groups in the benefits of increased social mobility, economic development, and the general effects of modernization during the years 1933 to approximately 1941. Regarding the more extreme goals, particularly the treatment of the Jews—as long as this hostility remained in the open—Otto Dov Kulka and David Bankier have indicated a growing measure of acceptance and an even wider background of indifference and inertia.[28] These findings have to be qualified to a point, as far as the early phase of the regime is concerned, by a measure of noncooperation of those sectors of society that could derive some advantage from continuing relations with Jews (the peasantry, e.g.).[29] Over the years, this noncooperation was eliminated by the elimination of the Jewish presence as such. In general terms, the growing support for the regime, also as a result of the modernization process, had a numbing effect on any adverse reactions to the massive persecution of the Jews and other groups, even if Nazi ideological tenets did not penetrate the wider reaches of society to any depth.[30]

It is within this context that Christopher Browning's work on those "ordinary men" of "order police" unit 101—who from being ordinary policemen in Hamburg became murderers without being an ideologically committed group and without being coerced by threatening orders—raises a basic issue.[31] Were these policemen merely "ordinary men," or were they "ordinary Germans," the product of a German society totally suffused by centuries old "eliminationist" anti-Semitism, as claimed in Daniel Goldhagen's *Hitler's Willing Executioners?*[32] One could argue, in fact, that Browning's "ordinary men" were not entirely unideological after all, since as late as the 1960s they still used Nazi terminology in order to explain how they could recognize the Jews whom they chased and killed in the forests of eastern Poland. They were probably not even aware of the ideological tenets that they had internalized during the thirties. Moreover, serving in the police was not identical to being an ordinary person of the kind one found outside of the network of official agencies and organizations. As for Goldhagen's position, it would be tenable if it were reformulated in a much less extreme form, with the main emphasis on the impact of the political culture produced by the Third Reich and not on an age-old German anti-Semitic tradition. It is unlikely that, in its present uncompromising form, Goldhagen's interpretation will have much impact on current historiography, notwithstanding its extaordinary success with the wider public in a number of countries, particularly Germany.

On the Origins of the "Final Solution"

Even with regard to the general background of the "Final Solution," the approach which I defined as traditional and *some* of the new trends may converge. In the debate as it is circumscribed here, the issue is not that of the date of the order of total extermination but rather that of the historiographical interpretation of the genesis of that order, either as a direct result of Hitler's anti-Jewish fury carried to its ultimate pitch by the new circumstances of the Russian campaign, or as the result of a huge extension of the plan for the annihilation of groups "unworthy to live," a view closely linking the onset of the "Final Solution" to the ongoing murder of tens of thousands of German mental patients.[33] In the first instance we would be facing the ultimate consequence of the impact of the deadly myth of the Jewish world enemy, that is, the ultimate consequence of redemptive anti-Semitism; in the second case, one could argue for the convergence of a gruesome instrumental logic with some general tenets of racism.

The point of convergence lies in the fact that both redemptive anti-Semitism and the policies of racial extermination of groups "unworthy of living" were fostered at the same time by Hitler and by party and state agencies as entirely compatible though distinct elements of the overall worldview. There seems to be little doubt that redemptive anti-Semitism was Hitler's dominant obsession and that it inspired the guidelines that determined the fate of the

Jews and established the framework for their extermination. But, as we well know, general racial "cleansing" was also on Hitler's agenda and, thus, radical anti-Semites and diverse categories of more "scientifically" oriented race specialists readily cooperated by furthering their own murderous agendas.

At this point, however, brief mention of a seemingly related historiographical interpretation is necessary, namely, that propounded over a number of years by Götz Aly and his different coauthors. In most of his work, until his recent synthesis on the "Final Solution," Aly stressed the central importance in the planning of Nazi exterminations of a group of middle-ranking economists and demographers who, free of anti-Semitic or other racial, ideological motivations, were calculating the cost-benefit effect of the extermination of millions of human beings. In this view, the "Final Solution" was the first result of this program of economic rationality, although it was merely the beginning of a much wider extermination process.[34] I would have presented the extremely cogent arguments formulated by Graml, Browning, Diner, Herbert, and others against these propositions had Götz Aly himself not recently again changed the focus of his interpretation. In his interpretation of the "Final Solution" published in 1995, Aly now perceives the evolution of the increasingly murderous policies directed against the Jews to be the result of the massive transfers of populations that the Nazis started in Eastern Europe after the conquest of Poland.[35] Such explanations leave out too many elements of the overall scene (such as the inclusion of the Jews of Western Europe in the extermination process) to be in any way convincing.

The main issue in the "Historians' Debate" of 1986 was the comparability of Nazi exterminations with those of other totalitarian regimes. Yet the comparison as such was not the main element of the debate but rather its use in order to downplay the nature of Nazi crimes. The Soviet Union became a model of major import and, as Ernst Nolte argued, the Gulag was the original of which Auschwitz was only a copy. Nolte's general thesis about the relation between bolshevism and fascism (Nazism) has recently found the unexpected support of one of the most prestigious historians of the French Revolution, François Furet, though not without some major objections.[36] A new debate on significant historiographical issues may be appearing in regard to the relation between Nazism and bolshevism and the significance of "totalitarianism" as a generalized explanatory framework for Nazi exterminations and the "Final Solution."

NOTES

1. For the major points of contention in the *Historikerstreit,* see Charles S. Maier, *The Unmasterable Past: History, Holocaust, and German National Identity* (Cambridge: Harvard University Press, 1988); Richard Evans, *In Hitler's Shadow: West German Historians and the Attempt to Escape the Nazi Past* (London: I. B. Tauris, 1989); Peter Baldwin, ed., *Reworking the Past: Hitler, the Holocaust, and the Historians' Debate* (Boston: Beacon Press, 1990). See also Saul Friedlander, "West Germany and the Burden of the Past: The Ongoing Debate," *Jerusalem Quarterly* 42 (Spring 1987); Steven E. Aschheim, "History, Politics and National Memory: The German *Historikerstreit,*" *Survey of Jewish Affairs* (1988).

2. For a perceptive overview of the German scene (mainly of the Berlin scene), see Jane Kramer, "The Politics of Memory," *New Yorker* 14 August 1995.

3. For the growth and impact of the *völkisch* ideology, see, for example, George L. Mosse, *The Crisis of German Ideology: Intellectual Origins of the Third Reich* (New York: Universal Library, 1964); for the convergence of the various ideological trends in Nazism, see Karl Dietrich Bracher, *The German Dictatorship* (Harmondsworth: Penguin University Books, 1973); and for recent surveys of the *Sonderweg* debate, see Jurgen Kocka, "German History before Hitler: The Debate about the German *Sonderweg,*" *Journal of Contemporary History* 23 (1988); Steven E. Aschheim, "Nazism, Normalcy, and the German *Sonderweg,*" *Studies in Contemporary Jewry* 4 (1988).

4. Detlev J. K. Peukert, "The Origins of the Final Solution," in Thomas Childers and Jane Caplan, eds., *Reevaluating the Third Reich* (New York: Holmes & Meier, 1993).

5. Peukert, "Origins of the Final Solution."

6. Eberhard Jäckel, *Hitler in History* (Hanover, NH: University Press of New England, 1984).

7. As far as the most general aspects of this position are concerned, see, for example, from a conservative and apologetic angle, Michael Prinz and Rainer Zitelmann, eds., *National-Sozialismus und Modernisierung* (Darmstadt:

Wissenschaftliche Buchgesellschaft, 1991). For an entirely different approach, see Zygmunt Bauman, *Modernity and the Holocaust* (Ithaca, NY: Cornell University Press, 1989). A leftist-oriented interpretation finds its most systematic presentation in a number of publications by Götz Aly and different coauthors, as indicated below.

8. Each of the elements referred to in this sentence has been dealt with in an immense historiography. For an altogether nuanced and precise illustration of these approaches, see Philippe Burrin, *Hitler and the Jews: The Genesis of the Holocaust* (New York: Routledge, Chapman & Hall, 1994). For an interesting distinction between Nazi irrationalism and Nazi counter-rationality, see Dan Diner, "Historical Understanding and Counterrationality: The *Judenrat* as Epistemological Vantage," in Saul Friedlander, ed., *Probing the Limits of Representation: Nazism and the Final Solution* (Cambridge: Harvard University Press, 1993).

9. For the first aspect, see mainly Michael Burleigh and Wolfgang Wippermann, *The Racial State: Germany 1933–1945* (Cambridge: Cambridge University Press, 1991); for the second aspect, see Götz Aly and Karl-Heinz Roth, *Die Restlose Erfassung: Volkszählen, Identifizieren, Aussondern im Nationalsozialismus* (Berlin: Rotbuch Verlag, 1984); Götz Aly and Suzanne Heim, *Vordenker der Vernichtung: Auschwitz und die deutschen Pläne für eine neue europäische Ordnung* (Frankfurt/M.: S. Fischer Verlag, 1991); Götz Aly, *"Endlösung": Volksverschiebung und der Mord an den europäischen Juden* (Frankfurt/M.: S. Fischer Verlag, 1995).

10. Max Horkheimer and Theodor W. Adorno, *Dialectic of Enlightenment* (New York: Herder & Herder, 1972 [1947]); Bauman, *Modernity and the Holocaust*; Aly and Heim, *Vordenker der Vernichtung*; also Peukert, "The Origins of the Final Solution."

11. This is to be the guiding theme of Ian Kershaw's forthcoming Hitler biography.

12. See Ian Kershaw's indications in his *The Nazi Dictatorship: Problems and Perspectives of Interpretation* (London: E. Arnold, 1993); see also the synthesis of these various approaches in Burleigh and Wippermann, *Racial State*.

13. For a discussion of "redemptive anti-Semitism," see my *Nazi Germany and the Jews*, vol. 1, *The Years of Persecution, 1933–1939* (New York: Harper Collins, 1997).

14. Peukert, "Origins of the Final Solution."

15. Paul Lawrence Rose, *Revolutionary Anti-Semitism in Germany from Kant to Wagner* (Princeton: Princeton University Press, 1990); Paul Lawrence Rose, *Wagner, Race, and Revolution* (London: Faber, 1992).

16. Norman Cohn, *The Pursuit of the Millennium: Revolutionary Messianism in Medieval and Reformation Europe and Its Bearing on Modern Totalitarian Movements* (New York: Harper, 1961).

17. According to my interpretation it is in Bayreuth and within the "Bayreuth Circle" that these tendencies converged. For an excellent presentation of the ideological positions of the Bayreuth Circle, see Winfried Schüler, *Der Bayreuther Kreis von seiner Enstehung bis zum Ausgang der wilhelminischen Ära* (Münster: Aschendorff, 1971).

18. For each of these stages successively, see Geoffrey G. Field, *Evangelist of Race: The Germanic Vision of Houston Stewart Chamberlain* (New York: Columbia University Press, 1981); Norman Cohn, *Warrant for Genocide: The Myth of the Jewish World Conspiracy and the Protocols of the Elders of Zion* (London: Eyre & Spottiswoode, 1967); Ralph Max Engelman, "Dietrich Eckart and the Genesis of Nazism," Ph.D. diss. (Ann Arbor: University Microfilms, 1971).

19. For one of the most recent and nuanced restatements of Mommsen's position on Hitler's role, see Hans Mommsen, "Reflections on the Position of Hitler and Göring in the Third Reich," in Childers and Caplan, *Reevaluating the Third Reich*; also "Hitler's Position in the Nazi System," in Hans Mommsen, *From Weimar to Auschwitz* (Princeton: Princeton University Press, 1991).

20. Apart from Prinz and Zitelmann, *Nationalsozialismus und Modernisierung*, see also Rainer Zitelmann's short biography of Hitler, *Eine politische Biographie* (Göttingen: Muster-Schmidt, 1989), as well as Uwe Backes, Eckhard Jesse, and Rainer Zitelmann, eds., *Die Schatten der Vergangenheit: Impulse zur Historisierung des Nationalsozialismus* (Berlin: Propylaen, 1990).

21. Jäckel, *Hitler and History*; Martin Broszat, "Hitler and the Genesis of the 'Final Solution,'" *Yad Vashem Studies* 13 (1979).

22. On this dual role, see my *Nazi Germany and the Jews*.

23. Dieter Rebentisch, *Führerstaat und Verwaltung im Zweiten Weltkrieg* (Stuttgart: F. Steiner Verlag Wiesbaden, 1989).

24. Ian Kershaw, "'Working towards the Führer': Reflections on the Nature of Hitler's Dictatorship," *Contemporary European History* 2.2 (1993).

25. Raul Hilberg, *The Destruction of the European Jews* (Chicago: Quadrangle Books, 1961); the same basic position informs the updated German edition, *Die Vernichtung der europäischen Juden*, 3 vols., (Frankfurt/M.: Fischer Taschenbuch Verlag, 1990). As for Hans Mommsen's argument, see especially "the Realization of the Unthinkable: The 'Final Solution of the Jewish Question' in the Third Reich," in Mommsen, *From Weimar to Auschwitz*.

26. For a minor illustration of this general situation, see the description of the paralysis of all German state agencies in regard to the *Haavara* agreement until Hitler's much delayed decision in Avraham Barkai, "German Interests in the Haavara—Transfer Agreement 1933–1939," *Leo Baeck Institute Yearbook* 35 (London: Secker and Warburg, 1990).

27. Ian Kershaw, "Improvised Genocide? The Emergence of the 'Final

Solution' in the 'Warthegau,'" *Transactions of the Royal Historical Society,* ser. 6, vol. 2 (1992).

28. Otto Dov Kulka, "Public Opinion in Nazi Germany and the 'Jewish Question,'" *Jerusalem Quarterly* 25 (Fall 1982); David Bankier, *The Germans and the Final Solution: Public Opinion under Nazism* (Oxford: Basil Blackwell, 1992).

29. On this issue, see my *Nazi Germany and the Jews.*

30. On the nonpenetration of Nazi ideology in the wider strata of the population, see mainly Martin Broszat's studies of everyday life, as well as his theoretical arguments around the notions of ideology, modernization, and *Resistenz* in Martin Broszat, *Nach Hitler: Der schwierige Umgang mit unserer Geschichte* (Munich: Oldenbourg, 1987), and particularly in Martin Broszat, "A Plea for the Historicization of National Socialism," in Baldwin, *Reworking the Past.* For a debate on these issues, see my essay "Some Reflections on the Historicization of National Socialism," in Baldwin, *Reworking the Past,* as well as Martin Broszat and Saul Friedlander, "A Controversy about the Historicization of National Socialism," in Baldwin, *Reworking the Past.*

31. Christopher Browning, *Ordinary Men: Reserve Police Battalion 101 and the 'Final Solution' in Poland* (New York: HarperCollins, 1992).

32. Daniel Jonah Goldhagen, *Hitler's Willing Executioners: Ordinary Germans and the Holocaust* (New York: Alfred A. Knopf, 1996).

33. The traditional presentation of the origins of the "Final Solution" is most cogently presented in Christopher R. Browning's collection of essays, *The Path to Genocide: Essays on Launching the Final Solution* (Cambridge: Cambridge University Press, 1992). For the direct link between euthanasia and the 'Final Solution,' see Peukert, "The Origins of the Final Solution," as well as the series of articles and documents published by Götz Aly and Susanne Heim under the general title *Beiträge zur Nationalsozialistischer Gesundheit- und Sozialpolitik* (Berlin: Rotbuch, 1991). For the most recent statement of this argument, see Henry Friedlander, *The Origins of Nazi Genocide: From Euthanasia to the Final Solution* (Chapel Hill: University of North Carolina Press, 1995).

34. Götz Aly and Susanne Heim, *Vordenker der Vernichtung.* For the criticism directed against Aly and Heim's positions, see mainly the essays published in Wolfgang Schneider, ed., *'Vernichtungspolitik': Eine Debatte über den Zusammenhang von Sozialpolitik und Genozid im nationalsozialistischen Deutschland* (Hamburg: Junius, 1991).

35. Götz Aly, *"Endlösung": Volkerverschiebung und der Mord an den Europäischen Juden* (Frankfurt/M.: S. Fischer Verlag, 1995).

36. François Furet, *Le Passé d'une Illusion: Essai sur l'idée communiste au* xxe *siècle* (Paris: Robert Laffont; Calmann-Levy, 1995). See in particular pp. 195–96n.

TWO

Unrepresentable Identities

The Jew in Postwar European Literature

MICHAEL ANDRÉ BERNSTEIN

IGNORANCE ABOUT THOSE WHO HAVE DISAPPEARED
UNDERMINES THE REALITY OF THE WORLD.

—ZBIGNIEW HERBERT, "MR. COGITO ON
THE NEED FOR PRECISION"

I

INITIALLY, THE TALE MAY SEEM all too familiar. After so many similar narratives, this story's trajectory from the gradual, piecemeal reconstruction of a family's devastation at the hands of the Nazis to bitter disappointment at the postwar German legal system's callous refusal of justice, let alone of repentance, for that murderous brutality moves us less by its scrupulously assembled details than by our always freshly triggered incomprehension at the sheer repetition of such facts. This time, the first incarnation of the story is as a combination memoir, detective story, legal brief, and carefully restrained *cri de coeur* by journalist Peter Finkelgruen in his 1992 text, *Haus Deutschland: oder Die Geschichte eines ungesühnten*

Mordes.[1] Finkelgruen is a German Jew, and although this fact is the foundation of his story, it is *not* especially highlighted in the story's actual telling. Briefly summarized, the book recounts how a writer, returning "home" to Germany in the summer of 1988, accidentally comes across a small newspaper article describing the imminent deportation "home" from Italy of Anton Malloth, a former guard at the Theresienstadt concentration camp. The two notions of being-at-home become crucial, if antithetical, in the course of the book. For Peter Finkelgruen this small shred of newsprint opens a complex double movement, on the one hand into his family's past, and on the other into the tortuous legal bureaucracy of his country's present.

The Finkelgruens, we quickly notice, begin to seem as emblematic of modern German Jewish family history as, say, the Buddenbrooks do for an earlier and decidedly different social dispensation. Their fate is recorded as a kind of *Entbildungsroman,* similar to that endured by millions of others like—and, equally important, *unlike*—them, although each member of the family is always meticulously individualized in spite of the leveling assaults directed at them by a regime that insisted that all Jews were fundamentally identical in their difference from humanity. *Haus Deutschland* covers three generations, beginning with Martin Finkelgruen, the successful businessman and decorated World War I veteran who flees to Czechoslovakia after the NSDAP assumed power. From Karlsbad, Martin Finkelgruen moved on to Prague, and from there, unable to keep running faster than the advancing *Wehrmacht,* he was deported to Theresienstadt where, on 10 December 1942, he was beaten to death by Malloth in the infamous *kleine Festung.* His son Hans tried to reach the United States but ended up in Shanghai, where he died in the Jewish ghetto set up by the Japanese occupiers. Hans's and Esti's son, Peter Finkelgruen, did survive, however, and although he lived abroad for some time, he eventually returned to Cologne, where he became a successful writer.

Haus Deutschland is not just a family history, though as such, it is an engrossing addition to the genre—almost as compelling, if narrower in its historical compass and anecdotal richness, as works like the Austro-Jewish story, *Das waren die Klaars*.[2] But Finkelgruen's account is also a legal murder-mystery, or rather, since there is no mystery and no legal process, an indictment of a judicial refusal that stands for all the greater refusals of a system and its practitioners. Malloth had already been condemned to death in absentia by a Czech court for war crimes, but the German authorities ruled that there was "insufficient evidence" to substantiate the charges against him and declined either to proceed further on their own or to extradite him to the waiting Czech police.

With all the technical expertise of a professional reporter and the growing intensity of a man who feels it is his own intimate history that is at issue, Peter Finkelgruen proceeds to assemble ever more convincing proof of Malloth's crimes, including eyewitness evidence that the guard had brutally murdered Martin Finkelgruen in front of numerous other prisoners. But in spite of the new evidence so meticulously provided by Peter Finkelgruen, the state prosecutor continues to resist trying Malloth, and at the end, it is the murderer who goes free, now safely "at home" in *Haus Deutschland* while an inconvenient reminder of the past like Peter Finkelgruen has been made to realize he is clearly less than completely welcome there.

But my own story only begins here, just as Peter Finkelgruen's book itself soon takes on another form. Not long after the publication of *Haus Deutschland*, the Düsseldorfer Schauspielhaus commissioned the Israeli dramatist Yehoshua Sobol to write a play based on Finkelgruen's book. That play, called *Schöner Toni* (Handsome Tony), after one of Anton Malloth's nicknames, was translated from Hebrew into German by Finkelgruen himself, with the assistance of Gertrud Seehaus, and had a successful premier in Düsseldorf in June 1994.[3] Sobol follows the book quite closely, but with instinctive dramatic intelligence he narrows the focus to two settings: the Finkelgruens' temporary, and ultimately, vain Prague refuge, and the grandson's futile search for justice in present-day Germany. But Sobol also highlights the non-Jewish women who accompanied the Finkelgruen men, especially Martin's Czech lover, Anna, who survives Auschwitz, and Hans's wife, Esti (Ernestine), who comes back from Shanghai completely broken by her ordeal. The play also contains some comically grotesque dialogues of silence between the public prosecutor, eager to discover nothing, and a Malloth obviously eager to oblige him. But what interests me more is what the noted director, Bruno Klimek, added to the text of the play to heighten the audience's sympathy for the characters. When we first meet Anna, for example, she is singing a Yiddish song, a detail for which there is no warrant in either *Haus Deutschland* or the text of *Schöner Toni*; and at a number of points the Finkelgruens are endowed with a kind of touching *Yiddishkeit* that is bound to surprise anyone who is familiar either with the actual story, or indeed with the class of German Jews that *Haus Deutschland* so ably portrays. In fact, all of the Finkelgruens, three generations of them—Jews, Aryans, and what the Nuremberg decrees so carefully demarcated as "Mischlinge erster Klasse"—are shown in Peter Finkelgruen's narrative to be thoroughly and completely German, identical in mannerisms, tastes, customs, and habits to the people from whom they were ferociously excised. Why, then, does Bruno Klimek, a genuinely gifted theater director and a man of impeccably antifascist and anti-anti-Semitic convictions, add such details, almost as if they were a matter of course, to his production?

I am not concerned here with suggesting that Bruno Klimek's addition of a visual and audible "Jewish" dimension to his characters, the surplus, in a sense, of an immediately decipherable network of codes designed to make it easier to identify the category of "being a Jew," stems from anything but the most unimpeachable of motives.[4] But I do think that what it highlights is just how troubling the issue of Jewish identity, and more specifically, the *representation* of European Jewish identity, has become in the aftermath of the Shoah. Nor is it only a matter of exotic stereotypes that all Jews are somehow supposed to embody, although elements of this belief can easily be shown to haunt philo-Semitic, as well as anti-Semitic, imaginings. Rather, it is as though in order for Jews to be represented at all by postwar European artists, they first need

to be "made visible" by bringing out those features that endow
them with a distinct, but supposedly communal, identity. For a
dramatist, filmmaker, or novelist to show us a European Jew in
the years before the Shoah, that Jew is almost always figured
through a set of conventions as formulaic and unindividualized as
the stock epithets used by oral poets as mnemonic devices to help
listeners grasp instantly who is being talked about. Given the
history of European Jewry, especially between 1932 and 1945, it
is no doubt inevitable that the question of how—indeed, for most
German and Austrian artists it should really be phrased as *a question of whether*—it is possible to represent Jews at all except by
regarding them as "proto-victims of the Holocaust."

To put the matter as starkly and polemically as possible, I want
to suggest that while it is possible for German and Austrian writers to sympathize, and even to sympathize deeply, with the catastrophic suffering inflicted on the Jews, it is much harder for them
to imagine that many of those Jews could have been indistin-
guishable *in every way* from their neighbors, that they did not
even possess any definably Jewish "family resemblance" that
linked all those sentenced to extermination—except, of course,
for the absolute universality of that sentence itself. To set into
motion, and come very close to succeeding in, a plan to extermi-
nate an entire race no doubt touches some absolute limit of
representability in the sense of actually letting us feel with any
inwardness, or even fully comprehend intellectually what took
place.[5] But it can nonetheless be symbolically figured, difficult
though the idea may be to admit, so long as any member of the
group can be pictured as standing in for—which means in some
immediately graspable way being identical to—everyone else for
whom the same fate is intended. But if the victims are *not* distin-
guishable from the murderers until they have been made recognizable as victims by continuous ill-treatment, if their only all-
pervasive, shared characteristics are those imposed by their killers
(on the model of the Nazi decree ordering all male Jews to add
the name Israel and all females the name Sarah to their identification documents), then the original indistinguishability of killer

from killed, the extermination, in this sense, of like by like, becomes a slaughter of identity rather than the attempted eradication of difference; as such it poses a much more intractable problem of both artistic and theoretical representation. If the murdered were as diverse as the murderers, then the metonymy on which a supposedly illustrative drama, film, or novel about the Shoah depends would be radically subverted; and while it remains possible to create a representation of an individual's entrapment within the Nazi killing machinery, it is not possible to make that person's catastrophe representative of the whole except in its ultimate terminus in death.[6]

But even if it could be argued that hunger, fear, exhaustion, terror, and hopelessness did indeed give the Jews imprisoned in the ghettos, and even more, those in the concentration camps, a set of common traits, this is manifestly not true of European Jewry before the Nazi victories. Elsewhere I have suggested a way of understanding how the annihilation of European Jewry in the Shoah has led writers, by what I call "backshadowing," to project a series of judgments, almost invariably negative ones, onto the daily lives of a large and heterogeneous population that is portrayed primarily—and uniformly—as "victims-in-waiting" of the coming genocide.[7] "Backshadowing" in this sense is a way to endow the past with the coherence of a linear unfolding: it works by a kind of retroactive foreshadowing in which the shared knowledge of the outcome of a series of events by narrator and listener is used to judge the participants in those events *as though they too should have known what was to come.* Thus, our knowledge of the Shoah is used to condemn the "blindness" and "self-deception" of Austro-German Jewry for their unwillingness to save themselves from a doom that was supposedly clear to see. I was struck by how often writers, especially Jewish writers—whether social historians, biographers, or novelists—in looking back from a postwar perspective on the life of Austro-German Jewry, found it hard to register, without the acquired certainty of backshadowing and the tone of patronizing incredulity to which it gives rise, that there is nothing self-evidently deluded in the fact that it was the *wrong* prediction, the fatally *incorrect* interpretation of public events that won the intellectual and emotional allegiance of the vast majority of European Jews. Or, to phrase the issue still more polemically: the wrong prediction did not have to be wrong; and its failure was, if anything, a good deal less likely than the (retrospectively) more accurate, pessimistic prognosis. My point here, though, is not to repeat arguments made in more detail elsewhere but to suggest that in the hands of postwar German and Austrian imaginative writers, dramatists, and filmmakers, backshadowing often works in a radically different way from the model I proposed in *Foregone Conclusions*.

In the hands of a philo-Semitic writer who wants to trouble the too easy sleep of his countrymen's conscience, a combination of compassion for the victims—rather than a judgment upon their supposed self-deception—fuses with an aesthetic need to make the victims both recognizable and representative in order to create a standardized and frequently sentimentalized figure whenever they depict European Jews in the years before the Nazi state. From the first moment we encounter such figures, no matter what activities they seem to be engaged in or the vicissitudes of their moment-by-moment existence, both their clear difference from the non-Jewish characters and their highlighted vulnerability mobilize our affective identification solely through their role as "soon-to-become victims" of a waiting terror. Whether it is the thoroughly assimilated Finkelgruens suddenly manifesting touching snatches of *Yiddishkeit,* or the very few Jews appearing in the supposedly even-handed Austrian bestselling novel, *Puntigam, oder, Die Kunst des Vergessens*—who are scarcely individualized at all and are only referred to in such general terms as "your famous grain Jews"—the Jew as an individual whose traits are not instantly universalizable hardly figures at all.[8] There is, in other words, a curious symmetry in the way backshadowing has structured the figuring of prewar European Jewry by postwar Jewish writers versus by Austro-German ones. In both cases, the Jewish community tends to be portrayed as a single, homogeneous entity. But where a writer like Aharon Appelfeld will satirize the self-delusion of Jews who act, think, talk, and live like other Austrians, thereby only blinding themselves to their preordained fate, postwar Austrian and German writers, if they are able to incorporate Jews into their fictions at all, will tend to standardize them in the exactly opposite direction. They tend to make each of them a visible, audible, and even gestural incarnation of a universal Jewishness whose inevitable destruction the audience ought to mourn and even feel a certain uncomfortable guilt about—much, perhaps, as American liberal audiences are expected to deplore the brutal but, it is also clearly implied, inescapable annihilation of the Native American tribes— who are invariably portrayed in *bien pensant* films and novels as the repositories of all the wished-for virtues lacking in the social fabric of present-day America. More often, however, it is the absence of Jews in Austro-German works that is most noticeable, for example, the painfully labored—because so overemphatic—avoidance of Jewish characters in Edgar Reitz's *Heimat* or, just as interesting, the astonishing decision in staging Erwin Sylvanus's 1957 play, *Dr. Korczak und die Kinder,* to represent the murder of Korczak and his orphans as a kind of Pirandellian *Sei personaggi in cerca d'autore* performed by a contemporary troupe of German actors without a single Jew in the company.[9] It is as though in order for the audience to "take in" even the barest facts of the Shoah, it is first necessary to make certain that they are not, as it were, doubly embarrassed by also having to confront a living Jew on the stage. The *Publikumsbeschimpfung* is difficult enough for the audience to endure when it is addressed to them by a good German "dressed up" as a Jew; if it were articulated by a real Jew, enacting what was once done to his people by men and women intimately related to those purchasing tickets for that night's performance, then the collapsing of the distance between "spectacle" and history would become too troubling to put up with.

But I would also want to argue that when Jews do appear, the backshadowing of the genocide makes them in some fundamental way unrepresentable in their specificity and particularity. In a sense, the negative sublime of the Shoah itself, its ultimate unrepresentability, has been transferred wholesale to European Jewry almost independently of when or where they lived. For a contemporary German or Austrian writer to take on the voice of a Jew, to embody the consciousness of a Jew, even in a work set before the Nazi accession to power, means to have figured the Jew as he will be seen in the black light of genocide; but in so doing, the lure of sympathetic representation inevitably collapses into an erasure of the difference upon which real meaning depends. No wonder then that for most writers, it is easier simply to do without Jews altogether.[10]

In a way, of course, the Shoah gives only a guilt-induced "positive" turn to a centuries-long fundamental European difficulty in imagining Jews as particularized at all. At least since the eighteenth century, the Jew has been a phantasmic figure for the two most powerful political and theoretical movements of the Western imagination: the Enlightenment on the one hand, and its negative emanation, loosely definable as the anti-Enlightenment, on the other.

For the Enlightenment, with its cult of progress, faith in universals, and formally abstract notions of citizenship and community, Jewish particularism was inherently retrograde, tribal, and doomed to extinction by the rational process of human civilization itself. Jews could become full citizens precisely and only by ceasing in any significant sense to be or to think of themselves as Jews.[11] For anti-Enlightenment thinkers though, it was only the local, the communal, and the specific that gave one a real identity. The difficulty for Jews in this scheme of things, however, was that while they were undeniably "particular," they were also and always the incarnations of that most oxymoronic concept—a deracinated particularism. Jews were simply never "in the right place" or endowed with the "right roots" to be seen as individuals: they had local customs, but the wrong ones; their language as Jews (whether Yiddish or Hebrew) was not that of the province in which they lived; and their customs, though venerable enough, had no mystical connection to the soil or tribal practices of the region where they dwelt. For the Enlightenment, that is, Jews typified a distasteful particularism, no more representable than was Othello's handkerchief upon a neoclassic Parisian stage; to the anti-Enlightenment, Jews were the very *exemplum* of a sterile, vitiating universalism that lacked all of the vital, blood-and-soil nourished specificity that alone made a densely individualized representation imaginable.

II

I THINK THERE ARE AS MANY WAYS OF SURVIVING SURVIVAL AS THERE HAVE BEEN TO SURVIVE.

—PHILIP K., QUOTED IN LAWRENCE LANGER, *HOLOCAUST TESTIMONIES*

If there is one genre that by its very nature ought to resist these forms of radical reductionism, it is surely the survivor memoir. And indeed, it is striking how often such memoirs succeed in portraying the pre-Shoah life of the writer without relying upon the kind of historical backshadowing I have been tracing. It is their portrayal of the sheer variety of prewar European Jewish life, its irreducibility to any monological categories, whether of "self-deluding assimilationism" or "Yiddish communalism," that is ultimately almost as instructive in these memoirs as their testimony about the horrors of the ghettos and camps. Survivor memoirs show how deeply intertwined the problems of individuality and representation are, since every survivor's story is utterly unique and yet each also bears witness to a fate that, in one way or another, was endured by all those caught up in the Nazi death machinery. What these memoirs enact, in other words, is an exemplary lesson in how the identical end planned for all Jews by the Reich, and the similarity of suffering inflicted by the Nazis upon every Jew in their grasp, need not be projected backward to represent a standardized European Jewish life and consciousness *before* the Shoah.

But the very fact that we know the Shoah did take place, as well as our response to the individual experience of the survivor witness, has decisively changed the terms in which we theorize the limits of representation today. And in this domain, it is as senseless to seek any consensus among the survivor witnesses as it is to expect their picture of pre-Shoah European Jewry to share a set of common characteristics. Indeed, it is again the *differences* in the way survivors such as Primo Levi or Jean Améry understand their relationship to European culture that is so revelatory of the incoherence of the very category of "the survivor" as a group identity. For all the technical expertise and even occasional bravura of recent philosophical debates about representation and identity, I know of none that approach the depth and seriousness of that between Levi and Améry; and if I gesture only briefly toward a moment in their texts, it is because even in its most condensed formulation, the implications of their positions and the resonance they carry will be readily apparent.

Writing on the Shoah has repeatedly turned on the antithesis between identity as the set of individuating, singular traits that made up prewar Jewish existence, and identity as the obliteration of all difference, whether in the Reich's anti-Semitic legislation, in the camps themselves, or in the postwar representation of European Jewry. One side of the antithesis is unforgettably crystallized in Jean Améry's bitter formulation: "no bridge led from death in Auschwitz to *Death in Venice*."[12] The experience of torture and the death camp gave Hans Maier not merely a new name but a new identity, one that erased forever the consciousness that had constituted and understood itself through its relationship to culture. Representation itself had failed Améry. With nothing left to draw upon except his permanently reexperienced ordeal ("Anyone who has been tortured remains tortured"), Améry's post-Auschwitz identity remains—on principle—forever identical, not merely to what *he* became under torture, but to the new category of "the intellectual at Auschwitz."[13] Hence, of course, Améry's wounded reaction to Primo Levi, whom he called "The Forgiver"—not because Levi ever "forgave" the Nazis but because for Levi, personal identity remained profoundly linked to representation, not merely representation of one's biographical experiences, but the act of cultural imagining and representation itself. This, surely, is the central meaning of the much-analyzed chapter "Il Canto d'Ulisse" in *Se questo è un uomo*.[14] Directly contrary to Améry's dictum, culture, in the specific form of Dante's lines about Ulysses in *Inferno* XXVI, *did* help Levi maintain a sense of identity, and even of continuity with his pre-camp self. Levi's recollection of Dante's great canto did not provide a bridge *to* Auschwitz; instead, it gave him a momentary bridge *back* to a way of thinking about himself that enabled him to answer in the affirmative to the question: "Is this a man?" On his first day in Auschwitz, Levi tried to grab an icicle to quench his unendurable thirst, "but at once a large, heavy guard . . . brutally snatched it away." When Levi asked, "Warum?," he received his first real lesson in the infernal logic of the camp: "Hier ist kein Warum." But in Dante's represented Inferno, rather than in the Nazis' actual one, explanation for each divine judgment is the principal thematic concern of the various *canti*. More pertinently still, the *form* of the poem, the strict *terza rima* that determines the shape and sound of every single line, is what helps Levi both to recall many of the crucial verses from the Ulysses canto as well as to realize which ones he has forgotten. In the rhyme scheme itself, in other words, there is a clear, formal *warum* for every lexical decision. It is this principle of form-giving imagination, of representation as a human activity, on which identity in the individualizing, anti-camp, and ultimately, contra-Améry sense, is shown to depend. Paradoxically, to maintain an individual identity is to be committed to representation; and the need to draw on cultural models to confirm one's humanity is ultimately a gift, not a lack or a weakness in either oneself or one's heritage.[15]

III

THEY WILL EVEN TAKE AWAY OUR NAME: AND IF WE
WANT TO KEEP IT, WE WILL HAVE TO FIND IN OUR-
SELVES THE STRENGTH TO DO SO . . . SO THAT BE-
HIND THE NAME SOMETHING OF US, OF US AS WE
WERE, STILL REMAINS.

—PRIMO LEVI, *IF THIS IS A MAN*

There are many ways that a distrust of representation can work to nullify individual identity. In a curious sense, the insistence on the uncrossable abyss between Hans Maier's prewar Austrian culture and Jean Améry's forever frozen moment in the SS torture cellar at Breendonk is not unrelated to Bruno Klimek's addition of a sentimentalized *Yiddishkeit* to the characters in *Schöner Toni*. A radical severance from one's roots as an intellectual, assimilated *Austrian* Jew and a sentimentalizing of the German *Jew* as a type, are eerily consonant in their insistence on a single mode of existence, expressed through a fixed repertoire of tones that are supposedly common to all Jews whose lives were devastated by the Shoah. Klimek probably does not realize that he is removing any humanly specific identity by imposing traits on the Finkelgruens that make recognizable a *type,* not a person, nor that his reliance on the most readily available ethnic stereotypes only obscures the very identity to which he is trying to give form. But if Klimek falls *below* the challenge of representation, Améry, as his Nietzschean title makes clear, wants to find a new identity and discourse *outside* the canon of pre-Shoah figuration altogether.[16] It is as though the Nazis' creation of a system and a language beyond any humanity permanently obliges a Jew to bear witness in a mode beyond any form of cultural representation linked to a time before the Shoah. Lucidly, and with enormous, though ultimately, I think, self-damaging strictness, Améry denies any authenticity to the effort of sustaining, through individualized representation and cultural memory, a continuity of personal identity extending from a prewar self through the experience of the Shoah.

To the question of how a non-Jewish, Austrian or German writer today can represent Jews without either evading the issue of what was done to them or of letting that communal cataclysm obscure the individuality of the victims, I think Thomas Bernhard's 1988 play, *Heldenplatz,* provides one possible answer.[17] Set in a present-day Vienna that is saturated with the ugliest venom of its Nazi past, *Heldenplatz* is more than merely a brilliant dramatization of history as a "return of the repressed." Nor is it, as Viennese critics, both sympathetic and hostile, seem to have felt, only an indictment of Austria for its anti-Semitism, opportunism, and venality. The play is all these things; but for my purposes, it is also a work that shows it is possible to represent Jews as victims of Nazism without sentimentalizing or, for lack of a better term, "ghettoizing" their behavior and traits.[18] So deeply have the scars of Nazism marked the play's characters that the whole piece begins only after the suicide of its most important character, Professor Josef Schuster, who has killed himself out of fear and disgust at the lack of any real change in the mentality of his countrymen. Schuster, a refugee who returned from his Chair at Oxford to a position at the University of Vienna in a desperately miscarried attempt to rebuild something of his prewar life, has the futility of that hope brought home to him with a virulence that places Bernhard's perspective squarely on the side of the most pessimistic judgments in Jean Améry.[19] But even as the appalling memory of the *Anschluss* begins more and more to flood the consciousness of the surviving Schuster family members, and as the remembered cries of the delirious crowd hailing their *Führer* from the Heroes' Square of the book's title become increasingly audible to actors and audience alike, until the raucous noise fills the whole theater, the Schusters continue to be the idiosyncratic, difficult, and in many ways personally unsympathetic people they have always been. They remain, that is to say, themselves—true to their own particular identities, though their identity as Jews has made any kind of existence in Austria utterly impossible.[20] The contemporary Viennese Nazi

apologists and anti-Semites are incalculably worse, but the contempt Bernhard feels for them is secure enough of its grounds and
precise enough in its focus that it need not insist upon the sanctity
or uniformity of the victims. Nor is Bernhard concerned to
"charm" his audience's sympathy by giving to the Jews he represents a set of endearingly ethnic—and hence, to a Viennese audience, reassuringly distancing—touches.

In Aharon Appelfeld's novel *Badenheim 1939,* one of the characters, uncomfortable with his Jewishness—as indeed are most of
them—reacts to a question about his origins by insisting that he
is "an Austrian citizen of Jewish origin."[21] In Appelfeld this is
clearly an absurd reply, another sign of the suicidal self-delusions
of a community whose toadying assimilationism and lack of authenticity, as much as the loathing of their enemies, made their
annihilation a foregone conclusion. The phrase "an Austrian citizen of Jewish origin" is meant by Appelfeld to sound bathetic—an
index of the depth of the speaker's willful obtuseness about the
truth of his position. The words are risible because they have no
meaning; and all of *Badenheim 1939* is intended to show that the
words were *always* meaningless, and not only after the application
to Austria of the Nuremberg Decrees, which formally stripped
Austrian Jews of their civil rights and citizenship. If the words ever
had any meaning, the implicit argument runs, the Shoah could
never have happened. But if Appelfeld's vacationing Jews all resemble one another in their self-alienation and refusal to see what
is happening everywhere around them, Thomas Bernhard's Schuster family, if it were so inclined, could accurately say of itself that
by mannerism, education, and even, in a sense, by cultural arrogance, it is composed of "Austrian citizens of Jewish origin," without either an iota of self-hatred or the slightest delusion that the
truth of the statement would save them from the malice of the
country's anti-Semites. The Schusters—and their author—already
know that the fury breaking out around them has nothing to do
with their personal behavior or characteristics. Anti-Semitism, in
this play, is a problem of the anti-Semite, not of the Jews, and once
the implications of this perception *for artistic representation* are

fully understood, the issue of identity can at last be extricated from both the condescending judgments and the clichéd sentimental-izations of backshadowing.

In a letter to Alexander Pushkin, Beztuzhev-Marlinsky wrote: "We have a criticism, but no literature."[22] So far, I admit that what I have offered here is little more than a theory in search of a literature-to-come.[23] And if much of twentieth-century Jewish his-tory militates against the likelihood of that literature ever being written, it is also true that such an effort must be made if European Jewry is to be represented in all its vital complexity and not merely as an ineluctably foredoomed museum or, more often still, ceme-tery culture.

NOTES

1. *Haus Deutschland: oder Die Geschichte eines ungesühnten Mordes* (Berlin: Rowohlt Verlag, 1992).

2. George Clare, *Das waren die Klaars* (Berlin: Verlag Ullstein, 1980). Clare's own English version has a more melodramatic title, *Last Waltz in Vienna: The Destruction of a Family, 1842–1942* (London: Macmillan, 1981), but is otherwise identical to the German text.

3. I would like to thank the staff of the Düsseldorfer Schauspielhaus, and especially Barbara Reitz of the Dramaturgie-Sekretariat, for their unfailing and prompt help with all my inquiries. Her assistance included providing me with a copy of the theater's own working text of Sobol's play, which was invaluable for my research.

4. An analogous problem, for example, arises for American Jewish nov-elists when they wish to show that their characters, though fully integrated into society as a whole, are to be regarded as essentially and distinctively Jewish. A complex, but in principle, I think, definable set of conventions intended to accomplish precisely this kind of "rapid deciphering of ethnic-ity" can be found in the work of novelists such as Saul Bellow, Bernard Malamud, and Philip Roth. For a fine discussion of this question, see Ben-jamin Harshav, *Language in Time of Revolution* (Berkeley: University of Cal-ifornia Press, 1993). But the resonance and implications of such conventions are profoundly different depending on whether they are employed on a German stage or in an American novel; and this fact alone has interesting implications for the ways in which history and immediate context decisively influence how formally similar codes actually function.

5. Of the enormous literature on this question, I have found these studies to be the most helpful: Berel Lang, ed., *Writing and the Holocaust* (New York: Holmes & Meier, 1988); James E. Young, *Writing and Rewriting the Holocaust: Narrative and the Consequences of Interpretation* (Bloomington: Indiana University Press, 1988); and Saul Friedlander, ed., *Probing the Limits of Representation: Nazism and the "Final Solution"* (Cambridge: Harvard University Press, 1992).

6. There is an exact analogy to the leveling of individual differences among the Jewish victims of the Shoah in the equally clichéd representation of the Nazi murderers as identical to one another. The "stage Nazi," that is, corresponds perfectly to the stereotypical Jew. But homogenizing the murderers turns history into a kind of puppet show devoid of individual decisions, choice, and, ultimately, moral responsibility. The readiness to participate in the genocide was always personal and could never be predicted, let alone, in any way "justified" on the basis of monolithic categories such as "German obedience," "national character," or any of the other readily available—and all too often invoked—typologies.

7. Michael André Bernstein, *Foregone Conclusions: Against Apocalyptic History* (Berkeley: University of California Press, 1994).

8. Gerald Szyszkowitz, *Puntigam, oder, Die Kunst des Vergessens* (Vienna: Paul Zsolnay Verlag, 1988). An English translation by Adrian Del Caro, with a preface by Simon Wiesenthal, and an afterword by Jurgen Koppensteiner, is available as *Puntigam, or, The Art of Forgetting* (Riverside, Ca.: Ariadne Press, 1990). It is worth mentioning in this context that throughout *Puntigam*, there is a good deal of discussion of Nazi brutality, but almost exclusively as it was exercised upon local Austrian patriots, *not* on the Jews. We read, for example, that "one heard it whispered that in Mauthausen they had again hanged someone from *Sveti Jacob* [an anti-German irredentist movement] "but *nothing* about the Jews who were murdered at Mauthausen" (p. 187 of the English text).

9. Erwin Sylvanus, *Korczak und die Kinder* (Hamburg: Rowohlt Verlag, 1957). The play is available in an English translation by George E. Wellwarth in Michael Benedikt and George E. Wellwarth, eds., *Postwar German Theatre: An Anthology of Plays* (New York: E. P. Dutton, 1967). For a more detailed study of this issue, see Anat Feinberg, *Wiedergutmachung im Programm: Jüdisches Schicksal im deutschen Nachkriegsdrama* (Cologne: Prometh Verlag, 1988). I would like to thank Dr. Jeanette R. Malkin of The Hebrew University, Jerusalem, for recommending Anat Feinberg's book to me, as well as for suggesting the pertinence of the production of Dr. *Korczak und die Kinder* for my argument here.

10. For a lucid discussion of the way postwar German filmmakers have represented the Third Reich, see especially Anton Kaes, *From Hitler to*

Heimat: The Return of History as Film (Cambridge: Harvard University Press, 1989).

11. On the theological roots of the conflict between a supposed Jewish "particularism" versus a Christian "universalism," see Daniel Boyarin, *A Radical Jew: Paul and the Politics of Identity* (Berkeley: University of California Press, 1994).

12. Jean Améry, *At the Mind's Limits: Contemplations by a Survivor on Auschwitz and Its Realities*, trans. Sidney Rosenfeld and Stella P. Rosenfeld (Bloomington; Indiana University Press, 1980) 16.

13. Améry's dictum, for all its dark brilliance, needs to be carefully questioned, not merely recited; it may perhaps open, rather than shut off, a whole series of questions on the relationship between pre-Nazi culture and the Holocaust. Améry seems to indict Mann's novella, and metonymically culture as a whole, for the absence of such a bridge. But would not a culture that provided this "bridge" be much more alarming? What if, in other words, there were not a chasm, but rather, as has been argued by many people, a *continuity* between the Nazi atrocities and the highest forms of German creativity? In this context I am less concerned to explore that question than to ask in more general terms why we ought to require of any work of art that it serve as preparation for, or as a link to, the experience of torture and genocide? As I have argued elsewhere, to indict culture because of its helplessness either to prepare one for, or somehow actually to restrain, an event as lethal and cataclysmic as the Holocaust profoundly misunderstands the relationship between culture and lived experience: Very little about either cultural or individual human values can be learned from how they bear up in a situation *in extremis*, and the Shoah is not an appropriate, let alone a privileged, gauge for the authenticity or legitimacy of those values. See Michael André Bernstein, "Against Comfort," *Times Literary Supplement* 5 May 1995: 9–10.

14. Of the numerous critical pieces on the function of Dante in Levi's texts, the two I have found most useful are: Lynn M. Gunzberg, "Nuotando altrimenti che nel Serchio: Dante as vademecum for Primo Levi," in *Reason and Light: Essays on Primo Levi*, ed. Susan Tarrow (Western Societies Program, Occasional Paper No. 25, Center for International Studies, Cornell University, 1990), and Dalya M. Sachs, "The Language of Judgment: Primo Levi's *Se questo è un uomo*," *Modern Language Notes* 110.4 (September 1995); 755–84.

15. For a different reading of the Levi-Améry connection, see Alvin H. Rosenfeld, "Primo Levi: The Survivor as Victim," in James S. Pacy and Alan P. Wertheimer, eds., *Perspectives on the Holocaust: Essays in Honor of Raul Hilberg* (Boulder, CO: Westview Press, 1995) 123–44. By looking at Levi both from the vantage point of the still-unresolved issue of whether or not his

death was a suicide brought on by the memory of his time in Auschwitz, as well as from the undeniably darker and more pessimistic tones of his late texts such as *The Drowned and the Saved*, Rosenfeld questions the ultimate value of literary memory and representation as a means of self-preservation for Levi's consciousness.

16. The English translation of Améry's title, *Jenseits von Schuld und Sühne*, literally "Beyond guilt and repentance," as *At the Mind's Limits*, though it captures some of the sense of a boundary, completely loses the deliberate invocation of Nietzsche's *Jenseits von Gut und Böse* (Beyond good and evil).

17. My discussion of *Heldenplatz* here is obviously not intended to suggest that it is the only possible model, or that Bernhard is the only writer to have made an attempt to represent Jews without backshadowing or sentimentalization. My intent is not to provide an exhaustive inventory of texts and authors, but rather, to highlight a specific set of theoretical and practical dilemmas. And in this context, it is worth stressing that a list, no matter how complete, is not an argument, and an inventory, no matter how scrupulously assembled, is not an explanation, and all too often the compilation of discrete items of information is seen as a sufficient answer to problems of interpretation and understanding. See Thomas Bernhard, *Heldenplatz* (Frankfurt: Suhrkamp, 1988).

18. For a useful analysis of the play from a political and ideological perspective, see Eckhard Gropp, *Thomas Bernhards "Heldenplatz" als politisches Theater* (Bad Honnef: E. Keimer Verlag, 1994).

19. My linking of Bernhard's play with Améry's writings is far from arbitrary; not only are both writers centrally concerned with a crisis of representation and cultural memory/amnesia in postwar Austria, but it is also widely accepted that Bernhard's Professor Schuster was directly inspired by Améry himself.

20. For a fascinating instance of how determined many Austrian Jews were to preserve as much as possible of their pre-*Anschluss* cultural habits and attitudes, even in exile in Bolivia, see Leo Spitzer, "Andean Waltz," in Geoffrey Hartman, ed., *Holocaust Remembrance: The Shapes of Memory* (Cambridge: Basil Blackwell, 1994) 161–74.

21. Aharon Appelfeld, *Badenheim 1939*, trans. Dalya Bilu (Boston: David R. Godine, 1980) 21.

22. This is quoted in Michael Holquist, *Dostoevsky and the Novel* (Princeton: Princeton University Press, 1977) 12.

23. Recent American fiction offers an interesting parallel to some of the formal directions that the kind of representation I have been championing might explore. In 1982, Toni Morrison wrote a short story, "Recitatif," which narrates a lengthy relationship between two women, Twyla and Roberta. One of these women is black, the other white, and the whole story turns on racial

questions; indeed, issues of race form the core of every incident in "Recitatif" and largely define the dialogues between the women. Yet, we are never told who is white, and who black, and the ambiguity is strictly maintained throughout the narrative. Morrison herself has said that she intended the uncertainty to be unresolvable and deliberately removed any authorial cues that might decisively settle the question. "Recitatif" appears in *Confirmation: An Anthology of African American Women*, ed. Amiri and Amina Baraka (New York: Quill, 1983) 243–61. For a searching analysis of Morrison's story, see Elizabeth Abel, "Black Writing, White Reading: Race and the Politics of Feminist Interpretation," *Critical Inquiry* 19 (Spring 1993): 470–98. Although I think "Recitatif" is only partially successful, it is a fascinating attempt; and it would be interesting to imagine a similar story, but with a German and a Jew as its protagonists, endlessly discussing Christian-Jewish relations, the Shoah, postwar Jewish reactions to the reemergence of Germany as a world power, and so on, yet also leaving the reader unable to decide which speaker is which.

THREE

Holocaust Movies and the Politics of Collective Memory

ILAN AVISAR

THE PROMINENCE OF IMAGES in our culture, and the special place of photographic pictures in relation to the history of Nazism, render cinema a source of collective memory and a reincarnation of collective memory. The evident connection between film images and public memory is further reinforced by striking similarities between the process of filmic representation and the act of memory. In both, reality elements are inscribed as vivid pictures; stock narratives are repeated and recycled; and past experiences are translated into two-dimensional, arresting images and gripping dramatic actions. Richard Terdiman stated that "memory [is] pretty much coincident with representation—with the function by which symbols, or simulacra, or surrogates, come to stand for some absent referent."[1] In sum, both cinema and memory engage in framing the past, editing the past, and reifying the past in pictures and narratives.

In Holocaust films, as in all historical dramas, the presentation of the past is the meeting place of historical fact and the forces of politics and popular imagination, which exploit images and stories for a variety of psychological needs and political gains. The critical arena for the struggle of ideological forces over historical defi-

nitions is the national context, because collective memory, or public memory, is crucial for the formation of national identity. Pierre
Nora noted that modern people's need for identity has created a
"demand for history that has largely overflowed the circle of professional historians."[2] And John R. Gillis adds a significant obser-
vation, pointing out that "modern memory was born not just from
the sense of a break with the past, but from an intense awareness
of the conflicting representations of the past and the effort of each
group to make its version the basis of national identity."[3]

To be sure, each society is liable to confront the horrors of the
Holocaust with considerable difficulty. A truly honest reckoning
deals with the burden of guilt and the traces of a traumatic experience. Political interests provide another significant complication
in coping with the past from the perspective of the present; and in
fact, Holocaust films reflect the accommodation of historical memory to contemporary political needs. In addition to the political
context and the specific national experience during the war years,
each national cinema exhibits its own modes of representation as
they have evolved from cultural tradition. When images and narratives are shared by both memory and cinema, the mode of past
representation—in terms of stylistic decisions—is not simply a matter of aesthetic choice; it also implies a claim to being the proper
approach of representation and hence the appropriation of memory.

One generation after the end of the war, three major bodies of
film offer representations that have a stake in the universal memory
of the Holocaust. These are Claude Lanzmann's *Shoah*, the works
of the New German Cinema, and American movies, especially
Spielberg's highly popular *Schindler's List*. These works are distinguished by the fostering of national interests and ideology as definitive claims to the historical memory of the Holocaust. A comparative analysis will demonstrate disturbing political differences in the
current points of view of those associated with victims, bystanders,
or the perpetrators of the Holocaust. Additionally, since each work
is characterized by a distinct artistic approach toward history, conclusions will apply to the connection between the aesthetic visions
of naive realism, modernism, or postmodernism and the ideology

of representation in relation to the shaping of historical memory from a national perspective.

Claude Lanzmann's *Shoah* (1985) has been recognized as a documentary masterpiece by film critics and as a canonical text in Holocaust studies primarily because of its relentless presentation of the core of the horrors, its consistent attention to the details of the mechanism of genocide, and its formal strategies for bridging the chasm that separates the viewer from the unimaginable. The title of Lanzmann's work indicates an attempt to provide a definitive representation of the genocide and a statement on the adequate parameters of historical memory vis-à-vis the event.

The extraordinary length of the film defies the expectations of conventional narrative and places a demand on the viewer to appreciate the enormity of the historical trauma. (Lanzmann has objected to any attempts to show the film in a series of four or more parts, agreeing only to a division into a two-part showing.) Suggestion of the incomprehensibility of Auschwitz is a strategic goal of the film presentation, leading to a special concentration on physical evidence and concrete details whose unsettling content simultaneously conveys the haunting unreality of another planet and the stark factuality of the horrors.

But the principal channel to the past is ultimately memory. The avoidance of any archival footage further enhances the reliance on personal memories as the sources of knowledge, while the camera documents the ongoing dramatic processes of painful recollection. The anguished descriptions of eyewitnesses are coupled with a sense of a moral imperative to tell and record the recounted or recollected facts of the genocide. On the other hand, the stark evil of the perpetrators is conveyed not only by their deeds but also by the lack of any remorse on the part of those interviewed in the present. Indeed, the degree of memory may also reflect moral integrity, as evidenced in the case of the German woman from Chelmno, who remembers only that the number of Jews killed in her town of residence was "four something. Four hundred thousand, forty thousand."[4] Lanzmann relentlessly presses with questions for more details, at times appearing to disregard the pain of the survivor in order to obtain more information and full testimony. The scene that demonstrates this approach most powerfully is one with a former haircutter from Treblinka, Abraham Bomba; it is set in a barber shop in Tel Aviv. The climactic moment in this scene occurs when Bomba relates the story of a fellow inmate, who had to cut the hair of his wife and sister before they were killed in the gas chamber. As Bomba chokes and the camera follows him in his efforts to regain composure, viewers become sharply aware of the horrifying past and the drama of memory in the present. A haunting question emerges in these moments: whose story is it that the survivor is unable to complete? Is it Bomba's story applied by him to another person?[5] Can we assume that he identified with the other person because he experienced a similar horror, or is the shock so great because of his proximity to the atrocity and the fact that his memory compels him to relive the horror?

Lanzmann's approach features the drama of memory as a battle-ground of the haunting forces from the past against the present drives that seek to exorcise the trauma. The fixation on the con-temporary look of old sites of atrocity and the central focus on interviewees trying to come to terms with their own emotional development render the Holocaust as a past that is still present. The drama of memory exhibits the existential pain of the survi-vors, the immoral evasion of former perpetrators, and the lingering attitudes of anti-Semitism on the part of the complacent bystand-ers. The act of memory is also recognized as a complex cognitive mechanism and a special challenge for artistic representation. This idea is manifest in such textual strategies as the foregrounding of the filming process, the solemn pace created by long takes and long pauses that maintain a sense of wonder toward the incredible and incomprehensible atrocities, and the fact that the film does not bother to clarify or eliminate several minor inconsistencies in the survivors' accounts. Indeed, Lanzmann's *Shoah* conveys the painful recognition that memory is the only cognitive avenue to the unimaginable. As Saul Friedlander puts it: "Reality is there, in its starkness, but perceived through a filter: that of memory (dis-tance in time), that of spatial displacement, that of some sort of narrative margin which leaves the unsayable unsaid."[6]

Lanzmann's cinematic approach can be traced to a specific

French tradition of filmmaking that combines modernist sensitivities with recognition of the unique ontological truth of the photographic image (Bazin) or the reality effect of the movies (Christian Metz). This cinematic tradition has also accounted for the achievements of *Night and Fog* and *The Sorrow and the Pity*. Apart from the artistic tradition, French culture provided a specific context of public attitudes, fostered by *cinéma retro,* the new preoccupation with World War II in French cinema that followed upon *The Sorrow and the Pity*. Films such as *Lacombe Lucien, Mr. Klein, Les Violons du Bal,* and *The Last Metro* treated the incidence of collaboration in French history, but they were also characterized by their aesthetic stylization of the past. Lanzmann's insistence on hard-core factual details countered the glossy romanticization of the *retro* movies and was declared by Lanzmann himself to be an effort to stimulate viewers who had a sense of superficial saturation created by the *retro* movies.[7]

Yet Lanzmann's national perspective is not so much French as it is Jewish, sustained by the moral conviction that it is necessary to focus on the plights of the victims. One generation after the Holocaust, during a time when Israeli cinema has been limited in its resources and concerns—examining the Holocaust only in terms of its presence in contemporary Israeli reality[8]—and American Jewish filmmakers have subscribed to assimilationist attitudes that have deemphasized the Jewish catastrophe,[9] Claude Lanzmann has emerged as the voice of the people who were subject to genocide (hence the Hebrew title). He adopts the division into perpetrators, bystanders, and victims, addressing the connection between national traditions and historical roles. The national identity and cultural heritage of Germans, Poles, and Jews appears as a crucial factor in the unfolding of the historical tragedy. The magnitude of the destruction is clearly connected with the specific German qualities of discipline, industriousness, organization, and technological excellence. The genocidal drive is associated with Christian-based anti-Semitism, a position supported by the lucid explanation of the distinguished historian Raul Hilberg and the mindless stories of rural Poles. The bystanders reveal a large range of responses, from despicable anti-Semitism, to puzzling indifference, to pathetic or heroic efforts to aid the victims. The survivors project human dignity and the sense of mystery that always accompanies their unimaginable and incomprehensible experiences. The national identity of the victims is portrayed with reference to the identification of many of them with their own European society, yet their unique status of victimhood is not compromised by facile analogies with other Nazi victims. Lanzmann avoids any "ideological conclusions" or specific readings of the history of the Jewish people in the modern era in light of the attempted genocide. His political views can be found in two other films he made before and after *Shoah: Pourquoi Israel* (1973) and *Zahal* (1995).

The impact of Lanzmann's film ultimately derives from his commitment to the basic, incontrovertible truths of the Holocaust. *Shoah* is based on the modernist conviction that art can create insightful understandings of reality, without compromising reality's complexity and its challenge to expression or representation. This belief has remained untarnished by the trendy postmodernist critique that ideological positions actually inform any and all forms of discourse. A contrasting view of historical truth and its presence in cultural texts dominated the works of the New German Cinema.

The New German Cinema is the term used for the remarkable works of filmmakers from West Germany in the seventies and early eighties; most of the filmmakers were born during World War II. For critics and film historians, the spate of serious movies by Fassbinder, Herzog, Wenders, Schlöndorff, Kluge, Syberberg, and others formed a distinct wave of art films and a novel treatment of topics related to the Nazi era. As Thomas Elsaesser put it: "The New German Cinema would have become a 'national' cinema, by helping to undertake the 'mourning labor' for Germany."[10]

Ironically, the view that the works of the young German filmmakers represented a significant cultural chapter was held primarily by people outside Germany itself. The enthusiastic reception by foreign critics reflected a conscious desire on the part of the filmmakers to appeal to international audiences and a less conscious concern with the image of modern Germany abroad.[11] These interests resulted in formal experimentations that challenged dominant forms of cinematic expression and in a defiance of dominant views of history that were understood to be part of an American ideological hegemony. Wim Wenders's well-known reference to the colonization of the German subconscious by American culture claims that the Germans are the apparent victims in the ideological conflict between the powerful West and other weak cultures. The specific national context of this position, especially in relation to Germany's Nazi past, is implied in Wenders's following statement: "I speak for all those who, in the past years, after a period of emptiness, have begun again to produce images and sounds in a country that has an infinite mistrust of images and sounds that speak of itself, a country that for this reason has for thirty years greedily soaked up all foreign images."[12]

The showing of Gerald Green's NBC teledrama *Holocaust* (1978) in Germany was a dramatic illustration of the impact of foreign images on German culture. Indeed, Green's film practically introduced the Holocaust into the public discourse of modern Germany. Edgar Reitz's *Heimat* (1984) was specifically designed to counter the images introduced into German homes by the American series, and the resulting epic drastically minimizes the period of the Third Reich as a negligible element in German historical consciousness. Most critics writing about *Heimat* have exposed the film's consistent avoidance of the harsh implications of the Third Reich for Reitz's characters and his vision of modern Germany. However, glossing over the disturbing aspects of German history was no embarrassment for Reitz but was an expression of a defiant triumphalism of German aggrandizement, presented in the fashionable discourse of anticolonialism. This agenda is evident in the nearly megalomaniacal scope of *Die Zweite Heimat* (1994) and in its vainglorious central theme—the special invention of the young Germans in film technology that superseded all other efforts in the field. *Die Zweite Heimat,* a mammoth production of 25 hours, 32 minutes, subtitled "Chronicle of a Generation in 13 Films," systematically ignores the Nazi era except for some passing comments on the similarities between the war in Vietnam and World War II. The only figure who is associated with the Third Reich, a former high-ranking officer in the SS, is the father of the Jewish woman in the story, Esther. When she mentions that her mother was gassed, her lover, the scriptwriter, declares: "Your story is now my story." He refers to his finished script, called "Deutsche Angst," which he plans to be filmed in Wannsee (the notorious site near Berlin, where Heidrich organized a meeting of Third Reich officials to discuss the details of the Final Solution).

Indeed, the works of the New German Cinema often combine national self-pity with an unabashed national assertiveness. The fourth part of Syberberg's *Hitler: A Film From Germany* (1978) is entitled "We Children of Hell." The title of Syberberg's impressive spectacle implies a strain of national arrogance, related to the filmmaker's belief that he masters the "art of the twentieth century: film" with "the subject of the twentieth century: Hitler."[13] From this assumed privileged cultural position, Syberberg's film refers to "Auschwitz as a battlefield of the race wars. It is a question of finding the cosmically guilty." In a similar vein, the interest in Nazism as a grand spectacle and the confusion of moral categories in connection with the atrocities of World War II are the premises of Fassbinder's *Lili Marleen* (1981). This film pays homage to a popular song from the Nazi era that moved, in the words of the film, "six million German soldiers." These soldiers appear as wretched victims in dirty ditches and bloody battlefields, given some rare moments of joyful grace when they hear the sentimental song on the radio. The drama focuses on the singer, who tries to assert her performing ambitions in Hitler's regime. However, the theme of the artist in a fascist regime and the combination of emotional melodrama with Brechtian alienation devices—which attracted the most critical attention—appear in a narrative that profoundly confuses the historical roles of victims and victimizers, to the extent that the German protagonist is a helpless woman, victimized by both SS threats and the manipulations of wealthy Jews living safely in Switzerland.

The most extreme example of self-pity and historical revisionism is Helga Sanders-Brahms's quasi-autobiographical *Germany, Pale Mother* (1980), which focuses on the ordeals of a mother and her daughter during the war years. This film indulges in scenes of victimization and suffering, concentrating on the predicament of German characters in the context of the Holocaust. Thus the notorious pictures of the *Einsatzgruppen* killings are staged in order to present the anguish of the German soldier—the killer in the scene! Camps surrounded by barbed wire and watchtowers appear as the site of dead Germans; the bombing of German cities is presented in extensive newsreel footage; and the narrative features the plights of German citizens as refugees of the massive bombardments. The conclusion of the film shows the removal of the mother's teeth as an act of a painful national catharsis (an insipid echo of the exploitation of dead victims' teeth by the Nazis in the camps). Curiously, the film outraged German critics, who objected to the relentless and shameless appropriation of images associated with the Nazi crimes to promote self-pity.[14] On the other hand, the focus on two female characters allowed for sympathetic feminist interpretations, which stressed the predicament of women during the war. The effective treatment of feminist concerns must have influenced Annette Insdorf, whose favorable discussion of the film ends with the statement: "Mother Germany—even purged of Nazis—continues to suffer quietly."[15]

The efforts to revise historical memory one generation after the fall of the Third Reich are manifested in numerous texts of the New German Cinema. Beyond the expected universalization and relativization of the Nazi crimes, the chief strategies of revisionism include the presentation of Germans as victims of the Nazis, the promotion of a notable degree of self-pity, which stresses German suffering during the war years ("one country defeated by the rest of the world"), or cultivating the myth of German resistance, which, in numerous works, exhibits this phenomenon in ways that were disproportionate to the pathetically few cases of the actual German opposition to Hitler (*The White Rose, The Plot to Kill Hitler, The Last Five Days*). Other films exhibit remorseless nationalist triumphalism in the glorious past of Germany's cultural tradition

(Herzog's neo-expressionist *Nosferatu* and his treatment of Faustian tyrants in *Aguirre* and *Fitzcarraldo*), or an unabashed celebration of war heroics, as in the highly popular *Das Boot*. In sum, under the guise of "coming to grips with the past," the films of the New German Cinema have engaged in the subversion of historical memory, seeking to expunge the traces of a shameful past. Furthermore, it is not only that these films were a far cry from the Mitscherlichs' call for "mourning labor" in German society, they actually sought to inscribe new memories outside the borders of Germany.

Ironically, most critics found in the works of the New German Cinema a new awareness of the past, which was taken as a significant change from the previous years of willful amnesia. The sophisticated aesthetics of Fassbinder and Syberberg, the stated challenges to Hollywood hegemony by Reitz and Wenders, and the treatment of some trendy and politically correct themes by such feminist filmmakers as Sanders-Brahms have also contributed to sympathetic reviews. Many films contained odd elements whose fresh contradiction of the history of the Holocaust was taken as a challenge inspiring critical interpretation rather than as a provocation deserving swift condemnation. The postmodernist deconstruction of categories of truth, the encouragement of multiple readings and alternative narratives, and the new agendas that elevate issues of gender, postcolonialism, and class have conditioned a critical reception that has ignored or downplayed the manifestations of historical revisionism and their function in fostering the return of a repressed German nationalism, purged of the disturbing implications of Nazism.[16] The most eloquent summary of this critical attitude can be found in Anton Kaes's appraisal of the New German Cinema: "The historical films of the New German Cinema are meant to preserve the past and to jog the memory of the living. They provide alternative ways of seeing with their self-reflexive narrative and visual style, their autobiographical tone and experimental form, and, above all, their refusal for the most part to recycle endlessly repeated and clichéd images of the Third Reich."[17]

Thus, whereas Lanzmann demonstrates commitment to the incontrovertible truths of the Holocaust and a quasi-religious fixation on the unsettling facts of history, the German filmmakers offer a sophisticated subversion by defining historical facts as elements of memory that can be subject to "jogging," or "recycled" images that can be revitalized through revisionist renditions. However, Anton Kaes's favorable judgment is rooted in the consideration of the distorting or numbing effects associated with images of the Third Reich in popular culture. Popular culture usually means "Hollywood," whose most recent contribution to the discourse of the Holocaust is Spielberg's *Schindler's List* (1993).

Unlike the drastic changes in the treatment of Nazism and the Holocaust in German cinema (a move from ignorance and repression to excessive and problematic obsession), American cinema displays a consistent pattern of continuous interest, albeit one that has been limited to a few remarkable productions each decade that have had a considerable social impact upon their release. Hollywood usually treats the Holocaust as a central event of modern history and as a compelling human experience. The combination of impassioned moral interest and a limited involvement with the actual historical events has generated a specifically American presentation of the Holocaust, a presentation that frames the event as a grand drama, depiction of which is cathartic and inspiring, instructive and full of pathos. At the same time, American films resort to naturalistic reenactments of the past. Creating a replica of the Franks' secret annex, filming in former concentration camps, or utilizing documentary records and reliable memoirs for narrative details displays a drive for truthful realism. The filmmakers' statements about fidelity to truth and the need for public enlightenment are rooted in a premodernist, realistic vision, characterized by gratification through spectacle and a predilection for moralizing. The manifestly didactic approach displays a disturbing triumphalist appropriation rather than humility—intellectual, artistic, or political—in the face of the extreme horrors; for the limits of comprehension and representation have not been acknowledged in these films.

Steven Spielberg's *Schindler's List* is essentially a product of the traditional patterns that characterize the treatment of the Holo-

caust in American cinema and of the specific national mood at
the historical moment of its production. Like all other American
films on the Holocaust, it was based on a published book. But
in this case, Spielberg took a fairly marginal text on the history
of the Holocaust and tried to elevate it to central canonical status.
This process began with the hype surrounding the decision of
the Hollywood wunderkind to deal with the subject of the Holocaust, continued with reports on the attempt to film in Auschwitz, and culminated with the highly publicized screenings
with distinguished celebrities and heads of state. The Oscar
awards capped the massive campaign that promoted the film as
a special cultural event.

Spielberg declared that his film is a document. He displayed his
claim for documentary truth value by filming much of the movie
in Kraków, the area where most of the historical events took place;
he had even planned to shoot scenes in Auschwitz but yielded to
opposition from Jewish organizations. He also chose to use black-
and-white photography and many shots made by hand-held cameras, supposedly in order to recreate the authentic conditions of
reality and its historical representations.

Despite Spielberg's claim to documentary truth, *Schindler's List*
ought to be recognized as a film that marshals the familiar codes
of Hollywood cinema. At an early stage of its critical reception,
the debate revolved around the trivializing effects of Hollywood
slickness, on the one hand, and the proven impact of reaching
many viewers with the uneasy subject of the Shoah, on the other.
In this respect, *Schindler's List* has made a limited contribution to
the critical discourse on the problematics of Holocaust representation. The issues involved in compromising the harsh realities of
the concentration camp universe in popular formulae of commer-
cial cinema—including the consideration of public enlightenment
and emotionally effective communication—also informed the debates over *The Diary of Anne Frank* and the TV series *Holocaust*.

In the case of Spielberg's film, however, the real issues eclipse the
arguments of popularization or trivialization. In the first place,
while the TV series clearly manifested its generic premises and

inherent shortcomings in the treatment of a vast and complex historical material, *Schindler's List* usurped the privileged position of a serious art work that makes a definitive statement about the Holocaust (the length of the film, 185 minutes, conveys a sense of its generic identity as a historical epic, and of a demanding viewing experience mandated by the weight of the subject). Hence, it is essential to expose the film's manipulative techniques and its attempt to mold historical memory according to its own ideological convictions. Indeed, the black-and-white photography signifies this drive, for public memory of the past has been inscribed in black and white by still pictures, newsreel footage, and wartime movies. Framing the main story in color pictures from the present is another act that delegates the narrated events to the realm of memory. The question then is what kind of memory Spielberg attempts to shape—how he frames the past, edits the past, and re-presents the past, and to what ends. Ultimately, I submit, Spielberg's film is a document of ideological positions that foster particular national values and celebrate certain fundamental values associated with "the American way" in reference to the Holocaust.

Spielberg does not display any of the restraints, hesitations, or stammers that have become characteristic of authentic artistic responses to the Holocaust.[18] Rather, he delves into the heart of darkness with complete confidence that his mastery of film art—in the style of Hollywood norms and conventions—can produce adequate images of the unimaginable. The result is a finely crafted film. The actors give memorable performances, with the leading parts of Schindler and Goeth allowing Liam Neeson and Ralph Fiennes to climb quickly to film stardom. The black-and-white photography accounts for an amazing visual texture, much different than the grainy pictures of the wartime high-speed film stock. The "superb cinematography uses shadows like prosody—illuminates with shadows."[19] The rich visual texture, the ornamental touch of the red dress of the little victim, and John Williams's accompanying music (with Itzhak Perlman doing violin solos) are conspicuous formal elements that stylize reality. In addition to an exciting narrative, rich scenery, fascinating acting, beautiful photography, and emotional music, the editing has been praised for its "intensity and line, never breathless, always fast."[20] (The effects of editing are especially apparent in the selection scene, and during the intercutting of the Jewish wedding, Oskar's party, and Goeth's victimization of Helen Hirsch.) The contradiction between this exquisite stylization and the real horrors is probably best seen in the oxymoronic comments of critics who referred to the "artlessness" of the camera and the construction of the "greatest sequences of chaos and mass terror ever filmed."[21]

The character of the camp commandant, Goeth, is arguably the most vicious villain ever to appear on the screen. He kills people for breakfast, practices shooting on living targets, murders twenty-five prisoners in cold blood after an attempted escape, and exercises the terror of a menacing maniac in his treatment of a helpless maid (Helen Hirsch). And yet, for Moshe Beisky, a survivor who became a supreme justice in Israel, the film character doesn't even come close to the cruelty, sadism, and brutality of the real Goeth![22] Making a character more evil may arguably go beyond the limits of artistic expression. The most authentic and effective Holocaust accounts are those that make reference to this impossibility in their text, either by admitting the inherent shortcomings of their discourse or by offering a device that transcends art and calls on the evidence of the real sources. In the case of Spielberg's film, the impression is that Goeth, and for that matter all other details of the horror, offer a truthful recreation of history. The film conveys no sense that the events were much worse, indeed unrepresentable, unimaginable, incomprehensible.

A significant dimension of Spielberg's politics is evident in the cautious and calculated approach toward character presentation in terms of its implications for national generalization. The treatment of the perpetrators displays "political sensitivity," pitting a malicious German (Goeth) against a good German (Schindler). This balance naturally diminishes the crucial role of the Germans in the Final Solution and may explain the favorable reviews of the film in Germany.[23] The Polish bystanders have only a limited presence—the one moment in which a young woman shouts with passion in support of the deportation of the Jews is a passing and timid reminder of what was, in fact, a far more pervasive anti-Semitism. Significantly, while trying to offer a narrative that encompasses most of the important stages of the genocide (ghetto, deportations, labor camps, selections, death camps), Spielberg refrains from any references to anti-Semitism as a driving force for the Holocaust or to Germany as the state apparatus that organized the destruction.

The Jewish characters have elicited a range of responses from viewers. Some have felt that the business dealings in the church performed by the young Jews, Stern's cold calculations, and Helen Hirsch's status as an object of desire are narrative elements or character traits that echo offensive Jewish stereotypes. Others have felt uncomfortable with the presentation of the Jews as passive victims.[24] The final sequence showing the Jewish survivors' respect for the man who saved them contains the visible cross on his grave, displaying a humble respect for the Christian symbol that may have the effect of suppressing the Christian contribution to anti-Semitism and the attempted genocide. It is the Christian "savior" who ends up in the highest moral position—even accusing himself of not doing more for the Jews. (His superior moral status is disturbingly manifest in relation to other Jews, especially in the relationship with Stern. It is the Jewish manager who instructs the reluctant Schindler about giving birthday gifts to SS officials; and in another scene, Schindler stresses to a worried Stern that he doesn't want his factory to produce anything for the Nazis' military effort—otherwise he would be "very unhappy.") On the other hand, the film's ending stresses the connection between the Holocaust and the Jewish state. Linking the Holocaust and the State of Israel is, however, problematic from the perspective of the historical chain of events.[25] But in Spielberg's film, ideology combines with aesthetic effect as the linkage creates a narrative closure that deemphasizes the horrors of the genocide in the context of Jewish revival and independence in Israel.

The film that has quickly come to be regarded by many as the most effective presentation of the attempted genocide of the Jews is about a person who saved Jews. In the fifties and sixties, Hollywood films made a considerable contribution to the distinction between "Germans" and "Nazis," serving Western interests in the Cold War and expressing faith in a denazified postwar Germany. In the nineties, *Schindler's List* makes a contribution to a cultural mood that shifts attention from murderers and victims to rescuers and survivors. It is impossible and immoral to ignore or underestimate the former inmates of the camps or those who risked their lives trying to save Jews; still, the message implied in Spielberg's project is one that focuses on exhilarating qualities of courage and moral strength at the expense of an excruciating recognition of the genocidal evil that prevailed over a period of years and at the cost of millions of lives.

This point is symptomatic of the thrust of *Schindler's List,* which is faithful to the American optimism that is celebrated in so many popular Hollywood movies. Of the Holocaust films, *The Diary of Anne Frank* ends with birds in the sky; *The Young Lions* ends with the union of Noah and Hope; and *Sophie's Choice* ends with the protagonist's reference to the beginning of a new day.[26] Beyond the issue of happy endings, American optimism also defines a belief in the power of the individual to determine his/her fate. But trust in human will, resourcefulness, courage, tenacity, and other positive virtues that enable man to struggle with difficult ordeals was, in fact, usually defeated by the infernal conditions of Nazi terror. Almost all survivors stress the elements of luck or coincidence that saved them from the genocidal assault. Yet *Schindler's List* falls into the trap of well-made Hollywood narratives, which provide motivation, choices, and closures based on character actions. All the principal Jewish characters that elicit our emotional involvement manage to survive, with many demonstrating their ability to actively avert their death.[27] The film includes scenes that show the scope of mass destruction, but the narrative gratifications associated with the stories of the saved victims deflect the paralyzing horror involved in the realization of the deaths of the millions who perished. Thus, when Schindler rescues Stern from the train to the death camp, the camera focuses in medium shots on the tense march to freedom of the two men, while the thousands of other victims sent to the gas chambers fade out in the background.

Spielberg's treatment of Schindler is a clear-cut morality tale. The conflict of good and evil is expressed in the rivalry between Schindler and Goeth. Observing the numerous Jewish prisoners from the top of the commandant's veranda, or looking at the ghetto liquidation from a hill, both Goeth and Schindler are like the devil and God, competing over the fate of human beings in the lower spheres. (This competition takes on another form in the card game for the life of Helen Hirsch.) The moral conception of Schindler is dominated by the narrative development of the main character. The beginning of the film shows the protagonist's questionable traits—he is a member of the Nazi party, a womanizer, drinker, and gambler. But as the movie progresses, his negative side disappears and he ends up looking like a saint. The film ignores the possibility that the intimate relations that Schindler had with the Nazis could not have left him totally untainted. It also ignores the evidence of many that he was possibly always motivated by power and prestige. I wish to emphasize that what is at stake is not an assessment of Schindler's character, whose historical act dwarfs all other character weaknesses. However, the man of enigmas and contradictions appears as a clear case of moral transformation—a Rick-like character (*Casablanca*), who starts out as an egocentric manipulator and ends up as a war hero. Schindler is the individual entrepreneur, a hedonistic businessman turned moral agent and savior—a possible parallel to Spielberg's career in making this movie.

Some have noted that it was no coincidence that Spielberg identified with a character named Oskar. Spielberg's motives in making the film are not simply the stuff of vicious gossip, and his conduct during and after the production is quite instructive. The preview in *Time* magazine describes Spielberg as being energized by the filming and quotes him as saying that he "felt liberated for the first time in my career"; he saw the project as a "dream" he was realizing. The article mentions that the ghosts of the past also made the experience special.[28] A *Newsweek* article quotes Spielberg as explaining how he overcame the depressing subject: "So every

single day was like waking up and going to hell, really. There were
no jokes on the set. No funny outtakes to show at the wrap party.
Twice in the production I called Robin Williams just to say, Robin,
I haven't laughed in seven weeks. Help me here. And Robin would
do 20 minutes on the telephone."[29] And finally, the Oscar awards
ceremony provided another display of colossal insensitivity when
Spielberg mentioned the "six million who can't be watching this
among the two billion that are watching this telecast tonight."

Indeed, in the case of *Schindler's List*, the Holocaust became
almost a backdrop for the story of the wunderkind. Note the
following statements, from two of the most enthusiastic reviews
of the film in America. Terrence Rafferty, in the *New Yorker*, compared Spielberg's act to Schindler's! "What Spielberg achieves in
Schindler's List is nearly as miraculous. (His accomplishment is less
inspiring than his hero's only because art is less important than
life.)"[30] And Janet Maslin's review in the *New York Times* stipulates:
"Rising brilliantly to the challenge of this material and displaying
an electrifying creative intelligence, Mr. Spielberg has made sure
that neither he nor the Holocaust will ever be thought of in the
same way again."[31] This confusion of cinema with life, of Hollywood representation with the realities of the Holocaust, was also
evident in recent programs on Oskar Schindler at the Holocaust
museum in Washington and in the ceremonial naming of a street
in Tel Aviv, which gave prominent attention to Spielberg's presence.
American cinema displays a national appropriation of Holocaust
representation, implying that America and its popular films have
a decisive role as the guardians of the memory of the Holocaust
and its universal lessons. Accompanying this claim is a rejection
of the devastating inhumanity associated with the Holocaust and
an abstraction of the evil into general terms that drain out the
specific Jewish predicament in history and exploit the tragedy for
reasons of facile moralization. The accommodation of the Holocaust to American culture and values is also accompanied by the
celebration of the American way of life, the empowerment of its
entertainment industry with supposedly serious moral obligations,
and the cult of its prominent personalities as special historical

figures. The popularity of *Schindler's List* is above all a testimony to the successful dissemination of American values according to Hollywood's norms and worldview. Schindler is the benevolent businessman who musters his moral faculties to perform heroic acts in the service of humanity; Spielberg is the wunderkind of popular hits who matures into a filmmaker tackling serious issues; the Holocaust was a terrible event of shocking atrocities, but ultimately good triumphed over evil, and the survivors and their families are proof of the defeat of the Nazi plan of genocide. These are reassuring attitudes, to be sure, but they are not compatible with the unambiguous existence of the evil of the architects of genocide and of the fate of the millions who perished.

Any discourse of the Holocaust is liable to reduce its subject by accommodating the unprecedented enormities to existing states of cognition, representation, and ideological competition. The previous modes of universalization of the Holocaust, the notion of man's inhumanity to man or crimes against humanity that characterized the postwar years, and the sixties' existentialist reflections on survival that intermixed different moral categories—all these have been replaced by new modes of evasion and deception, which today exploit the Holocaust for a variety of national concerns and the concerns of group identity politics. This is also a time in which cinema has assumed a cultural function that screens the past and produces images whose implied claim as a representation of reality actually serves for memory construction and identity formation. And yet any truly creative and responsible treatment of the Holocaust cannot ignore the demanding moral aspects of the subject, which call for a consideration of the enormity of the event and the limits of its representation, together with the imperative to remember, the necessary caution involved in what to remember, and the humility required when approaching how to remember.

NOTES

1. Richard Terdiman, *Present Past: Modernity and the Memory Crisis* (Ithaca: Cornell University Press, 1993) 8.

2. Pierre Nora, "Between Memory and History: Les lieux de mémoire," *Representations* 26 (Spring 1989): 7–25.

3. John R. Gillis, ed., *Commemorations: The Politics of National Identity* (Princeton: Princeton University Press, 1994), introduction, "Memory and Identity: The History of a Relationship".

4. Claude Lanzmann, *Shoah: An Oral History of the Holocaust* (New York: Pantheon Books, 1985) 94.

5. In *Writing and Rewriting the Holocaust: Narrative and the Consequences of Interpretation* (Bloomington: Indiana University Press, 1988), James E. Young mentions Bomba's story as referring to "his own family" (168).

6. Saul Friedlander, ed., *Probing the Limits of Representation: Nazism and the "Final Solution"* (Cambridge: Harvard University Press, 1992) introduction, 17.

7. See André P. Colombat, *The Holocaust in French Film* (Metuchen, NJ: Scarecrow Press, 1993) introduction, xv.

8. For the treatment of the Holocaust in Israeli cinema, see Ilan Avisar, "Personal Fears and National Nightmares," in Efraim Sicher, ed., *Breaking Crystal: Writing and Memory after Auschwitz* (Urbana: University of Illinois Press, forthcoming).

9. On the Holocaust in American films, see Ilan Avisar, *Screening the Holocaust: Cinema's Images of the Unimaginable* (Bloomington: Indiana University Press, 1988) ch. 4.

10. Thomas Elsaesser, *New German Cinema* (New Brunswick, NJ: Rutgers University Press, 1989) 243.

11. For an analysis of critics' views of the New German Cinema, see Ilan Avisar, "The New German Cinema and the Politics of Critical Reception," *Tel Aviver Jahrbuch für deutsche Geschichte* (1994): 401–11.

12. Quoted in John Sandford, *The New German Cinema* (Totowa, NJ: Barnes & Noble; London: O. Wolff, 1980) 154–55.

13. See Susan Sontag's preface to the published script of Hans Jürgen Syberberg, *Hitler: A Film from Germany* (New York: Farrar Straus & Giroux, 1982) ix.

14. Anton Kaes, *From Hitler to Heimat: The Return of History as Film* (Cambridge: Harvard University Press, 1989) 149 note 6.

15. Annette Insdorf, *Indelible Shadows: Film and the Holocaust* (Cambridge: Cambridge University Press, 1989) 188.

16. A German-inspired universalization of the Holocaust is an act of disburdening of national responsibility. The successful transposition of guilt is evident in Paul Monaco's conclusion for his chapter on German cinema, "The Bitburg Syndrome," in his book *Ribbons in Time: Movies and Society since 1945* (Bloomington: Indiana University Press, 1987) 91–92: "we acknowledge that Nazism must be viewed as a human and not a German

failure. Are the Nazis not still for us today the 'shadow' of our own inner failings, historical references to the darker side of human action and cunning, both loathed and strangely admired simultaneously?"

17. Kaes, *From Hitler to Heimat* 197.

18. See Alvin H. Rosenfeld, *A Double Dying: Reflections on Holocaust Literature* (Bloomington: Indiana University Press, 1980), esp. ch. 4, "Poetics of Expiration."

19. Stanley Kaufmann, *New Republic* 13 December 1993: 30.

20. Ibid. 30.

21. *Time* 18 December 1993.

22. In an interview with Israeli TV, channel 2, 28 February, 1994.

23. See "Good Germans," *New York Times* 12 June 1994.

24. See Frank Rich, "Extras in the Shadows," *New York Times* 2 January 1994. For Art Spiegelman, "these Jews are slightly gentrified versions of Julius Streicher's *Der Sturmer* caricatures"; see *Village Voice* 29 March 1994. The same view was expressed by Philip Gourevitch in his "A Dissent on *Schindler's List*," *Commentary* February 1994. The numerous responses to Gourevitch's article, published in the June issue of *Commentary,* reflect the multiple reactions to the presentation of Jewish characters in Spielberg's film.

25. See Yehuda Bauer, *A History of the Holocaust* (New York: Franklin Watts, 1982) 348: "The State of Israel did not result from the Holocaust; in fact, had the Holocaust not occurred, it is more than likely that Israel may have arisen quicker, and better and more securely."

26. On the imposition of optimistic visions on the concentration camp universe, see Alvin H. Rosenfeld, "The Americanization of the Holocaust," in this volume; Lawrence Langer, "The Americanization of the Holocaust on Stage and Screen," in *From Hester Street to Hollywood: The Jewish-American Stage and Screen,* ed. Sarah Blacher Cohen (Bloomington: Indiana University Press, 1983) 213–30.

27. One notable exception is the scene in which the Nazi gun miraculously fails to shoot, and the rabbi's life is saved. In a program on Israeli television (see note 17 above), former inmates of the camp referred to it as a popular yet fictional story. In the film, Spielberg made it a highly effective moment of tension and relief. Notwithstanding the apocryphal status of the incident, the connection between a rabbi and a miraculous act has cultural roots that offset the notion of pure luck even in this context.

28. *Time* 18 December 1993.

29. *Newsweek* 20 December 1993.

30. Terrence Rafferty, "A Man of Transactions," *New Yorker* 20 (December 1993): 132.

31. Janet Maslin, review of *Schindler's List* in the *New York Times* 13 December 1993.

PART TWO

The Holocaust, the Zionist Movement, and the State of Israel

FOUR

The Holocaust and World War II as Elements of the Yishuv Psyche until 1948

ANITA SHAPIRA

WE ARE STILL INCAPABLE—DUE TO THE SHORT DIS-
TANCE IN TIME BETWEEN US AND THOSE EVENTS—TO
UNDERSTAND THE SIGNIFICANCE OF ALL THAT WE
HAVE LIVED THROUGH AND SUFFERED, TO GRASP IT IN
THE INTELLECTUAL AND SCIENTIFIC SENSE. IT IS SIM-
PLY IMPOSSIBLE YET TO DRAW CONCLUSIONS. WHEN
IN 1492 CAME THE GREAT HOLOCAUST OF THE EXPUL-
SION OF THE JEWS FROM SPAIN, AND SUDDENLY ONE
OF THE GREATEST, MOST THRIVING, MOST SPIRITU-
ALLY IMPORTANT BRANCHES OF THE JEWISH TREE OF
LIFE WAS CUT OFF, THE PEOPLE NEEDED A LONG TIME
UNTIL THEY WERE ABLE TO REACH A TRUE ASSESS-
MENT, TO CONFRONT WHAT HAD HAPPENED TO THEM.
IN THE 16TH CENTURY IT TOOK TWO GENERATIONS
UNTIL THEY REACHED THIS STAGE, AND CERTAINLY IT
WILL NOT BE MUCH DIFFERENT THIS TIME. I DON'T
BELIEVE THAT WE, THE GENERATION OF THOSE WHO
LIVED THROUGH THIS EXPERIENCE . . . THAT WE ARE
ALREADY CAPABLE TODAY OF DRAWING CONCLUSIONS.
BUT THE IMPACT OF ALL THAT HAS HAPPENED, THE
IMAGE OF THE HOLOCAUST, OF NECESSITY WILL DOM-
INATE THE AGENDA OF JEWISH STUDIES. . . .

—GERSHOM SCHOLEM[1]

THE YEARS 1945-1949 WERE pivotal in the formation of Israeli identity. These were the years in which the struggle for the establishment of a Jewish state in Palestine reached its dramatic climax. From the blood and fire and columns of smoke of the War of Independence the State of Israel was born, and the circumstances of its birth determined the central myths of its society, myths that remained in force for an entire generation. The legendary figure of the *tsabar,* the archetype of the new Israeli, became the primary symbol of the Israeli identity that was then being born. The War of Independence was, however, preceded by two other crucial events—the Holocaust and World War II. What role did these two events play in the formation of this early Israeli identity?

The further we move from the events of World War II, the larger the Holocaust looms in our consciousness. Now, fifty years after the war, it seems that the Holocaust—an event that most of the histories of the war do not mention, or mention only in passing— has become the most salient symbol of that war. The Holocaust's massive presence in the cultural discourse of our times has implications for the study of the past. We tend to examine the past in line with our current sensitivities, and we therefore expect to find that the Holocaust had the same presence in the past as it does today.

The question of the relationship between the Holocaust and the war in the consciousness of the 1940s presents difficult methodological problems. The first is the question of the credibility of our sources. Can rhetoric about the Holocaust, manifested in the speeches of functionaries, politicians, members of youth movements, rabbis, writers, and others, serve as proof that the Holocaust had made an impression on people's consciousness, that it had penetrated into the private and public psyche, that it had been internalized by the people of the Yishuv and of the newborn state? The question is a difficult one: the rhetoric in question consists of slogans and clichés that were de rigueur at public events. The rhythmic repetitions, with greater attention given to the sound of the words than to their content, give these speeches the character of prayers or eulogies. The reference to the Holocaust in these contexts was, in fact, a display of typical Jewish mourning customs, which seek the community's participation in bereavement as in celebration. The clichéd quotes and tired slogans and descriptions—"If I forget thee, O Diaspora," "Do not be silent," "For these I mourn," "*hurban*" (meaning "calamity," with associations of the destruction of the Temple)—were taken from accepted paradigms of Jewish mourning after mass disasters dating back to the Middle Ages. That people used such rhetoric tells us nothing about whether they had or had not internalized the Holocaust. It can only illuminate the accepted cultural norms of the time.

A good example of the difficulty inherent in such judgments may be found in the debate over Ben-Gurion's attitude toward the Holocaust.[2] Can his prewar expressions of fear for the fate of European Jewry, or his impassioned statements about the Holocaust during and after the war, be taken as evidence of his attitude? The first type of statement was common among members of the Mapai leadership and represented what has been termed "catastrophic Zionism," the doctrine that the Jewish people could not survive in Europe. The second type of statement was familiar Holocaust rhetoric. On the basis of this sort of evidence, it is difficult to assess what Ben-Gurion's attitude really was.

But if rhetoric cannot prove or disprove that people internalized the Holocaust, can the absence of any discussion about the Holocaust be evidence that it was considered unimportant, and that it was *not* internalized? Can evidence of Ben-Gurion's alleged silence after his visit to the Displaced Persons (DP) camps in Germany be taken as an indication that he did not care about what he saw? Does the absence of reactions from Israel Galili and Yigal Allon after their visit to Auschwitz in 1946 indicate that the Yishuv's young people were apathetic about the subject?[3] The answer to this question is not a simple one, because there are people who give vent to feelings of pain and anger, and there are others who keep their emotions inside. The question of what conclusions we may draw from silence is a key one in the study of the Holocaust's impact. At the current stage of historical and psychological research I would hesitate to reach any conclusions.

How then may the impact of the Holocaust be measured? What do we expect to find in the documents? What will indicate a high or low level of sensitivity? Since public speaking about the subject seems to have been no more than a reflection of contemporary cultural norms, we have to search for indirect indications of the Holocaust's impact. Did people talk about it in private conversations? Did they mention it in letters, or diaries? We can learn about the Holocaust's place in public discourse by examining the plays presented in the theaters at the time, the books people read, the educational programs that were formulated, the way people treated the survivors. Did the Yishuv agenda change in the wake of the Holocaust? Did people search their souls, change their worldviews, revise their beliefs and opinions?

When we wish to compare the impact of the war to that of the Holocaust, our task is even more complicated. After all, in many instances the two experiences were interwoven. Could anyone relate to the war in isolation from the Holocaust? In the consciousness of the people of that time, was not the war identified with the Holocaust and the Holocaust with the war? Nevertheless, I think that the same indirect method outlined above may enable us to locate differences in attitudes to the war and to the Holocaust and illuminate their respective effects in shaping the public's consciousness. This consciousness was, of course, central in shaping the Israeli identity that appeared in the wake of the War of Independence.

An in-depth analysis of attitudes to the war and the Holocaust requires a comprehensive survey of the period press, as well as of collections of letters, diaries, memoirs, memorial books for those who fell in the War of Independence, the literature that came out of that war, and the literary works that appeared between 1943 and 1952. All this, of course, in addition to the scholarly literature.

I have examined only a part of this material. I have gone over some of the period press, memorial books, and diaries.[4] I have also surveyed *Alon Hapalmach,* a newsletter put out by the Palmach; *The Palmach Book;* minutes from writers' conventions, and writers' meetings with Ben-Gurion; as well as other sources. This essay should be seen as the fruit of research that is still in progress, presenting not-yet-final conclusions, but based nevertheless on a large range of primary sources.

My thesis is as follows: during the first years after World War II, and even after 1948, the Holocaust was referred to on the rhetorical-ritual level more frequently than was the war. However, the war was at least as much of a presence as was the Holocaust in the generation's consciousness, probably even a greater one. Moreover, if we focus on the "native generation," the generation of *tsabarim*, there can be no doubt that in their consciousness World War II played a larger role than the Holocaust. In time, these positions reversed, both in people's consciousness and in their memories. While the memory of the war faded in the consciousness of the collective, the memory of the Holocaust grew stronger, to the point where the memory of the war was eclipsed by that of the Holocaust. Simultaneously, the status of the *tsabar* as the epitome of Israeli identity was undermined. Rivals for the title appeared, among them survivors of the Holocaust and their children—the "second generation."

During the war, one of the Yishuv's most prominent publishing houses, Am Oved, published a series of books called *Min Hamoked*—"From the Conflagration." As its name indicates, the series was meant to be "the first expression of the Holocaust that has in our times afflicted the human race in Europe, and our people in particular."[5] The very use of the word "Holocaust" (*Shoah*) in the context of the fate of the European peoples, as well as the fate of the Jewish people, demonstrates that the difference between the two fates was not yet clear and sharp. Nevertheless, this series represented a considerable effort to give some expression to the disaster that befell European Jewry. It issued testimonies of refugees who had escaped from Europe after the outbreak of the war (*Twelve Refugees*) and published a collection of letters from the ghettos (*The Voice of the Blood of Brothers* [1943]). Despite this conscious effort, an examination shows that the series issued more books about the war than about the Holocaust. What does this fact teach us? It may simply mean that not many books on the

Holocaust had been written, and that their time would come later. Such a claim is not without validity—there were indeed very few books written by survivors during these years.[6]

However, we have some primary evidence of the contemporary reading public's interest in the war and the Holocaust—the testimony of Am Oved's editor, Berl Katznelson. In the summer of 1944, he spoke with young people attending a youth seminar on Mount Carmel about their attitude toward what was happening in Europe. Speaking of the "Hebrew reader's" interest in the Holocaust, he noted that books dealing with the war, recounting battles fought by the British, the Norwegians, and the Russians (*The Blitz, Moonless, The Immortal People*) had been well received and were circulating widely. In contrast, books on the Holocaust, such as the above-mentioned collections of letters from the ghettos, remained on the shelves unbought. "I don't think that these horrors, which everyone knows about in the upper reaches of his consciousness, are affecting us as a personal experience of our own, as our own fate," Katznelson observed regretfully.[7]

The difficulty of internalizing the Holocaust was something that existed in different forms in various strata of the Jewish public in Palestine. Beyond the different reactions to the same event by people with different personalities, the significant difference was a generational one. There seems to have been a direct correlation between people's ages and the degree to which they internalized these events. The older people were, the more they identified with European Jewry. For the sake of convenience, we will call them the older generation and the younger generation. For the older generation, that of the parents, the life of Diaspora Jewry was a reality that they knew and had experienced, even if they had rebelled against it. They intuitively identified with their fellow Jews in the Diaspora. For them, the *shtetl* was not a literary term— it was a living concept that was associated with family members, friends, and childhood haunts. They could not cope with the horrifying facts that began to trickle into Palestine, and did not know how to assimilate them. So they did what is natural in pressured situations—they repressed information too harsh to bear and continued with their everyday lives as if nothing was happening. One expression of this tendency was the repertoire of the theaters, which continued to be composed of the usual plays: *Hamlet, Oedipus Rex, Phaedra,* Molière's comedies, and dramas about the war. There were some attempts to dramatize the Jewish experience (David Bergleson's piece, "I Shall Not Die But Live"), but these were premature and, according to the critics, not very successful. People also wanted entertainment—these were the great years of Hamatateh, the famous satirical company that lashed out at left and right and especially at the British, the hated rulers of Palestine, providing the public with comic relief from the traumas they were living through.[8]

Professor Fischel Schneerson, a psychologist who was one of the leaders of Al Domi, an organization that strove to heighten awareness of the Holocaust during the war years, in 1945 offered an interesting analysis of the parent generation's silence during those years. "There is a very paradoxical psychology at work here," he noted. "I would say that the Jewish people still doesn't know what happened to it." He saw it as a reflection of a traditional Jewish behavioral pattern for coping with catastrophe. "We have here some mysterious power that lies behind our national consciousness and which does not allow us to observe the calamities we have experienced," he maintained. He added: "the Jewish people evades facing up to its calamities. We have encountered a historic phenomenon—the Jewish people distracting itself from its afflictions. This is our habit—after a massacre there is a fast day, [we set up] a pogrom relief committee, and then we go on with our business.[9]

This, to a great extent, reflects the behavior of the parents' generation—there is pain and identification, but also a desire to get back to normal as quickly as possible. The Holocaust did not induce a new perception of reality. There is a nostalgic tendency to hark back lovingly to Jewish cultural models that were considered "diasporic," and a demand that renewed legitimacy be granted to those ways of life that the revolutionary Zionist movement had rejected in the past. Great emphasis is placed on the motif "the whole world is against us," a motif that had existed before but which now received great force—but no more than that. The level on which the Holocaust had an immediate effect was in the field of culture. Dov Sadan, for instance, was emotionally incapable of choosing which of two translations of *Faust* should receive a prize. How could he award a prize for German literature, even for Goethe, at a time like this?[10] There was talk of boycotting German music, which resulted in the ban on Strauss and Wagner. Is it not significant that the practical conclusions drawn from the Holocaust were restricted to the cultural sphere?

In all Yishuv debates, the Holocaust served to strengthen traditional views rather than to make people rethink their positions. Hence, those who had believed in catastrophic Zionism saw the Holocaust as the vindication of their prognosis. Likewise, those who had supported the Biltmore plan for the establishment of a Jewish state after the war (a plan that was formulated before information about the Holocaust arrived, and which was based on an estimate of a million Jewish refugees leaving Europe for Palestine after the war) continued to support it even after the news of the death of those potential immigrants arrived. The points used to support the Biltmore program did, however, change—the reason for establishing a Jewish state was now to save those who survived. The political plan itself did not change, though. By the same token, those who had opposed the Biltmore plan out of concern that it would lead to a Jewish-Arab conflict did not change their positions after the Holocaust. Those who had opposed mass immigration, like Hashomer Hatsa'ir (and this was one of the central arguments that the movement made against the Biltmore plan), continued to oppose it even then. Indeed, there was no gathering in the Yishuv in which the memory of the Holocaust was not evoked. But public life in the Yishuv revolved around internal political issues—the splits and mergers of political parties, such as the split in Mapai and the establishment of the new Le'ahdut Ha'avoda party, and afterward the founding of Mapam. These political realignments were spurred by debates over orientation (pro-Western or pro-Soviet), over socialist ideology (Marxist or anti-Marxist), and over the issue of whether or not Palestine should be partitioned. None of them had anything to do with the Holocaust. At the important postwar Zionist Congress (Basel, December 1946), the debates focused on Zionist tactics in the face of British policy. The Holocaust was marginal.[11]

This phenomenon is even more pronounced when we turn to the younger generation. The 1940s and the beginning of the 1950s saw the flowering of Canaanism, a cultural-political trend that considered the nation forming in Palestine and Israel a local tribe, directly linked to the peoples of the ancient Mediterranean basin, to pagan myths, to the Semitic world. The Canaanites wanted to detach the Hebrew nation in Palestine from the Jewish tradition of 2,000 years of exile, to throw off its links to the Jewish people in the Diaspora, and to dispense with Jewish universal commitment in favor of local particularism. They sought a direct link among territory, language, origin, and national identity. Canaanism was restricted to a fairly small group of intellectuals, most of whom came from the extreme right. The Labor movement, which was the linchpin of the Yishuv, never countenanced these views. Labor nevertheless contained an undercurrent of Canaanite sympathy. This was evident in Ben-Gurion's views regarding the direct link between the new Jews and the ancient Hebrews and in his total rejection of Jewish Diasporic ways of life. An intuitive Canaanite ideology was apparent among broad circles in the younger generation, including in the youth movements and the Palmach, the flower of the Yishuv's youth. This Canaanite periphery did not accept that part of the doctrine that severed the link between the Jews in Palestine and the Jewish people in the Diaspora, nor was it attracted by Canaanism's pagan elements. But these Palestine-bred young men and women felt that they were different from the newcomers, a distinctive unit whose character was formed by the sense of freedom and possession they enjoyed in Palestine. This sense of being different was interwoven with a sense of superiority toward the Diaspora Jew. Modern Hebrew literature (Berdyezewski, Brenner, Judah Leib Gordon, Devora Baron, Agnon) was rich with negative images of the Diaspora Jew, and the "native sons" accepted these representations as real. The encounters with new immigrants, including Holocaust survivors, did not breed empathy but reinforced alienation. The immigrants looked different, smelled different, sounded different. The world of the Yishuv youth was a small, intimate, familiar one. The Holocaust remained an experience external to this world.[12] Dan Horowitz, brought up as a member of the veteran Yishuv elite and later a professor of political science at the Hebrew University, wrote in his memoirs: "The first news of the Holocaust—a horror story that penetrates the consciousness but which remains incomprehensible on the emotional level, alien, not from our familiar world." He went on to state that "the ghetto uprising was easier to understand, closer to the associational frameworks of a member of a youth movement in Palestine, and therefore more easily accepted as an object of identification.[13] This alienation is manifest in the primary sources: the December 1942 issue of *Alon Hapalmach* reports on a meeting of Company A. The meeting was opened in the evening with a lecture from a senior member of the Hagana, who spoke of the "terrible news coming from the Diaspora, and our role at this time." In the wake of his speech there was an evening devoted to the victims. There was mournful music, a pageant, and a reading of "Baruch of Mainz," a poem by Saul Tchernichowsky on Jewish martyrdom during the Crusades. Immediately afterward the pamphlet reports on the following day's sports competition and the fact that the scores were relatively low because of a lack of training.[14] At every celebration, such as on Hanukkah, there was a talk about the Holocaust. These talks were generally accompanied by a call to action: "The unforgivable fault of weakness, and the debt of blood that can never be repaid—will these not awaken among us a great yearning for a Hebrew force and for the simple right to fight for one's life?"[15] The main issues were usually defined as follows: "The problems of Zionism and the role of the youth at this hour, in the face of the Holocaust of Diaspora Jewry and the restrictions imposed on us in this country."[16] With this formula, the Zionist struggle in Palestine coopted the Holocaust. The equation of the "Holocaust of Diaspora Jewry" with the "restrictions imposed on us in this country," the role of youth being defined by the concrete needs of the struggle for Palestine, at this stage reserved for the Holocaust only a ceremonial, ritualistic role.

The reaction of these young people to the Holocaust was a mixture of rage and thirst for revenge on the gentiles and revulsion and shame for the Jews. The Germans were far away and inaccessible, so concrete anger was directed at the British, who were viewed as frustrating Jewish efforts to establish a state in Palestine. As with their elders, the Holocaust created no new sense of commitment among the young but rather sharpened and reconfirmed old beliefs. The younger generation's psychological distance from the Holocaust was apparent in their lack of interest in anything connected to the Holocaust proper and in anything that had to do with the old Jewish world that had been destroyed. In 1948, the newspaper *Hapo'el Hatsa'ir* printed a discussion of the younger generation's approach to modern Hebrew literature. The main assertion was that young people had no interest in Hebrew literature because it portrayed a Diaspora reality that was alien to them. "Now that the Jewish Diaspora has been destroyed . . . our children have another reason for avoiding it. They, in their natural approach to all the questions of our life [in contrast with the Diaspora approach] see the annihilation of the Diaspora as the distressing and very unfortunate end of the abnormal life that the Jews lived there, and, in the final analysis, the demise of a world that was past and gone and buried."[17]

In contrast with the Holocaust, which was shunted into the margins of public consciousness in those years, the war itself was a constant presence. The war set private and public schedules. The main question during the initial years was whether the Yishuv would or would not be saved from German occupation. The war was felt in the street, in everyday life. In 1940 Tel Aviv and Haifa were bombed by the Italians. Gas masks were distributed to children and everyone was trained in civil defense against gas attacks. At night there were total blackouts; when they ended in 1944, the change in the public atmosphere was tangible.[18] Churchill's speeches and the Battle of Britain were experienced with great emotion in the Yishuv.[19] V-E Day was celebrated, though with mixed feelings: people were aware that the victory had come too late for Europe's Jews and that the war for the Jewish state was still before them. Still, there were celebrations in Tel Aviv and at the kibbutzim. A young man wrote that day in his diary: "I am of the generation of the war. The war was the framework within which my spiritual makeup was formed. It made me understand the meaning of life and society. I saw how nations surrendered, betrayed, and changed sides once more, and how nations fight to the last man and do not give up. I saw the clash of world views, and I witnessed how yesterday's masters of the world became the defeated of today."[20]

During the war the press devoted its front pages to news from the front. Cinema newsreels provided the first visual reports of the fighting. In the wake of the Barbarossa operation (June 1941), the war became something close, intimate. The campaign in Western Europe was indeed traumatic, but it remained foreign to those of Eastern European origin. The battles in Eastern Europe, however, raged through the childhood homes of most of the members of the Yishuv. Radio Moscow became the primary source of news; relatively few understood the BBC's English, but many understood Yuri Levitan, Radio Moscow's Jewish newscaster. People's days began with the six o'clock news from Moscow. War books also played an important role. Even though *For Whom the Bell Tolls,* a Hebrew best-seller, was about a different war, it became part of the experience of World War II. Soviet war books soon appeared and captured the market: *How the Steel Was Tempered, Rainbow, The Young Guard, The One-Legged Pilot.* The most popular of them was Beck's *Panfilov's Men.*[21] Selections from this book were published in the *Alon Hapalmach* newsletter beginning in 1943, and the book soon became legendary. Movies did not lag far behind the books— Hollywood and Moscow and even London flooded Palestine with romantic patriotic films about the war. The spectrum of subjects and artistic value ranged from *Casablanca* through *Waterloo Bridge* to *The Fall of Berlin;* there were stories about the war itself, about the resistance movement and the partisans, about the cruelty of the Hun occupiers, and about the heroics of the underground fighters. In addition to all this there were songs. The most popular ones, enthusiastically sung by the youth movements, the Palmach, and later in the Israeli army for decades thereafter, were Hebrew translations of patriotic Soviet war songs. The songs, the novels, and the films were the agents that brought the war into everyone's consciousness. This is a good example of Karl Mannheim's dictum that the strongest messages are transmitted without the sender and the recipient being aware of them.

The "Jewish" news was hidden in the margins of the papers; the war was in the headlines. This was true not only of the press and the other media but also of public awareness. There was a feeling that this was a fateful war that would determine the future of the world. It was not just a Jewish war: the entire globe was battling the forces of evil. This awareness was very encouraging for the Jews—they were involved in a universal struggle, not some particularist Jewish matter. Participating in the war made the Yishuv part of the enlightened world, no longer just a victim or just a provincial community. It also served as a response to those who claimed that the Jews had been abandoned to their fate, that world solidarity did not apply to them: the Jews were not fighting alone, they were part of the great alliance fighting Nazism.

War has attractive attributes: it is an opportunity for self-sacrifice, dedication, for putting the common good before one's own selfish interests. It is the appropriate time to paint reality unambiguously in black and white, right and wrong. This approach was applicable to the Palestinian reality: the education of young people during the 1940s was governed by the upcoming struggle with the Arabs for mastery of the land. Dedication to the common good was a cherished value, as is evident in all the memoirs and diaries from those years. "We always await the command," sang the Palmach members. The exhilarating example being set by the partisans in their fight against the foreign invader, the heroism of the fighters at Stalingrad or of the conquerors of Berlin—these were the educational models for the Yishuv's youth.

The figure of the partisan was of special significance — the Palmach fighters' self-image was that they were fighting a popular, anti-imperialist war of national liberation. This image, a powerful one in the confrontation with the British, modeled itself on the experiences of the resistance movements of World War II — and especially on the struggle of the Soviet underground groups in the territories under Nazi occupation — and on Tito's ragtag Yugoslavian resistance army against the Germans. The need to adopt guerrilla tactics against the British made these the practical models for the Jewish army in formation. By the same token, the War of Independence was perceived as an anti-imperialist war in which the experience of the World War II guerrilla fighters was used to fight the regular armies of the Arab countries.[22]

The Soviet influence was overwhelming: when Abba Kovner, then the Givati Brigade's cultural commissar, issued a "battle sheet" to raise morale among the fighters, he took his cue from Soviet propaganda: "Death to the Invader" was a key slogan. New immigrant recruits in the nascent Israeli army used battle cries they had learned in Russia: "For the motherland and Stalin!" The terms *politruk* and *commissar* were used interchangeably to refer to battalion cultural officers. Kibbutz Negba, fighting for survival against the Egyptian expeditionary force, hung a slogan attributed to Stalin in its dining hall: "Not the tank, but man, will prevail."[23] The literature of the War of Independence made intensive use of models provided by so-called literary "socialist realism."

The myth of Stalingrad was of special importance to the Jews of Palestine. Even though it had been the battle of El-Alamein that had repulsed the threatened German invasion of Palestine, it was Stalingrad, the fortress on the Volga, that captured the Yishuv's imagination. Bearing Stalin's name, it symbolized unrelenting resistance to the German enemy. The Soviet Union's heroic battle for survival was an inspiration even to those whose sympathies were not with the left. The League for Friendship with the Soviet Union of those years had many members who were far from being Communists but who saw the tenacious struggle of this power as evidence of the Soviet system's superiority over the hesitant, flaccid

Western powers. Later, the USSR was seen as the ally who was willing to bring Nazi murderers to justice, unlike the overly merciful West.[24] When Eliahu Golomb, the leader of the Haganah, recalled the plan to defend the Yishuv by making Mount Carmel a fortress of resistance against a possible invasion by Rommel in 1942 (a plan which, luckily, never had to be put to the test), he said that it would have been "our Stalingrad, before Stalingrad."[25] When Meir Ya'ari wanted to reeducate immigrant resistance fighters who had been through the war in the Soviet Union and who had been more impressed by Soviet anti-Semitism and repression than with the wonders of socialism, he argued that they had seen only part of the reality and thus "could not explain from what sources Stalingrad drew its heroism."[26]

The decade after Stalingrad was marked by boundless admiration for the Soviet Union on the Israeli left. It reflected the same tendencies that had previously been manifested in the widespread interest in the war—the desire to change the focus of interest from specifically Jewish issues to universal ones. People wanted to concentrate on the future rather than deal with the past, and they wished to belong to the progressive camp, which was also the victorious one. The Holocaust, in contrast, transmitted messages that were Jewish-particularist, pessimistic, and isolationist. During the War of Independence these themes grew even stronger: now, as in the world war, good would defeat evil. Just as the victory in World War II had reflected the vitality of the victors' regime and society, so would the victory in Palestine. Equating the strong, victorious side with the right side was one more lesson of the war transferred to the Israeli landscape.[27]

Compared with the heroics of the war, the ordeal of the Holocaust seemed miserable, even repulsive. One could talk endlessly about the war, tell stories, wax enthusiastic about acts of bravery. But it was very difficult to talk about the Holocaust. People did not know how to handle the horror stories and did their best to avoid hearing them. The tendency of survivors to tell and retell what they had been through seemed masochistic, like refusing to let wounds heal. "The refugees' memories are incomprehensible to us," wrote one young man sent to assist the survivors who were deported to Cyprus by the British.[28] Soldiers were received as heroes; survivors seemed to arouse, at best, compassion. The only Holocaust story that seemed fit to tell was that of the Warsaw Ghetto uprising. It was no coincidence that this rebellion was coopted into the Israeli mythology, and its leaders presented as if they had been part and parcel of the Yishuv, who had only happened by chance to be in Poland. In this sense the rebellion served as a kind of mediator between the positive, strong war experiences and the repressed, gloomy experiences of the Holocaust. Other links between these two polarized sorts of awareness were the Jewish Brigade and the illegal immigration operation. The Brigade's soldiers symbolized the Yishuv's participation in the war, and they were also the first to make contact with the surviving remnant of European Jewry. They were thus able to fuse the memory of the war with that of the Holocaust. However, historians estimate that the Brigade's activities among the survivors "were not only not directed from Palestine, but were almost unknown there."[29] So their encounter with the survivors remained a personal experience and did not become part of the communal one. Illegal immigration, however, was at the top of the Yishuv agenda in the years 1945–1947. It combined by association the issue of the Jewish refugees—linked with the war and the Holocaust—and the struggle for free Jewish immigration to Palestine, which was the focus of the Zionist campaign at the time. It was also consistent with the pervasive Yishuv self-image—activist and militant, sending its fighters to organize illegal immigration. It also fit the common image of the refugees—passive, miserable, in need of saviors. Those involved in the illegal immigration operation who were also in contact with the survivors encountered the Holocaust face-to-face; but these were few. The great majority, even in the Palyam (the Palmach unit in charge of overseas operations), not to mention those who never left Palestine, considered illegal immigration to be first and foremost a theater in the battle for the Jewish state. The link with the Holocaust was indirect.

The illegal immigration operation enhanced the memory of the war, being in many ways a kind of continuation of the war in the underground, without the dangers involved in a real underground. It was no coincidence that former resistance leaders in Europe assisted the illegal immigration organization, Hamossad Le'aliya Bet—anyone who had trouble with the transition from the excitement of the war period to the daily routine of peacetime found in the illegal immigration operation a kind of war game: one deceived the authorities, broke the rules, engaged in romantic international adventures with a sheaf of false passports in one's pocket.

When the War of Independence broke out, the associations with World War II grew stronger. The establishment of the State of Israel was not perceived by the Yishuv as resulting from the Holocaust; rather, it was perceived as the outcome of immanent processes precipitated by the heroic struggle against the British. It is true that the destruction of European Jewry in World War II was mentioned in the Declaration of Independence, but it appears only as one—and hardly the most important—of a series of factors meant to give the new state legitimacy. The policy of attributing to the Holocaust a predominant role in the establishment of the state was to appear much later. When Ezriel Karlebach, one of the most important journalists in the country and founder of the evening newspaper *Ma'ariv,* listed the reasons why it was no longer possible to delay the establishment of the state, he recorded a long list of occurrences, all of them having to do with the Yishuv; the Holocaust was not mentioned at all.[30] Historical-philosophical comments regarding the state's establishment were couched in historical-redemptional terms regarding the end of Exile, without relating to contemporary history. The Crusades and Chmielnicki starred in the descriptions of Europe's treatment of the Jews, not the events of the immediate past. There was, however, a subtext relating to the Holocaust—when Karlebach wanted to reassure Jews apprehensive about fighting a war of independence, he proclaimed that in the entire war fewer Jews would be killed than in a single day in Majdanek.[31] By the same token, when he described the fratricidal battle over the arms ship *Altalena,* he called it "a more horrible sight than all the horrors of Majdanek."[32]

Karlebach's writing reveals a hidden stratum in relating to the Holocaust. While people's minds and hearts were immersed in the apocalyptic events of the birth of the nation, their associative and metaphoric worlds were unconsciously drawing from the Holocaust. This is a reservation that qualifies my findings about the secondary place of the Holocaust in the public discourse of the time.

The War of Independence seemed like an epilogue to World War II: the fighting, the types of weapons, the lexicon, even the foreign press reports from the battlefields, all had the same feel as World War II. The Jewish recruits from abroad who volunteered to fight for the Jewish state brought with them the routines and slang of the world war. The logistics, the tactics, the strategy—they were all products of the lessons learned the last time around. It was thus only natural for World War II to be a strong presence in the country in those years. The experience of the war as an entity reshaping Israeli reality made people identify the war "there" with the war "here." One of the young fighters in the War of Independence wrote: "We are children of the war. Even before we had time to understand anything, around us millions of people were already being killed and destroyed."[33] The continuity between the two wars was taken for granted.

The extent to which the Holocaust had not yet penetrated people's consciousness may be seen in Ben-Gurion's meetings with writers and intellectuals, after the guns of the War of Independence had fallen silent. He held two such meetings in 1949.[34] The Holocaust was mentioned by the participants, but it remained on the margins, a tangential subject, that could hardly even be called a subtext. Hugo Bergman, for instance, was concerned about isolationist and nationalist tendencies he diagnosed in the younger generation. Symptomatic of this, in his view, were young people painting out foreign-language signs on city streets and the cutback in the hours devoted to the study of English in the high schools. Martin Buber expressed his concern that mass immigration (of European survivors!) was flooding the country with newcomers who lacked convictions. He was worried that the new immigrants would dilute the influence of the elite, veteran elements. Another example of the failure to internalize the Holocaust during these years may be seen in the educational program outlined by Ben-Gurion for new immigrants, whom the army was to provide with a basic Israeli education. The immigrant soldier was to be given knowledge of the Hebrew language and a basic course on the history of the Jewish people in its land as well as on "What is exile and how the Jewish people overcame it." "We have to put it into their heads," the Prime Minister stated, "how the Jewish people survived for four thousand years." In this framework he also wanted to acquaint the recruits with a bit of Bible and a bit of modern Hebrew literature. A subject of central importance in Ben-Gurion's curriculum was knowledge of the Land of Israel and its geography. An analysis of this program reveals that Ben-Gurion continued in 1949 to speak in the same historical terms he had used forty years earlier.[35]

It is possible to argue, with justification, that World War II occupies no place in these discussions either, and that it is no less absent than the Holocaust. But, in the first decade after its end, popular culture helped strengthen awareness of the war, while it did not do so for the Holocaust. Cinema, literature, theater, and radio were full of the glory of the war, and this continued throughout the 1950s. Moreover, the War of Independence was the foundation myth of the state and a focus of the new Israeli identity. Local experiences played a central role in this identity. Its symbol was the young *tsabar*, forged in battle. The perceptions of the two wars converged in the *tsabar*'s image into one continuous impression. The experience of the Holocaust remained external to it.

In 1952 the opposition to the Mapai government latched on to the Holocaust as a convenient issue on which to attack the establishment. This happened in the debate over the reparations treaty with Germany, and with even greater force during the Kastner trial. Even so, the Holocaust still played no important part in the lives of the great majority of Israelis, especially those of the younger generation. One important milestone in the change of atmosphere was the Eichmann trial; another, the waiting period before the Six

Day War and the deep anxiety that accompanied it. The real, fundamental change did not take place, however, until after the Yom Kippur War in 1973, which symbolized the decline of the *tsabar* as the epitome of Israeli nationhood and the appearance of a new Israeli identity. This new identity internalized the Holocaust as one of its symbols. The process was accompanied by a changing of the guard in the Israeli elite and the first appearance of the children of Holocaust survivors as a cultural and public force.

As the Holocaust and World War II grew more distant in time, the war lost its significance. Other wars came and replaced it as foci of heroism. In contrast, the distance in time worked in favor of the memory of the Holocaust. Such distance was necessary for people to be able to confront the subject. The changes in the Israeli ethos and in the elite groups that signified it during the 1970s allowed the Holocaust to be internalized and adopted as one of the central components of Israeli identity.

NOTES

All sources are in Hebrew unless otherwise stated.

1. Gershom Scholem, "Judaic Studies," in *Explications and Implications* (Tel Aviv, 1989) 140.

2. On the debate over Ben-Gurion's attitude toward the Holocaust see Tuvia Friling, "*The Seventh Million* as the Zionist Movement's March of Folly and Iniquity," *Iyunim Bitekumat Yisrael* 2 (Sde Boker, 1992) 317–67; see also Shabbetai Tevet "The Black Hole," *Alpayim* 10 (1995); 111–95.

3. On Ben-Gurion's visit, see Ruth Klieger's testimony, Ben-Gurion Heritage Institute (Sde Boker); the material on Galili's and Allon's visit is based on Galili's personal testimony to the author.

4. See, for example, Re'uven Avinoam (Grossman), ed., *Gevilei Esh* [published in English as *Such were our Fighters*] (Ministry of Defense, 1952); Menachem Bergman (Aham), *Native Son* (Tel Aviv, 1947); and commemoration books such as the following: Nehemia Shein, *A Year after His Fall* (Ein Harod, 1947); Yehiam Weitz, *Letters* (Tel Aviv, 1948); Matti Megged, ed., *On the Path of the Palmach* (Jerusalem, 1958).

5. Yosef Seh-Lavan, "The *Min Hamoked* Library," *Hapo'el Hatsa'ir* 44 (year 37).

6. Yosef Kornianski and Renia Hershkowitz arrived in Palestine in early

1944 and related their stories at length. Hershkowitz's memoir was published at the end of that year: Renia Hershkowitz, *Wandering and Underground* (Ein Harod: Hakibbutz Hameuhad, 1944–1945). Kornianski's testimony was published in 1944 in Moshe Bassok, ed., *The Young Pioneer* (Ein Harod: Hakibbutz Hameuhad, 1944) 399–407; his complete memoir was published later; see J. Kornianski, *On the Pioneers' Mission* (Beit Lohamei Hagetaot: Hakibbutz Hameuhad, 1979). Two important books were published in 1946: *Flames in the Ashes* by Ruzka Korczak (Merhavia: Sifriat Hapoalim, 1946); and *Salamandrah* by Ka. Tzetnik (Tel Aviv: Dvir, 1946). Other books by survivors were published in the 1950s.

7. Berl Katznelson, "A Discussion on the Diaspora," *Writings*, vol. 12 (Tel Aviv: Mapai, 1950) 217–18.

8. The sources are issues of *Hapo'el Hatsa'ir* dealing with the Habima, Ha'ohel, and Hamatateh theaters in the years 1944–1950.

9. Fischel Schneerson, Writers' Convention at Ma'aleh Hahamisha, 25 Elul 1945 (*Moznayim* 21 [Tishrei-Adar 1945–1946], 77–78).

10. Dov Stok, Convention of Hebrew Writers in Palestine, 6–7 Hanukkah 1945–46, (*Moznayim* 21 [Tishrei-Adar 1945–1946]; ibid. 255–57).

11. For a broader discussion of this issue, see Anita Shapira, *Land and Power* (in English) (New York: Oxford University Press, 1992) 319–42.

12. For more on this, see Anita Shapira, "Native Sons," *Alpayim* 2 (1990): 178–203.

13. Dan Horowitz, *Blue and Dust, the Generation of 1948: A Self-Portrait* (Jerusalem: Keter, 1993) 37ff.

14. *Alon Hapalmach* December 1942.

15. M., "The Right to Fight," *Alon Hapalmach* September 1943.

16. Ibid.

17. Ya'akov Midrashi, "Youth and Hebrew Literature," *Hapo'el Hatsa'ir* 27 (year 41) 23 March 1948.

18. Horowitz, *Blue and Dust*, pp. 37ff.

19. See, for example, Moshe Salomon, diary entries, 23 June 1941 and 14 December 1941, *Gevilei Esh* 390–91.

20. Moshe Salomon, diary entry, 7 May 1945, *Gevilei Esh* 397.

21. Ernest Hemingway, *For Whom the Bell Tolls* (Merhavia: Hakibbutz Ha-artzi, 1942); Nikolai Alexevitch Ostrovsky, *How the Steel Was Tempered* (Ein Harod: Hakibbutz Hameuhad, 1946); Vanda Vasilevska, *Rainbow* (Merhavia: Hakibbutz Ha-artzi, 1948); Alexander Alexandrovitch Fadeyev, *The Young Guard* (Merhavia: Sifriat Hapoalim, 1947); Alexander Alfredovitch Beck, *Panfilov's Men* (Ein Harod: Hakibbutz Hameuhad, 1946); Boris Nikolaivitch Pollevoy, *The One-Legged Pilot* (Tel Aviv: Y. Shimoni, 1950).

22. See, for example, *Alon Hapalmach* November 1945; *Alon Hapalmach* May 1946; *Alon Hapalmach* March 1947.

23. On the *politruk*, see *Alon Hapalmach* June–July 1946; on the influence of the Soviet model on education in the army, see the minutes of a meeting to consider the question of cultural activity in the Israel Defense Forces (IDF), Hakirya, 19 September 1949, Ben-Gurion Heritage Archives 35. On the slogan at Negba, see *Gevilei Esh* 474.

24. On the Soviets' readiness to fight to the end, see Ben-Zion Grudzensky, 25 February 1945, *Gevilei Esh* 699; on bringing Nazis to justice, see Avraham Kritzman, 25 June 1944, *Gevilei Esh* 712.

25. *Alon Hapalmach* July 1944.

26. Meir Ya'ari, "Not Wayworn but Trailblazers," Meir Ya'ari Archives, A–D, 7.95, Givat Haviva. Quoted in Anita Shapira, *Walking on the Horizon* (Tel Aviv: Am Oved, 1989) 340.

27. Ben-Zion Grudzenski wrote 21 March 1948, during the siege of Jerusalem: "And we, the young generation . . . upon seeing that after such great victories for the vast armies of Germany, it could be beaten into the dust, we begin to think that apparently history has some force that acts against evil lest it come to rule the world. And we can only believe that what the Yishuv and the Jewish people are undergoing is a bad dream that will soon end. And until then we are obligated by destiny to be prepared to sacrifice all that is dear to us and to be ready for anything that will be required of us to defend our interests" (*Gevilei Esh* 699).

28. Shlomo Mautner, *Gevilei Esh* June–September 1947(?) 198–99.

29. Yoav Gelber, *History of Enlistment,* vol. 3 (Jerusalem: Yad Ben Zvi, 1983) 430; quoted in Hanna Yablonka, *Foreign Brothers* (Jerusalem: Yad Ben Zvi, 1984) 53.

30. Ezriel Karlebach, "For [Our] Sin," in *Sefer Hatekumah* (Tel Aviv: Sifriat Ma'ariv, n.d.) 64–67.

31. Karlebach, "For [Our] Sin" 157.

32. Karlebach, "For [Our] Sin" 260.

33. Yosef Ohali, *Gevilei Esh* (18 March 1948) 500.

34. Discussions with writers at two meetings called by the Prime Minister, the first on 27 March 1949 and the second on 11 October 1949. Ben-Gurion Heritage Institute Archives (Sde Boker).

35. Meeting on the question of cultural activities in the IDF, ibid., Hakirya, 19 September 5–6.

FIVE

The Zionist Leadership between the Holocaust and the Creation of the State of Israel

JEHUDA REINHARZ AND EVYATAR FRIESEL

THE CENTRAL TASK OF THE Zionist leadership in the 1940s was rooted in a prewar event: the White Paper of May 1939. The White Paper represented a major crossroads in the political life of the movement, and the Zionist leaders had to consider ways to cope with the new circumstances resulting from it. Very soon, however, all the deliberations and calculations of the Zionists were in disarray due to the systematic destruction of European Jewry. Thus, the most vital source of human power and ideological support of the Zionist movement—the Jews of Eastern Europe—would disappear by the end of World War II.

In 1939, the leadership of the Zionist movement was theoretically divided between the Executive of the World Zionist Organization (WZO) and the Executive of the Jewish Agency (JA). In practice, the same group of about twenty men led both bodies. Most of them lived in Palestine, but some lived in England and in the United States. The seat of the Zionist Executive was in Jerusalem.

The President of the World Zionist Organization was Chaim Weizmann, the towering figure of the movement. Weizmann had been deposed from the presidency of the WZO in 1931 but was reelected in 1935 as a result of the support of Mapai, the largest labor party in Palestine. Ideologically, Weizmann was a man of the center with progressive leanings but no party affiliation. His re-election began a period of political collaboration between Weizmann and Mapai, which was to continue, in one form or another, until Weizmann's death in 1952.

The second most prominent figure in the movement was David Ben-Gurion. Ben-Gurion had built a political basis in the Yishuv in the 1920s and 1930s as secretary-general of the Histadrut, the general association of workers, and after 1930 as the leader of Mapai. At the Zionist Congress in 1935 Ben-Gurion had been elected chairman of the Zionist Executive and of the Executive of the Jewish Agency. Other members of Mapai occupied key positions in the Agency. It marked the beginning of the predominance of the labor movement in the political leadership of the Zionist movement and later in the State of Israel; this would continue for more than forty years.

A figure of growing importance in the Zionist leadership was Nahum Goldmann, who until 1939 was the representative of the Zionist Organization at the League of Nations. At the beginning of World War II Goldmann moved to the United States, where he represented the Jewish Agency and became an influential Zionist figure. Moshe Shertok (later Sharett), the future Foreign Minister of Israel, was another important member of the Zionist Executive. Later on, in 1945, three central figures of the American Zionist movement were added to the Zionist Executive: Abba Hillel Silver, Stephen S. Wise, and Louis Lipsky. Silver would become the main spokesman in American Zionism during the crucial 1945–1948 period. In Britain, the movement was also represented by Executive members Selig Brodetsky and (after 1945) Berl Locker.[1]

Until the publication of the White Paper of May 1939, Zionist foreign policy had been based on the collaboration with Great Britain, the mandatory power in Palestine. The White Paper put an end to a British policy regarding Palestine that was influenced, however tenuously, by the Balfour Declaration. The underlying assumption of the White Paper of 1939 was that a thriving Jewish national home *had* been established in Palestine. Consequently, it was thought by the British that His Majesty's Government had fulfilled its moral obligation to the Jews and its political obligations under the terms of the Mandate. With war in Europe looming on the horizon, the British were keen to implement political conditions in Palestine in accordance with what they saw as the new constellation of forces in Palestine and Great Britain's larger interests in the Middle East. Those interests dictated that new and effective political arrangements should be established with the various Arab leaders and countries in the region.[2]

As the historical understanding between the Zionist movement and Great Britain reached a crisis, the Zionists found themselves at a serious strategic disadvantage. One of the implicit assumptions of the "Palestine triangle" of Jews, Arabs, and the British was that every political step supported by any two of the three had a fair chance to succeed. If the Arabs and the British agreed now on Arab statehood in Palestine, it could possibly become a reality. For the Zionists, the situation thus created was as ominous as it was simple. Only one solution remained: to accept the idea of an imminent *Jewish* state in Palestine. The British decided to create statehood, that is *Arab* statehood. The Zionists, forced to accept this turn of events, turned toward the creation of *Jewish* statehood.

In fact, the issue of statehood imposed itself now upon the Zionist leadership—if not ideologically, certainly tactically. The situation was clearly recognized by David Ben-Gurion. Speaking before the Twentieth Zionist Congress in August 1939, he proclaimed: "The 'White Paper' has created a vacuum in the Mandate. For us, the 'White Paper' does not exist in any form, under any condition, under any interpretation. For us there is only the vacuum created within the Mandate, and it is up to us to fill this vacuum, by ourselves alone. . . . We ourselves shall have to act as if we are the state in Palestine . . . in order that we shall become the state in Palestine."[3] Chaim Weizmann soon reached similar conclusions about Jewish statehood in Palestine.[4]

The end of the political connection with Great Britain posed before the Zionists an additional question. It was one of the fundamental tenets of political Zionism that in order to realize its aims in Palestine, the movement must associate itself with a major power. The principle had been formulated by Theodor Herzl and had been explicitly or implicitly accepted by the Zionist movement ever since.[5] The political understanding with Great Britain had been the most concrete as well as the most creative and rewarding implementation of that concept. Now, faced with the end of its association with Britain, the Zionist leadership began to consider new options for a powerful connection.

Because of the war against the common German enemy, a measure of collaboration was maintained between the Zionist movement and the British between 1939 and 1945. Simultaneously, however, David Ben-Gurion had already proclaimed in mid-1939 that the main instrument of the new Zionist policy should be massive *aliyah,* or immigration, legal if possible, "illegal" if all else failed.[6] Weizmann, Ben-Gurion, and the other members of the Zionist leadership were in basic agreement regarding the major elements of the new political line of the movement. In spite of growing difficulties, Jewish statehood remained the goal of Zionist policy throughout the 1940s. Indeed, from a Zionist perspective, there was no other alternative.

The Turn to American Jewry

Although never the subject of a formal resolution, the turn to the United States was one of the major decisions in Zionist history. Support by a major power was a necessity for the Zionists, since the Zionist movement and the Yishuv in Palestine were too small and their influence too limited to succeed on a political path of such far-reaching significance as Jewish statehood. In terms of backing, there was of course world Jewry, but it has been rightly stated that although the concept was "used by Jews, as well as their friends and enemies, [world Jewry] has never existed as political reality."[7] There was little or no coordination between the Jewish parties or communities. The only existing semirepresentative body that served (supposedly) as an umbrella organization for all Jews was the World Jewish Congress, a voluntary association of representative Jewish communities and organizations. Founded in 1936 by delegates from thirty-six countries, it was headed by one of the leaders of the American Zionist movement, Stephen S. Wise; the chairman of the executive board was another prominent Zionist, Nahum Goldmann. Obviously (and with good reason), the WJC was seen as a front for the World Zionist Organization.

The turn toward American Jewry and, with its aid, to the American government, was a development that had some past history. Since World War I, the United States had been one of the main arenas of Zionist activity. Louis D. Brandeis was a Zionist of great national, even international, stature who had bestowed upon the movement much prestige. Ben-Gurion had lived in America for several years. Weizmann was a frequent visitor to the country and in the 1920s had established close relations with leading American Jewish personalities and organizations. The collaboration between Weizmann and Louis Marshall, the powerful president of the American Jewish Committee, had been the foundation on which the establishment of the enlarged Jewish Agency was built in 1929. Finally, the concentration of the main Diaspora activities of the Zionist movement in the United States implied a judgment about the political strength of the other Jewish communities outside the European (and soon German-dominated) continent. It meant, in fact, that little support was expected either from the Jews in less well-established, non-European Jewries,[8] or from the leadership of British Jewry. Regarding the latter, it was clear from meetings Weizmann and his colleagues had with them in September 1941 that on the whole they continued to be negatively inclined toward Zionism.[9]

The change from a British to an American-oriented Zionist policy started soon after the Twentieth Zionist Congress. Weizmann and Ben-Gurion visited the United States several times in 1940, 1941, and 1942. Nahum Goldmann soon settled there. In the early

1940s, the main efforts of the Zionist leadership were directed more toward American Jewry than toward the American government. For Weizmann, Ben-Gurion, and other Zionist leaders it was conventional wisdom (in historical hindsight, unsupported by facts) that access to the American government was in the hands of a small group of distinguished American Jews and should be pursued through them. This impression about the influence of distinguished American Jewish figures was not unjustified. To mention but a few examples, Justices of the Supreme Court Louis D. Brandeis and Felix Frankfurter were old Zionists who had many influential contacts. Benjamin V. Cohen and Rabbi Stephen S. Wise, veteran Zionists, were counted among the close associates of President Roosevelt. Indeed, there was no other country where Zionists and Jews were as numerous and as influential as in the higher echelons of the American administration during Roosevelt's presidency. In addition, Zionist aspirations were supported by large sectors of the Jewish community. It was commonly assumed that the political potential of American Jewry had never been fully mobilized for Zionist purposes.

Nevertheless, to attain the support of American Jewry for the Zionists' plans would prove to be a very complex and frustrating experience. American Jewry was probably weaker and less well organized in the late 1930s and early 1940s than it had been ten years earlier, at the time of the founding of the enlarged Jewish Agency. After Louis Marshall's death, in 1929, no person of similar prestige and standing had emerged in the community. The Jewish Agency had not accomplished the tasks its founders had set for it. The 1930s were a time of economic hardship in the United States, a situation which did not enhance Jewish communal collaboration. Although the United Jewish Appeal was established in 1939 (and part of the money collected was earmarked for Palestinian purposes), it had a difficult start.

The intentions of Weizmann and Ben-Gurion to organize the support of American Jewry for Zionist plans in Palestine after the war was based on their experiences during World War I. In 1914, a Zionist umbrella organization had been formed, the Pro-

visional Committee for General Zionist Affairs (PZC), headed by
Louis D. Brandeis. The PZC had brought together the other leading institutions of American Jewry, and after long negotiations,
the first American Jewish Congress had emerged. The Congress
had been a most forceful presence at the Peace Conference in
Paris in 1919.[10]

Similarly, in mid-1939 an Emergency Committee for Zionist Affairs (ECZA) was established in New York.[11] As in 1914, its main
participants were the Zionist Organization of America, Hadassah,
Poale Zion, and Mizrahi. Smaller Zionist groups were also invited.
Stephen S. Wise, certainly the most prominent figure in American
Zionism at that time, was elected chairman. In 1914, Shmarya
Lewin, a member of the Smaller Actions Committee (the executive
body of the Zionist movement), had been designated liaison between the international leadership and the PZC. Now, on the eve
of World War II, the same task was assigned to Jewish Agency
member Nahum Goldmann. Last, there was another lesson remembered from the success of the American Jewish Congress: it
was necessary to assure the support of the non-Zionists, and particularly of the influential American Jewish Committee. The Zionist leadership in America grasped well one of the differences between conditions in Europe and the United States: unlike their
European counterparts, American non-Zionists could be persuaded—under certain conditions—to endorse at least some of the
plans of the Zionist movement. It had happened during World War
I and again in 1929.

However, during the early 1940s Zionist efforts did not bear
fruit. The Emergency Committee for Zionist Affairs proved ineffective. Much effort was expended on debates with the Revisionists
and like-minded groups, who were agitating for a Jewish army and
against British policy in Palestine. The political work of the ECZA
in Washington was thus almost negligible, which prompted the
Jewish Agency to establish, in 1943, its own representation in the
capital, headed by Nahum Goldmann. Although Rabbi Stephen
Wise had obviously passed his prime, it was not until August 1943
that Abba Hillel Silver, a prominent Reform rabbi from Cleveland

and a former national chairman of the United Palestine Appeal, was chosen to be co-chairman of the ECZA.[12]

Furthermore, no understanding was reached with the non-Zionists, specifically with the small and oligarchic, but highly influential, American Jewish Committee. Weizmann tried hard in 1940 and 1941 to get their financial and political support, but to no avail.[13] There was no repetition of the situation in 1916, when the Committee had participated in the American Jewish Congress, and its leading personality, Louis Marshall, had become one of the most effective Jewish spokesmen in the negotiations for Jewish rights at the peace conference in Paris.

In historical perspective, the reticence of the American Jewish Committee in the early 1940s appears quite understandable. The Committee still represented the "German" segment of the American Jewish community. Most members of the Committee belonged to the older sector of the Reform movement, which was opposed to the Zionist's concepts of Jewish nationality and peoplehood. True, in those years American Reform Judaism was undergoing significant changes: many second-generation members from the younger Jewish settlement, of East European origin, were beginning to participate in Reform congregations. The sociological change also had consequences for Jewish self-definition among growing sectors of the movement. At the 1937 meeting of the Central Conference of American Rabbis, the rabbinical association of the Reform movement, new principles were formulated, recognizing that the Jews were not only a religious denomination but a people. Support was also expressed for the Jewish settlement in Palestine.[14] In 1941, Rabbi James Heller, an active Zionist, had been elected president of the CCAR, which seemed a sure sign that times had changed. However, the new openness toward Zionism by the Reform movement was more apparent than real. When, at the CCAR meeting in 1942, a resolution was approved endorsing the formation of a Jewish army in Palestine, the simmering tensions between Zionists and anti-Zionists in the Reform movement came to a head. A significant number of anti-Zionist rabbis claimed that the conference had been manipulated by Rabbi Heller.

Although a split in the CCAR was avoided, tensions in the Reform movement continued to mount. The anti-Zionist rabbis were joined by lay leaders and formed a new association, which later became the American Council for Judaism. Although small in numbers, the Council was financially well-endowed, and during the 1940s it became the most vociferous opponent against Zionism within American Jewry.[15]

It was against this unfavorable situation of intensified debate and boiling crisis in the older sector of American Jewry that the Zionist leadership, headed by Weizmann and Ben-Gurion, tried to obtain the support of the non-Zionists for their plans in Palestine. Furthermore, what was now asked of the non-Zionists was much more than in 1916. The issue was no longer a general statement of support for the development of the Jewish settlement in Palestine, but the backing of a Jewish army to fight against Germany and for Jewish statehood in Palestine. Given the conditions of the early 1940s, these were propositions that the heads of the American Jewish Committee were unable to accept.

The Zionist leaders decided to turn to the large Zionist and pro-Zionist sectors of American Jewry and bring about their activation within the framework of a new political statement of Zionist goals. Prodded by Weizmann and Ben-Gurion, the Emergency Committee for Zionist Affairs called in May 1942 a national conference of Zionist representatives at the Biltmore Hotel in New York. The resolutions adopted there became known as the Biltmore Program. Article six called for the rejection of the White Paper of May 1939. Article eight represented a new landmark of Zionist policy. It urged that the "gates of Palestine be opened; that the Jewish Agency be vested with control of immigration into Palestine and with the necessary authority for upbuilding the country . . . and that Palestine be established as a Jewish Commonwealth integrated in the structure of the new democratic world."[16]

The Biltmore Program represented the first fundamental response of the Zionist movement to the political challenges that had arisen as a result of the Palestine White Paper of 1939. The resolutions summed up thoughts and feelings that had begun to develop among Zionists at that turning point. Due to the difficult circumstances of the war, it had taken the Zionist Executive exactly three years to produce a full response. By the end of 1942, the Biltmore Program was adopted by a majority of the Executive of the Jewish Agency and by the Zionist Smaller Actions Committee and thus became the official policy of the movement. The drive toward the creation of a Jewish state had now been publicly proclaimed, and in spite of numerous political fluctuations, it was to remain the central objective of Zionist policy in the coming years.

The subsequent goal of the Zionist leadership was to win the backing of American Jewry at large for the Biltmore Program. Again, the tactics were similar to those applied at the time of the first American Jewish Congress during World War I. With the help of Henry Monsky, president of the Order B'nai B'rith, an American Jewish Conference was called in August 1943; it was attended by the major organizations of American Jewry. The Conference approved the Zionist program for Palestine, but again there was a repetition of what had happened at the CCAR meeting a year earlier: the important non-Zionist participants, whose presence had been assured after many efforts, resigned from the Conference.[17]

It is still an open question as to how sensitive, or even how knowledgeable, the European and Palestinian Zionist leaders were to the internal situation of the non-Zionist segments of American Jewry. Since they worked closely with the leadership of the American Zionist movement—who supposedly knew their own community well—we may assume that during the negotiations in 1943 the urgent needs of the Zionist movement were given more weight than the ideological sensitivities of the non-Zionists. The result was that from the early 1940s onward, Zionist political activities in the United States could not count on the collaboration of the American Jewish Committee and the influential circles connected with it. The effectiveness of the Zionists' efforts was thus much diminished.

Faced with the outcome of the American Jewish Conference, the American Zionist leadership (obviously supported by the heads of the Jewish Agency) decided to concentrate their activities on an exclusively Zionist constituency and through it reach for the broadest support possible of the community. In 1943 the American Zionist Emergency Council was established. Forcefully led by Rabbi Abba Hillel Silver, the AZEC would lead political activity in the United States on behalf of Jewish statehood in Palestine.[18]

Confrontations within the Zionist Leadership

During the deliberations at the UN in 1947–1948, the Zionist political machinery would function like a well-oiled machine. It was difficult to remember that only five years earlier two parallel power struggles within the Zionist leadership had seriously hampered the political work of the movement, and at a time when collaboration between all Zionists, indeed, between all Jews, was vital. On the international level, Ben-Gurion had locked horns in a fierce confrontation with Weizmann. In the United States, a monumental clash between Abba Hillel Silver and Stephen Wise had practically stopped all political activity in the American movement.[19]

In spite of his enormous achievements as the leading figure of Zionism in the 1920s and 1930s, there were two factors that gradually undermined Weizmann's standing. First, he never bothered to build a party of his own in the movement. Consequently, Weizmann was left open to criticism from all Zionist quarters with no political shield to protect him. The absence of a party structure under his direct control had been the major reason for his forced departure from the presidency of the movement in 1931. His return in 1935 was possible mainly due to the support of Mapai, the major Labor Zionist party, which was related to conditions and expectations that Weizmann hardly bothered to consider. The second factor was the alliance between the Zionist movement and Great Britain, of which Weizmann was the foremost Zionist representative. As long as the historic understanding between the British and the Zionists held, however tenuously, Weizmann was the indispensable leader of the Zionist movement. The White Paper of 1939, however, had put an end to the British-Zionist understanding.

All through the 1940s, there was a great measure of agreement between Weizmann and Ben-Gurion on the strategic posture of Zionism. Both recognized that the only possible answer to the 1939 White Paper was Jewish statehood in Palestine. Both emphasized the importance of aliyah as an expression of Zionist ideology, as a political means for strengthening the Jewish community in Palestine, and later on, after the war, as the best way to save the remnants of the European catastrophe. Both recognized the importance of American Jewry in any Jewish or Zionist political maneuvers during and after the war. Therefore, it was no coincidence that the most embarrassing of their clashes occurred in the United States.

There were significant tactical differences between the two men. Due to his life-long affinity for Great Britain, Weizmann was slow in reaching the radical conclusions that characterized Ben-Gurion's position. As preached by Ben-Gurion, the new activist line of the Zionist movement accepted the possibility, in fact, the probability, of a struggle, almost certainly an armed one, against the Arabs and perhaps also against the British. For Ben-Gurion, the White Paper and the consequent steps for its implementation had put an end to his belief in the Zionist alliance with Great Britain. The British refusal in November 1941 to allow the formation of a Jewish fighting force only reinforced the conclusions he had reached in 1939.[20] Weizmann, on the other hand, despite his growing appreciation for the importance of the United States, did not fully abandon his old relationship with the British. In mid-1943 he still believed that "our fate is bound up with England."[21] After all, these were the days of the Cabinet Committee on Palestine formed by Churchill, which revived the partition plan for Palestine.[22] It was only in 1945–1946, after his disillusionment with the recently elected Labor Party in Britain and "Black Saturday" in Palestine, that he was forced to recognize that there was no longer any real hope for a positive collaboration between Zionism and Great Britain.[23]

Fully cognizant of the far-reaching significance of the Biltmore resolutions, Ben-Gurion decided to reach for the leadership of the

Zionist movement and to depose Weizmann. First in the United States, later also in Palestine, Ben-Gurion tried at the very least to neutralize Weizmann, hoping eventually to force him to give up his position altogether. Although in poor health and deeply depressed over the death of his son Michael, Weizmann was able to fend off Ben-Gurion's attack without much effort. His prestige among Jews and Gentiles went far beyond Ben-Gurion's capacity to upset his standing. It was only in December 1946, at the twenty-second Zionist Congress, that the struggle came to an end. Weizmann was not reelected president of the World Zionist Organization. It was Ben-Gurion, chairman of the Jewish Agency, who was to lead the Zionist movement in the decisive stages of the struggle for Jewish statehood.

In spite of the different circumstances, there were many similarities between the Ben-Gurion–Weizmann dispute on the international level and the Silver–Wise confrontation in the American movement. Like Ben-Gurion, Silver represented a younger generation in Zionist politics and the more radical approach that developed in the 1940s. Wise had been one of the founders of the American movement in 1898; Silver had first appeared on the American Zionist scene in 1920. Since then he had built an influential rabbinical career in Cleveland. Wise was a long-time Democrat, known for his close relations with President Roosevelt; Silver was an active Republican, and he considered Wise's Democratic connection a handicap, since it hindered him from making more forceful demands on the White House. Interestingly, both men were Reform rabbis, a movement whose attitude toward Zionism was, on the whole, rather negative.[24]

A man of impressive presence, Silver was one of the great orators of his age, highly focused and quite aggressive.[25] In 1943, the cause of his confrontation with Wise was the leadership of the American Zionist Emergency Council. Simultaneously, a rivalry was brewing between Silver and Nahum Goldmann, the representative of the Jewish Agency, regarding Zionist activities in Washington. Silver accused Goldmann of interfering in activities that were the rightful concern of AZEC. It was only in mid-1945 that an understanding was reached in the American leadership that in fact guaranteed Silver's primacy in the Council. A somewhat precarious modus vivendi was also reached between Silver and Goldmann. From then on, Silver was to lead American Zionism and significant parts of American Jewry in the fight for Jewish statehood. This relative stability did not eliminate tensions between a number of outstanding personalities, regardless of their political or strategic orientation. Between 1944 and 1948, Silver alternately allied himself or quarreled with Weizmann (who in 1941 had brought him into the American Zionist leadership), with Goldmann (who was more of a diplomat than Silver), or Ben-Gurion (who while recognizing Silver's qualities, preferred using him without allowing him to become too powerful).

The parallel confrontation between Ben-Gurion and Weizmann for the leadership of the international movement, and between Silver and Wise for control over American Zionism, occurred at a time when overwhelming problems and dangers burdened both European Jewry and the Zionist movement. Obviously, the consequences of such struggles between the important figures of the movement distracted them from the needs of the Jews in Europe and from the interests of Zionism in general. Nevertheless, on the whole, these struggles were over style, emphasis, and tactics. Basically, all the figures involved were in agreement regarding the essentials: Jewish statehood; Zionist activism in Palestine and in the Diaspora; the development of a political working relationship in the United States, both with the Jewish community as well as with the American administration; and covert consensus over the partition of Palestine.

Reactions to the Holocaust

In the ongoing debate over the behavior of the Jews inside and outside Europe during the period of the Holocaust, poignant questions have been asked in the last two generations about the attitudes and policies of the Zionist leadership. Until the last few years the main criticism has been directed against the general Jewish leadership and the Jewish Councils (Judenräte) established by the Germans in the lands under their occupation. It is recognized that the Zionists were among the most active among the Jews in the struggle against the Nazis and in the efforts to save Jews from German-occupied Europe. Nevertheless, there are scholars who claim that Zionist policy was too much focused on its own aims and relegated the rescue of the Jews trapped in Nazi-dominated Europe to a secondary position. The discussion, it should be stressed, is about Jewish behavior in general, and within this framework, the activities of the Zionists have also been scrutinized. The critical arguments of one group of scholars have, not surprisingly, been vigorously refuted by other researchers.[26]

Whatever recriminations there are against Zionist policy during the Holocaust, in most cases they are built on the inaccurate premise that there was an intrinsic and interdependent connection between the destruction of European Jewry and the Zionist plans in Palestine. In the 1940s, the Jewish people were confronted with two pressing but diverse challenges: one was how to save the Jews caught in the European inferno, and the other was how to react to British policy in Palestine. The change of British policy in Palestine was the result of internal developments in Great Britain itself that had nothing to do with the situation of the Jews; nor did the Zionist goals in Palestine have immediate connection to the plight of European Jewry.

It has been repeatedly argued that against the Nazi determination to "solve" the "Jewish Question" there was little that the Jews could have done.[27] Nevertheless, in Jewish quarters there were differences of attitudes concerning the ability to act—which was limited—and the notion of what actually should be done in order to alleviate the situation of the Jews in Europe—a precondition to any action. The Zionist leadership was far better prepared to consider these matters than any other group. The Zionists were in favor of the evacuation of the Jews, to Palestine if possible, and if not to Palestine, to any other place. The non-Zionist leadership in such important countries as the United States and Britain held to the principle of the resettlement of the Jewish refugees in their countries of origin. Another fallacy—rejected by the Zionist leaders but accepted by many Jewish personalities—was the idea, much cherished in British official circles and also in the American administration, that the best way to save the Jews was to concentrate *all* the efforts in the fight against Nazi Germany. In practice, it meant doing nothing to save the Jews trapped in Europe.[28]

Only after the war did the leaders of the American Jewish Committee conclude that to force the survivors of the Holocaust, languishing in Displaced Persons (DP) camps in Europe, to rebuild their lives in their former countries made no sense and would be unacceptable. Even then, practical reasons, and not ideological arguments brought them around to support the immigration of the survivors to Palestine: the will of the DPs themselves and the absence of other alternatives. Immigration to Palestine was not necessarily related to the partition of Palestine and even less so to Jewish statehood; these realities were again matters that were only slowly and painfully accepted by the leaders of the AJC and the sectors of American Jewry close to them.[29]

One important occasion when the broadest representation of Zionist leaders from Europe and from the United States met and discussed current conditions and future plans was the Biltmore Conference in May 1942. The minutes of the conference show that both the White Paper of May 1939 and the plight of European Jewry were uppermost in the minds of the speakers.[30] The arguments touching on the fate of European Jewry, while displaying anxiety, were couched in rather general terms. Reference was made to "Nazi persecutions" but there was no mention of a Holocaust or of massive extermination of the Jews. Weizmann expressed the fear that up to 25 percent of the East European Jews might be "liquidated" during the war. The remainder, two to four million Jews in his estimation, would be uprooted from their homes and "left as a floating population between heaven and hell, not knowing where to turn." He recalled his earlier warning in 1936, when he had said that for European Jewry the world was to be "divided in two parts: the countries where they cannot live and the countries they cannot enter." But in spite of all this, Weizmann was still optimistic about the ultimate survival of European Jewry. His experience during World War I led him to hope that once again European Jewry would survive pogroms and persecutions and re-emerge stronger than ever.

While Weizmann's position had been more Diaspora-oriented, Ben-Gurion had concentrated on the situation in Palestine. He demanded the fulfillment of the original terms of the Mandate, criticized the 1939 White Paper, and suggested solutions to the Arab problem.[31] Both leaders were still unaware—as were almost all the other delegates to the Biltmore Conference—that total destruction threatened European Jewry. The only hint of the magnitude of the catastrophe came from Nahum Goldmann. He alone suggested that the large majority of European Jewry might not survive the war, and that those who might would be left without the strength to rise again and rebuild their shattered lives and communities.[32]

Nevertheless, there was a built-in contradiction in the Biltmore resolutions, which was to surface again and again in future discussions. Had the delegates known about the extent of the European disaster, their position would have been even more difficult: the destruction of European Jewry undermined the main premises on which the Biltmore platform rested. Ben-Gurion was aiming for the immediate transfer of about two million Jews from Europe to Palestine after the war as the basis for the Zionist demand for a Jewish Commonwealth.[33] But what if those Jews were no longer alive? Here again was expressed the intrinsic contradiction between the Holocaust and Jewish statehood. After the war, the number of DPs on whose future the Zionists based their political plans for Palestine was reduced to some 250,000 Jewish survivors.[34]

Altogether, the influence of the Holocaust on the attitudes of the Zionist leadership should be understood within the framework of the general behavior of the Jews outside Central and Eastern Europe. The facts are grim but have to be recognized as they were.

None of the classic disputes between the Zionists and the non-Zionists, or between the different Zionist factions, or between the diverse movements in non-Zionist Jewish society, or the patterns of relations between Jews and Gentiles, were significantly influenced as a result of the Jewish tragedy unfolding in Europe.

Toward Confrontation in Palestine, 1945-1948

The war in Europe ended in May 1945. In July 1945 there were elections in Great Britain, and the Conservatives were defeated. The Labour Party, now in power, was on record as being pro-Zionist.[35] Close personal relations existed between several of the Zionist-Socialist leaders and members of the Labour Party. For a short time there were great hopes among the Zionists that the new British government might bring about a radical change in its anti-Zionist policy in Palestine.

The disappointment was all the more harsh. By the fall of 1945 it had become clear that under the Labour government there would be no change in British policy regarding Palestine. On the contrary: One of the justifications of the 1939 White Paper had been the precarious strategic situation of Great Britain in the Middle East during the approaching war. Now that the war was over it became evident that the pro-Arab orientation of the British in the Middle East had been based on much broader political considerations and continued without any change. Forcefully headed by Ernest Bevin, the Foreign Office continued to be in charge of British policy in the Middle East and undermined the more cautious approach of the Colonial Office.[36] The position of the Foreign Office, which had crystallized in discussions inside the British government during the second half of 1937, was totally Arab oriented.

At the end of the war in Europe, the Zionist leadership called for broad consultations to consider its next steps. A World Zionist

Conference, convened in London in August 1945, affirmed the resolutions of the Biltmore Conference. The 1939 White Paper was declared "devoid of any moral and legal validity." The conference demanded free Jewish immigration into Palestine, the right to control and develop the land and power resources of the land, and "that an immediate decision be announced to establish Palestine as a Jewish state."[37] Eighteen months later, in December 1946, the twenty-second Zionist Congress met in Basel and reaffirmed the resolutions of the Zionist Conference.[38] In the meantime, however, the confrontation between the Zionists and the British had reached a critical stage.

Back in 1939, Ben-Gurion had declared that aliyah, by any means, would be the principal instrument of the Zionists' struggle against the White Paper policy. Efforts to rescue Jews from Europe and to bring them to Palestine had been attempted during the war. The effort made had been immense, the results, rather disappointing.[39] Now, after the defeat of Germany, a major effort of the Zionist movement was to bring the survivors of the Holocaust, most of them languishing in camps in the American zone in Germany, to Palestine, and this in spite of the opposition of the British authorities. Most of the ships with so-called "illegal" immigrants were intercepted and their passengers interned on Cyprus.[40]

Until the end of April 1946—when the recommendations of the Anglo-American Committee of Inquiry were published—the Zionist leadership continued to search for political solutions to the impasse with the British. Until then, few lines of communication had been established between the Zionist leadership and the American government. However, the negotiations with the British brought none of the results hoped for. The fact that the British government seemed closed to any of the Zionists' demands strengthened the radical line of action represented by Ben-Gurion. The burden of the growing confrontation with the British was on the Jewish community in Palestine, and there the more moderate position of Weizmann was less influential than in the Diaspora. Among the American Zionists the more radical approach also gained the upper hand. Led by Abba Hillel Silver, the American

Zionist Emergency Council was gradually preparing American Jewish public opinion for the nearing political struggle for Jewish statehood in Palestine. At the same time, both in the United States and in Palestine the Zionist leadership had to cope with an extremist fringe. In the United States, the activities of the Bergson Group were concentrated on huge announcements in the press. In Palestine, however, armed resistance was becoming part of the political effort. While the Haganah, the army of the Jewish community, was controlled and directed by the institutions of the community, the two smaller resistance groups, the Etzel and the Lehi, were motivated by other political and ideological guidelines. Small and dedicated, operating as urban guerrillas, both organizations declared a private war on the British. They were as effective as groups of their kind usually are. By 1946 their activities and British intransigence had created a dangerous crisis in the relations between the British and the Jewish community.[41] In the end, though, these organizations were one of the factors that influenced the British decision to turn over the Palestinian problem to the United Nations.

The brewing crisis in Palestine was brought to new heights as a result of the recommendations of the Anglo-American Committee of Inquiry.[42] The Committee was formed to look into the situation in Palestine, to study the problem of the Jewish refugees in Europe, and to suggest solutions concerning both. Some of the recommendations of the Committee were hardly satisfying to the Zionists, such as the postponement of independence for Palestine. However, the second recommendation proposed that 100,000 Jewish refugees should be admitted immediately into Palestine. The recommendation was accepted by the Americans but rejected by the British, although there was a previous understanding that any recommendations unanimously endorsed would be binding on both governments.[43] Furthermore, the work of the Committee of Inquiry had additional results. It was the first major American involvement in the Palestinian problem, the beginning of a new trend that was welcomed by the Zionist leadership.

From the point of view of the Zionist leadership, the result of the Committee's labors brought the relations between the movement and the British government into a phase of serious and open confrontation. Acts of sabotage increased, "illegal" immigration reached a peak, and clashes between the British army and the various resistance groups brought Palestine to the verge of large-scale rebellion. In June 1946 the British launched Operation Agatha: the headquarters of the Jewish Agency in Jerusalem were occupied and search and arrest operations took place all over the country. About 2,700 Jews were arrested, among them members of the Jewish Agency. In July 1946 the Etzel group, commanded by Menahem Begin, demolished part of the King David Hotel, which housed several branches of the British administration. Almost one hundred people were killed.[44]

In spite of the worsening spiral of violence, the Zionist leadership and the British did not stop political contacts altogether. Yet, the longer negotiations with the British went on, the clearer it became that their political aims in the Middle East were geared to an understanding with the Arab states and leaders. The fact that the Arabs had embarked on a line of total rejection of any and all of the Zionists' political demands made the Zionists' position, if not easier, certainly simpler. Again and again, exhaustive discussions between the Zionist leaders and the British came to naught since any concession was rejected by the Arabs.[45]

In such an increasingly complex situation, the Zionist leaders worked to guarantee the concentrated support of the largest possible part of the Jewish people for its political aims. The first of those aims had been decided during the war: Jewish statehood in Palestine. The second was now considered: partition of the country. A third goal complementing the first two was to assure the American government's support for the Zionist plans. In the circumstances of the postwar years, American backing was of decisive importance for the realization of the Zionist plans in Palestine.

For a considerable time, the political relationship between the Zionist movement (and later, the State of Israel) and the United States remained a one-sided affair. As mentioned, the Zionist leadership had tried since 1939 to establish contact with the American administration, with mixed results. The pro-American tendency of the Zionist (and later Israeli) side was not encouraged by the American government, certainly not during World War II, and only marginally afterward. Even the White House remained ambiguous concerning the Zionist overtures, in spite of President Truman's assistance on a number of critical occasions. Seen from a larger historical perspective, Truman's pro-Zionist actions were the exception in America's Middle Eastern policy during that period.[46] In the Americans' attitude there was none of the spiritual background that had made the British receptive to an understanding with the Zionists in the days of World War I. In fact, in the 1940s, the American policy regarding the Middle East was not very different from the British one. It too was Arab-oriented, although not as sharply crystallized and certainly less self-assured than British policy.

In spite of all this, when in 1947 the issue of Palestine came before the United Nations, the Zionist leadership considered American support essential for the success of their plans. True, there was also a Soviet option worth considering. In Palestine and in the Diaspora there were Jewish political circles very keen for an understanding with the Russians. However, Soviet policy had until then been consistently anti-Zionist. The later support of the Soviet Union for partition (September–November 1947) would come as a surprise to everybody, including the Zionists.[47] As matters stood in mid-947, the pro-American tendency of the Zionist leadership reflected strategic foresight and subjective leanings but was not based on any factual understanding with American policy-makers.

Jewish statehood in Palestine considered as an unavoidable Zionist reaction to the British White Paper of 1939, there still remained the question as to whether the Jewish state should encompass all of Palestine or whether partition was acceptable as an alternative. The issue was not without its difficulties. Some influential sectors in the Zionist movement, for example, claimed that the Land of Israel had already been partitioned once: in 1922, when Transjordan had been separated by the British and by the League of Nations from that part of the Palestinian Mandate wherein a Jewish National Home was to be established. When partition of Palestine west of the river Jordan had been brought up in 1937 by the Royal Palestine Commission, the Zionists had vacillated, the Arabs had opposed the plan, and soon the British changed their mind as well. The Biltmore Program of 1942 had spoken of Palestine being established "as a Jewish Common- wealth," which literally meant the whole of Palestine. In fact, however, partition was in the air. Weizmann had mentioned it in his negotiations with the non-Zionist leaders of the American Jew- ish Committee in 1941–1942. After the war other Zionist leaders also indicated that partition was not an issue beyond discussion.[48] Even Silver, the radical leader of the American Zionist Emergency Council, was ready to consider it.[49] Nevertheless, for tactical rea- sons the Zionist leadership held to the "Palestine *as*" formula- tion—against the "*in* Palestine" usage—of the Balfour Declaration. If there was to be partition, the Zionist leaders preferred that it be suggested by the British or the Americans.[50] This was a vain hope: the British would not antagonize the Arabs, and the Arabs rejected partition in principle.

In February 1947 the British government decided to refer the question of Palestine to the United Nations. The Zionist leaders were unsure as to the consequences of this new step and there was a general feeling of apprehension about the chances of the Zionist case at the UN.[51] Obviously, the British acted as they did because it seemed to serve their own interests well. In addition, the Arabs were strongly represented at the UN. In fact, the result was entirely different. Once Palestine became an international issue, the inter- national organization began to look at it from its own point of view. British intentions, Zionist fears, and Arab hopes were all turned upside down. The General Assembly decided to establish a commission to examine the case—the United Nations Special Committee on Palestine. UNSCOP visited the DP camps in Europe and spent several weeks in Palestine listening to all sides involved in the conflict.

The Zionist leadership quickly understood that the activities of the United Nations could have very positive results. They made every effort to explain the Zionist case to the members of UNSCOP as convincingly as possible, both in Europe and in Palestine, while the Palestinian Arabs decided to boycott the commission.[52] The American Zionist Emergency Council, skillfully led by Silver, created a background of favorable public opinion for the Zionist case in the United States. The fact that the Jewish Agency was now recognized as a body entitled to participate in the UN discussions dealing with Palestine gave the Zionists an additional boost. The Zionist leadership concentrated on partition, a solution now also supported by large segments of the non-Zionist American Jewry. Even Joseph Proskauer, the influential president of the American Jewish Committee, came to recognize that partition was the most practical solution to the Palestinian imbroglio.[53]

The report of UNSCOP, published at the end of August 1947, recommended the partition of Palestine. In the months between September and November 1947, the Zionists worked very hard to assure the approval of partition by the General Assembly, which indeed approved it on 29 November 1947.[54] Since the decision was adopted by a very small margin, it is most probable that the efforts of the Zionists made the difference.[55]

Although the partition resolution was greeted by the Zionist leaders and their supporters as a great victory, it brought little respite from tension. It merely marked the beginning of another difficult period, which extended until 14 May 1948, when the State of Israel was proclaimed. At that time, the Zionist struggle acquired a military dimension as a result of increasing Arab guerrilla warfare in Palestine and the threat from neighboring Arab states. The situation was complicated by an arms embargo on Palestine imposed in January 1948 by the Americans and other Western states but not by the Communist bloc.

Ironically, the most difficult obstacle on the way to Jewish statehood now became none other than the American administration. Unconvinced as to the advantages of the partition resolution and faced with a significant worsening of the security situation in Palestine in early 1948, the State Department engineered a new political solution—a plan for a UN trusteeship for Palestine, which it presented before the Security Council in March 1948.[56]

Although obscured by the drama of the proclamation of the State of Israel two months later, the American political change of heart represented a most delicate, even dangerous, moment in the political fortunes of the Zionist movement. It proved how tenuous American support was for the Zionists' plans.[57] The Zionists rejected the American plan and proceeded with their preparations toward the establishment of the Jewish state. The Zionist leadership continued to work harmoniously during the ongoing debate on the future of Palestine that continued until the proclamation of the State of Israel in mid-May 1948. Ben-Gurion was in Palestine, mostly occupied with security matters. Silver and Goldmann directed the political efforts in the United States and represented the Jewish Agency at the UN. Moshe Shertok (Sharett) had the overall responsibility for the diplomatic work, and he coordinated efforts between the headquarters of the Jewish Agency in Jerusalem and the Zionist delegations in Washington and New York. Weizmann, by 1947 without any formal standing but still the bearer of huge moral authority, was in the United States. Although sick and spent, some of his interventions were significant, such as his meeting with President Truman in March 1948. Berl Locker represented the Jewish Agency in London. His was a delicate task: to keep open channels of communication with the British government, still the mandatory power in Palestine but by now committed to ending its presence in Palestine with as little trouble for itself as possible.

At this difficult hour, the majority of the non-Zionist Jewish organizations in the United States stood by the Zionists (or at least did not oppose them) in their thrust for Jewish statehood in Palestine. The Jewish left-wing organizations, their hesitations neutralized because of the support for partition on the part of the Soviet bloc, even intensified their support for partition. The influential Order B'nai B'rith did likewise. The American Reform movement adopted neutrality, although the majority of its members supported partition. Neutrality was also the stance of the American Jewish Committee, in spite of the pro-partition position of its president, Joseph Proskauer.[58] Only the American Council for Judaism continued to oppose Jewish statehood, but by now it was quite isolated. It should be stressed that adoption of the position taken by American non-Zionists represented no small feat: opposing the official line of the government was something unheard of among Diaspora Jews in modern times. The non-Zionist leadership of British Jewry, for example, never went that far. In March 1948, at the peak of the Zionists' struggle, Sir Robert Waley-Cohen, president of the prestigious Anglo-Jewish Association, expressed support for a UN trusteeship in Palestine.[59] However, his position was meaningless. When in May 1948 the hour of political decision regarding Palestine arrived, most sectors of the Jewish people, right and left, religious and secular, Zionists and non-Zionists, fully supported the establishment of a Jewish state.

Conclusions

Tracing a pattern of coherent policy is the privilege of historians. In real life, statesmen mostly muddle through. Up to a point, this is what happened to the Zionist leadership in the fateful years that preceded the creation of the State of Israel. Nevertheless, there were three major decisions that directed the overall strategy of the Zionist leadership: the recognition that the political relationship between the Zionist movement and Great Britain had come to an end; the focus of Zionist foreign policy on the United States; and finally, the determination to strive for Jewish statehood.

Basically, all three decisions had already emerged in 1939, as a result of the White Paper on Palestine. The elaboration of the new policy occurred during the war, between 1939 and 1945; and expression of the policy worked in favor of the unification of American Jewry, at least for the support of Zionist aims in Palestine. The first steps, so-called illegal immigration to Palestine, were the main weapon to be used in the impending struggle against the British White Paper. The preparation of military means, among them the Haganah and the Palmach, for a probable struggle against the Arabs and, if necessary, against the British, were likewise part of the strategy to prepare for Jewish statehood.

All these steps were accompanied by a realignment of the Zionist leadership. On the international level, David Ben-Gurion gradually took over from Chaim Weizmann. Less important but not less dramatic were the changes in the American movement, where Abba Hillel Silver stepped in for for Stephen S. Wise. Unavoidably, these confrontations also gave rise to personal accusations and tensions between the various leaders. Nevertheless, in historical perspective the struggle between Ben-Gurion and Weizmann belongs more properly to the folklore of the movement than to its ideological or political core. It was little more than the personal aftershock of a major political earthquake—a turning away from Great Britain, and perhaps even against the British—which affected Weizmann's personal standing. This, added to his other limitations—age, poor health, personal tragedy, the lack of internal political support—made Weizmann's position at the head of the movement untenable. Ben-Gurion was the driving force during this new era, which had its beginnings in the Zionist movement in 1939. It was only a matter of time until he fully took over the leadership of the movement at the twenty-second Zionist Congress in December 1946.

The years from 1945 to 1948 were a period of struggle. It was a struggle whose aims and methods had been established in the first half of the 1940s. There were severe limitations on the means available for Zionist or Jewish political action. Public support was doubtful. The practical significance of such widely used concepts as "World Jewry" or "American Jewry" was, in fact, highly questionable. There was little cooperation between the Jewish communities of the diverse lands or between the different Jewish parties. "American Jewry" existed as a sociological reality but not as a unified body willing to act in concert except during some emergencies. The idea of the "unification" of American Jewry was and remained mainly a Zionist goal.

The practical results of these limitations were evident everywhere.

True, significant sectors of American Jewry mobilized behind the activity of the American Zionist Emergency Council, forcefully led by Abba Hillel Silver; however, it remains an open question as to how effective the AZEC actually was.[60] No understanding was possible with the American administration, in spite of the helpful but isolated decisions of President Truman in 1948. "Illegal" immigration into Palestine had an important psychological effect, but meager results in terms of the numbers of actual immigrants who arrived. The military preparations of the Yishuv went on, but they were barely sufficient to meet the needs which materialized later, after the partition decision of the United Nations in November 1947.

Nevertheless, during the crucial years from 1946 to 1948, the Zionists managed to resolve their leadership problems. The leaders of the movement, supported by whatever sectors of "World Jewry" that were active, were united in the thrust toward Jewish statehood in the United Nations, in the United States, and in Palestine. To everybody's surprise, they succeeded. Historians still marvel at the outcome. As Roger Louis wrote more than a generation later, "one way of interpreting the sequence of these complex events would be to maintain that it was the Zionists' year for a miracle."[61] As miracles go, this one was as well-prepared as possible under quite adverse circumstances.

The more one researches the events of the fateful years between 1945 and 1948, the more tenuous the connection between the Holocaust and the creation of Israel appears. It is difficult to point to a direct influence of the Holocaust on the shaping of Zionist policy or the political behavior of the Zionist leadership. The decision to change the strategic course of Zionist policy—to direct it to Jewish statehood, to build a strong American connection— was taken as a result of the 1939 White Paper. The Biltmore Conference took place before the news about the systematic destruction of European Jewry filtered through. The confrontation between Ben-Gurion and Weizmann, or between Silver and Wise, had nothing to do with the tragedy which befell European Jews. All through the war, important and leading non-Zionists within

American and British Jewry held to the notion that the best way to save European Jewry was to support fully the general war effort, that to defeat Nazi Germany was the best way to save the remnants of European Jewry.

Moreover, the Zionist movement that led the struggle for Jewish statehood in 1947–1948 was a very different one from the movement ten years earlier. It was much smaller and weaker. The vital part of the Zionist constituency, the Jews of Eastern Europe, had been exterminated during World War II. The most vigorous among the Jewish communities, the East European Jewry that created the Jewish National Home in Palestine prior to 1939 and that would have been the most able and best prepared to complete the task, existed no longer. The State of Israel was reborn during the darkest hour of the Jewish people. Under such conditions, the creation of Israel was indeed something close to a miracle.

NOTES

1. World Zionist Organization and the Jewish Agency for Palestine, *Reports of the Executive Submitted to the Twenty-second Zionist Congress at Basle, December 1946* (Jerusalem, 1946) 6–7.

2. See Michael J. Cohen, "Appeasement in the Middle East: The British White Paper on Palestine, May 1939," in Michael J. Cohen, *Palestine to Israel: From Mandate to Independence* (London: Frank Cass, 1988) 101–28; Yehuda Bauer, *From Diplomacy to Resistance: A History of Jewish Palestine, 1939–1945* (Philadelphia: Jewish Publication Society, 1970) 28–43; and Nicholas Bethell, *The Palestine Triangle: The Struggle between the British, the Jews and the Arabs 1935–1948* (London: Futura Publications, 1970) ch. 2. The text of the White Paper is found in John N. Moore, ed., *The Arab-Israeli Conflict*, vol. 3, Documents (Princeton: Princeton University Press, 1974) 210–21.

3. David Ben-Gurion, *Bamaarakha 2* (Tel Aviv, 1957) 188–89.

4. See Chaim Weizmann, "Palestine's Role in the Solution of the Jewish Problem," published in *Foreign Affairs* 20.2 (January 1942): 324–38.

5. See Jehuda Reinharz, "Zionism and the Great-Power Connection: A Century of Foreign Policy," Leo Baeck Memorial Lecture (New York, 1994).

6. See Yitzhak Avnery, "Immigration and Revolt: Ben-Gurion's Response to the 1939 White Paper," in Ronald W. Zweig, ed., *David Ben-Gurion, Politics and Leadership in Israel* (Jerusalem: Y. I. Ben-Zvi, 1991) 99–123. Avnery

rightly emphasizes the aliyah theme in Ben-Gurion's policy, but it seems that aliyah was the means to his strategic end, Jewish statehood.

7. See Walter Laqueur, in *The Terrible Secret: Suppression of the Truth about Hitler's 'Final Solution'* (London: Weidenfeld and Nicolson, 1980) 158.

8. Regarding the Jews in Latin America, see Haim Avni, "Patterns of Jewish Leadership in Latin America during the Holocaust," in Randolph L. Braham, ed., *Jewish Leadership during the Nazi Era: Patterns of Behavior in the Free World* (New York: Institute for Holocaust Studies of the City University of New York, 1985) 87–130.

9. See Richard Bolchover, *British Jewry and the Holocaust* (Cambridge: Cambridge University Press, 1993); Gideon Shimoni, "The Non-Zionists in Anglo-Jewry 1937–1948," *Jewish Journal of Sociology* 28.2 (1968): 90; Bernard Wasserstein, "Patterns of Jewish Leadership in Great Britain during the Nazi Era," in Braham, ed., *Jewish Leadership* 29–43.

10. See Yonathan Shapiro, *Leadership of the American Zionist Organization 1897–1930* (Urbana: University of Illinois Press, 1971), ch. 4; Oscar I. Janowsky, *The Jews and Minority Rights (1898–1919)* (New York: Columbia University Press, 1933) ch. 7.

11. See Doreen Bierbrier, "The American Zionist Emergency Council: An Analysis of a Pressure Group," *American Jewish Historical Quarterly* 60 (September 1970): 82–83.

12. Bierbrier, "American Zionist Emergency Council" 84–85.

13. Menahem Kaufman, *An Ambiguous Partnership: Non-Zionists and Zionists in America 1939–1948* (Jerusalem: Magnes Press; Detroit: Wayne State University Press, 1991) 58–61.

14. See Howard R. Greenstein, *Turning Point: Zionism and Reform Judaism* (Chico, CA: Scholars Press, 1981) 28–32; Marc Lee Raphael, *Profiles in American Judaism* (San Francisco: Harper and Row, 1984) 55–63. On developments in the American Jewish Committee, see Naomi W. Cohen, *Not Free to Desist: The American Jewish Committee 1906–1966* (Philadelphia: Jewish Publication Society, 1972) 249–64.

15. Cohen, *Not Free to Desist* ch. 2.

16. *Book of Documents Submitted to the General Assembly of the United Nations Relating to the Establishment of the National Home for the Jewish People,* ed. Abraham Tulin (New York: Jewish Agency for Palestine, 1947) 226–27; Yehuda Bauer, *From Diplomacy to Resistance: A History of Jewish Palestine 1939–1945* (Philadelphia: Jewish Publication Society, 1970) 234–43; see also David H. Shpiro, "The Political Background of the 1942 Biltmore Resolution," in *Essays in American Zionism 1917–1948* (*Herzl Year Book*, vol. 8), ed. Melvin I. Urofsky (New York: Herzl Press, 1978) 166–77.

17. Kaufman, *An Ambiguous Partnership* 108–57.

18. On AZEC, see Samuel Halperin, *The Political World of American Zion-*

ism (Detroit: Wayne State University Press, 1961), esp. ch. 10; Bierbrier, "American Zionist Emergency Council." On AZEC and Silver, see Marc Lee Raphael, *Abba Hillel Silver: A Profile in American Judaism* (New York: Holmes & Meier, 1989) chs. 4–7.

19. See Bauer, *From Diplomacy to Resistance* 233–42; Yosef Gorni, "Ben-Gurion and Weizmann during World War II," in Zweig, *David Ben-Gurion* 85–98; Michael J. Cohen, *Palestine: Retreat from the Mandate. The Making of British Policy, 1936–45* (London: P. Elek, 1978) ch. 7: "Zionist Leadership in Crisis"; Melvin I. Urofsky, "Rifts in the Movement: Zionist Fissures, 1942–1945," in Urofsky, *Essays* 195–211.

20. See Cohen, *Palestine* 128–29.

21. Weizmann to B. Dugdale, 1 June 1943, Central Zionist Archives, Jerusalem, Z5/1385.

22. See Ronald W. Zweig, *Britain and Palestine during the Second World War* (Woodbridge, Eng.: Boydell Press for the Royal Historical Society, 1986) 107–13, 171–76.

23. See his letter to the Chief Rabbi of Palestine, Isaac Herzog, 21 July 1946, *The Letters and Papers of Chaim Weizmann, Series A–Letters,* vol. 22, 169–73 (Jerusalem: Israel Universities Press, 1979).

24. See Raphael, *Abba Hillel Silver,* esp. ch. 6; see also Urofsky, "Rifts in the Movement."

25. He was described by Nahum Goldmann as follows: "Above all he had unyielding strength of will. He was a typical autocrat, possessing the authority and self-confidence to command, but not the flexibility to understand his opponent. . . . He was a loyal friend to all those who followed his orders absolutely. Anyone who fought him politically became his personal enemy. He could be extremely ruthless in a fight, and there was something of the terrorist in his manner and bearing" (quoted by Urofsky, "Rifts in the Movement" 201).

26. Lucy S. Dawidowicz, "Could the United States Have Rescued the European Jews from Hitler?" *This World* 12 (Fall 1985): 15–30. Dawidowicz's argument is more exhaustively treated in her book *The War against the Jews* (New York: Holt, Rinehart, and Winston, 1975); Dawidowicz argues against the position of David S. Wyman, *The Abandonment of the Jews* (New York: Pantheon Books, 1984).

For a partial list of works on the Jewish reactions to the Holocaust in the United States and in Great Britain, see Richard Bolchover, *British Jewry and the Holocaust* (Cambridge: Cambridge University Press, 1993) 157. Regarding the Jewish leadership in different countries, see the essays in Braham, *Jewish Leadership.* On reactions in Palestine, see Dina Porat, *The Blue and the Yellow Stars of David: The Zionist Leadership in Palestine and the Holocaust 1933–1945* (Cambridge: Harvard University Press, 1990) 239–62;

Yoav Gelber, "Zionist Policy and the Fate of European Jewry (1939-1942)," *Yad Vashem Studies* 13 (1979): 169-210. For an overview of the diverse approaches, see Michael R. Marrus, *The Holocaust in History* (Hanover, NH: University Press of New England, 1987) chs. 6-7.

The activities of the Jewish Councils represent the centerpiece of the debate over Jewish behavior. See Raul Hilberg, *The Destruction of the European Jews* (Chicago: Quadrangle Books, 1961) esp. 662-69; Hannah Arendt, *Eichmann in Jerusalem: A Report on the Banality of Evil* (New York: Viking Press, 1964) esp. 117-20, 123-25. For an analysis of those views, see Yisrael Gutman, "Jewish Resistance—Questions and Assessments," in Yisrael Gutman and Gideon Greif, eds., *The Historiography of the Holocaust Period: Proceedings of the Fifth Yad Vashem International Historical Conference* (Jerusalem: Yad Vashem, 1988) 641-77; Aharon Weiss, "The Historiographical Controversy Concerning the Character and Functions of the Judenrats," in Gutman and Greif, *Historiography of the Holocaust Period* 679-96; regarding the Jewish Councils, the standard work remains Isaiah Trunk's *Judenrat: The Jewish Councils in Eastern Europe under Nazi Occupation* (New York: Macmillan, 1972).

27. The case is forcefully presented by Dawidowicz in "Could the United States Have Rescued the European Jews from Hitler?" and by Marrus, *Holocaust in History.*

28. See Bolchover, *British Jewry and the Holocaust* 103-20, 146.

29. See Menahem Kaufman, "An Uneasy Relationship: American non-Zionists and the Issue of a Jewish State (1940-1948)," *Jerusalem Cathedra* 3 (1983): 295, 296-99.

30. Minutes of the Extraordinary Zionist Conference (Zionist Archives and Library, New York). The resolutions were published in Tulin, ed., *Book of Documents* 226-27.

31. *Minutes.* Ben-Gurion's speech was published in David Ben-Gurion, *Rebirth and Destiny of Israel* (New York: Philosophical Library, 1954) 113-32.

32. Ben-Gurion, *Rebirth.*

33. Bauer, *From Diplomacy to Resistance* 234, 260.

34. Yehuda Bauer, *Flight and Rescue: Brichah* (New York: Random House, 1970) 320.

35. See Joseph Gorni, *The British Labor Movement and Zionism 1917-1948* (London: Frank Cass, 1983) chs. 10-11.

36. See Gorni, *British Labor Movement;* Michael J. Cohen, *Palestine and the Great Powers 1945-1948* (Princeton: Princeton University Press, 1982) 16-28; W. Roger Louis, *The British Empire in the Middle East 1945-1951: Arab Nationalism, the United States and Postwar Imperialism* (Oxford: Oxford University Press, 1984).

37. *Book of Documents,* ed. Tulin, 238-42.

38. *Book of Documents*, ed. Tulin, 304–308.

39. See Jon Kimche and David Kimche, *The Secret Roads: The "Illegal" Migration of a People 1938–1948* (London: Secker & Warburg, 1955) 45–106; Porat, *Blue and Yellow Stars of David* 229–38.

40. See Bauer, *Flight and Rescue;* Zeev (Venia) Hadari and Zeev Tsahor, *Ships of a State* (Tel Aviv and Beer Sheva, n.d., in Hebrew) 12–32; Kimche and Kimche, *Secret Roads* chs. 13–15.

41. See Cohen, *Palestine and the Great Powers* ch. 4.

42. *Report of the Anglo-American Committee of Enquiry Regarding the Problems of European Jewry and Palestine*, 20 April 1946, Cmd. 6808; see also Michael J. Cohen, "The Genesis of the Anglo-American Committee on Palestine, November 1945: A Case Study in the Assertion of American Hegemony," in *Palestine to Israel* 175–97; and Louis, *British Empire in the Middle East* 397–419.

43. Statement by President Truman, 30 April 1946; statement by Prime Minister Clement Attlee, 1 May 1946 in *Book of Documents*, ed. Tulin, 267–68.

44. Cohen, *Palestine and the Great Powers* 85–93.

45. Cohen, *Palestine and the Great Powers* chs. 7–8.

46. See Jehuda Reinharz, "Zionism and the Great Powers" 13–14, 21.

47. See Yaacov Ro'i, "Soviet-Israeli Relations, 1947–1954," in Michael Confino and Shimon Shamir, eds., *The U.S.S.R. and the Middle East* (New York: J. Wiley, 1973); and Cohen, *Palestine and the Great Powers* 261–63.

48. Cohen, *Palestine and the Great Powers* 136–37.

49. Cohen, *Palestine and the Great Powers* 174–75.

50. See Bauer, *From Diplomacy to Resistance* 258–59; and Cohen, *Palestine and the Great Powers* 174–75.

51. Yehoshua Freundlich, *From Destruction to Resurrection: Zionist Policy from the End of World War II to the Establishment of the State of Israel* (Tel Aviv: Mifalim Universitaiyim, 1994, in Hebrew) 63.

52. Freundlich, *From Destructon to Resurrection* 67–72.

53. Kaufman, *An Ambiguous Partnership* 265–269. The American Jewish Committee itself remained neutral in the matter of partition. See Menahem Kaufman, "The American Jewish Committee and Jewish Statehood, 1947–1948," *Studies in Zionism* 7.2 (1986): 259–75.

54. Cohen, *The Great Powers* 260–300; Louis 464–94; Freundlich 199–201.

55. Freundlich 104–14; Cohen, *Palestine and the Great Powers* ch. 11.

56. See the chapter "American Retreat from Partition," in Zvi Ganin, *Truman, American Jewry, and Israel, 1945–1948* (New York: Holmes & Meier, 1979) 147–69.

57. Ganin 169.

58. See Kaufman, *An Ambiguous Partnership* 323–31.

59. Kaufman, *An Ambiguous Partnership* 323–31. On the internal situation of the leadership of British Jewry in 1948, see Shimoni, "Non-Zionists in Anglo-Jewry" 100–110.

60. See Samuel Halperin, *The Political World of American Zionism* (Detroit: Wayne State University Press, 1961) 270.

61. Louis, *British Empire in the Middle East* 395.

PART THREE

The Impact of the Holocaust on
American Jewish Life and Thought

SIX

The Americanization of the Holocaust

ALVIN H. ROSENFELD

FIFTY YEARS AFTER THE END of World War II, how do we look back upon and understand that catastrophic event? And from the perspective of half a century, what do we make in particular of the almost total devastation of European Jewry?

In an effort to discover answers to questions of this kind, the American Jewish Committee has recently carried out a series of studies to determine what people in several different countries — among them, the United States, France, Germany, and Great Britain — know about the Holocaust.[1] The findings are not encouraging, especially with respect to the levels of historical knowledge among Americans. When asked, "What does the term 'the Holocaust' refer to?" 38 percent of American adults and 53 percent of high school students either do not know or offer incorrect answers. Higher percentages of American adults (65 percent) and high school students (71 percent) seem not to know that approximately 6,000,000 Jews were killed by the Nazis and their allies. Presented with the names "Auschwitz, Dachau, and Treblinka," 38 percent of the same adults and 51 percent of the high school students fail to recognize these as signifying concentration camps. Fifty-nine percent of the adults and the same percentage of the students do not know that the symbol that Jews were forced to wear during the war was the "yellow star." It is little wonder, then, that the scholars who carried out this survey conclude that a "serious knowledge gap exists for both adults and youth in the United States with regard to basic information about the Holocaust."[2]

The Europeans do better, with adults and students in Germany scoring the highest among the national population groups surveyed in these studies. But then we confront a seeming paradox, for while the Americans know the least about the Holocaust, they seem to *care* the most, with large percentages of those polled replying that they deem it "essential" or "important" that Americans "know about and understand the Holocaust."[3] Given the shockingly low levels of their own knowledge and understanding, how is it that these Americans—only 21 percent of whom are able to recognize that the "Warsaw ghetto" had some connection to the Holocaust—regard the Holocaust as "relevant" today and strongly hold to the opinion that Americans should know about it?[4] What do Americans mean by the Holocaust anyway, and how do they come to these meanings? What are their sources of information about the Holocaust, and what images do these sources project to them? How, in sum, do they come to know whatever it is they do know? These are the kinds of matters I wish to reflect on in this essay, but before proceeding it will be helpful to draw attention to a few more general concerns.

We can begin by noting that for most people a sense of the Nazi crimes against the Jews is formed less by the record of events established by professional historians than it is by individual stories and images that reach us from more popular writers, artists, film directors, television producers, political figures, and the like. We live in a mass culture, and much of what we learn about the past comes to us from those forms of communication that comprise the information and entertainment networks of this culture—novels, stories, poems, plays, films, television programs, newspaper and magazine articles, museum exhibitions, etc. By way of illustration, it is worth recalling that tens of millions of Americans watched the NBC docudrama *Holocaust* when this popular television miniseries was first shown in the spring of 1978. More recently, a mass audience perhaps equally as large has seen Steven Spielberg's *Schindler's List*. It does not detract in the least from the scholarly value of a work such as Raul Hilberg's magisterial study, *The Destruction of the European Jews*, to recognize that far more people are likely to learn about Jewish victimization under the Nazis from these films or from reading Anne Frank's *The Diary of a Young Girl* than from reading Hilberg.

In considering the term "Holocaust" itself, one recognizes that although it is widely used today, those Jews who suffered in the ghettos and camps of Nazi-occupied Europe did not think of themselves as victims of a "Holocaust." Nor did most of them use such terms as "Churban" or "Shoah," which today sometimes alternate with "Holocaust" in popular usage. Rather, in referring to their fate, one typically spoke, in the immediate postwar years, about the "catastrophe," or the "recent Jewish catastrophe," or the "disaster." These more or less general terms remained dominant through the latter 1940s and into the early 1950s, when "Holocaust," or "The Holocaust," gained currency and took on the connotations it has largely had until today.[5] The writer Elie Wiesel had a prominent role in popularizing "The Holocaust" as the term of choice to designate the Nazi assault against the Jews, though it is not at all clear that he actually coined the phrase. In Wiesel's usage and, following him, in that of countless others, "The Holocaust" has been intended as an exclusive term to point to the sufferings and intended genocide of European Jewry. There are others who have preferred to widen the application of the language of "Holocaust" so that it includes all those who perished at the hands of the Germans and their allies.[6]

The debate between those who reserve the term "Holocaust" specifically and exclusively for the Jewish victims of Nazism and those who opt for much wider inclusion of victim populations is an ongoing one. It is a debate of great consequence, for in terms of projecting an image of what the Holocaust was, a great deal depends on the numbers employed and the sense of the past that these numbers imply. Following Simon Wiesenthal, for instance, President Carter, speaking on Holocaust Remembrance Day in

Washington in 1979, referred to 11 million victims of the Holocaust, among them 6 million Jews and 5 million non-Jews.[7] More recently, the language of "Holocaust" has been used by those who want to draw public attention to the crimes, abuses, and assorted sufferings that mar the quality of social life in today's America. In the passionate debates that are underway about abortion, for instance, one frequently encounters terms such as "the abortion Holocaust," the "killing centers" where a "genocide" is being carried out against unborn baby "victims," etc. Following this turn — and it is characteristically American in its intent to be broadly inclusive — "Holocaust" or "The Holocaust" is in the process of being transformed from a proper noun to a common noun, a semantic switch that signifies an important conceptual and ideological transformation as well. As a result, language that hitherto has been employed to refer primarily to Nazi crimes against the Jews is now frequently applied to social ills and human sufferings of diverse kinds.

There are those who oppose this tendency but also those who favor it. The Israeli scholar Yehuda Bauer has spoken out strongly against it, arguing that in the process of becoming Americanized, the Holocaust is in danger of becoming de-Judaized. As Bauer puts it, "In the public mind the term 'Holocaust' has become flattened" so that "any evil that befalls anyone anywhere becomes a Holocaust." Bauer recognizes that the semantic extension of the term "Holocaust" is accompanied by a cognitive shift, resulting in what he fears will be a "total misunderstanding" of the historical event that the term was originally meant to designate. What underlies this development? Its causes are various, but in Bauer's view, much of it relates to those people who were charged with the responsibility of creating the United States Holocaust Memorial Museum in Washington, D.C. They were faced with a difficult dilemma, moreover, one of a specifically American kind: "It was unclear how the uniqueness of the Holocaust and its universalist implications could be combined in a way that would be in accord with the American heritage and American political reality."[8]

Bauer did not spell out what constitutes the "American heritage," but anyone familiar with the ideological tendencies that inform American political culture would be able to fill out the picture for him. It is part of the American ethos to stress goodness, innocence, optimism, liberty, diversity, and equality. It is part of the same ethos to downplay or deny the dark and brutal sides of life and instead to place a preponderant emphasis on the saving power of individual moral conduct and collective deeds of redemption. Americans prefer to think affirmatively and progressively. The tragic vision, therefore, is antithetical to the American way of seeing the world, according to which people are meant to overcome adversity and not cling endlessly to their sorrows. Because Americans are also pragmatic in their approach to history, they are eager to learn what "lessons" can be drawn from the past in order, as many are quick to say, to prevent its worst excesses "from ever happening again."

If it is values such as these that Bauer had in mind when he referred to the American heritage, it is little wonder that he found Americans culturally predisposed to "misunderstand" the Nazi persecution and mass murder of Europe's Jews. The right to life, liberty, and the pursuit of happiness, after all, had no place in Auschwitz, which denied its inmates all rights and subjected them instead to the punishments of forced incarceration, constant misery, and mass death. These cruelties and deprivations, systematized by state policy and willingly carried out by large numbers of its citizens, are so antithetical to the American mind and moral imagination as to be virtually incomprehensible.

The Holocaust has had to enter American consciousness, therefore, in ways that Americans could readily understand on their own terms. These are terms that promote a tendency to individualize, heroize, moralize, idealize, and universalize. It is through such cognitive screens as these that human behavior is apt to be refracted within American cultural productions, and they have helped to shape the ways in which the Nazi Holocaust of European Jewry has been represented in this country on the popular level.

While significant attention has been focused on the Holocaust in recent years, we would do well to remind ourselves that during

the war itself and for a number of years afterward, the fate of
Europe's Jews under Hitler was not a matter of central concern
within American political and cultural life. Consider American
films on the subject, for instance. According to Ilan Avisar, who
has given us an important book on *Screening the Holocaust,* Hollywood produced some five hundred narrative films on the war
and war-related themes during the years 1940–1945. "In examining this harvest," Avisar writes, "we find striking avoidance of any
explicit presentation of the Jewish catastrophe during the course
of the war. *The Great Dictator* (1940) was a remarkable exception.
. . . [Otherwise], Hollywood completely ignored the contempora-
neous, systematic extermination of European Jewry."[9] Furthermore, Avisar notes, it was not until 1959, in filming the diary of
Anne Frank, that Hollywood "addressed itself directly to the Nazis'
genocidal treatment of the Jews."[10]

It is a matter of no small interest that it was the figure of Anne
Frank that helped to break the relative silence within American
culture about Jewish fate under Nazi tyranny. Anne Frank's diary
was a popular success from the start, and to this day it can be
taken as paradigmatic of the American reception of the Holocaust.
First published in English translation in 1952, *The Diary of a Young
Girl* remains one of the best-known and best-loved stories of
World War II. The book was made into a popular play by Frances
Goodrich and Albert Hackett and produced on Broadway in 1955;
four years later it was screened as an equally popular full-length
film. The book, the play, and the film remain in circulation to this
day, so much so that it is fair to say that more Americans are
familiar with Anne Frank's story than with any other single narrative of the war years. For millions of young Americans in particular, the Holocaust is first made known and vividly personalized
in the image of Anne Frank.

What is it that defines her image for people in this country, and
why have they come to cherish it so? There is a vague understanding that Anne Frank was a Jew and for this reason was also a
victim, but the stage and film translations of her diary do not make
her appear "too Jewish," nor do they make her status as a victim

too unbearably harsh. It is notable, for instance, that at no time during the play does a Nazi soldier or Gestapo agent ever appear on the stage. Consequently, one can leave the theater feeling somehow uplifted by Anne Frank's story rather than deeply disturbed.

The early reviews of the Broadway production of the diary register these feelings in unambiguous ways. Writing in the *New York Herald Tribune* on 6 October 1955 about the play's debut at the Cort Theater, Walter Kerr had this to say: "Nearly all of the characters in 'The Diary of Anne Frank' . . . are doomed to death. Yet the precise quality of the new play at the Cort is the quality of glowing, ineradicable life—life in its warmth, its wonder, its spasms of anguish, and its wild and flaring humor." William Hawkins, writing in the *New York World Telegram and Sun* on 15 October 1955 concurred: "Producer, playwright, director, and actors have united to make a truly uplifting adventure out of as terrifyingly sordid a situation as it is possible to find in history. . . . One leaves the theater exhilarated, proud to be a human being." John Beaufort, the reviewer for the *Christian Science Monitor* wrote on 15 October 1955 of *The Diary of Anne Frank* as "an exquisite play which endows the deeper grief of its subject with a shining and even triumphant humanity." He went on to say that the play "moves one as readily to laughter as to tears. . . . The spirit of man, including his comic spirit, is by no means extinguished." Richard Watts, Jr., the reviewer for the *New York Post* (26 August 1956), saw the play as "an inspiring drama, not a wrathful one. [The play] makes audiences feel that inspiration, that pride in mankind's potential courage, as members of the human race and not of any particular branch of it. To that extent, it is universal in interest, though its main characters are Jewish."[11]

These reviews, and numerous others like them, reveal clearly enough the terms in which Americans of the mid-1950s were prepared to confront the Holocaust: it was a terrible event, yes, but ultimately not tragic or depressing; it was an experience shadowed by the specter of a cruel death, but at the same time it was not without the ability to inspire, console, uplift. Still today, among those who come to know Anne Frank through the pages of her diary or the stage or screen versions of it, responses are remarkably similar to those cited above. Harry James Cargas, a contemporary American literary scholar and theologian, has recently written about Anne Frank in terms that hardly differ from those of the 1950s: "This compassionate child, never forgetting to go beyond herself, to see the miserable condition of others rather than to wallow in her own situation as many of us might have done, despite all, evinced hope. Each time I read the Diary I am uplifted. Anne's spirit gives me hope. Each time I read the Diary I cannot help but feel that this time she'll make it, she'll survive."[12]

She did not survive, as we know, but went to a miserable death in Bergen-Belsen before she was sixteen years old. Nevertheless, the survival fantasy that is triggered in Cargas's encounter with Anne Frank is common among American audiences. Who, after all, wants to stare into the abyss and discover only blackness? Few people have the nerves to sustain so dark a vision of life. Consequently, Americans are typically given stories and images of the Nazi Holocaust that turn upward at the end rather than plunge downward into the terrifying silences of a gruesome death. The stage production of *The Diary of Anne Frank* ends with Anne's voice repeating what has become her signature line, informing us, as if from the heavens, "In spite of everything, I still believe that people are really good at heart." To which her father replies, humbly and affectionately, "She puts me to shame." Following these words the curtain comes down, ending Anne Frank's story not on a disconsolate note but an uplifting one.[13]

It is on a similar note that Gerald Green ended the NBC miniseries, *Holocaust*; that William Styron chose to end his popular novel, *Sophie's Choice*; and that Steven Spielberg ends his extravagantly acclaimed film, *Schindler's List*. As in these instances and others like them, it is almost a general requirement of American cultural engagement with the Holocaust that audiences not be subjected to unrelenting pain. Indeed, American "civil religion," as it has been called, places the stress emphatically on closures that are optimistic and affirmative. Consider, as one more example of this tendency, the following passage, taken from a widely circulated

letter from the United States Holocaust Memorial Museum solic-
iting funds for new membership:

> Visitors will learn that while this is overwhelmingly a story about
> the extermination of the Jewish people, it is also about the Nazis'
> plans for the annihilation of the Gypsies and the handicapped, and
> about the persecution of priests and patriots, Polish intellectuals
> and Soviet prisoners of war, homosexuals and even innocent chil-
> dren.
>   Then, finally, when breaking hearts can bear it no longer, visitors
> will emerge into the light—into a celebration of resistance, rebirth,
> and renewal for the survivors—whether they remained in Europe,
> or as so many did, went to Israel or America to rebuild their lives.
> And having witnessed the nightmare of evil, the great American
> monuments to democracy that surround each departing visitor will
> take on new meaning, as will the ideals for which they stand.[14]

The topographical reference that gives rise to this note of American triumphalism is an important feature of the overall message
that the United States Holocaust Memorial Museum means to
convey. The museum is advantageously situated adjacent to the
National Mall in the historic and cultural center of Washington,
D.C. The Washington Monument and the Jefferson Memorial are
nearby and easily visible. These national monuments have the
effect of reestablishing museum visitors in the familiar and con-
soling realities of American space, and in so doing they can also
have the effect of telling them that the exhibits they just saw, for
all of their horror, signify an essentially European event. To identify it as such is not to diminish the significance of the Holocaust
for Americans; but it is to mark it as an alien experience, one that
took place far from America's shores and even farther from the
American spirit of fair play, decency, and justice for all. It is imperative, therefore, that some means to return people to this spirit
be built into how the Jewish catastrophe in Europe is to be presented to the citizens of this country. In conformity with this need,
the letter from which I have quoted above concludes by urging all
of us to remember "the six million Jews and millions of other

innocent victims who died in the Holocaust" and, at the same time, to "also remember and renew our own faith in life . . . in civilization . . . in humanity . . . and in each other."

It is noteworthy that as visitors enter the Holocaust Museum, they are greeted by words from America's hallowed Declaration of Independence, prominently engraved on a nearby wall, extending to all citizens the rights to "life, liberty, and the pursuit of happiness." They might also be fortified against the terrifying pictures they are about to see by some famous words of America's first president, which likewise are prominently displayed near the museums's entrance: "The government of the United States . . . gives to bigotry no sanction, to persecution no assistance." It is, of course, bigotry and persecution in the most extreme sense that viewers will soon be staring at as they tour the Holocaust Museum's exhibits, but by bracketing the horror with some of the noblest principles of America's national credo, the museum's architects and program designers remind their visitors that the American vision of life is altogether different from that which brought on the catastrophe that is about to unfold before their eyes.

Given the story it tells in powerfully graphic fashion, the Holocaust Memorial Museum is not and cannot be a pleasurable museum to visit. Its aim is to educate the American public about a historical experience of a kind so excruciatingly painful that it would be a rare visitor who could emerge from this place unmoved. Just what it is that people take away with them and retain as permanent knowledge, however, we do not yet know. I suspect that the following account, which concludes an article by Estelle Gilson describing her own visit, may be representative of the responses of many of those who come to the Holocaust Museum:

> Do I think the United States Holocaust Memorial Museum will protect Jews in the future? Highly unlikely. Will it protect other minorities from genocide? Not likely. But it does what the United States does best. It informs. It bears witness to the Holocaust's existence, and provides a warning to whomever wishes to learn from it, that those who would dehumanize people in order to destroy them, dehumanize themselves as well.

To have walked through this exhibition alongside fellow Americans—Caucasian Americans, African Americans, Hispanic Americans, Asian Americans, and yes, Jewish Americans—all in their bright summer tourist garb, left me feeling strangely comforted and surprisingly proud.[15]

Comfort and pride are no part of what one feels upon leaving the remains of the Nazi camps in Germany or Poland or upon concluding a visit to Yad Vashem in Israel. Why, therefore, are such feelings evoked at the United States Holocaust Memorial Museum? The answer probably lies less in what is shown in the one place and not in the others than in the site itself and the democratic ideals that America's capital exemplifies. If one is to subject oneself to a serious confrontation with the history of the Nazi Holocaust at all, therefore, it is probably easier to do so at the National Mall in Washington, D.C., than it is anywhere else in the world.

Although still very new, the United States Holocaust Memorial Museum has already drawn exceptionally large crowds, and everything about it suggests that for years to come it is destined to be a powerful instrument for educating millions of Americans and others about the Holocaust. That is all to the good. As the museum grows and matures, however, it may be that its conceptual base will broaden, in familiar American fashion, to embrace a wider sense of its mission.

Michael Berenbaum, the former director of the museum's research institute, has argued that the "Holocaust is only 'Americanized' insofar as it is explained to Americans and related to their history with ramifications for future policy. The study of the Holocaust can provide insights that have universal import for the destiny of all humanity. A national council funded at taxpayers' expense to design a *national* memorial does not have the liberty to create an exclusively Jewish one in the restricted sense of the term, and most specifically with regard to audience."[16]

Expanding on the connection between a museum's presentations and its audience, Berenbaum has also written that as the United States Memorial Council took up its task of telling Americans about the Holocaust, it realized that "the story had to be told in such a way that it would resonate not only with the survivor in New York and his children in San Francisco, but with a black leader from Atlanta, a midwestern farmer, or a northeastern industrialist." Connecting such a diverse audience to history, Berenbaum noted, means connecting them to the past in a way that "inform[s] their current reality," including what he calls their current "social need."[17] The social needs of the different American types that he describes, however, are of a diverse sort, and it is hard to imagine narrating any story of the crimes of the Nazi era that will remain faithful to the specific features of European-based historical events of two generations ago and, at the same time, address a multiplicity of contemporary American social and political agendas. Berenbaum's formula for resolving such potential problems is to recognize that while the Holocaust was a unique event, it carries universal implications. That is no doubt the case. As some of his colleagues develop their own understandings of this formula, however, the "uniqueness" of the Holocaust may begin to yield some of its priority in historical fact to what is taken to be its wider metaphorical ramifications for today's American visitors. Naomi Paiss, the museum's director of communications, has said that "the museum's ultimate goal was an 'en-masse understanding that we are not about what the Germans did to Jews but what people did to people.'"[18] If the Washington museum ever adopts a broadening of its mission that is that large—and the temptation to engage in such a universal reach is a recognizable part of the American cultural reflex—it will no longer be a museum devoted to educating the public about the Nazi Holocaust but something else.

We need not wonder what this "something else" might look like, for it is already upon us, if not at the United States Holocaust Memorial Museum in Washington, D.C., then at the Simon Wiesenthal Center's Museum of Tolerance in Los Angeles and elsewhere. The mission of the Los Angeles museum is twofold: to inform visitors about the history of racism and social prejudice in America and to represent what the museum calls "the ultimate example of man's inhumanity to man—the Holocaust."[19] Both are noble aims, but by situating the Holocaust within an historical framework that includes such quintessentially American experiences as the Los Angeles riots and the struggle for black civil rights, both of which are prominently illustrated, the Museum of Tolerance relativizes the catastrophe brought on by Nazism in a radical way. America's social problems, for all their gravity, are not genocidal in character and simply do not resemble the persecution and systematic slaughter of Europe's Jews during World War II. To mingle the victims of these very different historical experiences, therefore, is ultimately to broaden the conceptual base of the Nazi Holocaust to the point where it begins to metamorphose into that empty and now all but meaningless abstraction: "man's inhumanity to man."

This tendency to relativize and universalize the Holocaust has been a prominent part of the American reception of Holocaust representations from the start. It is strong today and seems to be growing, especially within those segments of American culture that are intent on developing a politics of identity based on victim status and the grievances that come with such status.

To cite one egregious example among many, consider the most recent work of the feminist artist Judy Chicago. Chicago (née Gerowitz) claims descent from twenty-three generations of rabbis; but until the age of forty-five, as she freely admits, she knew virtually nothing about either Judaism or the Holocaust. She has now produced a large and ambitious art installation entitled the *Holocaust Project,* which combines her own work in several media with the work of her husband, the photographer Donald Woodman. The *Holocaust Project* had its opening at the Spertus Institute of Jewish Studies in Chicago in the fall of 1993 and since then has shown at museums in Boston, Los Angeles, and other cities. Those who do not actually get to see the photo-paintings, tapestries, and stained glass productions that make up this exhibition can have access to Chicago's work through an illustrated, oversized volume, also entitled *Holocaust Project,* which carries colored plates of the artwork along with numerous preliminary sketches, historical and contemporary photographs, excerpts from the artists' readings, and a detailed and highly revealing personal journal that Chicago kept as she set out to educate herself about the Holocaust.[20]

Her search, which she describes as one in quest of her latent Jewish self as well as of knowledge about the Nazi crimes, was intensive and demanding. It continued on over a period of six or seven years and took Chicago and Woodman on trips to former camp sites and other places of wartime interest in France, Germany, Austria, Czechoslovakia, Poland, Russia, Latvia, and Lithuania. Journal entries, drawings, and photographs illustrate this ambitious itinerary and make clear that Chicago's search was not just for knowledge in the cognitive sense but, more passionately, for an emotional sense of the "Holocaust experience." To make this "experience" her own, as it were, Chicago did some things that go well beyond ordinary tourist behavior. During a visit to the former Natzweiler/Struthof concentration camp in France, for instance, she had herself photographed lying down on one of the long iron shovels that had been used to feed the bodies of victims into the flames of the crematorium oven. The large picture of her stretched out and seemingly entering the mouth of the oven is accompanied by a brief explanatory note: "When I lay on the shovel that carried bodies into the crematorium, I realized that, had I lived in Europe during the war, this would probably have happened to me. (Donald is too young.)"[21]

The Holocaust Project includes other "revelations" of this order. In translating them into her artwork, Chicago was guided by a point of view that, as she says, set her and her husband apart from most members of "the Holocaust community." Specifically, Chicago's "more comprehensive approach" situates the Holocaust as one "victim experience" among many and finds the root of all of these in "the injustice inherent in the global structure of patriarchy and the result of power as it has been defined and enforced by male-dominated societies."[22] Having sighted the enemy and given him his proper name, the artist then set out to make his violence graphic.

The artwork itself reflects these emphases and understandings. One finds images of Nazi brutality side by side with images of slavery, atomic warfare, animal vivisection, and evil-looking gyne-cologists. Women are everwhere abused, attacked, tormented. A large tapestry entitled *The Fall,* conceptualized along the lines of a "battle of the sexes," depicts naked women being attacked by knife-wielding men while other women are being burned alive. In this same piece, a black slave plows furrows into the weeping earth-mother; a gaunt Jesus-like figure hangs helplessly in the background; other men wield bloody swords or feed people into the flaming ovens; and still others flay the hides of pigs and women hung side by side on a rack. In the middle of all this torment is a reworking of Leonardo's *Vetruvian Man,* which, an explanatory note tells us, is meant to show that the Holocaust had its true origin in "that moment in human history when men consolidated patriarchal power through force."[23] In Chicago's conception of his-tory, all of our later troubles, including those brought on by the Nazis and their allies, have their roots in the overthrow of matri-archy by cruelly aggressive, domineering "men."

The last piece, entitled *Rainbow Shabbat,* is a departure from all that precedes it and is intended to close the exhibit on a prayerful note. It is "an invocation for human awakening and global trans-formation," as the artist puts it.[24] A large stained glass production, *Rainbow Shabbat* depicts twelve people around a sabbath table. At one end of the table there stands a woman, covered in a traditional prayer shawl, blessing the candles. At the other end, a man, also in a prayer shawl, is making the traditional blessing over wine. Between these two and seated around the table are representatives of the world's people—an Arab in kaffiyeh headdress, a Christian minister or priest with a large crucifix dangling on a chain beneath his clerical collar, Vietnamese, blacks, women, children, assorted whites. The ten people all face away from the man and toward the woman, for it is through her and not him that the world will find whatever renewal and redemption may be possible. The faces of these sabbath celebrants are expressionless but, inasmuch as they all have their arms about one another and seem to fall within the embrace of the praying woman's outstretched arms, we are given to understand that all is now well with the world or soon will be.

Rainbow colors fill out the table scene from top to bottom, and on flanking side panels a large Jewish star, also surrounded by these bright colors, is inscribed with words that end the *Holocaust Project* on a prayerful note: "Heal those broken souls who have no peace and lead us all from darkness into light."[25]

It would be easy to see the *Holocaust Project* as one giant cliché from start to finish and dismiss it without any further ado. That would be a serious mistake, however, for Ms. Chicago's version of the Holocaust embodies a number of trends that inform the American cultural and political mood today. We live in an age that is marked by narcissistic indulgences of a relentless sort. In such a time, everything is drawn back to the self and its desires, the self and its needs, the self and its pains. Combine this extreme emphasis on subjectivity with an increasingly intrusive political correctness and you get not only a production like the *Holocaust Project* but many another invocation of the Holocaust dragged emblematically into the contemporary American debates about AIDS, abortion, child abuse, gay rights, the rights of immigrant aliens, etc. In fact, these are all matters of legitimate and serious social concern; but the analogy with the Nazi destruction of Europe's Jews adds nothing but sensationalism to the public discussion of what truly ails American society. And while the sensational is guaranteed to draw attention, it obfuscates and obscures more than it enlightens.

It also tends to make people lose their hold on reality. Listen to Judy Chicago as she contemplates painting a rape scene for one of the panels of her *Holocaust Project:* "I am exhausting myself and depleting all my life's energy in fighting for the truth to be seen and heard. . . . I need to rest before I begin the rape image. Not only is it an intense, painful image, but it makes me very anxious. I keep thinking: am I going to get raped after I do this image? . . . But of course, I have no choice — so I'll just have to hope that art won't translate into life."[26] In this imaginary world, Holocausts threaten from every corner, and all are victims or potential victims. In more or less the same psychological register, even though with an eye on a different enemy, listen to the evangelical preacher Pat

Robertson: "Just what Nazi Germany did to the Jews, so liberal America is now doing to evangelical Christians. . . . It's no different; it's the same thing. It is happening all over again. It is the Democratic Congress, the liberal-biased media, and the homosexuals who want to destroy all Christians. It's more terrible than anything suffered by any minority in our history." We read that as the Reverend Robertson made this speech over his Christian Broadcasting Network, "footage of Nazi atrocities against the Jews appeared on screen."[27]

How, one wonders, does the Reverend Robertson's audience respond to rhetoric of this kind? Will most people recognize it as trumped-up, a form of religio-political hysteria and, as such, seriously out of line with reality; or will they be prone to believe it? Does the Reverend Robertson himself believe it? We do not know, anymore than we know how much genuine belief Judy Chicago has invested in her own seriously skewed version of the Holocaust. What we do know is that if you expose thinking people long enough to images of atrocity, they will no longer remain fully thinking people, capable of recognizing differences and making distinctions between one order of human experience and another. Given the penchant among growing numbers of Americans to proclaim themselves "victims," one cannot help but wonder if the spread of Holocaust images throughout the various layers of our culture may not be having such a self-deluding effect.

Until recently it has been generally understood that, in Raul Hilberg's words, "a variety of perpetrators, a multitude of victims, and a host of bystanders"[28] made up the essential core of the Holocaust in its time. In more recent years, however, as thinking and writing about the Nazi crimes have taken a figurative turn, there has been a substantial augmentation of this core and also a shift of emphasis within it. I refer especially to the emergence of the "survivor" and "rescuer" as prominent and popular types, along with the "liberator," the "resister," the "second generation survivor," and the Holocaust "revisionist" or "denier." Interest in all of them has broadened the focus of the Holocaust "story" and influenced the point of view from which it is both narrated and received. In what follows, I want to examine the prominence that two of these types have enjoyed of late, namely the "survivor" and the "rescuer." To focus these observations, I turn to Steven Spielberg's hugely successful film, *Schindler's List,* and to the nature of the response to it among American filmgoers and critics.

For a number of years following the end of World War II, relatively little public attention was paid in this country to those people who had managed to survive the Nazi assault against European Jewry and resettle in the United States. Their status was that of the "DP," the "immigrant," the "war refugee," or the "greenhorn"; and attitudes toward them were hardly adulatory. Generous-hearted people did what they could to help these newcomers adjust to their new circumstances in America and rebuild their lives here; others more or less ignored them. Throughout the late 1940s and well into the 1950s, a prevalent attitude was to put all of "that" behind one and get on with life.

Here is how the sociologist William Helmreich describes the situation:

> Most immigrants quickly learned not to talk about the war, often rationalizing their reluctance by saying that the stories were too horrible to be believed. Americans frequently responded to such stories with accounts of how they too had undergone privation during the war, mostly food rationing. Moritz Felberman [a survivor] was told by his aunt: "If you want to have friends here in America, don't keep talking about your experiences. Nobody's interested and if you tell them, they're going to hear it once and then the next time they'll be afraid to come see you. Don't ever speak about it."[29]

Just when this period of relative muteness broke is hard to say with any precision, but beginning in the late 1960s and continuing up to the present day, a radical change of attitude has taken place, so much so that today the "survivor" is a much-honored figure and, in some instances, enjoys something close to celebrity status. The writer Elie Wiesel has played an important role in this regard, as have others. The result is that those who formerly had been regarded as "war refugees" have given up that unenviable status and taken on new symbolic importance as "Holocaust survivors."

As "survivors" these aging men and women are frequently sought as platform speakers at Yom HaShoah commemorative programs and other public occasions during the year, and sizable audiences are likely to turn out to hear them tell their tales. Survivor memoirs have been published in large volume and by now constitute a significant subgenre of Holocaust literature. In addition, such institutions as the Fortunoff Video Archives at Yale University and Steven Spielberg's Holocaust Foundation have been engaged in ambitious efforts to interview these aging witnesses and get their stories on tape while it is still possible to do so.[30] In short, the survivor now enjoys a greatly heightened public profile and has about him an aura that elicits honor, respect, fascination, and no small degree of awe. Leon Uris has recently summed up these attitudes by stating the case forthrightly: "These men and women are to be looked upon with wonderment."[31] And so, increasingly, they are.

Schindler's List, dedicated as it is to narrating the story of 1,100 Jews rescued from what doubtless would have been a gruesome death for most, is a film that celebrates "survivors." As such, it builds upon a momentum within segments of American culture, and especially American Jewish culture, that has developed over a number of years. Many of those who managed to survive the ghettos, camps, and assorted hiding places of Nazi-occupied Europe have done well in this country, and in their latter years they have dedicated themselves energetically and successfully to seeing to it that their stories and the wrenchingly painful story of their era are preserved for future generations. Without the extraordinary commitment of these people there would be no United States Holocaust Memorial Museum, no video archives for Holocaust testimony, no endowed chairs at American colleges and universities for the teaching of the Holocaust—and no *Schindler's List.* Their success in this respect is truly remarkable. The latest catalogue of the Association of Holocaust Organizations, for instance, lists more than 100 Holocaust institutions throughout the United

States and Canada, all of which are dedicated to educating the public about the Holocaust. These places exist largely because Holocaust survivors in North America have seen to it that they exist. Their mission, simply stated, is to carry on in perpetuity the memory work of a traumatized generation of European Jews who, in the short space of a generation, have transformed their former status as victims into unprecedented positions of influence and respect. Abandoning the reticence that marked their situation in the immediate postwar years, they have gained their voice and are not reluctant to use it when the need arises. No one who recalls the Bitburg affair in the spring of 1985 will soon forget that it was a "survivor" who faced the President of the United States and, with all of the world's television cameras recording the moment, "spoke truth to power." Who but Elie Wiesel—a figure who has come to symbolize the moral authority of his generation—would have dared to publicly tell the President of this country that it was "not [his] place" to travel to Germany to join Chancellor Kohl for ceremonies at the military cemetery at Bitburg?[32]

The newly found strength, self-confidence, and self-assertion of survivors reached its high point during the 1994 Academy Awards ceremony when Branko Lustig, himself a survivor, and Steven Spielberg stepped before a vast and inordinately appreciative television audience and, in the name of the survivors as well as in the name of "the 6,000,000," accepted their Oscars as producer and director of *Schindler's List.*

As *Schindler's List* makes clear, if this is the age of the "survivor," it is also the age of the "rescuer." For along with a high degree of public attention being turned on the "survivor," we have seen and continue to see the elevation through the popular media of "righteous Gentiles," "helpers," "liberators," "rescuers," and "saviors." These are the people who, in many instances, helped the "survivor" to survive, and so they, too, are to be looked upon with a degree of wonderment. These people are now frequently regarded as the "moral heroes" of the Holocaust, the ones who managed to exemplify virtue during a time when basic human goodness was otherwise scarcely to be found. Those who speak of them unfailingly revert to such religious or quasi-religious metaphors as "the light that pierced the darkness," "the righteous," "the just," "the good Samaritans," etc. In this regard, it is notable that the United States Holocaust Memorial Museum in Washington, D.C., is situated on Raoul Wallenberg Place, a designation rich in symbolic implications and one that helps to "balance" the horrors awaiting visitors inside the building with a sense of righteousness duly honored on the outside.

Thanks to Steven Spielberg's film, the Swedish hero Wallenberg has now been joined by the German Oskar Schindler as another one of the "righteous among the nations." Moreover, the attention newly focused on Schindler's wartime deeds of rescue has had the effect of renewing or creating interest in the stories of others who acted similarly—Aristedes de Sousa Mendes, Sempo Sugihara, Hermann Graebe, Miep Gies, Pastor André Trocmé and the people of Le Chambon, the Danes, etc. Each of them put their lives at risk to help protect and save Jews during the war; and while their numbers are not huge, their actions were clearly exemplary. The question that arises with respect to the "rescuers," therefore, is not one of their inclusion or exclusion from narrative accounts of the Nazi era but chiefly one of proportion: how central or peripheral are these "moral heroes" of the Holocaust to the overall story of the Holocaust?

Schindler's List answers this question in a way that moves "rescuers" like Schindler from the margins to the precise center of events. By doing that as successfully as he has, Spielberg has in effect repositioned the terms of the Holocaust "story" away from those favored by Hilberg and others—the Holocaust encompassing essentially "perpetrators," "victims," and "bystanders"—and has placed the emphasis squarely on "rescuers" and "survivors." *Schindler's List,* after all, is a Holocaust film that focuses chiefly on the Jews who do *not* die at the hands of the Nazis but who, on the contrary, are actually saved by a Nazi who undergoes a moral conversion to goodness. If, as claimed by some, Spielberg's film is to be regarded from this point on as the "definitive" Holocaust film, and if, as claimed by others, it may actually do more to educate vast numbers of people about the history of the Holocaust than all the academic books on the subject combined, one has to recognize that it has achieved these ends as the result of a paradigm shift of significant proportions. In their viewing of this film mass audiences are exposed to a version of the Holocaust that originates in long-standing American preferences for "heroes" and "happy endings," preferences that Schindler's List satisfies through its artful employment of tried-and-true Hollywood conventions of cinematic storytelling. To say this much is not to call into question Spielberg's achievement in Schindler's List, which is considerable; but it is to point up the fact that this is a film that presents a characteristically American way of reading and resolving an extreme history.

As for its impact, there was an extraordinary amount of press interest in Schindler's List even before the film had its premiere showing. Since then commentary on the film has grown exponentially and reveals both laudatory and highly critical attitudes. No less a political figure than President Clinton has "implored" people to see Schindler's List, and others, including the governors of California and New Jersey, have likewise given the film their public endorsement and promoted it as a primary source of historical information and moral education. Following its garnering of no less than seven prizes at the 1994 Academy Awards presentations, Schindler's List was even more lavishly acclaimed as a "great film," "a masterpiece," "an astounding achievement." Stephen Schiff, writing about the film for the New Yorker, has said that it is the "finest fiction feature ever made about the century's greatest evil. . . . It will take its place in cultural history and remain there." Terrence Rafferty agrees with this evaluation and has called Spielberg's film "by far the finest, fullest dramatic film ever made about the Holocaust." Jeffrey Katzenberg, at the time head of Walt Disney film studios, remarked that Schindler's List "will wind up being so much more important than a movie. . . . It will affect how people on this planet think and act. . . . It will actually set the course of world affairs."[33]

At the same time, the film has had its critics. James Bowman, writing in the *American Spectator,* denounced *Schindler's List* as a film that "cheapens and trivializes the enormity of the Holocaust" and offers "no sense whatever of the political realities that allowed such things to happen." J. Hoberman, film critic of the *Village Voice,* found the film "sentimental," too much of a "feel-good" movie, and therefore bound to encourage attitudes of "complacency" in viewers. Donald Kuspit sees *Schindler's List* as "stereotypical," the work of an artist who simply does not "understand" the history of the Holocaust: "*Schindler's List* is a triumph of simplemindedness—always Spielberg's strength." Claude Lanzmann, the creator of *Shoah,* denounced Spielberg's film as one that is essentially false to the essential facts of the Holocaust: "To tell the story of the Holocaust through a German who saved Jews can only lead to a distortion of the truth, because for the overwhelming majority of Jews things like this did not happen."[34]

While critical opinion on the film is clearly divided, there is no question but that Spielberg's cinematic statement is a major one and that from this point on *Schindler's List* is destined to play an influential role in determining how millions of people in this country and elsewhere will come to remember and understand the Nazi Holocaust. In light of this prospect, one is moved to ask: what version of the Holocaust does this film project? In particular, what images of Germans and Jews does Spielberg present in *Schindler's List?*

The fundamental dramatic confrontation in the film is not one between Jews and Germans but one between an evil German (Amon Goeth, the commander of the Plaszów labor camp) and a German who comes to exemplify righteous behavior (Oskar Schindler). As the movie progresses, the face-off between these two intensifies and takes on allegorical dimensions; in the balance hangs the fate of the Jews. Otherwise, the Jews in *Schindler's List* are weakly imagined figures, for the most part either passive victims of random atrocity or venal collaborators with their persecutors. In just about every case they are presented as nondescript, anonymous figures or appear in stereotypical fashion, the men among them associated with money deals and other sorts of scheming and the women as temptresses and seductresses. Itzhak

Stern, the only Jewish character developed at any length, is an inflexible, soulless type, whose expression throughout the film rarely changes from that of the professional bookkeeper that he is. In just about every other respect, the Jews in *Schindler's List* are irrelevent to the major drama of the film, which focuses on Oskar Schindler and Amon Goeth, the chief embodiments of "good" and "evil." In the contest between the two, of course, it is Schindler who prevails and who, at film's end, is the recipient of the Jews' gratitude, respect, and love.

This ending takes Schindler and the Jews through two major rites of passage, both of which have about them an aura of the morally sublime, if not indeed of the sacred. Through the presentation of a gold ring, the *Schindlerjuden* in effect "marry" themselves to this man out of heartfelt gratitude for his righteous deeds. And in the final cemetery scene, these same Jews, now elderly, pay their respects to the memory of their savior through the ritualistic placing of tokens of honor and love on his grave. Both scenes convey tender feelings of affection, respect, and reconciliation— and both project Schindler as a figure defined by overtly Christian symbolism. In the first scene, he holds forth in a dramatic speech that recalls Jesus's Sermon on the Mount; and in the second, the camera pans lovingly over the crosses in Jerusalem's Latin Cemetery, coming to rest on the gravesite where Schindler himself is buried.[35] These two scenes bring to culmination and closure the career of a man who may have been a morally flawed character in many other respects but who is depicted as nothing short of a saintly hero with respect to the Jews.

As the Holocaust enters American public consciousness through *Schindler's List,* therefore, it may have the effect of dislodging earlier and more difficult feelings of shame and guilt that typically accompany reactions to images of the persecution and mass slaughter of Europe's Jews. The political dimensions of Nazi behavior go altogether unexplored in *Schindler's List,* and in their stead one encounters raw sadism of an extremely personal rather than systemic kind. Identification with such a character as Amon Goeth, who is the incarnation of the murderous passions of limitless evil, is out of the question for most filmgoers, who are far more likely to align themselves sympathetically with the "good" German, Oskar Schindler, the "rescuer" of the Jews, rather than with Goeth, the ostensibly mad and vicious killer.

What version of the Holocaust, then, does *Schindler's List* present? Michael André Bernstein is correct when he writes that by concentrating "on a small group of Jews who survived and on the good German who aided them rather than on all the millions who did not live and the millions of Germans and German sympathizers who did nothing to help," Spielberg satisfies "a characteristic American urge to find a redemptive meaning in every event."[36] That urge is not felt in such films as Alain Resnais's *Night and Fog* or Claude Lanzmann's *Shoah,* nor does one find it satisfied in the Auschwitz memoirs of such European writers as Primo Levi or Jean Améry. By contrast, it is on a note of redemptive promise that American productions on the Holocaust are likely to end. To reach such endings, however, it is necessary that a new paradigm of narrative construction be advanced, one focusing prominently on the more "affirmative" figures of the Holocaust story, notably "survivors" and "rescuers." *Schindler's List* is the most recent and also the most powerfully articulated example of this paradigm shift, but it hardly stands alone. For increasingly one finds a desire for a greater degree of "balance" in representing the Holocaust, a "balance" that might be achieved by modulating somewhat an emphasis on the Jewish victims and their German torturers and murderers and focusing a new kind of attention on the "righteous Gentile," or "rescuer."

Within the American context, this search within the darkness and evil of the Holocaust for figures of luminosity and goodness seems to be part of a larger cultural quest for religious meaning or what today is loosely called "spirituality." As Eva Fogelman states the case in her *Conscience and Courage: Rescuers of Jews during the Holocaust* (1994), "People in the 1990s are hungry for role models," for inspiring examples "of moral courage during an immoral time." Her book is but one of many that identifies these role models with the "rescuers," whom she does not hesitate to define as the "spiritual heirs to the *Lamed Vav*—the thirty-six people of Jewish tradition whose sole task it is, in every generation, . . . to do good for their fellow men."[37] And Eva Fogelman is hardly alone in "wanting to give altruism back its good name."[38] Indeed, since 1980 we have been given at least forty films and thirty-five books that relate stories of Christian rescue of Jews, and most of these have appeared in the last ten years. Seen within this context, Steven Spielberg's film, far from being exceptional in its focus on "rescue," is the culmination of a development in Holocaust narrative that has been building momentum for a number of years now.

In Eva Fogelman's view, it is not difficult to explain what it is that accounts for this development: "The brutal testimony of the Eichmann trial set off an urgent quest for evidence of human kindness during the war. People around the world needed to feel that the heart of man was not unrelievedly black. Rescuers were discovered."[39]

Within the American discourse on the Holocaust, the person who has done the most to advance this discovery is Rabbi Harold N. Schulweis. In 1963, on the heels of the Eichmann trial, Rabbi Shulweis founded the Institute of Righteous Acts at the Judah Magnus Museum in Berkeley, California. Some twenty years later he went on to establish the Jewish Foundation of Christian Rescuers (Eva Fogelman served as its first director), which is now an integral part of the Anti-Defamation League's International Center for Holocaust Studies. In addition to his work in establishing these institutions, Rabbi Schulweis has published several articles on "rescuers," and he devotes a full chapter to them in his most recent book, *For Those Who Can't Believe* (1994).

Through all of these writings Rabbi Schulweis has consistently argued that in transmitting knowledge of the Holocaust, nothing should be done to mitigate the severity of the Nazi crimes against the Jews but that everything must be done to identify and call attention to those good people who put themselves at risk to protect Jews whose lives were imperiled. In his own words, "In remembering the cruelty and barbarity of the Holocaust, we must not forget the moral heroes of conscience. In an era of the anti-hero, the heroes of conscience must be exalted."[40] Rabbi Schulweis looks upon memory as a "healing art," one characterized by the imperative to establish "balance." In this view, memory is most meaningful when it is dedicated to the purposes of "moral education." Consequently, with respect to recounting the story of the Holocaust, Rabbi Schulweis argues that we face a question that is fundamentally ethical in its thrust: "How are we to remember without destroying hope?"[41]

In setting forth answers to this question, Rabbi Schulweis has developed both a pragmatic and a didactic approach to history and memory, one that seeks to interpret the Holocaust in ways that are fundamentally constructive. "Memory," he writes, "contains an ambiguous energy. It can liberate or enslave, heal or destroy. The use of memory carries with it a responsibility for the future." Thus, "it is to the moral act of remembering that we must be dedicated. How are we, as moral educators, to make memory the father of conscience and of constructive repentance?" His answer, not surprisingly, is to look to the "righteous among the nations" as a positive counterweight to what is otherwise an overwhelmingly negative and depressing record of villainy. "There is a moral symmetry in man," Rabbi Schulweis insists, and to help restore it, we must become newly attentive to the voices of heroism: "The world is hungry for moral heroes . . . , heroes whose altruism is lived out in action; models of exemplary behavior who realize our abstract ideals, human beings to be emulated." Hence, the discovery and promotion of Oskar Schindler and the other "rescuers."[42]

These figures serve as a bridge in advancing the aims of Jewish-Christian dialogue in America, but beyond this pragmatic purpose they have reached a level of importance in Rabbi Schulweis's thinking that elevates their goodness to a theological principle. "Where was Adonai in Auschwitz?" Rabbi Schulweis asks. While numerous other religious thinkers have raised similar questions about God's absence or presence in the Nazi death camps, it would be rare to find among them very many who answer as Rabbi Schulweis does:

> Where was Adonai in the Holocaust? Adonai was in Nieuvelande,
> a Dutch village in which seven hundred residents rescued five hun-
> dred Jews. . . . Adonai was in Le Chambon-sur-Lignon, whose citi-
> zens hid and protected five thousand Jews. . . . Adonai was in the
> rat-infested sewers of Lvov, where Polish sewer workers hid seven-
> teen Jews. . . . Adonai was in Bulgaria . . . in Finland. . . . Adonai
> was with the Italian troops stationed in the southwestern half of
> Croatia . . . in Yugoslavia, Greece, southern France, Albania. . . .[43]

The litany goes on and on, an "affirmative" antiphony to that strain of severe religious doubt, if not outright theological despair, that has entered the post-Holocaust religious consciousness of so many other writers. One recalls the broken, stuttering prayer that concludes Schwarz-Bart's *The Last of the Just:* "And praised. *Aus-chwitz.* Be. *Maidanek.* The Lord. *Treblinka.* And praised. *Buchen-wald.* Be. *Mauthausen.* The Lord. *Belzec.* . . ."[44] Schwarz-Bart seems to reach the melancholy conclusion that the Nazi assault against the Jews was so overpoweringly destructive as to bring to an end the ancient Jewish tradition of the Just. Rabbi Schulweis, by con-trast, not only revives this tradition but, on the basis of its Chris-tian exemplars, actually presumes to locate God *within* the Holo-caust. Rabbi Schulweis thus inscribes a characteristically American script for narrating the story of the Holocaust, one that has yielded a large and still growing corpus of "rescue" literature and film, of which Spielberg's *Schindler's List* is, for the moment, the culminat-ing expression.

In writing about the film, Rabbi Schulweis has argued that if *Schindler's List* "has become the defining symbol of the Holocaust, it is . . . not because of its artistry alone, but because it enables the viewer to enter the dark cavern without feeling that there is no exit. . . . Memory of the Holocaust is a sacred act that elicits a double mandate: to expose the depth of evil and to raise goodness from the dust of amnesia."[45] Eva Fogelman has put the same "mandate" in the form of a question: "Every child knows the name of Hitler, but how many know the name of Raoul Wallenberg?"[46]

The fact is that in the American population at large, and not only among children, pitifully little is known about either Hitler or Wallenberg.[47] But even if it were the case that knowledge of the former ran deep and knowledge of the latter was all but absent, the case for "balance" would not be a convincing one. There was not nor can there be any "symmetry" in the historical weights of Hitler and Wallenberg, or Hitler and Schindler, or Hitler and the good people of Le Chambon. The deeds of the righteous are assuredly worthy of remembrance, but by placing them on an almost equal level with the deeds of Hitler and encompassing both within a "double mandate" of Holocaust memory, one ends up reshaping the history of the Holocaust in ways that are bound to obscure how truly horrendous the Holocaust actually was. It is no part of Rabbi Schulweis's intention to bring about such a consequence — indeed, he has declared himself emphatically on this point time and again. Nevertheless, the inevitable end point of his moral "art of memory" is clear: by projecting "rescuers" as central figures in narrative accounts of the Holocaust — as if the morality of Wallenberg or Schindler truly were on a par with the evil of Hitler — one changes the core of Holocaust remembrance in ways that will almost certainly vitiate any sober understanding of the deeds of the murderers and the sufferings of the victims.

The Israeli writer Aharon Appelfeld has written on this matter in a way that restores some much-needed perspective: "During the Holocaust there were brave Germans, Ukrainians, and Poles who risked their lives to save Jews. But the Holocaust is not epitomized by the greatness of these marvelous individuals' hearts. . . . I say this because survivors sometimes feel deep gratitude to their rescuers and forget that the saviors were few, and those who betrayed Jews to the Nazis were many and evil."[48] A similar sense of perspective is required in considering other contemporary distortions introduced by the continuing popularization of the Nazi destruction of European Jewry.

NOTES

1. These studies, the first of which appeared in 1993, have been published by the American Jewish Committee as a series of "Working Papers on Contemporary Anti-Semitism." Titles to date include: *What Do Americans*

Know about the Holocaust? (1993), *What Do the British Know about the Holocaust?* (1993), *What Do the French Know about the Holocaust?* (1994), *What Do Australians Know about the Holocaust?* (1994), *Current German Attitudes toward Jews and Other Minorities* (1994), and *Holocaust Denial: What the Survey Data Reveal* (1995); they are available from the American Jewish Committee, 165 East 56th Street, New York, N.Y. 10022–2746. An earlier version of this article was presented at the University of Michigan as the 1995 David W. Belin Lecture in American Jewish Affairs.

2. Jennifer Golub and Renae Cohen, *What Do Americans Know about the Holocaust?* (New York: American Jewish Committee, 1993) 13.

3. Golub and Cohen, *What Do Americans Know about the Holocaust?* 38–40.

4. Tom W. Smith, *Holocaust Denial: What the Survey Data Reveal* (New York: American Jewish Committee, 1995) 31.

5. For an early but still useful study of terminological origins and changes, see Gerd Korman, "The Holocaust in American Historical Writing," *Societas* 2.3 (Summer 1972): 251–70; see also Zev Garber and Bruce Zuckerman, "Why Do We Call the Holocaust 'The Holocaust?' An Inquiry into the Psychology of Labels," *Modern Judaism* 9.2 (May 1989): 197–212.

6. Zev Garber and Bruce Zuckerman advocate a broader conception of what the "Holocaust" was, and they are therefore open to the same historical criticism that Bauer levels at Simon Wiesenthal: "[The Holocaust] becomes a warning of what too easily can happen at any time, at any place, with anyone in the role of victim or victimizer. This is the way 'The Holocaust' should be characterized and especially how it should be taught. . . . The 'six million' figure, often invoked in characterizations of 'The Holocaust,' points up the problem of stressing uniqueness and chosenness over commonality. The truth is that eleven million people were killed by the Nazis in the concentration camps. Nearly half of these are excluded in most characterizations of 'The Holocaust,' and this seems to imply that Gentile deaths are not as significant as Jewish deaths" (Garber and Zuckerman, "Why Do We Call the Holocaust 'the Holocaust?'" 208). The authors cite no sources to corroborate their reference to "eleven million" people killed in the concentration camps and probably look to Wiesenthal as their authority on this matter.

7. See "Address by President Jimmy Carter," printed in "President's Commission on the Holocaust" 27 September 1979.

8. Y. Bauer, "Whose Holocaust?" *Midstream* 26.9 (November 1980): 42.

9. Ilan Avisar, *Screening the Holocaust: Cinema's Images of the Unimaginable* (Bloomington: Indiana University Press, 1988) 96–97.

10. Avisar, *Screening the Holocaust* 116.

11. For more on the reception of Anne Frank's diary in its book and stage versions, see Alvin H. Rosenfeld, "Popularization and Memory: The Case of

Anne Frank," in *Lessons and Legacies: The Meaning of the Holocaust in a Changing World*, ed. Peter Hayes (Evanston, IL: Northwestern University Press, 1991) 243–78.

12. Cited in Dienke Hondius, "The Holocaust and Us," *Reconstruction* 2.3 (1994): 95.

13. Frances Goodrich and Albert Hackett, *The Diary of Anne Frank* (New York: Random House, 1956) 174.

14. Undated, four-page letter of solicitation by Miles Lerman, Chairman, United States Holocaust Memorial Museum.

15. Estelle Gilson, "Americanizing the Holocaust," *Congress Monthly* (September/October, 1993): 6.

16. Michael Berenbaum, *After Tragedy and Triumph: Essays in Modern Jewish Thought and the American Experience* (Cambridge: Cambridge University Press, 1990) 22.

17. Berenbaum, *After Tragedy and Triumph* 20.

18. See the *New York Times*, "Crowds Strain U.S. Museum on Holocaust" 23 December 1993.

19. These aims are set forth in a Simon Wiesenthal Center–Museum of Tolerance promotional brochure.

20. Judy Chicago, *Holocaust Project: From Darkness into Light*, with Photography by Donald Woodman (New York: Penguin Books, 1993).

21. Chicago, *Holocaust Project* 36.

22. Chicago, *Holocaust Project* 27, 31.

23. Chicago, *Holocaust Project* 90.

24. Chicago, *Holocaust Project* 138.

25. Chicago, *Holocaust Project* 139.

26. Chicago, *Holocaust Project* 132.

27. Quoted in an article, "ADL Hits Christian Fundamentalists," in the *Forward* 10 June 1994.

28. "ADL" ix.

29. William Helmreich, *Against All Odds: Holocaust Survivors and the Successful Lives They Made in America* (New York: Simon & Schuster, 1992) 38.

30. The Fortunoff Video Archives for Holocaust Testimonies at Yale University has been engaged in filming the testimonies of Holocaust survivors for a number of years now and is a major resource of its kind. At least two books have already been produced on the basis of these archival holdings: Lawrence Langer, *Holocaust Testimonies: The Ruins of Memory* (New Haven: Yale University Press, 1991); and Shoshana Felman and Dori Laub, *Testimony: Crises of Witnessing in Literature, Psychoanalysis, and History* (New York: Routledge, 1992). In addition, Steven Spielberg has recently established a foundation whose purpose will be to record and videotape the testimonies of tens of thousands of Holocaust survivors.

31. Leon Uris, foreword to Ernst Michel, *Promises to Keep* (New York: Barricade Books, 1994) xiii.

32. For more on the Bitburg affair, see Geoffrey H. Hartman, ed., *Bitburg in Moral and Political Perspective* (Bloomington: Indiana University Press, 1986).

33. Stephen Schiff, "Seriously Spielberg," *New Yorker* 21 March 1994; Terrence Rafferty, "A Man of Transactions," *New Yorker* 20 December 1993; the Katzenberg encomium is quoted in the Schiff article cited above.

34. James Bowman, "Lost and Profound," *American Spectator* February 1994; J. Hoberman, "Spielberg's Oskar," *Village Voice* 21 December 1993; Donald Kuspit, "Director's Guilt," *Artforum* February 1994; and Claude Lanzmann, "The Twisted Truth of *Schindler's List,*" *London Evening Standard* 10 February 1994.

35. Since the appearance of the film, Oskar Schindler's grave in the Latin Cemetery of Jerusalem has become something of a popular religious site for pilgrims visiting Israel. In addition, tourists can visit Poland on monthly tours called "Oskar Schindler's Poland." See Jack Schneidler, "The Ghosts of Poland's Past," *St. Petersburg Times* 9 October 1994.

36. Michael André Bernstein, "The *Schindler's List* Effect," *American Scholar* 63.3 (Summer 1994): 429–32.

37. Eva Fogelman, *Conscience and Courage: Rescue of Jews during the Holocaust* (New York: Anchor Books Doubleday, 1994), xix, 3.

38. Fogelman, *Conscience and Courage* xix.

39. Fogelman, *Conscience and Courage* 301.

40. Harold M. Schulweis, *For Those Who Can't Believe* (New York: HarperCollins, 1994) 150.

41. Harold M. Schulweis, "The Bias against Man," *Dimensions* 3.3 (1988): 5.

42. Schulweis, "Bias against Man" 4, 6, 8.

43. Schulweis, *For Those Who Can't Believe* 148–49.

44. André Schwarz-Bart, *The Last of the Just,* trans. Stephen Becker (New York: Atheneum, 1961) 374. For a brief but illuminating history of the Jewish folk legend of the "just man," see Gershom Scholem, "The Tradition of the Thirty-Six Hidden Just Men," in *The Messianic Idea in Judaism and Other Essays on Jewish Spirituality* (New York: Schocken Books, 1971) 251–56.

45. Schulweis, *For Those Who Can't Believe* 157.

46. Fogelman, *Conscience and Courage* 303.

47. The authors of *What Do Americans Know about the Holocaust?* and *Holocaust Denial: What the Survey Data Reveal* are in agreement about the knowledge level of Americans regarding the Holocaust and conclude that it is generally "shallow, incomplete, and imperfect." In their informed view, "Holocaust ignorance is widespread" (Smith, *Holocaust Denial* 3, 22).

48. Aharon Appelfeld, *Beyond Despair* (New York: Fromm Publishers, 1994) xiii.

SEVEN

To Seize Memory

History and Identity
in Post-Holocaust Jewish Thought

MICHAEL L. MORGAN

DURING THE LATE 1960s and the early 1970s a small number of
Jewish intellectuals attempted to articulate, for a North American
audience, an understanding of Judaism in a post-Holocaust situation. In this essay I will try to give an interpretation of their work,
of what is called "post-Holocaust Jewish thought."

What is the significance of these thinkers and their work? A
preliminary answer might be that any serious theological response
to the death camps would take the shape of an encounter with the
traditional problem of evil. This answer would lead us to think
that the main themes of post-Holocaust Jewish thought are God,
covenant, redemption, and providence, among others. But my proposal will point us in another direction. While I agree that themes
like these do arise in post-Holocaust Jewish thinking, I want to
focus on a different issue, one that concerns the very nature of
Jewish religious ideas and beliefs and specifically their relation to
history—that is, to temporality, objectivity, change, context, the
past, and other such matters. From another point of view, this
central issue concerns identity—in this case, religious identity—
and memory, or the past as it is present for the purposes of Jewish
self-understanding.

To many people it may seem obvious that the articulation of one's identity, in this case one's religious identity, is an historical task. After all, it takes place for a group at a particular historical moment, and it employs historical resources. But we must be cautious. The late 1960s and early 1970s were indeed a time when many groups sought a sense of self-identity through a return to the past; and national or public identity seems intrinsically historical, a nation's past being the most natural place to look for the constituent values and models that configure the national self. In the case of religious identity, however, things differ. Its construction may be historical, to be sure, and it may use historical resources as models or for symbolic purposes, but the assumption that religious self-understanding is historical through and through is less obvious and perhaps even wholly unlikely. Religious aspiration, like scientific inquiry and like philosophical thought, has always aimed at objectivity and transcendence. Religious communities, people, and institutions are certainly historical, but religious belief and the religious *Weltanschauung*—at least in the West— strive for a timeless, unconditional, and permanent comprehension of what is valuable and true about the world, human life, and the divine. Ultimately, Jewish belief, like all such religious belief, has conceived of itself along these lines. Although the historicity of national or public identity is obvious, the historicity of Jewish identity is hardly so to the theologians who took up the question of how to cope with the Holocaust and how to rethink Judaism in a post-Holocaust world. Indeed, if the prefix "post" had a strictly temporal or historical connotation, it might have made many in the late 1960s and early 1970s wonder at its propriety at all. To historians, change and temporality and development are taken for granted; this is not so for theologians and believers.

There are, moreover, additional reasons why one might doubt the propriety of history to the task of Jewish self-understanding. The 1970s saw the emergence of postmodernism and antirealism and hence the rejection of any sense that there are secure grounds for any self-interpretation, either in the self or in the resources which are employed. In such an atmosphere—neo-Nietzschean as some call it—the return to the past may seem unintelligible, for either the self provides no privileged standpoint for any process of interpretation, or the past should harbor no secret security of any kind. Rather the past should turn out to be as open and mutable as the present dictates. Seeking one's own identity in an understanding of history might seem to be a case of self-deception.[1]

In order to show that the connectedness of Jewish identity and history is central to the movement of post-Holocaust Jewish thought, I would like to perform three tasks. First, by drawing on the debates in West Germany in the 1980s concerning German identity and its relation to the Nazi period as an analogue, I will try to illuminate the connection between the Holocaust and debates about the relation between identity and history. Application of this theme to post-Holocaust Jewish thought is only plausible, however, if the movement and public attention to the Holocaust occurred at a historical moment when the reconstitution of group identity through an encounter with the past was urgent. In the case of American Jewry, this moment involves the Six Day War and the historical milieu of the late 1960s and early 1970s. Second, by examining American cultural and political life in the 1950s and 1960s, I will try to show that post-Holocaust Jewish thought arises and is received in just such a context. At that time, a variety of ethnic and interest groups in America were seeking to articulate their own identities in terms of a return to the past. Finally, I will consider briefly how the work of Emil Fackenheim, Eliezer Berkovits, and Irving Greenberg exhibits this appreciation of how history and the Holocaust are essential to Jewish self-understanding and Jewish identity.

I

In the course of the 1980s a number of events occurred within West Germany that raised the question of how the past is related to public memory and national identity. Specifically, the problem related to the role of the Nazi Period, 1933–1945, in German self-understanding. The events I have in mind include the showing of the American television miniseries *Holocaust*,[2] the plans to build national museums in Bonn and Berlin, the Reagan visit to Bitburg on 8 May 1985, and the *Historikerstreit,* or the Historians' Debate, with all of its complex literary encounters.[3]

The meaning of these events, as one might expect, is multifaceted. They, and especially the Historians' Debate, raise questions about historiography in general and in particular concerning the case of Nazi Germany. The general issues concern the legitimacy of studying everyday life and popular culture and social life without sufficient attention to major political and historical events, policies, and changes that frame the microcosm.[4] They also involve questions about objectivity and perspective, the context of historical inquiry and the goals of such investigation. Early on, for example, Jürgen Habermas challenged Andreas Hillgruber's proposal that the historian must worry about whose perspective, among those of his subjects, he should adopt.[5] Habermas had every reason to be puzzled by the fact that Hillgruber had raised the question; it is one that even Collingwood, with his commitment to the historiographical necessity of reenactment, would not ask.[6] The natural way of treating historical evidence is with critical detachment, and if reenactment is attempted, it should surely be sought for all relevant agents for whom sufficient evidence can be had so that reenacting their deliberations, choices, actions, and judgments is well-supported, illuminating, and informative.[7]

At certain points, general worries about the nature of historical investigation and specific ones about historiography relating to Nazi Germany converge. Saul Friedlander, Otto Dov Kulka, and others object, for example, to the attempts to historicize Nazism by normalizing it.[8] They debate with Nolte, Broszat, and others precisely because the latter fail to appreciate fully the moral dimension of the choice to diminish the special features of the Final Solution, trivializing the Holocaust by treating it as a Nazi defense against Bolshevist threats or by focusing on the continuities of normal, everyday life rather than on the extraordinary character of the death camps.[9] The point is that *no* history is *mere* inquiry; it is always loaded with political and moral freight. Decisions about emphasis, selection, and so on are not benignly academic; in the case of Nazi policy and practice, the Final Solution, and the special role of its victims, the moral freight has much to do with responsibility, honesty, and dignity.[10]

These issues, moreover, remind us that much of the meaning of the Historians' Debate and the surrounding events concerns German national identity and how that identity was viewed by neoconservatives and others in the 1980s.[11] In this respect the debate about how to understand the Nazi period and what role to assign the Final Solution and the death camps is a debate about the past and how it figures in one's self-understanding. Here, of course, the agent is a nation and not an individual; and the notion of a national or public memory is a metaphor for the ways in which a conception of national character and purpose is constituted by models, images, and figures from a nation's historical tradition.[12] In the case of German identity, the debate is about facing the past at all and hence about the possibility, indeed the threat of, total unqualified discontinuity. It is about a darkness so unyielding that everything else might be occluded, leaving a people without a positive sense of history and hence leaving it wholly trapped in the present. The neoconservative government of Helmit Kohl sought to enlist historians such as Michael Stürmer of Erlangen to retrieve the past and with it the pride of German national identity; but, as Habermas has argued, merely being a historian will not do.[13] What is needed is an honest encounter with a past that is ambiguous, an encounter that is not a politically motivated disposal of Nazi atrocities and the death camps undertaken in order to leap beyond it.[14] In short, Habermas argues that the issue is not a scholarly but a political-moral one and that it turns on honesty.[15] In terms that Paul Ricoeur has made famous, genuine German self-understanding requires a two-fold hermeneutical recovery of the past, a recovery that is both a retrieval of what is positive and a "suspicious" rejection of what is unacceptable, an appropriation of positive models and motifs and

an honest, responsible denial of the repulsive.[16] But even that rejection must be dialectically genuine, involving first an acceptance
of the horror for what it was and of the responsibility for it that
burdens even the present. Rejection, resistance, opposition, commitment to stand against any future recurrence—these can only be
authentic responses when built on honest recognition of what happened, why, by whom, and to whom.[17]

It is not surprising that the victims and their descendants, just
as the perpetrators and their progeny, have struggled and continue
to struggle with similar problems. Indeed, we can learn something
about the Jewish encounter with the memory of Auschwitz if we
compare that struggle with the problems generated by the Historians' Debate. Viewed formally, the two situations have deep similarities. Both are questions of identity and self-understanding, one
national or political, the other religious and ethnic, in the broad
sense. Both situations raise questions about the roles of the past
and of historical tradition in the constitution of that identity. And
both require confrontation with the question of whether the Holocaust and the death camps do cut off the present from any
meaningful recovery of the past and whether they aggravate an
attempt at flight from history altogether.[18] In short, in both cases,
the present confronts the past as discontinuity and continuity,[19]
leading one to wonder whether the two roles can occur at once
and together. I am not denying, of course, that the perspective of
agent and victim are fundamentally and importantly different. Certainly they are. The differences, moreover, are substantive and
affect the ways in which each engages the same dark time, what
that time does to one and to the other as they respond to the
necessity of memory and recovery. But even amid the differences,
there are similarities, and they too are important.

If it was the rise of neoconservativism in West Germany and the
breakdown of the antitotalitarian consensus of the 1960s that led
to the events we listed above, and eventually to the debates about
Nazism and German identity,[20] it was the disintegration of the
liberal consensus in America in the 1960s, coupled with the Six
Day War in 1967, that led to the emergence in the United States

of an effort to reconstitute Jewish identity in terms of a responsible and genuine encounter with Auschwitz. This effort was widespread, a dominant feature of the American Jewish community's attempt to reinterpret itself. It was also the central impulse for a small group of theologians or Jewish thinkers. By placing them, their work, and its reception within the proper historical context, we shall be able to understand the special significance of this "post-Holocaust" Jewish thought, the Jewish analogue to the more recent German effort to reconstitute identity in terms of an encounter with the past.[21]

II

In the United States, prior to 1967, at least two thinkers had written about the Holocaust and its impact on Jewish life and belief; but their work, while noticed, had not been influential.[22] I am referring to Elie Wiesel, whose autobiographical novel *Night* had appeared in English in 1960, and to Richard Rubenstein, whose collection of essays, *After Auschwitz,* was published in 1966.[23] In March of 1967, however, Steven Schwarzchild, the editor of the journal *Judaism,* hosted a symposium under the auspices of the American Jewish Committee entitled "Jewish Values in a Post-Holocaust Future." *Judaism* published the proceedings of the symposium in the summer of 1967, and this was the first phase in an increasingly influential set of responses to the currents of political and social anxiety, urgency, and elation of the period.[24] In addition to Wiesel and Rubenstein, the key figures were Emil Fackenheim, a participant in the symposium; Eliezer Berkovits; and Irving Greenberg. By the early 1970s, all had continued lines of thought first articulated earlier, had revived and revised their thinking, or had made major statements that established them as the central figures in the project of reconstructing Judaism after Auschwitz. For our purposes, we shall focus on Fackenheim, Berkovits, and Greenberg.[25]

The work of these theologians (two of them philosophers, one a historian) was received in a variety of ways by a complex and variegated Jewish community seemingly united in the anxiety and relief of the Six Day War.[26] With lightning efficiency the Israeli army had repelled Syrian and Egyptian attacks and won a decisive, thrilling victory that transformed the map of Israel, the institutional structure of American Jewish life, and the shape of Jewish consciousness. Israel, survival, a proud self-reliance, political awareness, militant self-expression—these became for many Jews the core, if not the totality, of Jewish identity.[27] And with these themes came an acknowledgment of the Holocaust, Auschwitz, the memory of catastrophe, victimization, and defeat, but no longer, as had been the case, as the catalyst of guilt and embarassment, but rather as objects of opposition and a new-found self-confidence, a sense of transcendence. As if miraculously, the American Jewish community was unburdened of its commitment to subordinate, even to *repress* the death camps, to set them aside as a deeply distressing wound, a painful memory that would not go away but also could not be assimilated. The victory in June 1967 made it possible to locate Auschwitz *before* the liberation of Jerusalem and hence to accept it not as an obfuscating, unintelligible darkness but rather as an object of opposition now and resistance then, as accepted but transcended. The everyday Jew, the common people, realized first what the thinkers only seemed to realize later, that Auschwitz could be honestly encountered only when it did not threaten to obliterate all of Jewish tradition and the Jewish past along with it.[28]

American Jews were helped to this insight by the Arab nations themselves, who repeated the Nazi language of destruction and hence participated in staging their own defeat as a belated response to Nazi Germany. But even such a catalyst could not have been effective if the situation had not been a receptive one. Nor was it effective for all Jews in the same way, for all were not the same.[29] What indeed was the situation of American Judaism in 1967? And what were its various constituencies?

The postwar period, from 1945 to 1960, saw the consolidation of a New Deal ideology that welded together welfare state policies, economic development and abundance, increased consumerism, anti-Communism, and a domestic ideal that encouraged a traditional family model in a new urban setting.[30] All of this was a perfect context for postwar Jews to occupy as they sought total acceptance into American life and culture.[31] But while they bought into the liberal consensus of the Eisenhower years, they did so both as participants and as critics. They lived the tension, endorsing many of the values that underwrote their acceptance into a tolerant and open society and capitalizing on new prosperity, wealth, and position. At the same time, Jews struggled with their distinctness, critical of injustice and inequality, wary of continued anti-Semitism, and ambivalent about tradition, practice, ritual, authority, and custom.[32]

When the civil rights movement exploded in Greensboro, North Carolina, in 1960,[33] and the student movement, the New Left, began to flourish a few years later,[34] many of the earliest white activists were the children of these second generation, affluent, liberal, suburban Jews.[35] It is often remarked that the children of the sixties—the New Left, the civil rights and antiwar activists, the hippies and experimenters with counterculture, the nascent feminists, and others—had more in common with their parents than we once thought.[36] What they shared were anti-Communism, a passion for America, dissatisfaction and discontent with consumerism and suburban isolation, with fixed, traditional roles; they shared a search for community and, if they were Jewish, a drive to be accepted fully in American life and culture—for what we might call Jewish dignity.[37] They were also deeply critical of the dissonance between American ideals and practice; they were devoted fighters against dishonesty and hypocrisy.

By and large, then, with many rabbis and a vanguard of Jewish college students leading the way, American Judaism bought into the 1960s, into that wave of critical enthusiasm for righting wrongs and purifying the American ideal. Moreover, by displaying the moral resources of the Jewish tradition, the prophetic morality of biblical faith, the Jewish community and especially its liberal elements, largely Reform and Conservative in affiliation, could treat its participation in American life as a genuinely Jewish act. Furthermore, this participation was a strategy for being authentically American and authentically Jewish that subordinated, if it did not altogether avoid, distinctiveness, diminished the importance of ritual, assimilated religious to moral faith, and turned religious education into moral and political training.[38] In the Jewish summer camps of the 1960s (and to this day), the songs of Pete Seeger, Bob Dylan, and Joan Baez were sung like liturgy and teenagers read Salinger, Ginzburg, and Kerouac as canonical texts.

In the mid-60s, however, a change or set of changes occurred that relocated rebellious youth and the liberal Jewish community. As always in this decade, the most influential shifts first took place in the civil rights movement.[39] When, in 1964 and subsequent years, the civil rights movement changed from nonviolent to militant and became increasingly exclusive and Black nationalist, this signalled an important shift in the structure and character of American social and political activism. To be sure, the seeds of such fragmentation and polarization were already present in the early 1960s; if not before, then certainly after the Atlantic City Democratic convention in August 1964 and the episode of the Mississippi Freedom Democratic Party, they grew and flourished, eventually producing a period of both left- and right-wing parochialism, from Black nationalism to the new ethnicity, from a virulent counterculture to the new feminism.[40]

From 1965 on, then, American social and political activism became increasingly fragmented, localized around a variety of causes and a host of special interest groups.[41] Some were political, others ethnic, racial, ecological, gender-specific, or cultural.[42] These interest group clusters just as often fought each other as they did the power of big business and government bureaucracy.[43] Moreover, as they fought each other and sought recognition and acceptance, these groups searched for viable traditions, histories, and roots. As America as a whole experienced its own political and cultural crisis of identity, so did each of these nuclei of interest, from the women's movement to the new ethnics to the ecologists, engage in similar struggles.[44]

III

It was in this context that the Six Day War occurred. Most books on American political and cultural life in the 1960s do not even mention the war except to comment that it did not take long for Black nationalists to side with the Palestinians and to attack Israel as an imperialist oppressor.[45] But while June 1967 may, on reflection, seem unimportant to American history in general, it was not so for American Jews. Indeed, the war stimulated massive support from the American Jewish community, altered the character and structure of American Jewish life, and redefined what Jewish fidelity and Jewish identity came to mean in the following years. It was, in short, momentous.

The Six Day War was also determinative for American Jews.[46] By 1967 those who had entered the 1960s as civil rights workers and student activists had been excluded from the former movement.[47] The student movement itself had become more militant, and its goals seemed increasingly hopeless.[48] With the flourishing of countercultural activity, drug use, and looser sexual practices, relations with mainstream Jewish life became more and more strained. Both within and without institutional Jewish life there were doubts about purpose and direction; and the fragmentation of style, conviction, and purpose exposed an American Judaism in disarray.[49] The Six Day War, at one level and if only temporarily, brought unity out of chaos. Moreover, it mobilized an historical and political unity that was compatible with the new ethnicity on the right and interest group polarization on the left.[50] For a moment, virtually all of American Judaism stood united against the Arab threat to Israel's existence, on behalf of Israeli self-defense and heroism, and in an encounter with the dark memory of Auschwitz.[51]

Radio Damascus, Jewish leaders, Christian theologians, and popular memory all conspired to cast the war against the background of the death camps and to blend in a celebration of national-religious pride the heroes of Masada and the Warsaw Ghetto with those of Sinai, the West Bank, the Golan Heights, and Jerusalem.[52]

The prominence of Israel and the sense of pride that accompanied a victory that was military, political, historic, and real brought with it the opportunity to return in memory to the death camps and honestly encounter them.[53] What occurred was a liberation for memory but only if that memory could be orchestrated with honesty and coordinated with pride.

Many Jews spoke about such memory, both leaders and lay people, but a few theologians engaged in the task of remembering and confronting Auschwitz with a deep appreciation of its implications for Jewish identity. Not all Jews were happy with their reflections or even with their emphasis on Nazi persecution, Hitler, and the death camps.[54] But for these thinkers the honest appraisal and understanding of contemporary Jewish life, the retrieval of Jewish tradition and the Jewish past, and the understanding of Israel's place in it—these could not proceed without a fully responsible encounter with the Nazi past and the Final Solution as a persisting trauma for the Jewish mind.

IV

I think that this challenge about history is one of the central lessons of the Jewish theologians' attempts to articulate a post-Holocaust Jewish identity; for these efforts incorporate a recognition that identity must be self-consciously historical and yet must somehow transcend its own historicity. Even a brief look at the work of Fackenheim, Greenberg, and Berkovits shows that they are indeed aware of the special role that Auschwitz requires for temporality and history in Jewish self-consciousness and Jewish identity.

Berkovits is perhaps less explicit about this issue than Greenberg or Fackenheim. His polemical and chauvinistic work, *Faith after the Holocaust*, attacks those who charge God or the Jewish people with major roles in the atrocities of Auschwitz.[55] It uses an antiquated distinction between fact and value to indict the modern world and to define the task of Jewish history; and it solves the problem of innocent suffering in a wholly traditional way that underwrites the voluntarism of Jewish destiny by appealing to the divine creation of human beings as free agents.[56] For Berkovits, the traditional problem of evil and its solution simply *is* the framework for understanding Auschwitz. To be sure, Berkovits does couch the "free will" solution to the problem of evil in biblical language—God's "hiding" of His face—and he does make it sound paradoxical; but it is nonetheless a traditional response. All of this and much more in Berkovits's account is unsurprising and even unpersuasive—or should be. But underneath his polemics, his inflated and florid prose, and his conventional philosophy, Berkovits makes a singularly important point; he raises a significant problem, and solves it in a creative way. The issue concerns the relation between history and identity and the problem of how to conceive of that relation after Auschwitz.

Berkovits emphasizes that the Holocaust raises no special difficulty for Jewish theology. As he puts it, "the suffering of a single innocent child poses no less a problem to faith than the undeserved suffering of millions." And, "the Holocaust does not preempt the entire course of Jewish history." We can rephrase Berkovits's point: Jewish belief is not essentially historical; no single event raises a unique problem for it; the Holocaust has no special theological implications. Jewish belief is, in a sense, timeless and absolute. It solves the problem of evil and innocent suffering as part of its general account of divine providence, human freedom, the meaning of history, and the role of the Jewish people in history. The Holocaust causes no theological changes and makes no theological difference.[57]

By themselves these commitments are wholly expected. Any traditionalist would surely agree that in essence Jewish beliefs are immune to historical influence in any essential way. One is reminded of Abraham Joshua Heschel's marvelous statement, "the Bible is not man's theology; it is God's anthropology." In addition to warning us about any pretense to knowledge of the divine mystery, this description points out that Jewish belief as articulated in revelation and the revelatory tradition is from a divine perspective, and that means from a transcendent, objective, nonsituated and hence ahistorical point of view. Berkovits's point is similar. But he adds to it a deep and sensitive need to take the Holocaust seriously and not to "normalize" or dispose of it as others do. In the early 1970s many Jewish intellectuals, for instance, Neusner and Wyschogrod, sought to do just this. They are the Jewish analogues to Stürmer and Hillgruber. To them the Holocaust is not singular or especially influential. Berkovits disagrees. Although the Holocaust is theologically normal, it is not in all its uniqueness unimportant, and no Jewish traditionalist can afford to neglect that importance. This is the challenge that Berkovits sets for himself: to cling to the absolute status of Jewish belief and yet to remain utterly sensitive to the importance of Auschwitz.

Berkovits's solution is to recall that the Jewish people has a moral purpose in history and to recognize that the Holocaust, while it has no effect on the nature of this project, does seriously influence the project's *history*. According to Berkovits, that is, the Holocaust has two roles. First, it is evidence that the powers of technology, self-interest, and bureaucratic domination have become so overwhelming that they threaten history itself. Second, this fact, coupled with the fact that this domination was aimed primarily at the Jewish people, has the psychological effect of destroying the will of the Jew to continue at his or her post, the project of bringing value and morality to a world of self-interest and power. Ultimately, then, the Holocaust must be confronted seriously for historical and psychological reasons and because Judaism is essentially engaged in an historical task. The event has no influence on theology, but it does affect the commitment to Jewish belief and Jewish destiny. At one level, the Holocaust must be normalized, but at another it cannot be.

In a sense, Berkovits uses a Kantian strategy of divide and conquer. How, Kant asked, can human beings be both causally determined and free? Because, he answered, man is free in the moral, noumenal world and causally bound in the scientific or phenomenal world. Similarly, for Berkovits, the Holocaust is assimilated to the universal in the world of belief and theology but uniquely influential in the world of history and action. This way of considering Berkovits's achievement, however, shows that a more radical dilemma is still possible: a more extreme traditionalist thinker might acknowledge the theological impact of Auschwitz and nonetheless believe that certain beliefs are immune to history. Irving Greenberg, I believe, is just such a thinker.

Greenberg, a traditional theologian and trained historian, is best represented in a famous, widely cited article that appeared in 1974 in the conference proceedings, *Auschwitz: Beginning of a New Era?* edited by Eva Fleischner. This piece—"Cloud of Smoke, Pillar of Fire: Judaism, Christianity, and Modernity after the Holocaust"—is probably Greenberg's most radical statement and represents his position at its most powerful. Unlike Berkovits, he announces at the outset his recognition that the relationship between Judaism or Christianity and history is central to his reflections on the impact of the Holocaust. He confronts explicitly, therefore, the problem raised by the Historians' Debate: how is history related to identity and in particular, how can we retrieve authentically Jewish history and tradition and yet take Auschwitz seriously?

According to Greenberg, Judaism is a religion of history, and thus it must be exposed to and influenced by changes in history. What happens influences what Judaism is. But this conclusion is too facile and ambiguous. As we have seen, Berkovits encourages us to distinguish between the ways in which Judaism is about history and hence the ways in which historical events affect Judaism. As Greenberg proceeds, it becomes clear that he believes that the Holocaust should alter the theological core of Judaism, its beliefs about human nature and about God. Moreover, Greenberg realizes that in order to do this, the Holocaust must itself be recovered for Jewish memory and for Jewish identity. In my estimation, the real novelty of Greenberg's view lies in the precise way in which he carries out and then employs this recovery.

At issue is the question of perspective and its relation to our access to the past. Hillgruber, in his disturbing reflections on the Eastern Front, had raised this question.[58] In order to understand the events of 1944–1945, with whom should the historian identify? Whose point of view should the historian take? As I already indicated, this question is confusing. R. G. Collingwood, in a classic discussion, and William Dray more recently, both argued that in order to explain why an agent did what he or she did, one should identify with that agent, reenact the agent's deliberations and choice, and articulate his reasons for doing what he did. Others have claimed that both explanation and narrative require a detached point of view, the historian's own, and that it be as immune to bias and presupposition as possible. More recently, however, especially among students of popular culture, the historian has sought to see and understand practices, rituals, images, and so forth as the common people did, in order to uncover their meaning for them.[59] Historiographically, Hillgruber's suggestion seems most akin to these latter historians; but its onesidedness nonetheless reflects poorly the goals of historical investigation.

Surely Saul Friedlander and others are right when they argue that this issue of perspective is a moral and political one, not restricted to its historical implications.[60] In Hillgruber's choice to ignore the relationship between the performance of the Wehrmacht in the East and the operation of the death camps, this becomes very clear. Hence, the question of perspective is one of importance, significance, and to a degree access. It is integral to the way that the past comes to mean something to people today. The question of perspective and identification is therefore partly about access to the past, about relating to it at all, and about meaning, aiming at a significance for the subject. Claude Lanzmann, for example, has characterized his interrogatory technique in *Shoah* as a device for giving the viewer access to events in the camps; watching participants recall the past *enables* access to the audience. Evidence, data, and remains require inference and reconstruction; remembering is a living, moving, and often painful experience that, almost like a moving conveyer, transports the viewer back to what the rememberer is calling to mind. One becomes a "passenger," as it were, on the remembering of others as that process returns to the past. Hillgruber's strategy is far more conventional and, this is the crucial point, it is not aimed at working through the relationship to Auschwitz but rather at avoiding such a task. What he seeks to do is to avoid just that reidentification with the perspective of perpetrator or victim that is crucial to coming to grips with the Holocaust. As Andreas Huyssen has shown, this access to the victims especially, so crucial to a German working through of the Nazi past, was precisely what the television miniseries *Holocaust* provided for so many Germans in the Federal Republic. It was just this mechanism for identification that was the reason for the incredible public impact of the series.[61]

Greenberg recognizes that an authentic encounter with Auschwitz—its meaning for the contemporary Jew—requires access to the event, and he provides that access in an especially powerful way. First, he locates a piece of testimony and interrogation from the Nuremberg trial record. In it a guard from Auschwitz is questioned by a Soviet judge about the conduct of the gassing and particularly about an occasion when infants were taken from their mothers—who were standing in line to enter the "showers"—and cast, alive and screaming, into a burning pit alongside the gas chambers. The judge finds this shocking, horrifying, and inexplicable, and he elicits from the guard the suggestion that this form of execution was done in order to save money. By itself, this is a terrifying, awful thought. But Greenberg does not stop here. He reenters the text and engages in a brief, almost mechanical historical clarification, in which he reconstructs the precise a-mount per life that was "saved" by this procedure. The effect on the reader is chilling—a montage of perspectives that focuses on atrocity and elicits a shocked, horrified amazement in response to it. Greenberg exploits that effect, moreover, when he announces his principle for uttering post-Holocaust beliefs: no statement, the-ological or otherwise, should be made that could not be uttered in the presence of the burning children.[62]

In Greenberg we have an explicit recognition that contemporary Jewish identity must expose itself to the past, and this means to a genuinely, deeply recovered past. This is, for Greenberg, a theological matter, for one result of such an exposure is what he calls "dialectical faith."[63] Furthermore, Greenberg realizes that in order to reappropriate the Jewish past and to recover such biblical models as Job and the Suffering Servant, one must first find some access to the Holocaust and then employ that access as a mechanism for determining its meaning for contemporary identity. Unlike Hillgruber, Greenberg rejects identification with the victims. In its place he gives us a low-ranking guard, an agent, and the Soviet judge's amazed and horrified response. To this he couples the historian's "coldly analytical" and detached supplement; but the impact is great, drawing the reader into the event, distancing him or her from it, and underscoring the judge's horrified amazement—deepened for us by the historical epilogue. This whole enables the contemporary theologian to remain present and yet to define his affirmations against the reality of the past. It enables us both to face and recover a dark past and then to face and recover a traditional past in these terms.

Greenberg does not explain with any precision how exactly the memory of the burning children will adjudicate or shape today's theological commitments. He suggests, in his account of the dialectical faith that will emerge, that memory will raise doubts about any continued faith, about its completeness, and about its fixity. We might put it this way: no theological statement is acceptable that, when uttered by a person with a vivid memory and understanding of the episode of the burning children and others like it, does not register doubt, uncertainty, and partiality. Nothing comes easy, and in place of rationality as a standard of acceptability, Greenberg identifies not the Holocaust but the individual's powerful, penetrating internalization of its horror, its utter disregard for, even denial of the value of human life.

The grounding of the horrified surprise is best explored in the work of Emil Fackenheim. Perhaps more self-consciously than anyone else, especially in the late 1960s and early 1970s, Fackenheim's response to Auschwitz involved a recognition of the role of history for Jewish self-understanding. Indeed, according to his own testimony, that recognition marked the major turning point in his intellectual career. One constituent of Fackenheim's post-Holocaust Jewish thought made him famous; one statement became widely quoted and showed that the Jewish community longed for a means to return to Auschwitz but only if such a return did not threaten the present. In 1967, for the first time, Fackenheim pronounced what he called the 614th Commandment: thou shalt give Hitler no posthumous victories. It was his way of saying "no," of making resistance, courage, and opposition to threat emblems of Jewish pride, and of showing how the Holocaust could be confronted honestly and yet, in a sense, transcended. It even implied why it was necessary for the Jew to do these things, although it did not show with sufficient clarity how it was possible for today's Jews to carry out such an incredible task of opposition. In a few central publications in the late 1960s, Fackenheim confronted the utter historicity of Jewish experience and the nemesis represented by that history and marked out a path to recovery, a path that he has spent over three decades elaborating and modifying.[64]

Fackenheim's utterance of the famous 614th commandment occurred at the *Judaism* symposium in New York on 26 March 1967, months before the Six Day War. Later he would acknowledge the sense of moral duty that arose for him at Schwarzschild's invitation. But that sense of duty would not have been sufficient to produce the result had Fackenheim not already seen his way toward confronting a dual challenge: to deal honestly and seriously with the death camps and yet to realize how Judaism could nonetheless survive and persevere. In principle the Holocaust might have threatened to destroy Judaism, but in fact it did not succeed. The first lesson he claimed to have learned from his study of Hegel and the vulnerability of the Hegelian system to unassimilable events; the second he learned from Elie Wiesel and from all those Jews whose indignation and anger did not subside but whose commitment to Judaism nonetheless remained alive and vital. All this was present to Fackenheim in March of 1967, long before the war. What that event added, however, was support for him personally and a receptive audience to hear his utterance. In part it was able to provide that audience because Jews in America were immersed in a period of shifting identities, and the fragmentation of American commitments was encouraging group affiliation and identification and a questing for rootedness and particularity. Confrontation with Jewish memory seemed dramatically appropriate at a time when the Jewish people had been singled out, forced both to "return into history" and to find a way to survive in history all at once.

Let me clarify Fackenheim's achievement by focusing on a few features of his thinking. First, prior to 1967, Fackenheim had vigorously clung to the transcendence of philosophical and religious thought. To him, philosophy was capable of objectivity, of arriving at some truths not tied to history in such a way that no historical event could possibly falsify them; and religion, especially Judaism, rested on the commitment to such unconditional, objective foundations. Indeed, he was convinced that even existentialist philosophy and religious thought could manage such transcendence, thereby avoiding historicism and ultimately relativism.[65] But in about 1967, Fackenheim came to realize that Judaism, at least, was not a set of absolute, true beliefs; rather, as he put it, the "Midrashic Framework" is open. Nothing in Judaism is immune to historical falsification; everything is vulnerable. At any given moment, no belief is in principle wholly independent in meaning and truth of the events of history and of our experience. Moreover, this is true not because of the nature of religion or philosophy or language or thought. It is true because of the Holocaust. That event shattered the security of all our conceptual systems and ways of thinking; honest encounter with it required the recognition that *here* thought may have reached a limit. In terms of Judaism, no belief we have about God or human nature, morality or faith or politics, is in principle inviolate after the death camps.[66]

Nonetheless—and this is the second point—the evil of that event is such that authentic response must oppose it and cannot either let it be or, God forbid, support it. Any genuine working through a return to Auschwitz must yield an obligation to oppose it, and that means to do what one can to make its repetition impossible—to oppose hatred of Jews, to serve the cause of human dignity, to oppose fascism, and more. The horrified surprise that arises when one confronts inexplicable evil cannot remain surprise or mere thought; it must become resistant action. Hence, a genuine confrontation with the Holocaust and an authentic cultivation of memory result in an obligation to opposition. In his early writings of the late 1960s, Fackenheim identified God and "Divine Command" as the ground of that necessity, although he cautiously recognized that only the believer and not the nonbeliever was able to hear that command. Still, in later years, this affirmation came to seem too glib, and Fackenheim increasingly abandoned any facile identification of the ground of the imperative to oppose Nazism and its purposes. Instead he became fond of recalling Nietzsche's cryptic remark from *Ecce Homo*—so often cited by Martin Buber—that there are times when one receives but does not ask who gives. What remains, then, is an unconditional commitment to opposition, interpreted by us in a variety of ways but as yet without a ground or foundation.

Finally, while the necessity of the obligation may have to be left without a foundation, the possibility of opposition to such an evil must be grounded in something. Human nature and divine nature, freedom and grace, can no longer serve to secure that possibility. After Auschwitz, one cannot simply posit human freedom as a divine gift or infer human capability from the existence of an obligation. Fackenheim therefore seeks a resistance in action that by itself constitutes a foundation, what he calls an "ontological novum," and he finds it in resistance by victims during the Holocaust to the evil itself. The actuality of such resistance makes subsequent opposition possible; if there had been no *actual* resistance during the event, then subsequent opposition would have been *impossible* or at best an act of willful pride or self-deception. Hence, Jewish commitment in the 1960s and beyond, commitment to the survival and recovery of Jewish life and principle, is possible only because resistance was actual in Nazi Germany and in the death camps. And the precise shape that contemporary Jewish identity takes arises out of a return to the traditional past that is mediated by a return to the experience of those dark years.

Fackenheim, even more explicitly than Berkovits and Greenberg, recognizes that after Auschwitz Jewish identity is essentially tied to history and indeed even to historicity. The death camps admit no prima facie transcendence and hence require that all Jewish belief be historical through and through. But they also loom as threatening obstacles to any facile recovery of tradition, history, the past. Our post-Holocaust situation, temporal and ideological, confronts the post-Holocaust Jew with the demands of continuity and the threat of discontinuity. Our task is to cope with both horns of this dilemma honestly and seriously. Fackenheim underscores this challenge with great clarity at the outset of a lecture on Hermann Cohen on the occasion of the fiftieth anniversary of Cohen's death:

> For a Jew of today to commemorate a fiftieth anniversary in Jewish history is an enterprise fraught with obligation and danger. We are on one side, the event to be commemorated is on the other, and between us yawns an abyss without equal in the annals of history. As we remember, we seek to bridge the abyss, for to save the past for the present is our obligation. Yet no less great is the obligation to remember the abyss itself. And in this double obligation, and the tension between them, lies the danger. We tremble lest, in an effort to save the Jewish past for the present, we pretend, if but for a moment, that the greatest catastrophe in Jewish history never happened. But we also tremble lest, overwhelmed by the catastrophe, we allow the Jewish present to be robbed of its past. To renew the past for present life has always been an essential obligation for the Jewish historian, philosopher and theologian. Never before has this task been both so indispensable and so difficult.[67]

In the Historians' Debate and the crisis of German identity, it was assumed that the past must play a central role in reconstructing the German self. But the principal problematic was how to acknowledge genuinely both the Nazi period and the German past.

Fackenheim accepts the same problematic for Jewish self-understanding: how to treat the Holocaust with full honesty and yet refuse to reject the entire past that stretches out beyond it; how, that is, to treat the traditional past as continuous and compelling and yet radically discontinuous with the present.

In 1967, when Fackenheim and the other Jewish thinkers began to be heard, the American Jewish community expressed a willingness to accept the burden of their special past, to acknowledge their status as a distinct people, to stare into the dark times of the Nazi destruction, and yet to build a posture for the present and the future. As I have tried to show, American political and cultural life had by 1967 begun a period of fragmentation and particularization. Commitments to common values needed to be channeled through the special interests of groups seeking identities and a sense of integrity for themselves. The Six Day War provided the political and religious *opportunity* for many American Jews to reconfigure their institutional and ideological lives. A central feature of that process was the act of returning to the Holocaust and learning how to cope with it. Such a return involved acknowledging the centrality of history to Jewish identity and self-understanding. More than others, the Jewish post-Holocaust thinkers recognized this centrality of history, and on that foundation they sought an honest and authentic confrontation with the horrors of Auschwitz in order to recover the traditional Jewish past—all on behalf of their ultimate goal of reconstituting Judaism for the present and the future.

NOTES

1. See Andreas Huyssen, *After the Great Divide: Modernism, Mass Culture, Postmodernism* (Bloomington: Indiana University Press, 1987) 171–72; cf. Charles Taylor, *Sources of the Self: The Making of the Modern Identity* (Cambridge: Harvard University Press, 1989), for a contrary argument, and Richard Rorty, *Contingency, Irony, and Solidarity* (Cambridge: Cambridge University Press, 1989), for an attempt to acknowledge the openness of interpretation and the need for principle.

2. On the screening of *Holocaust*, see Andreas Huyssen, "The Politics of

Identification: 'Holocaust' and West German Drama," in *After the Great Divide* (rpt. from *New German Critique* 19 [Winter 1980]: 117–36).

3. On the museums, see Charles Maier, *The Unmasterable Past: History, Holocaust, and German National Identity* (Cambridge: Harvard University Press, 1988); on Bitburg, see Geoffrey H. Hartman, ed., *Bitburg in Moral and Political Perspective* (Bloomington: Indiana University Press, 1986). Thanks to Peter Baldwin, an English-speaking audience now has excellent access to many of the original documents of the Historians' Debate. See Peter Baldwin, ed., *Reworking the Past: Hitler, the Holocaust, and the Historians' Debate* (Boston: Beacon Press, 1990); see esp. ch. 1, Baldwin's introduction, for an overview. Ian Kershaw, Richard Evans, Charles Maier, and Jürgen Habermas, among others, have already provided accounts of many dimensions of this ongoing debate about Nazism, the Final Solution, and German identity. See Ian Kershaw, *The Nazi Dictatorship: Problems and Perspectives of Interpretation*, 2nd ed. (London: Edward Arnold, 1989) chs. 8–9; Richard J. Evans, *In Hitler's Shadow: West German Historians and the Attempt to Escape from the Nazi Past* (New York: Pantheon Books, 1989); Maier, *Unmasterable Past*; see also Richard J. Evans, "The New Nationalism and the Old History," *Journal of Modern History* 59.4 (1987): 761–97; Saul Friedlander, "West Germany and the Burden of the Past," *Jerusalem Quarterly* 42 (Spring 1987): 3–18; Geoff Eley, "Nazism, Politics and the Image of the Past," *Past and Present* 121 (1988): 171–208.

4. On these issues, see Kershaw, *Nazi Dictatorship* ch. 8; Diner in Baldwin, *Reworking the Past* ch. 7; and Nolan in Baldwin, ibid. ch. 13.

5. Jürgen Habermas, *The New Conservatism: Cultural Criticism and the Historians' Debate* (Cambridge: MIT Press, 1989) 216–17.

6. On Collingwood's notion of rational reenactment, see R. G. Collingwood, *The Idea of History* (London: Oxford University Press, 1956) 205–334; see also William H. Dray, *Laws and Explanation in History* (London: Oxford University Press, 1957), and idem, *Perspectives on History* (London: Routledge and Kegan Paul, 1980) ch. 1.

7. Compare Maier, *Unmasterable Past* 19–23.

8. See Kershaw, *Nazi Dictatorship* 154–58.

9. See Evans, *In Hitler's Shadow* 73–80. There is also a worry that functionalist accounts of the establishment and operation of the death camps ignore the special role of anti-Semitism in Hitler's ideology and mitigate the roles of intention, moral responsibility, and the event's uniqueness; see Eberhard Jäckel, *Hitler's World View: A Blueprint for Power* (Cambridge: Harvard University Press, 1981) and *Hitler in History* (Hanover, NH: University Press of New England, 1984); G. Fleming, *Hitler and the Final Solution* (Berkeley: University of California Press, 1984). See Maier, *Unmasterable Past* 91–99, on the intentionalist/functionalist debate. Also, Christopher Browning, "The

Decision Concerning the Final Solution," in François Furet, ed., *Unanswered Questions: Nazi Germany and the Genocide of the Jews* (New York: Schocken, 1989) 96–118 (reprinted in *Fateful Months,* [New York: Holmes and Meier, 1985] ch. 1).

10. On the issue of moral weight, see the correspondence between Saul Friedlander and Martin Broszat in Baldwin, *Reworking the Past* ch. 6, esp. 129–31. See also Friedlander, "Some Reflections on the Historiography of National Socialism," in Baldwin, ibid. ch. 5; Habermas, *New Conservatism* 225; Maier, *Unmasterable Past* 13–16, on what he calls "Bitburg history," confusions about responsibility and ways in which Nazism was a special case.

11. See Evans, *In Hitler's Shadow* ch. 1; Maier, *Unmasterable Past* 4 ("effort to define national identity through history"), 6; 154–55 ("how in fact is history constitutive of collective identity?"); cf. Baldwin, *Reworking the Past* 27–30; Mommsen in Baldwin, ibid. 179–81: the Bolsheviks' responsibility for National Socialism has been eagerly taken up by groups lamenting the absence of a healthy German national consciousness.

12. See Habermas, *New Conservatism* 215, 259–66. According to Broszat, the attempt is to use history like a substitute religion to support the *status quo* (Evans, *In Hitler's Shadow* 119). The past is understood metaphorically and not as critically reconstructed by the historian.

13. On Stürmer, see Kershaw, *Nazi Dictatorship* 181–84, and the allusion to Orwell. Also, see Baldwin, *Reworking the Past* 10–21.

14. See Kershaw, *Nazi Dictatorship* 184–86; also Evans, *In Hitler's Shadow* 118–28.

15. Habermas, *New Conservatism* 226–27, 241–48.

16. See Maier, *Unmasterable Past* 58–59, where he notes that German history may be painful but that the responsible approach requires taking responsibility for a form of life in which Auschwitz was possible.

17. See Theodor W. Adorno, "What Does Coming to Grips with the Past Mean?" in Hartmann, ed., *Bitburg in Moral and Political Perspective.* See also Anson Rabinbach, "The Jewish Question in the German Question," in Baldwin, *Reworking the Past* 54–56, 66–68; Huyssen, *After the Great Divide* 97–114.

18. Habermas, *New Conservatism* 209–11.

19. Broszat worries about whether the Nazi period blocks historical understanding altogether in "A Plea for the Historicization of National Socialism" (Baldwin, *Reworking the Past* 82–83, 86–87); it may be a blockade, he says, hermetically sealed off, in moral quarantine.

20. Evans, *In Hitler's Shadow* 138. Habermas calls this neoconservative feature a "healthy sense of tradition" and "courage for the past" (*New Conservatism* 43) and a "public appropriation of tradition" (ibid. 187).

21. We should notice an important pair of differences between the two cases. In the German case, the stimulus is primarily a political one—the rise of neoconservatism to prominence in German national politics—and the key players are historians and intellectuals whose attention is focused on history. In the American case, the stimulus is a war of self-defense in Israel, and the context is the state of American political and social culture at the end of the 1960s. The chief protagonists, moreover, are theologians and religious thinkers, whose attention seems to be focused on traditional religious concepts and their continued propriety and acceptability.

The question of history for post-Holocaust Jewish thought involves four dimensions: (1) recognizing that Jewish self-understanding is fundamentally historical; (2) appreciating the centrality of Auschwitz to current Jewish self-understanding; (3) asking why and how a recovery of tradition and the past is necessary and possible; and (4) seeking grounds for unconditional standards in this historical, postmodern situation.

22. The lack of centrality of the Holocaust prior to 1967 and even avoidance of it is widely noted. See Nathan Glazer, *American Judaism* (Chicago: University of Chicago Press, 1957) 172–73; Charles E. Silberman, *A Certain People: American Jews and Their Lives Today* (New York: Summit, 1985) 183.

23. Elie Wiesel, *Night* (New York: Hill and Wang, 1960); Richard L. Rubenstein, *After Auschwitz: Radical Theology and Contemporary Judaism* (Indianapolis: Bobbs-Merrill, 1966). The earliest of the essays go back to 1956–1957, although the earliest ones dealing with Auschwitz date from 1960.

24. See "Jewish Values in a Post-Holocaust Future," *Judaism* 16.3 (Summer 1967).

25. I shall set Rubenstein and Wiesel aside for a variety of reasons. I shall also set aside George Steiner, a participant in the symposium and author of *Language and Silence* and *In Bluebeard's Castle,* both works of literary and cultural criticism aimed at confronting the death camps as expressions of Western, European culture. I also do not consider the deep and important work of Hannah Arendt on the camps, especially *The Origins of Totalitarianism.* Neither that work nor the later, controversial *Eichmann in Jerusalem* significantly influenced Jewish self-understanding. The major works of this period, the late 1960s and early 1970s, are: Emil L. Fackenheim, "Jewish Faith and the Holocaust: A Fragment," *Commentary* (1968), reprinted in *The Jewish Return into History: Reflections in the Age of Auschwitz and a New Jerusalem* (New York: Schocken, 1978) and in Michael L. Morgan, ed., *The Jewish Thought of Emil Fackenheim: A Reader* (Detroit: Wayne State University Press, 1987); idem, *God's Presence in History: Jewish Affirmations and Philosophical Reflections* (New York: New York University Press, 1970), reprinted by Dover; Eliezer Berkovits, *Faith after the Holocaust* (New York: Ktav, 1973); Irving Greenberg, "Cloud of Smoke, Pillar of Fire: Judaism, Christianity, and

Modernity after the Holocaust," in Eva Fleishner, ed., *Auschwitz: Beginning of a New Era?* (New York: Ktav, 1977).

26. On the impact of the Six Day War on the American Jewish community, I have consulted the following works: Nathan Glazer, *American Judaism* 2nd ed. (Chicago: University of Chicago Press, 1972, reprinted in 1989), epilogue, "The Year 1967 and Its Meaning" 151–86; Charles Silberman, *A Certain People* (New York: Summit Books, 1985) 181–208; Daniel J. Elazar, *Community and Polity: The Organizational Dynamics of American Jewry* (Philadelphia: Jewish Publication Society, 1976); Lucy Dawidowicz, "American Public Opinion," *American Jewish Year Book* 69 (1968): 198–229; Milton Himmelfarb, "The 1967 War," in *The Jews of Modernity* (New York: Basic, 1973) 343–60; Marshall Sklare, "Lakeville and Israel: The Six-Day War and Its Aftermath," *Midstream* (October 1968): 3–21; Chaim I. Waxman, *America's Jews in Transition* (Philadelphia: Temple University Press, 1983) esp. 121–23.

27. Glazer discusses what made such a sudden reversal possible; see *American Judaism* 169–76.

28. Silberman makes a similar point (*A Certain People,* 198): "Without Israel's victory . . . the Holocaust might have been too dreadful to contemplate; with it Jews have been able to construct a new mythology, in which Israel serves as a symbol of redemption." There is at least a partial truth here, even if Silberman's understanding of the Holocaust and Israel is too simplistic to recognize its importance and its real character.

29. See Elazar, *Community and Polity* 74–75, for an account of the different groups of Jews in America during the late 1960s.

30. My account of Cold War America and the 1960s is indebted to the following works: Godfrey Hodgson, *America in Our Time* (Garden City, NY: Doubleday, 1976); Frederick F. Siegel, *Troubled Journey: From Pearl Harbor to Ronald Reagan* (New York: Hill and Wang, 1984); Elaine Tyler May, *Homeward Bound: American Families in the Cold War Era* (New York: Basic Books, 1988); Sara Evans, *Personal Politics: The Roots of Women's Liberation in the Civil Rights Movement and the New Left* (New York: Knopf, 1979 [rpt. Vintage, 1980]); Wini Breines, *Community and Organization in the New Left, 1962–1968: The Great Refusal* (New York: Praeger, 1982); James Miller, *Democracy Is in the Streets: From Port Huron to the Siege of Chicago* (New York: Simon and Schuster, 1987); Allen J. Matusow, *The Unraveling of America: A History of Liberalism in the 1960s* (New York: Harper & Row, 1984); Clayborne Carson, *In Struggle: SNCC and the Black Awakening of the 1960s* (Cambridge: Harvard University Press, 1981); Steve Fraser and Gary Gerstle, eds., *The Rise and Fall of the New Deal Order, 1930–1980* (Princeton: Princeton University Press, 1989); Todd Gitlin, *The Sixties: Years of Hope, Days of Rage* (New York: Bantam Books, 1987); Jonathan Schell, *The Time of Illusion* (New

York: Knopf, dist. Random House, 1975); Daniel Bell, *The Cultural Contradictions of Capitalism* (New York: Basic Books, 1976).

31. On American Jewish life during the Cold War period, the synagogue, prayer, and the rise of the *havurah* movement after 1968 and in the early 1970s, see Riv-Ellen Prell, *Prayer and Community: The Havurah in American Judaism* (Detroit: Wayne State University Press, 1989).

32. Waxman, *America's Jews in Transition* 96–98, on the joint desires for assimilation and the maintenance of group identity; compare Charles S. Liebman, *The Ambivalent American Jew: Politics, Religion and Family in American Jewish Life* (Philadelphia: Jewish Publication Society, 1973).

33. See Carson, *In Struggle* chs. 1–3. On the sit-in in the Woolworth's in Greensboro, North Carolina, see Hodgson, *America in Our Time* 184–89; and Matusow, *Unraveling of America* ch. 3.

34. See Hodgson, *America in Our Time* chs. 14–17; Miller, *Democracy Is in the Streets* passim; Gitlin, *The Sixties*.

35. Gitlin, *The Sixties* 26, 96; see also the three anthologies on the Jewish radicals; *Response* magazine; and Prell, *Prayer and Community*.

36. See Maurice Isserman and Michael Kazin, "The Failure and Success of the New Radicalism," in Fraser and Gerstle, eds., *Rise and Fall of the New Deal Order* ch.8; see also Jonathan Rieder, *Canarsie: The Jews and Italians of Brooklyn against Liberalism* (Cambridge: Harvard University Press, 1985) 27, 43–54, on their humanism, faith in the democratic state, tolerance, concern for rights; and see Gitlin, *The Sixties* 19.

37. On the importance of community, and with it participatory democracy, as a New Left goal, see Breines, *Community and Organization*, and Miller, *Democracy Is in the Streets*. For the Jewish search, see Prell, *Prayer and Community*. The student activists were indebted to C. Wright Mills, Paul Goodman, Albert Camus, and Martin Buber (in some cases), for discussion of distance and intimacy, dependence and independence. For a discussion of their break with traditional politics and its connections to the War on Poverty and the issue of community control, see Matusow, *Unraveling of America* chs. 4 and 9 (on the Community Action Program); see also Gitlin, *The Sixties* 133–35.

38. For the way in which liberalism came to be viewed by some Jews in the early 1970s, see Rieder, *Canarsie*.

39. See Carson, *In Struggle* chs. 8–13, for an excellent account. See also Evans, *Personal Politics*, esp. ch. 7 and her discussion of the memo on the role of women in SDS and the Illinois Conference in 1965; and cf. Breines, *Community and Organization* 83–84; Matusow, *Unraveling of America* ch. 12, on the rise of Black Power and the role of the ghetto riots, for example, Watts (1965) and Detroit (1967). Among other things, the riots led to a

Jewish fear of black violence; see Rieder, *Canarsie* 67–79, esp. 70. See also Gitlin, *The Sixties* chs. 16 and 19.

40. See, on the new ethnicity, Michael Novak, *The Rise of the Unmeltable Ethnics: Politics and Culture in the Seventies* (New York: Macmillan, 1972). Waxman, *America's Jews in Transition* 130–34, 226–29, calls this the ideology of a new cultural pluralism; he associates with it the resurgence of Jewish religious commitment expressed in the early 1970s. Waxman sees the Jewish case against the background of the general theory of increasing postimmigrant generational assimilation and the diminishing of religious involvement.
On the civil rights movement and disenchantment with the liberal establishment, see Hodgson, *America in Our Time* ch. 10, esp. 213–17: "That was the moment when the more radical black leaders finally lost faith in the presidency, in the Democratic Party. . . ." On the Convention, see Matusow, *Unraveling of America* 140–52; Carlson, *In Struggle* 123–29; Gitlin, *The Sixties* 151–69.

41. See Gitlin, *The Sixties* chs. 2, 3, 8, and 9.

42. Hodgson, *America in Our Time* chs. 21–22; the various "movements" attended to environmental, peace, black, ethnic, homosexual, feminist, and religious issues (e.g., the "new majority"). See also Siegel, *Troubled Journey* ch. 10.

43. See Rieder, *Canarsie*, esp. 119–31.

44. See Huyssen, *After the Great Divide* ch. 9; see also Rieder, *Canarsie* ch. 5, esp. 141, 164 on the post-Vietnam retreat from the world and the "growth of historical wisdom."

45. See Carlson, *In Struggle* 267–69, on SNCC support for the Palestinians after the Six Day War and the Jewish responses, and compare the comments on 272. See also Gitlin, *The Sixties* 245; Prell, *Prayer and Community* 86–87; Glazer, *American Judaism* 173; Waxman, *America's Jews in Transition* 114–16.

46. For a nice summary of its impact, see Glazer, *American Judaism* xiii; Waxman, *America's Jews in Transition* 112–14.

47. Especially on campus, for students and intellectuals; see Silberman, *A Certain People* 205–208; Elazar, *Community and Polity* 369–73.

48. The militancy also became increasingly anti-Semitic; see Glazer, *American Judaism* 173–75, 179–84.

49. See Rieder, *Canarsie*.

50. Elazar, *Community and Polity* 263, 339; Glazer, *American Judaism* 174. Silberman, *A Certain People* 201, calls it a "celebration of distinctiveness" and a short-lived security (202–205).

51. Rieder, *Canarsie* 47—"But for virtually all the Jews in Canarsie, the observant and the faithless, Zionism was inseparable from the issue of communal survival"—as well as 163–64, 248. Also, Jews, frightened and angry,

would later compare themselves to Israelis threatened by the Arab nations (Rieder, *Canarsie* 79) during the busing crisis of 1972-1973. The unity was, of course, only apparent; on Breira, a short-lived organization of American Jewish liberal critics of Israel, its rise and demise, see Waxman, *America's Jews in Transition* 221-23.

52. Rieder recounts how some Jews, in opposition to busing, saw themselves as heroes of Masada (*Canarsie* 215). See also Elazar, *Community and Polity* 82-83, 288, 376-77; Waxman, *America's Jews in Transition* 119; Glazer, *American Judaism* xiii, 178-79; Silberman, *A Certain People* 185-99. The role of Israel for Jewish identity is important, but that role is, of course, complex, as have been the responses to it. And there is, for example, the Jewish abandonment of liberalism and the Democratic Party in 1972, later viewed by some as a self-betrayal; see Rieder, *Canarsie* 249-50. On Judaism and liberalism, see Glazer, *American Judaism* xiii; on Israel, see Silberman, *A Certain People* 199-201.

53. Rieder notes how the Jews' response to a busing crisis in Canarsie in 1972-1973 led to a recollection of 1967, the Holocaust, and Israel; see Rieder, *Canarsie* 206. A resurgence of Jewish pride was associated with the memory of the Warsaw Ghetto and the defense of Israel during the Six Day War.

54. Some criticized the emphasis on a negative event, or the apparent lack of attention to classic texts, to traditional ritual, prayer, Torah, or to the universality of moral principle. Some associated with the *havurah* movement turned during this period to a prayer aesthetic and were doubtless repelled by the emphasis on historical-political involvement. Among the vocal intellectual critics were Jacob Neusner and Michael Wyschogrod, but there were others then, in the early 1970s, and later.

55. In part, then, Berkovits is a belated response to Hannah Arendt and others who argue for the prominence of Jewish collaboration; his work is therefore also a response to the controversy that raged after the publication of Arendt's *Eichmann in Jerusalem* in 1963 and even before.

56. This solution to the problem of evil or theodicy, the free will response, is traditional both in the Christian and Jewish traditions, as well as in Western philosophy.

57. This is also a point that Steven Katz makes in his essay "The Unique Intentionality of the Holocaust," in *Post-Holocaust Dialogues: Critical Studies in Modern Jewish Thought* (New York: New York University Press, 1983) 287-317. The quotations from Berkovits are on pages 128 and 134.

58. Andreas Hillgruber, *Zweierlei Untergang: die Zerschlagung des Deutsches Reiches* (Berlin: W. J. Siedler, 1986); the book has been widely discussed, by Habermas and others. See, for example, Evans, *In Hitler's Shadow* ch. 3.

59. See, for example, Carlo Ginzburg, *The Cheese and the Worms: The Cosmos of a Sixteenth-century Miller* (New York: Penguin, 1982).

60. Ginzburg, *The Cheese and the Worms*.

61. See Huyssen, *After the Great Divide* 94–114, esp. 94–100, 112–14.

62. Greenberg, "Cloud of Smoke" 23.

63. This is not a notion that Greenberg clarifies with great precision. His discussion and examples suggest that what he has in mind is that no genuine post-Holocaust faith can be more than tentative, uncertain, questioning, complex, partial, and so forth. See Greenberg, "Cloud of Smoke" 22–34.

64. There are three classic texts for clarifying Fackenheim's original post-Holocaust Jewish thought: his contribution to the *Judaism* symposium of March 1967; his *Commentary* article, "Jewish Faith and the Holocaust: A Fragment"; and *God's Presence in History*, the Charles Deems Lectures given at New York University in 1968 and published in 1970, especially the third lecture. A revised version of the *Commentary* article was published as part of the introduction to his collection of essays, *Quest for Past and Future: Essays in Jewish Theology* (Bloomington: Indiana University Press, 1968). All of these texts are reprinted in Morgan, ed., *Jewish Thought of Emil Fackenheim*.

65. In a sense, he was convinced that neither modern philosophy nor religion need succumb to the Straussian worry, the total lack of unconditional standards and principles.

66. Fackenheim's recognition is like Quine's attack on the a priori and empirical distinction, or like Rorty's account of the historical character of all philosophy, or like Davidson's account of conceptual schemes, or like the denial of skepticism that follows the attack on foundationalism. A fundamental difference is that Fackenheim is stimulated to admit the openness of Jewish belief (what he calls "the Midrashic Framework") by Auschwitz, that is, an incommensurable event rather than an argument about the incoherence or impossibility of transcendence or complete objectivity. Fackenheim was convinced of the incommensurability of the Holocaust by his study of Hegel and his realization that Hegel's system could not and indeed would not accommodate the reality of the death camps.

67. "Hermann Cohen—After Fifty Years," *Leo Baeck Memorial Lecture* 12 (1969): 3; rpt. in Emil L. Fackenheim, *Jewish Philosophers and Jewish Philosophy*, ed. Michael L. Morgan (Bloomington: Indiana University Press, 1996) 41.

EIGHT

Rereading an Unsettling Past

American Jews during the Nazi Era

GULIE NE'EMAN ARAD

IN HIS CONTEMPLATIVE 1979 ESSAY, "Who Shall Bear Guilt for the Holocaust: The Human Dilemma," Henry Feingold reflected on the level of historical scholarship dealing with America and the Holocaust. Without dismissing the then available studies out of hand, he stressed the need to "recognize that they are as much cries of pain as they are serious history."[1] A decade later Michael Marrus observed a "growing shelf of books and a burgeoning file of articles" that uncovered "particular variations" on the theme of the bystanders' response to the Holocaust. Yet, he also noted the fact that with few exceptions, the detailed studies—about widespread indifference, unwillingness to change established policies to help the Jews, and the inability to grasp the information on mass extermination—had failed to produce "breaks in the pattern" of research.[2] In a similar vein Jonathan Sarna expressed doubts as to whether the subject of America and the Holocaust, as it had been approached, "warrant[s] continued investment of scholarly resources at the current extravagant level."[3] It appears that these three eminent historians were alluding to the fact that while the scholarly output had contributed much to our knowledge, it had added little to our understanding.[4]

Being in agreement with these observations, especially with regard to the American Jewish leadership's response, this essay will consider some of the factors that may have obstructed the bridging of the gap between "knowing" and "understanding." An undertaking of this kind entails probing the methodological and epistemological categorizations that frame the historical representation of this era as well as examining the "subject position" of the narrators.

It should be emphasized that it is *not* my intention here to *review* the historiography on American Jews and the Holocaust, a task that has been undertaken by others.[5] Rather, what follows is a *critique* of the prevalent historical-methodological approach. Re-evaluation of the analytical framework, the questions that are asked, and the basic assumptions that are used to support them may induce a rethinking of some *a*historical understandings that this body of research has promoted. The fact that certain central assumptions have been regarded as "major truisms" renders critique both difficult and "dangerous." However, precisely because such an approach can often nourish "erroneous assumptions about where bias and objectivity are located," this task must be embarked upon if we are to appraise the past and anticipate the future with realistic expectations.[6]

In focusing this essay on the historical representation of the American Jewish leadership, I propose to identify and explicate a number of ambiguous zones that defy a clear understanding of the response to the Nazi menace. Paramount among these issues are: "Auschwitz" as an impediment to historical understanding; an eschewed periodization; bystanders as a universal or particular category; the blessings and afflictions of tradition; the "subject position" of the historians; and the need for historicization.

"Auschwitz"—An Impediment to Historical Understanding

Stronger than the sum total of its *un*historical components—as a central element in the consciousness of humanity, a symbol of the profane in human behavior, and a reference point of our moral discourse—"Auschwitz" is the center toward which all historiography that covers the National Socialist epoch gravitates. However difficult the task may be, if we are to remain committed to *history*, the Nazi era cannot be analyzed within the closed referential framework of its catastrophic ending. Indeed, when adopting a "reverse chronology," historical questions become *supra*historical. Hannah Arendt's depiction of the victims' leadership and Saul Friedman's of the American Jewish leaders are two extremes, but certainly not the sole examples of ex post facto reasoning, according to which "Auschwitz" as a moral reference point serves as a venue for categorical indictment.[7]

In following such an interpretive course historians are pleading a case in the name of six million dead and are exonerating those who did not save six million lives. More than a moral signifier, "Auschwitz" has also become a quantitative signifier, a code that thrusts us toward a "numerical" orientation that makes it more "bearable" to overlook the fate of the tens, hundreds, and thousands of human lives that might have been saved.

However, it must be borne in mind that for humanity's collective consciousness, Auschwitz came to epitomize "a world gone mad" only some twenty years after the events.[8] Among American Jewish contemporaries who closely observed the Nazis' beastly intentions, the year 1933 was already anything but normal.[9] For Rabbi Stephen Wise, "the frontiers of civilization [had] been crossed" as early as April 1933,[10] while in May of that year Felix Frankfurter remarked that to understand what was happening in Germany required "a complete reorientation of one's sense of reality as well as one's historical sense."[11] Other Jewish leaders viewed the situation as "indescribably bad and absolutely unparalleled in modern times."[12] In contrast, it seems that in the representation of this history, whatever preceded the industrial killing, however horrific, has come to be accepted within the bounds of the normal. Viewed through the distorting prism of Auschwitz, the events of the preceding years are shifted out of historical focus.

Periodization

The ordinary holds little fascination for any form of narration; historical narratives are no exception. Hence, it is hardly astonishing that in constructing the history of Nazism in all its facets, and especially with regard to the Jews, the period between 1933 and 1938 is treated as little more than a prelude to the "Final Solution."[13] Yet the scant attention devoted to the bystanders' response prior to the *Anschluss* and the 1938 pogrom seems to suggest more than a fixation on the reality of the unimaginable.

The interpretation of the bystanders' conduct is dominated by two factors: need and fulfillment. With the end result known, rescue becomes the indisputable expectation and the six million victims the equally indisputable failure. Although strictly speaking such a reading of the past is *a*historical, under the circumstances it is perfectly understandable why it is the most widely embraced. Less to be expected, perhaps, is the prevalent acceptance among historians of a periodization template that seems to reinforce a misleading interpretation. The Jewish victims are regarded as "refugees" from 1938 to the end of 1941 and in need of "rescue" thereafter.[14] Indeed, when Feingold, for instance, separates the plight of the Jews into a "refugee" phase and a "rescue" phase, it apparently becomes tenable for him to argue that the "rescue campaign was lost largely during the refugee phase,"[15] because so very few who wished to escape found a place of asylum. In the same vein, when considering rescue options only from the fall of 1941, "the credibility problem" can become central to rationalizing the reaction of the witnesses. After all, as this historian maintains, the potential rescuers could not be expected to "react to something they did not know, or believe." In fact, he argued, "the problem of credibility takes us out of the realm of history."[16] Rather curiously, when employing such a division, the prospect of rescue is left altogether out of the realm of possibility. Yet, somewhat paradoxically, the core discussion of rescue is framed within the time span of mass killings, when it is generally accepted that both the options and capabilities for rescue were highly improbable.[17]

Historically speaking, the strongest case against America's "abandonment of the Jews," as David Wyman charges in his book by the same name, and against the nation's Jews who are blamed by Elie Wiesel for not having moved "heaven and earth,"[18] can be made for the years prior to 1939. Although there is much circumstantial evidence to weaken this case as well, the fact remains that it was during this period that the German quota was consistently underissued and that even the few Jews who perceived the danger, had the means, and wished to leave were turned away on grounds of "legal technicalities."[19] In 1933 some 37,000 Jews fled Germany. During that first year an additional 14,000 persons requested information about migration possibilities. Both numbers dropped consistently until 1939, at least partly because, as one communal official of the *Hilfsverein der deutschen Juden* in 1934 put it, "many have lost the courage and determination to leave because of the negative answers with reference to immigration. . . ."[20]

In a recent essay, Henry Feingold implies that he now reads his earlier periodization as erroneous, writing that "rescue possibilities were far more promising during the refugee phase," which he now dates back to 1933.[21] Why is it, then, that historians focus the blame on the later period, when the Nazis began implementing the solution to the "Jewish problem" in its most radical form and the United States became actively engaged in the global conflict? Was this, on the contrary, not the least promising time for rescue?

David Luebke, former historian of the United States Holocaust Memorial Museum, has suggested, for example, that the failure to bomb Auschwitz has become a crucial symbol of American indifference because it is so much more "emotion-laden" than the issue of restrictive immigration policies of the 1930s and 1940s. It is also easier, he noted, "to cope with helplessness after the fact, if you can convince yourself that mendacity, not circumstances, had produced it."[22]

Can one also speculate that the earlier years are largely absent because it was then that the American government and the Jews

could have done more and did not? Although such a question is
*supra*historical, it may assist us in discerning the *supra*historical
arguments that are adduced in support of the aforementioned periodization and categorization.

No one doubts that American Jewish contemporaries knew and
believed that Jews in Germany were being persecuted: their progressive exclusion from German social and economic life had culminated in the revocation of their citizenship in 1935 and in forced
expulsion. All of these circumstances were graspable; none were
outside the realm of the Jewish historical experience. Yet, in historical studies these conditions are not considered as warranting
"rescue" but rather as arousing less urgent expectations of "aid,"
"help," "relief," and the like. Undoubtedly as a result of the "Auschwitz" experience, the scale of what is to be recognized as victimization has been changed perceptibly. People who were
"merely" trying to escape legal discrimination, which may have
resulted "only" in hunger, disease, or homelessness, are no longer
considered to be in urgent or grave enough circumstances to merit
"rescue" operations.

In the context of the extreme "rational" brutality of mass industrial killing, rescue is imbued with a sense of the "divinely sacred"
mission. Indeed, much Holocaust discourse has been oriented toward the binary formulation of catastrophe and redemption, the
earthly and the sublime. This tendency also affects periodization
where it serves two opposing historical interpretations. For historians who are inclined to accuse Jewish leaders, "Auschwitz" is
more than sufficient evidence to charge them with being "passive
accomplices."[23] Yet at the same time, for those who opt to defend
the bystanders, "Auschwitz" as an end result renders any action
futile since "in neither period ['refugee' or 'rescue' phase] was there
much cause for hope."[24]

In recent years a new factor seems to have had an impact on the
periodization. The growing concern over "Jewish continuity" has
induced a search for a bonding agent that would serve to restore
a sense of community and Jewish identity. The past is a natural
domain for this quest, or rather an "agreeable" past, or one that

can be renegotiated to suit present needs. One such attempt is the retelling of history by Aaron Berman in his book, *Nazism, the Jews and American Zionism, 1933–1948*. Adopting a periodization that extends to the triumphant-redemptive conclusion of the creation of a Jewish state allows him to construct a narrative that enhances the role of American Jews in bringing about salvation while blurring failure during the "catastrophic" era.

Berman goes out of his way to celebrate American Jews' achievement and to offer a "happy end" to his narrative. By underscoring the "great cost and sacrifice" and "considerable amounts of energy and time" that the establishment of the state entailed, he can conclude with pride that "in spite of the great hardships *they* endured, the period between 1933 and 1948 ended triumphantly" for them. Berman's construction is appealing because it obscures American Jews' powerlessness in the face of the catastrophe. Washington's support for Jewish statehood is linked to the "long, hard political and propaganda struggle of American Zionists," who in this version are credited with the power to affect national policy. Even the "tragic cost" that the struggle for the state exacted, which according to Berman "handicapped any attempt to build a powerful lobby to force the American government to undertake the rescue of European Jewry," is attributed to misallocation of power rather than to lack of it.[25]

Retelling the past is not necessarily intended "to justify and legitimize contemporary Jewish political and institutional agendas,"[26] as some critics maintain. But when this is the aim, it preserves old and breeds new false assumptions whose outcome is inadmissible as history.

Bystanders: A Universal or a Particular Category?

The ability to understand and explain the bystanders' reactions to what began as a political-racial ideology and resulted in the murder of millions of human beings is likely to be obstructed by the nature of the event itself. The extent of the tragedy and the failure to minimize it, let alone prevent it, inspires a tacit moral-psychological posture that renders the bystanders guilty until proven innocent. Anchored, as it were, in the foregone moral verdict that in the face of the Holocaust all are guilty, this is a deeply felt, moral-emotional argument. But it is also deeply flawed. Although a "moral yardstick" should not be missing from the historians' tool box, it cannot replace the rules of evidence or the need for critical analysis. The reconstruction of the past cannot be based on pre-construed moral judgments.[27]

Another central problem that besets the representation of the bystanders' response to the Holocaust is that as a research category they defy precise "scientific" definition. The victims and perpetrators have essentially been depicted as absolutely innocent and absolutely guilty, respectively. Suffice it to recall the reactions to Hannah Arendt and Andreas Hillgruber, who "dared" to deviate from the consensual model, in order to demonstrate the strong objections on both scholarly and moral grounds to any questioning of these categories.[28] The bystanders occupy a priori an ambivalent middle position; they can be approached as potential saviors or as betrayers of the victims and hence can be exalted or condemned accordingly.

Post factum analysis of individual or collective behavior can rarely yield impartial results, all the more so when the objects under investigation, as in the case of American Jews, identify vicariously with the subjects of their response (the European Jews). Let me make clear my own position on this last point. While solidarity, empathy, comradeship, responsibility, and similar sentiments of affinity are obviously universal attributes, it would be to disregard collective social nature to deny that an essential element in invoking these feelings is a "common something"—be it a shared belief, morality, past, present, or an envisioned future—that creates expectations intrinsic to it. It is in the realm of both feelings and intentions that hopes and disappointments are born; such is human nature.

Opting to neutralize particular expectations may command "scientific respect," but it does not necessarily lead to a truer understanding of the subjects' response because, although the questions posed are universal, the interpretations are almost inevitably based on particular expectations. Hence, when Raul Hilberg includes American Jews under the heading of "Jewish rescuers," this definition is not based on critical analysis of historical evidence but rather on anticipations that are nourished by that particular group's historical consciousness.[29] What Hilberg seems to be intimating is that Jewish bystanders, by virtue of their historical, religious, and ethnic ties to the most singled-out group of victims, cannot be expected to function as anything *but* rescuers and hence are depicted as such.

Indeed, from a post-Auschwitz perspective, what has come to be expected of the bystanders can be summarily described as "rescue." However, at a point where millions had already perished and all the rest were targeted to die, there is an intuitive-moral inclination to evaluate the results of the bystanders' actions as a function of the sufferers' needs and not of the rescuers' means.

Moreover, awareness of the unprecedented dire calamity that befell Europe's Jews and the unparalleled dire needs that it presented, when fused with the difficulty of containing the moral outrage that Nazi barbarism provokes, tends to foster facile moral judgments instead of critical understanding. Indeed, in the writing of history, as Henry Feingold aptly observed, the "indictment against the witnesses is as predictable as it is irresistible."[30] Looking at the book titles alone, where expressions such as "American apathy," "no haven for the oppressed," "the abandonment of the Jews," "the Jews were expendable," "were we our brothers' keepers?" "the sacred and the doomed," "thy brother's blood," and "the deafening silence" are used, may suffice to prove the point.[31]

When historians feel a strong commitment to defending their subjects' heritage and tradition, they may be disposed to locate their analysis within a moral framework. Take, for example, Rafael Medoff, who repeatedly denounces American Jewish leaders for "lunching at the regular hour at their favorite restaurant," or going on "vacation," instead of devoting every moment to protesting against America's inaction;[32] or historian Haskel Lookstein, who concludes that "The Final Solution may have been *unstoppable* by American Jewry, but it should have been *unbearable* for them. And it wasn't."[33]

The Blessings and Afflictions of Tradition

To argue that the "Final Solution" may have been *preventable* by American Jewry is perhaps ludicrous, but it can nonetheless serve as a working hypothesis. To maintain that it should have been *unbearable* for them, *cannot*! For how can one determine what is tolerable short of submitting the subjects to trials that would prove to be intolerable? Nonetheless, many historical studies arrive at historical-moral conclusions that are based on idealized and somewhat outdated social and cultural traditions. For example, continued Jewish existence supports the belief in unity of fate as paradigmatic. In its social-secular version, this is considered the foundation of collective unity and solidarity. Similarly, in the writing of Jewish history, "Jewish Solidarity" is treated as a sacred precept. Assigned the imperative of a mission, it is often introduced into the narrative as an absolute behavioral role model. By extension, political and social processes are treated not as they actually were but as they should have been according to the solidarity maxim.[34] The subtext of such questions as "Was enough done?" "What might have been done? or "Could more have been done?"[35] reflects an expectation based on the "knowledge" that "all Israel are responsible for one another." Similarly, the question "What did they know?" or, in its updated version, "Had they known more, could they have done more?"[36] when posed within the context of assumed bonds of kinship, presupposes the existence of a direct correlation between "knowing" and "understanding" and further deduces that "understanding and action are expected to connect."[37] In the historiography of the period, these unstated conjectures have been "elevated from interpretative stance to historical truth," as, for instance, in the case of Wyman's approach to the issue of bombing Auschwitz,[38] or Friedman's claim that Rabbi Stephen Wise, by agreeing to withhold publication of the Riegner report on the "Final Solution" until the information was confirmed by the State Department, was directly responsible for the loss of up to 10,000 Jewish lives a week in the Warsaw Ghetto in the interim period.[39]

Although difficult to disclaim emotionally, Jewish solidarity is a suprahistorical term, geographically and temporally. When misused for reaching historical judgment it results in a curiously reconstructed past in which explanations are rendered by way of such worldly causes as xenophobia, anti-Semitism, war, and the like, but evaluations of the group's behavior are based on exalted relics of a traditional past that are molded as if they were "working" mottos for everyday life. Whereas American Jews have come to accept that the vision of America as a "haven for the oppressed" is a legacy of a golden, yet distant past, the psychological protective shield that a continued faith in Jewish solidarity provides has preserved that faith as a viable force in contemporary consciousness.

Timeless in its spirit and expression, the legendary notion of Jewish "oneness" fostered the belief that,

> Jewish unity is not of yesterday, not of thirty years ago. It was not created by any organization. It is a fact and has always been a fact. It is cemented by common sanctities and common sorrows. It is a real power in the world.[40]

In the interpretation of American Jewish behavior in the 1930s and 1940s, this notion is particularly conspicuous. Lack of Jewish unity is rated as *the* source of weakness and is accorded central importance in explaining the ineffective response to the Holocaust.[41] Even Henry Feingold, who concludes that had American Jewry "achieved unity, there is still no assurance that [it] would have been more effective in convincing the government to embark on a more active rescue policy," does so only after lamenting extensively about Jewish disunity as a source of powerlessness.[42]

"Power" has "an elusive, almost intangible, quality."[43] Although difficult to define, it is too tantalizing to discard, and historians let it creep into their narratives in disguise, using such terms as "influence," "control," "pressure," and the like. An admission to timidity and powerlessness, although it may provide a rationale for inaction and ease feelings of guilt for the past, may also prove counterproductive if that image continues to linger on into the present.[44] Indeed, Saul Friedman's list of indictments against American Jews is predicated on the assumption that they had the power, among other things, to resist the cooptation of the system and to demand emergency changes in the immigration laws. Yet, perhaps because he is primarily interested in repudiating the powerlessness image, he does not define what was their "real" power.[45] Henry Feingold comes much closer to the truth when he claims that American Jewish power "did not match the responsibilities assigned to it by yesterday's rescue advocates and today's historians."[46]

In part our expectations of American Jewry are based on the fact that it was (and still is) the "largest and most powerful Jewish community in the world."[47] But this unequivocal fact tells us virtually nothing about the nature and extent of its power or how and whether it could have influenced national policy. It does provide, however, fertile ground for nourishing false expectations and for encouraging unjustified accusations. If the more lenient interpreters of the Jewish leaders' response base their explanation on the Depression and the rising tide of domestic anti-Semitism,[48] the harsher critics concentrate on the missed opportunities and the misuse of resources.[49] Rafael Medoff, for example, sums up Hitler's first six months in power with the conclusion that while "Wise and his colleagues had hesitated," Hitler had consolidated his political power and, thus, "a crucial moment of historical opportunity for the American Jewish leadership had passed un- exploited."[50] There is not even a hint as to what this missed opportunity was or how it could have been exploited; both asser- tions are treated as axiomatic.

Related to the "unity" and "power" modules is what I call the "willingness factor." The dark shadow that eclipsed humanity after Auschwitz is reflected in the historians' moral world; the existence of absolute evil creates the need to invent an absolute good. In the historiography this tendency is revealed in the tacit expectation that American Jews should have identified totally with the plight of their European brethren. Analysis based on the falsified notion of unequivocal altruism has led to an equally fictitious conviction that no objective or subjective obstacles could have stood in the way of a determined rescue effort.[51] Analysis grounded in a uto- pian vision of kinship solidarity that idealizes Jews' human nature may be seen within the larger framework of the search for redemp- tive meaning by all who have lived through the long Holocaust night.[52]

When heedful of the contemporaries' "truth," one discovers a somewhat different reality. American Jews were "normal" in the sense that their self-preservation came first. Many Jewish leaders and politicians alluded to this throughout the period of crisis,[53] although few expressed it as candidly as the editor of the *Menorah Journal*, who wrote in early 1943:

> There is a strong pull, for the faithful, to regard Jewish life and interests as being always in the center of the world. To be sure, our enemies have been doing their cruelest to make them so. . . . Yet, as free men and women, our vital concerns with national and world politics, with social and economic problems, with science and liter- ature, art and music, transcend—however intensely they include— our Jewish devotions. There must be a sense of proportion. . . .[54]

Sentiments of this type are generally missing from historical narratives. Their absence points to yet another problem of the historical representation.

Who Is Writing History, for Whom, and for What?

Since "history," as we know, is written "by" and "for," its interest far transcends the aim of reaching "historical truth." The narrators, after they record what R. G. Collingwood called the "outside event," are expected to attend to the "inside events"—that is, to discern the thoughts of the protagonists by rethinking them in their own minds.[55] Accordingly, historians, however "objective," cannot be expected to be too distant from the period or event they investigate—all the more so, perhaps, when considering an event of such moral magnitude as the Holocaust, where the "demand for closure" and the desire to invest the response to it with "moral meaning" are most pronounced.[56]

Furthermore, if we accept that historians are not only critical observers of the past but also active, and not necessarily disinterested, agents in shaping the present and future, their claim to "scientism" is still narrower. It is confined to the ability to arbitrate between how they presently wish the past to have been—their "desire for the imaginary, the possible"—and how it was—their obligation to "the real, the actual."[57] Hence, the question about who is writing whose history and for whom merits our attention and is consequential, especially when the subject under investigation is one that challenges the historians' own personal and collective identity, which may further induce them "to condemn, rather than to explain."[58]

Writing about historians and the Holocaust, the late Lucy Dawidowicz asserted that there are "defects" that "universally afflict" those who write about "peoples other than their own." Of the opinion that historians and readers are "saddened and often displeased and angered" by the way the other historians portray them, she concluded:

> It was to be expected that non-Jewish historians would not approach the history of the murder of the European Jews with the same empathy and moral concern that they would normally apply when writing the history of their own people.[59]

Dawidowicz appears to be claiming that a certain fusion must exist between the narrator and the subject of his narrative; that shared emotions and principles are not only legitimate but a necessary prerequisite. For those who are adamant in their belief that only Jews can possess "empathy" and "moral concern" when writing about the Holocaust, this exclusivity may prove a blessing; but for the pre-postmoderns whose aim is historical truth, which does not mean that it is devoid of empathy and moral concern, it may prove a serious stumbling block.

If bystanders, as suggested before, can rarely be proven innocent, they can only seldom command moral authority as witnesses. By extension, common wisdom would have the recorders of their history guilty by association; consequently, the "truth" and authenticity of the historical accounts are questionable. Accordingly, "knowledge" alone may not qualify as an adequate "proof" of historical truth.

As a possible way out of this impasse, most historians load their accounts with empathy and moral judgments that often run counter to the evidence they present and the historical forces they describe. While to one extent or another all historians consider economic distress, anti-Semitism, restrictionist sentiments, diplomatic and military restrictions, and the like, as obstacles to initiating an active drive for mass rescue, at the same time they suggest that American Jews should have appealed to "high government officials" and mounted a "national campaign to publicize the mass killings with a view to directing public pressure on the Roosevelt administration and Congress."[60] The frustration born of the inability to reconcile what was actual and possible and what was desirable inevitably leads to moral condemnation and lamentations. No one could disagree with noble, humanitarian impulses of this kind. But in the writing of history, where interpretation of the possible or desirable must rest on concrete grounds, conclusions based on moral criteria alone fail to convince or provide understanding.

Some historians have elected to invest their narrative with the uniquely moral-authoritative truth of the survivor-witnesses. "The truth. But what was the truth?" Elie Wiesel asks readers in his introduction to *The Abandonment of the Jews, America and the Ho-locaust.* "Read David Wyman's courageous, lucid, painful book," he urges us, "and you too will learn it."[61] It is rather obvious that what Wiesel has endorsed is Wyman's ideological and moral stand, not his erudition as a historian. When recommending Lookstein's work *Were We Our Brother's Keepers? The Public Response of American Jews to the Holocaust, 1938-1944,* Wiesel urges us to read it for the sake of "ahavat Yisrael" (love of Israel) since, as the title makes clear, its intended audience is the historian's "own."[62] Rabbi Lookstein also sought advice from Wiesel, the "Professor" in this context, on "the choice of events to be studied."[63]

The charged "for" context in which this history is written — which will be dealt with from another angle later on — is further uncovered by the defensive polemics aimed at gaining credence with "implied readers." For David Wyman, the exceptional Other, the need for legitimacy as a narrator, emerges as particularly pressing. He meets the problem head on in the preface to his book by explicitly pronouncing his "subject position" as that of an "insider . . . a Christian, a Protestant."[64] Assuming that those who do not know may take him to be Jewish, he assures readers that he is an insider who should not be suspected of dual loyalty. Yet, it does not appear that Wyman's aim is to establish his credentials as an "objective" historian but rather to validate his "rights" to this specific subject. Hence, when listing his credentials as an American Protestant, he adds, "*But* I have advocated a Jewish state for a very long time. . . . Today I remain strongly pro-Zionist and I am a resolute supporter of the state of Israel."[65] However, even his long support of Zionism does not allow him to criticize the American Jewish leadership without apologetics. As an outsider to that community he confesses that he does so "reluctantly," for the sake of "honest and objective" reporting. But under the circumstances this confession may not be enough, and to be beyond reproach he bases his entitlement on the fact that several of the Jewish leaders "have since criticized their own failures in the face of the catastrophe."[66]

The case of Rabbi Lookstein, as can be expected, is less complicated. Although he is a trained historian, his role as spiritual leader appears to gain primacy. Lookstein is critical of the historians' "expectations and assumptions," which, he claims, "impinge upon" their "objectivity." Moreover, he questions their "standards of fairness." Yet in his attempt to bring about *Tikkun*, to revise the harsh judgments to which American Jews have been subjected by historians, he himself proves to be much less "objective." While taking pride in his "less judgmental" approach, Lookstein none-theless admits that some judgments (moral castigations seem more accurate) have remained in his text. But these, he tells us, "are intended in a spirit of love and empathy and are there solely as lessons for the future."[67]

With respect to the historians of America and the Holocaust, and more specifically of the American Jewish response, Dawidowicz's concern seems unwarranted: it is mostly Jews who have contributed to this historiography. Nonetheless, her appre-hensions may assist us to discover why we have been "blessed" with "cries of pain" more than with "serious history." At issue is a two-level transferential relationship that needs to be negotiated: a shared religious-ethnic-cultural identity between today's histori-ans and their historical objects of inquiry, and a likely attachment of a similar nature to their "implied readers" in the present.[68]

Few would disagree that historians' prime responsibility is to attempt a reconstruction of the past "as it was." But even fewer, perhaps, would accept the reconstituted "reality" as the absolute truth. Historical truth is always "truth limited"—circumscribed, as it were, by historians' re-visits to the past under present cir-cumstances. Traces of the social-cultural transformation that American society has been undergoing in the past two decades and more, the so-called "ethnic movement," are reflected not only in the present position of ethnic-minority subgroups but also in the retelling of their American past. Feeling more and more at home, the Jews, like other minorities, have been liber-ated from the unease of remembering and reminding others of the darker chapters in their American experience. Gone are the apprehensions which, in the immediate postwar period, for ex-ample, prevented American Jews from erecting a monument in memory of the six million Jewish victims in Europe because it was thought to be

> detrimental to the best interest of Jewry since it would stand as a perpetual reminder . . . that the Jews are a helpless minority whose safety and very lives depend upon the whim of the people among whom they live or the governments who control their destinies.[69]

The changed configuration in the public sphere is evident from the establishment of the United States Holocaust Memorial Museum and from the popularity of a film such as *Schindler's List*. In the 1980s the Jews of America did not flinch from putting up a public-political struggle to incorporate the "shameful" past into the enshrined space of America's national memory, nor did profit-motivated Hollywood recoil from investing in a "Holocaust" film. But it was a long journey. As is often the case, this uneasy subject was first broached in the mid-1960s by the investigating journalist Arthur Morse, who pierced the barrier for academics to follow. The first results were harsh criticisms of President Roosevelt and his administration and then of American Jewry. At about the same time and much for the same reasons, research on American anti-Semitism began to attract serious scholarly attention. Previously it had been widely believed, or rationalized, that a discussion of Jew-hatred would intensify its effects rather than lead to an understanding of bigotry. In the past two decades or so research in this field has been thriving.[70]

Yet, the growing acceptance of multi-ethnicity and cultural pluralism as the "true" definition of the American nation points to the existence of a curious paradox. Whereas the willingness to accept "Others" as others tends to attenuate particular identities, it is also considered by many to constitute a threat to "Jewish continuity."[71] These fears seem to be exaggerated, if for no other reason than because in the American kaleidoscope of race, ethnicity, and culture, the individual's "to be or not to be" is becoming increasingly dependent on belonging to a solidly defined sub-group. Such a sociopolitical climate has transfigured the legacy of oppression into "a vehicle for maintaining one's connection to, and even identification with, the past." As Michael Roth has suggested, remembering an oppressive past may have an extraordinary power at particular times for particular purposes; it may be "misused" for gaining "a moral superiority that our [American] culture often awards to acknowledged victims."[72]

Indeed, if throughout their history in America, Jews strained to repudiate their image as victims, as of late they appear to be straining their victimization to prove the reverse.[73] The current mood is supportive of an amended historical verdict—a lighter, if not a reversed, sentence for their failure to do more for their European brethren. In the introduction to the report of the "Commission on American Jewry during the Holocaust," its chairman, former Supreme Court Justice, Ambassador Arthur Goldberg, declared that American Jews were "also victims of Nazism."[74] Historian Leonard Dinnerstein also opined that "American Jewish leaders of the period were among the victims, not the perpetrators, of this nation's failure to achieve more."[75]

The urge to recast American Jews as victims has led another historian to intimate that they even share a similar experience of victimization. In the concluding chapter to his book Aaron Berman writes:

> American Zionists shared in the experience of their European co-religionists. Although they personally did not have to endure deportation to death camps . . . [they] were painfully aware of what was occurring in the Nazi murder factories.[76]

Such historical misrepresentation obviously trivializes the experience of the genuine victims; but it also distorts, if not to say falsifies, the Jews' experience in America. Although American Jews have never before been more mature and secure as they embark upon an "inward journey" to face their past "as it really was," they seem to embrace the highly dubious yet currently popular American fascination with victimization.[77]

By Way of Summation: A Call for Historicization

If the history of American Jewry is to receive the serious attention it merits, a process of historicization must begin. Why? Because if we were to stage an imaginary gathering with Jews of the 1930s and 1940s and ask them what they thought of their subsequent historical representation, it is quite likely they would answer that "as a tale, it isn't bad." And why? Because to speak of the response of the "American Jewish community" to the Nazi menace during the 1930s and 1940s is "the product of a messianic imagination."[78] More than describing the Jews' reality, it represents others' imaginary perception of them as a cohesive and powerful group. To speak of a "leadership" is no less deceptive. There was no united authority that could claim to speak for American Jewry.[79]

Yet, with very few exceptions, historical analysis is located within these two non-existing configurations: the American Jewish community and the American Jewish leadership.[80] Moreover, since the Jews' behavior is examined against the backdrop of the administration's response, the result is all the more imaginary. Whereas contextualizing the Jewish response is the only sound approach, to be persuasive it must point to the significant disparities that existed between the "dominant" and the "subordinate" cultures. Failure to define differences in means, opportunities and limitations, and neglect of the wider historical experience of the Jews in American society fosters the illusion that David and Goliath were equal partners to the same violation. The most conspicuous manifestation of this skewed interpretation is the often sweeping conclusion that the American government *and* American Jewry were "passive accomplices to a policy that closed the doors on the Jews of Germany," or even to the murder of the Jews.[81] It appears that conflating the Jews' powerlessness with the nation's apathy is easier to bear.

To write "serious history" of the American Jewish response to the Nazi menace calls for a "historicization" of the American Jewish experience. Breitman and Kraut, for example, while they predicted pessimistically in their 1987 book that "a final verdict grounded on scholarly investigation rather than on self-serving, accusatory exchanges . . . is probably years away," also noted that "available evidence . . . already suggests the need for a revised perspective on the prewar period."[82] Similarly, but more specifically, Henry Feingold points to the restraining impact of the twin forces of secularization and acculturation during the twenties and thirties on the American Jews' ability to respond to the crisis.[83]

There is no doubt that American Jewry underwent structural, cultural, and ideological changes during the interwar period that brought about greater diversity and weakened communal ties. However, if we opt to attain an "interpretative perspective" and even perhaps an "explanatory theory," both the time framework and the context must be expanded.[84]

The Jews who came to America from Eastern Europe toward the end of the nineteenth century, and constituted the majority during the 1930s and 1940s, did not arrive in America tabula rasa. The internal tensions that resulted from a concurrent attachment to traditional Jewish ways, on the one hand, and attraction to modernity, on the other, had to be negotiated within themselves and with the host culture. Older attitudes on both sides did not dissipate swiftly or easily.

For the Jews these tensions involved the strains of arrival; of being tolerated but not fully accepted; a struggle to break through the ghetto walls, to become Americans yet to remain Jewish; and to rework a history and tradition of two thousand years into a hospitable yet controlled new social experiment. And on the "American side" we cannot disregard the fact that political rights were not matched by social acceptance; that equality before the law, for those to whom it was granted, did not guarantee equality of opportunities. The change from an emerging frontier society to a modern nation-state also redefined America's relations with the world. As a world power America was obliged to accept the primacy of national sovereignty and the limitations such sovereignty imposes on intervention in the internal affairs of other nations. Since "humanitarian diplomacy" was out and "power politics" was in, many of the loopholes through which American Jews could plead the case of their distraught brethren abroad were sealed. Hence, to argue that American Jewry "had a good track record in nurturing beleaguered Jewish communities abroad" in the nineteenth century tells us virtually nothing about what was possible after World War I.[85] American society changed, and so, for better *and* for worse, did the opportunities that were available to America's Jews.

The toll in human lives and the moral magnitude of the Holocaust tend to make us psychologically predisposed to presume and even insist that the response of American Jews should have grown progressively more militant to match the escalating Nazi terror. But such an analytical framework supports the dubious assumption that an anomalous situation is bound to elicit a nonnormative response; it is justified by emotions rather than by observable conduct. Not only does it neglect tangible political-social-economic factors, it overlooks the force of continuity in human behavior.

To reinstate the response of the Jews to the Holocaust in a true temporal and historical setting calls for close consideration of multifarious changing circumstances, for tracing the configuration and reconfiguration that shaped American society and the minorities in its midst. Stated differently, a *longue durée* approach will both temper the observed inclination to emphasize the elements of "change" as well as attenuate the forces of the "continuum" that must be resisted.[86]

NOTES

1. Henry L. Feingold, "Who Shall Bear Guilt for the Holocaust: The Human Dilemma," originally published in *American Jewish History* 68 (March 1979): 261–82. Quoted here from the reprinted version in the 1980 edition of Feingold's *The Politics of Rescue* (New York: Holocaust Library, 1980) 309.

2. Michael R. Marrus, *The Holocaust in History* (London: Weidenfeld & Nicholson, 1988) 156.

3. Jonathan Sarna, "American Jewish History," *Modern Judaism* 10.3 (October 1990): 355.

4. In addition to this partial list of books, numerous articles have been

published and a good many dissertations have been written on various facets of America and the Holocaust. Among the most eminent for their for scholarship or passionate argumentation are: Arthur D. Morse, *While Six Million Died: A Chronicle of American Apathy* (New York: Random House, 1968); David S. Wyman, *Paper Walls: America and the Refugee Crisis, 1938-1941* (Amherst: University of Massachusetts Press, 1968); Saul S. Friedman, *No Haven for the Oppressed: United States Policy toward Jewish Refugees, 1938-1945* (Detroit: Wayne State University Press, 1973); Martin Gilbert, *Auschwitz and the Allies: The Politics of Rescue* (London: Joseph, 1981); Yehuda Bauer, *American Jewry and the Holocaust: The American Jewish Joint Distribution Committee, 1939-1945* (Detroit: Wayne State University Press, 1981); Moshe R. Gottlieb, *American Anti-Nazi Resistance, 1933-1941: An Historical Analysis* (New York: Ktav, 1982); David S. Wyman, *The Abandonment of the Jews: America and the Holocaust, 1941-1945* (New York: Pantheon Books, 1984); Monty Noam Penkower, *The Jews Were Expendable: Free World Diplomacy and the Holocaust* (Urbana: University of Illinois Press, 1983); Haskel Lookstein, *Were We Our Brothers' Keepers? The Public Response of American Jews to the Holocaust, 1938-1944* (New York: Hartmore House, 1985 [paperback edition, New York: Vintage Books, 1988]); M. J. Nurenberger, *The Sacred and the Doomed: The Jewish Establishment vs. The Six Million* (Oakville, NY: Mosaic Press, 1985); Richard Breitman and Alan M. Kraut, *American Refugee Policy and European Jewry, 1933-1945* (Bloomington: Indiana University Press, 1987); David Kranzler, *Thy Brother's Blood: The Orthodox Jewish Response during the Holocaust* (Brooklyn: Mesorah Publications, 1987); Rafael Medoff, *The Deafening Silence* (New York: Shapolsky, 1987); Aaron Berman, *Nazism, the Jews and American Zionism, 1933-1948* (Detroit: Wayne State University Press, 1990).

5. For reviews on the historiography, see, for example, Deborah E. Lipstadt, "America and the Holocaust," *Modern Judaism* 10.3 (October 1990); the introductory chapter to Breitman and Kraut, *American Refugee Policy;* Frank W. Brecher, "David Wyman and the Historiography of America's Response to the Holocaust: Counter-Considerations," *Holocaust and Genocide Studies* 5.4 (1990): 423–46.

6. Linda Gordon, *"AHR Forum, Comments on That Noble Dream," American Historical Review* 96.3 (June 1991): 684.

7. See Hannah Arendt, *Eichmann in Jerusalem: A Report on the Banality of Evil* (New York: Viking Press, 1963); Saul S. Friedman, *No Haven for the Oppressed* and his article "The Power and/or Powerlessness of American Jews, 1939-1945," appendix 8 in Seymour Maxwell Finger, ed., *American Jewry during the Holocaust* (New York: American Jewish Commission on the Holocaust, 1984).

8. Edward T. Linenthal, *Preserving Memory: The Struggle to Create America's Holocaust Museum* (New York: Viking, 1995) 6–10.

9. See Gulie Ne'eman Arad, "The American Jewish Leadership's Response to the Rise of the Nazi Menace," Ph.D. diss., Tel Aviv University, 1994.

10. Stephen S. Wise to Julian W. Mack, 8 April 1933, American Jewish Historical Society, Wise's Papers, Box 115.

11. Felix Frankfurter to James G. McDonald, 8 May 1933, Central Zionist Archives, Julian W. Mack Papers, A 405 84/B.

12. Cyrus Adler to Louis Ginzberg, 7 April 1933, reprinted in Ira Robinson, ed., *Cyrus Adler: Selected Letters*, vol. 2 (Philadelphia: Jewish Publication Society of America, 1985) 258.

13. With regard to the American bystanders, the two noticeable exceptions are: Breitman and Kraut, *American Refugee Policy*, and Berman's, *Nazism, the Jews and American Zionism*, who start their respective studies in 1933.

14. See, for example, Feingold, *Politics of Rescue* 301, and Wyman, *Paper Walls*. It is interesting that Feingold noted the fact that even in the critical year of 1941, only 47 percent of the German-Austrian quota was filled (*Politics of Rescue* 296).

15. Henry L. Feingold, *A Time for Searching: Entering the Mainstream, 1920-1945* (Baltimore: Johns Hopkins University Press, 1992) 234.

16. Feingold, *Politics of Rescue* 326.

17. This is true of Feingold, Wyman, Medoff, and Penkower. Breitman and Kraut, in *American Refugee Policy* 291n, are among the few who correctly argue that mass rescue was "infeasible."

18. The phrase is Elie Wiesel's in "Telling the Tale," *Dimensions in American Judaism* (Spring 1968).

19. Feingold, *Politics of Rescue* 3, 296, 327; Wyman, *Paper Walls* 221-22. The pressure for visas increased between 1938 and 1941 following the *Anschluss* and *Kristallnacht,* and indeed, it was only during fiscal year 1939 that the quota was filled for the first time since the crisis began. By late 1941 the American quota became immaterial; Nazi restrictions on legal exit from the German-controlled territories rendered it meaningless.

20. Quoted in Lucy S. Dawidowicz, *The War against the Jews, 1933-1945* (Harmondsworth: Penguin, 1986) 189.

21. Henry L. Feingold, "PBS's Roosevelt: Deceit and Indifference or Politics and Powerlessness?" in *Bearing Witness: How America and Its Jews Responded to the Holocaust* (Syracuse: Syracuse University Press, 1995) 187. An earlier and shorter version of this essay appeared in *Dimensions* 8.2 (1994): 9-14.

22. Cited in Linenthal, *Preserving Memory* 223.

23. On referring to America and its Jews as "passive accomplices," see Lookstein, *Were We Our Brothers' Keepers?* 69; Wyman, *Abandonment of the Jews* xiii, applies the term to the American government, public, and to American Jewry; Elie Wiesel, "Telling the Tale" 11, wrote: "Taken in by

Roosevelt's personality, they [American Jews, GNA], in a way, became accomplices in his inaction. . . ."

24. Feingold, "PBS's Roosevelt" 187.

25. Berman, Nazism, the Jews and American Zionism 179, 182–84.

26. Marie Syrkin, "What American Jews Did during the Holocaust," Midstream 28.8 (October 1982): 12. On the same issue, see also, Bernard Wasserstein, "The Myth of 'Jewish Silence,'" Midstream 26.7 (August–September 1980): 10; Lipstadt, "America and the Holocaust," 283–84.

27. For an attempt by a philosopher to probe the moral qualities of behavior during the Holocaust, see Berel Lang, Acts and Ideas in Nazi Genocide (Chicago: University of Chicago Press, 1990).

28. The references are to Arendt's Eichmann in Jerusalem, where she questioned the absolute innocence of the victims, and to Andreas Hillgruber's Zweierlei Untergang: Die Zerschlagung des Deutsches Reiches und das Ende des europäischen Judentums (Berlin: W. J. Siedler, 1986), where he claimed the right to express empathy for the heretofore eternally damned.

29. Raul Hilberg, Perpetrators Victims Bystanders: The Jewish Catastrophe, 1933-1945 (New York: Aaron Asher Books, 1992) 225.

30. Feingold, Politics of Rescue 309.

31. See note 4 above.

32. Medoff, Deafening Silence 11–15, 154.

33. Lookstein, Were We Our Brothers' Keepers? 216 (emphasis in the original).

34. Henry Feingold "Crisis and Response: American Jewish Leadership during the Roosevelt Years," Modern Judaism 8.2 (May 1988): 101.

35. Lookstein, Were We Our Brothers' Keepers? 213; Wyman, Abandonment of the Jews 331; Feingold, A Time for Searching 234.

36. See, for example, Walter Laqueur, The Terrible Secret, Suppression of the Truth about Hitler's "Final Solution" (Boston: Little, Brown, 1980); Walter Laqueur and Richard Breitman, Breaking the Silence (New York: Simon and Schuster, 1986); Yehuda Bauer, "When Did They Know?" Midstream IV (1968): 51–58; Henry Feingold, "Did American Jewry Do Enough during the Holocaust?" the B. G. Rudolph Lecture, Syracuse University (pamphlet, April 1984); and "The Government Response," in The Holocaust: Ideology, Bureaucracy, and Genocide, ed. Henry Friedlander and Sybil Milton, (Millwood, NY: Kraus International Publications, 1980), esp. 245–46.

37. Elizabeth Janeway, Powers of the Weak (New York: Knopf, 1980) 166 (emphasis added).

38. For updated views on this issue see, Linenthal, Preserving Memory 218-24, quote on 224.

39. Friedman, "Power and/or Powerlessness."

40. Rabbi Samuel Schulman of Temple Emanu-El in New York, in "American Palestine Campaign Launched," American Hebrew 20 (January 1933).

41. See, for example, Wyman, *Abandonment of the Jews* xv, 328.

42. See, for example, Feingold, *A Time for Searching* 156, 263, and ch. 8; Wyman, *Abandonment of the Jews* 328, maintains that the split over Zionism was the chief obstacle to forming a united drive for rescue.

43. Michael Parenti, *Power and the Powerless* (New York: St. Martin's Press, 1978) 3.

44. For a similar interpretation, see Lipstadt, "America and the Holocaust" 292.

45. Friedman, in "Power and/or Powerlessness," lists the counts as follows: American Jews *should* have (1) striven for greater unity and suppression of ego; (2) refused to be coopted by the system; (3) conveyed the news of Nazi extermination plans to their American countrymen and to Jews in Europe; (4) insisted upon the issuance of a statement by the Allied governments acknowledging the special tragedy befalling Jews in Europe; (5) publicly rejected the argument of military expedience as inapplicable to relief and rescue of European Jews; (6) pressed for emergency changes in their country's immigration laws; and finally, "American Jews *could* have withdrawn their political support from the Roosevelt Administration or registered a vote of no confidence in the Democratic Party."

46. Feingold, *Politics of Rescue* 322.

47. See, for example, Gottlieb, *American Anti-Nazi Resistance* xxi; Shlomo Shafir, "The Impact of the Jewish Crisis on American-German Relations, 1933–1939" (Ph.D. diss., Georgetown University, 1971) pt. 1, p. vi.

48. See, for example, Frederick A. Lazin, "The Response of the American Jewish Committee to the Crisis of German Jewry, 1933–1939," *American Jewish History* 68.3 (March 1979): 284; Wyman, *Abandonment of the Jews* passim and his interesting partial reversal in a note on page 330 of that work. Since his *Politics of Rescue,* Feingold has come to view anti-Semitism as a lesser factor in American Jewish life. See his "Finding a Conceptual Framework for the Study of American Antisemitism," *Jewish Social Studies* 47.2 (Spring 1985): 313–26.

49. See Friedman, *No Haven for the Oppressed* and his article "Power and/or Powerlessness"; Berman, *Nazism, the Jews and American Zionism*; and Medoff, *Deafening Silence.*

50. Medoff, *Deafening Silence* 31.

51. Such an expectation is evident in the following works: Friedman, *No Haven for the Oppressed* 139–54; Wyman, *Abandonment of the Jews* 321–29; Finger, ed., *American Jewry during the Holocaust* appendix 8; Leon Weliczker Wells, *Who Speaks for the Vanquished? American Jewish Leaders and the Holocaust* (New York: P. Lang, 1987); Lookstein, *Were We Our Brother's Keepers?*

52. On the search for meaning in the Holocaust see, Saul Friedlander, "Historical Writing and the Memory of the Holocaust," in Berel Lang, ed.,

Writing and the Holocaust (New York: Holmes & Meier, 1988); Harold Kaplan, *Conscience and Memory: Meditations in a Museum of the Holocaust* (Chicago: University of Chicago Press, 1994) esp. ch. 7.

53. See Ne'eman Arad, "American Jewish Leadership's Response" esp. chs. 4–7.

54. Henry Hurwitz in a signed opening statement of an issue devoted to the postwar reconstruction of Jewish life, *Menorah Journal* 21 (January–March 1943).

55. R. G. Collingwood, *The Idea of History* (Oxford: Oxford University Press, 1961 [1st ed., 1946]) 213–15.

56. Hayden White, *The Content of the Form: Narrative Discourse and Historical Representation* (Baltimore: Johns Hopkins University Press, 1990) 21.

57. White, *The Content of the Form* 4; Joan W. Scott, "Experience as Evidence," *Critical Inquiry* 17 (Summer 1991): 773–97.

58. Marrus, *Holocaust in History* 157.

59. Lucy S. Dawidowicz, *The Holocaust and the Historians* (Cambridge: Harvard University Press, 1981) 2 (emphasis added).

60. See, for example, Wyman, *Abandonment of the Jews* 327–28.

61. Wyman, *Abandonment of the Jews* viii.

62. Lookstein, *Were We Our Brothers' Keepers?* 12.

63. Lookstein, *Were We Our Brothers' Keepers?* 23.

64. Wyman, *Abandonment of the Jews* xvi.

65. Wyman, *Abandonment of the Jews* (emphasis added).

66. Wyman, *Abandonment of the Jews* xv–xvi.

67. Lookstein, *Were We Our Brothers' Keepers?* 13, 69.

68. It is in no way implied thereby that the need to negotiate "transferential relations to the object of study" is a unique dilemma for Jewish historians. See Dominick LaCapra, "Representing the Holocaust: Reflections on the Historians' Debate," *Probing the Limits of Representation: Nazism and the "Final Solution,"* ed. Saul Friedlander (Cambridge: Harvard University Press, 1992) 110.

69. Minutes of a meeting of an ad hoc committee to consider the American Memorial for Six Million Jews of Europe, Inc., held at the offices of the National Community Relations Advisory Council (NCRAC), March 9, 1948 (YIVO, American Jewish Committee Records, General Series 12, Box 102, NCRAC Ad Hoc Committees 1947–1952).

70. Two recent additions are Frederic Cople Jaher, *A Scapegoat in the New Wilderness: The Origins and Rise of Anti-Semitism in America* (Cambridge: Harvard University Press, 1994); and Leonard Dinnerstein, *Anti-Semitism in America* (New York: Oxford University Press, 1994). See particularly Dinnerstein's preface.

71. On the current discussion about the problem of "Jewish continuity,"

see Martin Lipset and Earl Raab, *Jews and the New American Scene* (Cambridge: Harvard University Press, 1995); Jonathan D. Sarna, "The Secret of Jewish Continuity," *Commentary* (October 1994): 55–58.

72. Michael S. Roth, "Victims, Memory, History" *Tikkun* 9.2 (March–April 1994): 60, 95. For a somewhat similar argument, see John Murray Cuddihy, "The Holocaust: The Latent Issue in the Uniqueness Debate," *Christians, Jews and Other Worlds: Patterns of Conflict and Accommodation,* ed. Philip F. Gallagher (Lanham, MD: University Press of America, 1988) 77.

73. On American society's celebration of victimhood see, Alvin H. Rosenfeld, "The Americanization of the Holocaust," *Commentary* (June 1995): 35–40.

74. See the foreword to the Commission's report, *American Jewry during the Holocaust,* ed. Finger, i, ii, iii.

75. Leonard Dinnerstein, "What Should American Jews Have Done to Rescue Their European Brethren?" *Simon Wiesenthal Center Annual* 3 (1986): 286.

76. Berman, *Nazism, the Jews and American Zionism* 182–84.

77. On the use of the Holocaust in the attempt to find a mode of memorializing other American traumas, see Miriam Bratu Hansen, "Schindler's List Is Not Shoah: The Second Commandment, Popular Modernism, and Public Memory," *Critical Inquiry* 22 (1995/96): 292–312.

78. Feingold, *Politics of Rescue* 322; see also Feingold, *A Time for Searching* 264.

79. See Henry L. Feingold, "Crisis and Response: American Jewish Leadership during the Roosevelt Years," *Modern Judaism* 8.2 (May 1988): 107; Benny Kraut, "American Jewish Leaders: The Great, Greater, and Greatest," *American Jewish History* 78.2 (December 1988): 201–36; Breitman and Kraut, *American Refugee Policy* 83.

80. For the exceptions, see the works cited in note 79.

81. The claim that failure to remember the victims would "mean to become accomplices to their murders" is from *Report to the President: President's Commission on the Holocaust,* Washington, D.C., 27 September 1979.

82. Breitman and Kraut, *American Refugee Policy* 80.

83. Feingold, *Bearing Witness* 244.

84. I borrowed these terms from Allan Megill, "AHR Forum, Fragmentation and the Future of Historiography," *American Historical Review* 96.3 (June 1991): 694, note 5.

85. See, for example, Feingold, *Bearing Witness* 243.

86. See Sarna, "American Jewish History" 355; Jacob Katz, "On Jewish Social History: Epochal and Supra-Epochal Historiography," *Jewish History* 7.1 (Spring 1993).

PART FOUR

European Jewry in the Postwar Period

NINE

Breaking the "Cordon Sanitaire" of Memory

The Jewish Encounter with German Society

FRANK STERN

IN HIS ESSAY "THE MEMORY of the Offense," Primo Levi describes the distortion of memory by many Germans in the last years of the Nazi regime: "The best way to defend oneself against the invasion of burdensome memories," he writes, "is to impede their entry, to extend a *cordon sanitaire*."[1] Historically this cordon sanitaire wards off the contents, forms, and structures of individual and collective experiences that have an imprint on historical consciousness. More than being just a complacent barrier, this act of keeping the painful elements of memory at a harmless distance is one of the most ambiguous legacies of the Third Reich. This distance, moreover, enabled many Germans to twist the cords of memory for legitimizing purposes as, for example, in the common German postwar myth of the so-called "decent soldier" or the widespread attitude among the civil population: "We didn't know." This cordon sanitaire created a major shield against moral awareness and the necessity of self-critical questioning. It became the

German postwar coat of arms, the main device in the German culture of forgetting. Ultimately, it created a deep historical dividing line in the historical consciousness of most of the Jewish survivors inside Germany in the spring of 1945, on the one hand, and the vast majority of the German people, on the other.

An insurmountable cultural barrier and emotional and intellectual alienation characterized German-Jewish relations after the downfall of the Third Reich. Consequently, German postwar society was defined by a culture of antagonistic memories whenever German-Jewish encounters took place.

In the following pages I will describe the situation of the Jewish survivors inside Germany, the nature of their plight, and their general experience with Germans in the postwar period. That experience led most Jewish women and men to rely almost entirely on the Allied occupation authorities, who guaranteed what might be called the "second emancipation" of the Jews in Germany.[2] Nazi Germany had abolished the earlier emancipation of the Jews, and the victorious Allies returned this most important of historical assets to the Jewish minorities living in occupied Germany. This situation created a historic triangle composed of the Allied authorities, postwar Germans, and the Jews who were situated between the two; that triangle continued to exist throughout the early formative years of postwar Germany.

Beyond the sphere of political and social history there were deeper layers involved in this historic triangle; they influenced German culture and historical perceptions, bringing to the fore new elements of German memory and works of art that tried to confront the recent past. The intellectual and aesthetic representations that gave expression to this specific situation and often tried to define shifting cultural identities were not so much inspired by distant recollections of former German-Jewish relations. At their center were individual and collective experiences that could either be warded off or painfully mirrored in the return of memory to everyday life, be it in a German or in a Jewish context.

Surviving on Borrowed Time—
Returning on Borrowed Memory

Fifty years ago, during Passover 1945, American troops captured Frankfurt and liberated the "remaining Jews in a few ghetto houses." The novelist Meyer Levin, then an officer in the American army, recalls that day:

> I went into Frankfurt and found the remaining Jews in a few ghetto houses. There were a hundred and six people out of a former population of forty thousand. It was strange how the Jewish GI's had already gravitated toward them. But according to military regulations, these Jews were German civilians, and fraternization with them was forbidden. So the GI's had left packages of matzoth for them on the doorsteps of the ghetto houses. The Jewish soldiers watched from across the street as the last Jews of Frankfurt slipped out, still fearful, and picked up the Passover food.[3]

In Cologne, Konrad Adenauer, the first postwar mayor of the city, asked British forces to assist with trucks in getting the Jews from Cologne who had survived in Theresienstadt back to their hometown. Most of them were old people.

In the vicinity of Berlin, a Jewish nurse survived in hiding. After liberation, she returned to Berlin and found her twelve-year-old daughter, who had been living in semilegality. The mother later recalled that her daughter "had never forgotten that as a very small girl once, wearing a Star of David, she had been beaten bloody. And now, after a short time she said she wouldn't have it, she wasn't going to go to school with German kids."[4] The girl was accepted into a Jewish youth home in northern Germany in 1946 and then emigrated to Palestine in 1947. Her mother remained, living until her death in East Germany.

Another characteristic example is reported by Martin Riesenburger, a rabbi in Berlin. He and about 800 Jews were liberated in May 1945 in the Jewish Hospital in Berlin-Wedding and in the Jewish Cemetery in Berlin-Weissensee. Among the survivors were 100 children.[5] They ranged in age from two to eighteen years. Half of them were from Berlin, the rest from Frankfurt and other cities. Besides the specific situation of this group, the Jewish Hospital had continued to work with Jewish physicians, nurses, and other members of the staff in the period 1943 to 1945. Sometimes, to illustrate the absurdity of this place, Jewish inmates were *cured to death*[6] since only healthy Jews were allowed to be deported by train. It was a kind of Jewish Ghetto that existed even after the offices of the *Reichsvereinigung* were closed in 1943 and its officials deported.[7] The Jewish Hospital, in fact, was the last official Jewish institution in Nazi Germany, tormented, terrorized, but somehow surviving "inside the vicious heart."[8] Most of the 100 children, mentioned above, were without parents or relatives. Immediately after liberation, some of them approached the rabbi after he advertised on the walls of the city center and over the radio. Jewish children who had survived were asked to contact him so that he could organize the first classes in Judaism following liberation. He writes in his memoirs that the teaching materials had been hidden in the Weissensee cemetery, and adds: "Now the flame of Judaism, whose glow had flickered for years beneath the ashes, but which we had never allowed to go out, began once again to burn brightly. The light had not been extinguished."[9] In May, the first Jewish wedding was celebrated, and it was not long before the first Jewish child was born in postwar Berlin. Other German Jews who had survived the extermination camps in the east or the death marches—however small in numbers—returned to their former hometowns, most of them from Theresienstadt.

Others, some immediately and some reluctantly, returned from exile in England, Sweden, Switzerland, Shanghai, Palestine, Mexico, or the United States. Many were cautious, waiting to return, and after observing political developments in Germany, settled in other states. Walter Mehring, Wolfgang Hildesheimer, Hermann Kesten, Robert Neumann, Jean Améry, Ludwig Marcuse, Carl Zuckmayer, Peter Weiss—to name just a few intellectuals—lived only temporarily in Germany or were just occasional visitors. Wolfgang Hildesheimer, in an autobiographical interview, said in 1989: "We are nowhere at home."[10] In the 1950s German culture quickly adapted to this "foreign" solution of the extended displacement and exile of its former countrymen. In high schools Carl Zuckmayer was taught as a Swiss author. It was easier to ward off memory if one saw Jewish writers largely as outsiders. In the eyes of most postwar Germans, so it seemed, German literature was not represented by the humanist encyclopedia composed of those titles that had been burned in May 1933 but through the hidden voices of inner emigration that came proudly forward now, looking disdainfully upon writers such as Thomas Mann and others who, for obvious reasons, had not been in the homeland, and who apparently did not know what had been going on inside the Reich. Consequently, most of the burned books were not reprinted in the first postwar years, although there were some serious efforts in East Germany to bring these books back. In terms of the new literary public sphere, the cordon sanitaire remained a delicate dividing line, a cultural twilight zone in which it could be understood that not too many Jewish authors should be printed. Besides, in these early years one could always pretend that there was a lack of paper, and, particularly, a lack of interest in Jewish authors among German readers. Although some Jewish women and men returned, most of the Jewish voices of Weimar culture remained part of a distant and silenced memory. After Hitler, the cordon sanitaire of memory even began to extend backward into the rich cultural German-Jewish life of the past.

At the same time, there also existed various Jewish perspectives on this painful situation. In January 1946, Hannah Arendt answered Karl Jaspers's invitation to publish in the new German periodical *Wandlung:* "It is not an easy thing for me to contribute to a German journal. . . . Yet one thing seems clear to me: If the Jews are to be able to stay in Europe, then they cannot stay as Germans or Frenchmen, etc., as if nothing had happened. It seems to me that none of us can return (and writing is surely a form of return) merely because people again seem prepared to recognize

Jews as Germans or something else. We can return only if we are welcome as Jews."[11]

Others, like former members of the group *Neu Beginnen*, returned and became active in the Social Democratic Party, and a number of Jewish Communists and those who had been close to the socialist movements of Weimar and in exile returned defining themselves as antifascists. At this time, antifascist attitudes ranged from the hope for the revival of the radical liberal temper in German culture to the leftist dream of a socialist Germany that would cure all the failures and mistakes of the socialist and communist movements of the 1920s and 1930s. The intellectual world of these individuals was formed by their experience of persecution, by their relationship with Germans, and by the intellectual controversies of exile. Most of these approximately 3,500 people settled in East Germany. They were driven by the intellectual and emotional urge to live within real history after they had so long participated in the shadowlike reproductions of memory. They wanted to participate in the economic, cultural, academic, and political reconstruction which, at that time, was defined as the creation of an antifascist-democratic order in the tradition of that other Germany, seemingly lost but nevertheless still envisioned by many.[12] It has to be stressed that the main difference between those Jewish survivors and returnees who chose to live in the West and those who chose to live in East Germany was that the decision for the East usually was a political decision.[13]

However, these returnees also confronted the demands of a very specific situation: their Jewish experience was politically silenced for the sake of socialism, for the sake of a new Germany that obviously had problems dealing with traditional German anti-Semitism and the Holocaust. These Jewish women and men, though, were only a minority among those survivors who stayed in Germany or returned in the immediate postwar years. It belongs to the historical dimension of German-Jewish relations since 1945 that, to a large extent, both German states and their political cultures warded off the memory of the Jewish survivors and returnees for the sake of the new and legitimizing discourse of postwar identities: Germans West in opposition to Germans East, and both opposing their common past: National Socialism.

In short, beneath the evolving East-West antagonism and the Cold War remained hidden another and much deeper layer of historical consciousness, represented by those persecuted by Nazism, particularly the Jewish survivors and their diverse recollections.

As all of these examples show, it is impossible to reduce the often-heard question, "How could Jews live in Germany after the Holocaust?" to a simple, straightforward answer.[14] One central aspect, however, cannot be overlooked: from a cultural, intellectual, and social perspective, it is indeed insufficient to reduce the reconstruction of Jewish life in postwar Germany to the reestablishment of Jewish religious-based congregations or to consider just the registered members of these communities as representing postwar Jewish life in Germany. It has to be stressed that most Jewish intellectuals, whether or not they returned, and numerous survivors of Jewish origin did not become registered members of the established congregational communities.

The Return to a German Place That Was Foreign

In the spring of 1945, a remnant of German Jewry and some 50,000–80,000 Jewish forced laborers from Eastern Europe had survived Nazi persecution and genocide within the very heart of the Third Reich. Between 20,000 and 40,000 German Jews could soon be counted in the "Altreich," that is, in German state territory within the borders of 1937. This was a mere fraction in comparison with the more than 500,000 German Jewish citizens in January 1933. These Jewish women and men, the German-Jewish part of *Sheerith Hapleita,* the Jewish remnant, resurfaced in German society although, at that time, the Jewish communities in many countries assumed that Hitler had been successful and that no Jews were left in Germany. All reports of the Allied military authorities show the contrary; although only few had survived in comparison with the huge number of those murdered, there were, in fact, some survivors.

This remnant of German Jewry had left the camps, their hiding places, or their lives in semilegality or underground and returned from abroad—unlike the great mass of Germans, not to their homeland. Rather, they came back to a "German place that was foreign"—"eine deutsche Fremde," as it was dubbed by the literary scholar, Hans Mayer, one of those returning from exile in Switzerland.[15]

At the same time, Jewish institutions were reestablished or resurfaced almost spontaneously. Already in early March 1945, the American Officer for Education and Religion granted Jewish survivors in Düsseldorf permission to hold religious services, and in April, the community, numbering 80 members, was reconstituted.[16] In and around Frankfurt, about 250 Jews had survived; in August they numbered about 650. In Munich a Jewish lawyer who had survived working in a munitions factory applied to reestablish the Jewish community there. About 400 Jews had survived in and around Munich, and 297 returned in June from Theresienstadt. In July 1945, the Berlin Jewish Community was reestablished.[17] In Dresden 134 survivors were counted, and in Leipzig there were 300, including those who returned from Theresienstadt.[18]

At this time, there existed two Jewish organizational structures in Germany: the newly founded congregations of German-Jewish origin, and the Jewish institutions and committees of the liberated Jewish forced laborers from Eastern Europe, now living in the camps for displaced persons.[19] The Jewish population of these camps numbered approximately 250,000. Anti-Semitic events in Poland, particularly the Kielce pogrom, and *Brichah,* organized Zionist activities to encourage and implement immigration to Palestine, led to the move of tens of thousands to occupied Germany, particularly to the American Zone in South Germany, which would situate these Jews close to Austria, Italy, and the Mediterranean harbors. Anti-Semitic events in camps where non-Jews and Jews were put together according to national origin, as well as the search of many Germans for scapegoats, led to a growing number of American reports of anti-Semitic incidents and in general of the unbearable situation of the Jewish DPs. In the summer of 1945, separate camps for the Jewish DPs were set up by the American military government. The *Central Committee of the Liberated Jews of Bavaria* was constituted in July 1945. Solutions that were thought to be temporary turned out to last for years since the British did not issue enough immigration visas for Palestine, nor were American officials all too eager to hand out the necessary documents to those who wanted to emigrate to the United States. As late as 1948, the *New York Times* wrote: "As matters stand, it is easier for a former Nazi to enter the United States than for one of the Nazis' 'innocent victims.'"[20]

Frictions between Jewish DPs and American soldiers, and between Jewish inmates of these camps and the surrounding German society, led to investigations and in the end to an official report to President Truman by Earl G. Harrison. *The Plight of the Displaced Jews in Europe* changed the American attitude toward the Jewish DPs. In summer 1945, General Eisenhower issued several orders concerning Jews living in Germany. However, these orders were not properly implemented in the field. Anti-Semitism among American GIs and the questionable position of General Patton concerning denazification contributed to a situation in which Truman approached the British to increase the immigration quota to Palestine. Britain, in turn, suggested the use of two camps in North Africa for these displaced persons. It was a deadlock situation.

American Jewish organizations became active, and the social and cultural situation in the DP camps slowly changed due to immense American support. For a short period there were more than 190 camps for Jewish displaced persons, largely isolated and often despised by the local German population. Samuel Gringauz, one of the leaders of the DP organizations, describes this situation for the period from autumn 1945 to summer 1947 and comes to the conclusion that despite all of the acts of German discrimination, "it was a period of moral and cultural rehabilitation, looking back, it seems a kind of golden age"[21] for the Jewish DPs. The Cold War changed this considerably, but with the founding of the Jewish state the vast majority of the Jewish DPs could leave Germany, either to go to Israel or to the United States and other countries. In the early 1950s, there still existed one DP camp in Bavaria, Föhrenwald, which was handed over to the German authorities in 1954 and dissolved in 1956. In the end, emigration to Israel and other countries and, for some 20,000 Jewish women and men, partial integration into German society, had brought an end to their existence as *displaced persons*. Most of them soon became members of local Jewish communities. Both groups merged, Jews of Eastern European origin becoming the majority of most of the congregational communities after many German Jews had left Germany.

In retrospect and considering the scholarly criticism of U.S. immigration policies, the role of American Jewry, and that of the leaders of the Jewish settlement in Palestine in the 1940s, one should not overlook one simple fact: with respect to the Jews living in Germany at the end of the 1940s, it has to be stressed that beyond the memory of the brutal face of Nazism another image has had a lasting imprint on Jewish memory: the helpful hand of the Allied liberator. It is this more kindly historical experience that created, among other things, a deep emotional and intellectual bond between American political culture and the Jewish survivors of the Holocaust.

The reestablishment of Jewish communities in the early months of the occupation period, on the other hand, meant the creation of a social and religious bond among the survivors as a group vis-à-vis the administration of the occupying authorities and the local German municipalities.[22] This situation and the fact that it was more than doubtful that there would be any long-term prospects for some sort of Jewish life in Germany shaped not only the sense of identity among Jews but also molded their attitude toward the German milieu and citizens.

By 1946, some fifty-five Jewish communities had been reestablished all over Germany, but only eight of them were in the Soviet Zone. The members of these new congregations lived in more than

500 cities, towns, and villages, the names of which generally re-appear in reports of anti-Semitic incidents. The reconstruction of Jewish communities on German soil after the Holocaust was a point of fierce debate among the Jewish survivors and returnees. Their own self-identity oscillated between being a "community in transit," a "community in the process of liquidation," or—soon in Berlin, Frankfurt, and Munich—a "Jewish new beginning." Many members and officials of these communities thought in the first few years that their activities were only a necessary part of the preparation for emigration or the result of unavoidable help for the elderly and needy. Their attitude toward postwar German so-ciety was highly ambiguous, and, as it was commonly put, "the suitcase remained packed." In the outstanding feature film *Long Is the Way,* produced in 1947 in the DP camps, a German-Jewish woman who had survived the concentration camp expresses a typical Jewish sentiment of the time: "I have to leave Germany. Here, one cannot forget."

Julius Posner, a British officer in North Rhine-Westfalia, de-scribed a conversation with a German woman in the autumn of 1945. She was contending that all Jews should come back and stay because Germany was now a country where Jews could live best. Besides, Jews could get business moving again, and this boost to the economy would be good for the Germans. Posner objected that many Germans would probably be somewhat reluctant to give back the formerly Jewish possessions that they had gotten used to. The German woman hesitated a moment, and then answered: "Well, maybe it would be better if not too many of them came back."[23]

The general German mood toward the Jews was one of social distance, influenced both by pre-Nazi economic anti-Semitic ste-reotypes and arguments in favor of a "balance of victims," equating the Germans who died as a result of Allied air raids with the Jews murdered in Auschwitz. Surviving German Jews were supposed to reintegrate into German society as "our" Jews, and the Jewish displaced persons were supposed to leave soon. Overt anti-Semi-tism was usually directed against these DPs. The Berlin newspaper

Der Tagesspiegel wrote on 5 December 1945 that once again "the Jewish problem" had to be solved: "This can be accomplished by the emigration of homeless Jews, on the one hand, and by the complete assimilation of Jews who wish to remain in Europe."

The terms of this solution, however, sounded very much like the refined upper middle-class anti-Semitic discourse of Weimar. Neither the first postwar German politicians nor the first government of the Federal Republic issued a public call addressed to the exiles explicitly asking them to return. A letter of 10 April 1945 by Konrad Adenauer, then mayor of Cologne, inviting a former Jewish acquaintance to come back, illustrates the hope of some prominent German politicians that former Jewish friends might come back and help with the reconstruction of Germany: "You know our country, and you know the USA. I believe that you could render the city of Cologne and Germany and our shared ideals many valuable services."[24]

There were indeed Jewish personalities who had already been active in politics in the years of the Weimar Republic who now returned and tried to become involved in the process of democratic reconstruction. But they did not represent the general mood, nor were they backed by a broad acceptance within the German population. When, in 1947, the British military returned the 4,350 Jewish women and men aboard the *Exodus* to Germany, newspapers in the American Zone called upon the German municipalities to provide these Jews with a home. Not a single town volunteered to do so. Instead, a wave of anti-Semitic letters reached the editors. A few months later, a movie with the famous Jewish actor Fritz Kortner playing a German-Jewish scholar who returns from his American exile, did not turn out to be a box office hit. The depiction of postwar German anti-Semitism was not exactly what the audience, longing for more traditional entertainment, expected.

Against this background it is apparent that cooperation with the military authorities, who represented the political government in Germany, was central, and that contacts with the reemerging local German administrations was fraught with difficulties. Continuities in the German bureaucracy enforced the tendency of the Jewish survivors and returnees to rely on the military governments. On the one hand, the Jews had to seek the assistance of the emerging German administrations that in some cases became more renazified than denazified. On the other hand, the Jewish communities had been reestablished by permission of the occupation forces, and their authority could be trusted.

In retrospect, it is clear that these postwar years were in a very specific way characterized by the historic triangle referred to earlier: occupiers, Germans, and the Jews in between. Jewish survivors, or returnees, particularly when in the uniform of the Allied troops, were perceived by Germans as belonging to the enemy, the conquerer, the "other." Negative attitudes toward the survivors, so widespread in the German populace, reinforced the cultural status of Jewish women and men as outsiders. As a consequence, many Jewish women and men now began to keep their Jewishness to themselves, to enforce a social cordon sanitaire from their side. Among most the general attitude was "wait and see."

Only very few Jews decided to become politically active in German politics or join the new political parties. And whenever they did become active, they could usually be found on the political left. Many Jewish survivors inside Germany, however, considered emigration. Particularly the younger generation and very often whole families left between 1945 and 1948. By 1948, a group of active spokesmen who had represented the Jewish cause in the weeks and months after liberation were deeply disappointed and left Germany. Others tried to resume their professional activities, businesses, or careers at the point where they had been forced to leave off in the 1930s. After the emigration of the majority of the Jewish displaced persons to Israel and to the United States, and after the founding of the two German states in 1949, only about 23,000 Jews remained registered members of the Jewish communities in West Germany. Most of the Jews in East Germany left for the West at the height of the Cold War and following anti-Semitic attacks disguised as political anti-Zionism in the early 1950s (in connection with the Slansky trial in Prague). About 1,200 registered members of congregations remained in East Germany.[25]

Concerning the German-Jewish history of assimilation, one has to add about 20,000–40,000 survivors of Jewish origin who did not become or remain members of the congregational communities but went on living in Germany as of the 1950s. All in all, they were a shadow part of German Jewry, often clinging to the remembrance of a lost past, and seldom successful in gaining a self-conscious identity. By their own definition they did not continue the history and tradition of German Jewry but saw themselves merely as Jews living in Germany. The term "living out of a suitcase" became a common self-definition. Until 1945, these Jews had survived on borrowed time, and now they were living on borrowed memory.

Following the early 1950s, some notable changes could be felt. More Jewish exiles returned, and since the 1960s, approximately 24,000 Israelis have come to live "temporarily" in West Germany; this has been followed since the late 1980s by a growing number of Russian Jews, probably numbering some 40,000 to date. Today, the Jewish community in united Germany is again growing and gaining a strong measure of diversity. But with the exception of Berlin and some other urban centers, the Jewish life we find is one outside of the defining parameters of a German-Jewish history before the Holocaust.

Breaking the Cordon Sanitaire: The Berlin Experience

For those Jewish returnees and survivors who, after 1945, lived in the Soviet Zone of occupation and later in the German Democratic Republic, official political antifascism shaped their Jewish identity to a certain extent and helped to replace the loss of a former German identity. Some rose to important positions in East German politics, society, and culture, and some became critics and opponents of the German version of Soviet communism and left the GDR. Others did not deal with politics at all and merely hoped that sometime there would be another and better Germany. Strange as it may sound, simply to remain or become a communist in the aftermath of the Holocaust and of exile and return could mean to preserve a very specific aspect of Jewish identity. Sometimes, when going through recollections of this group of German Jews, one is confronted with notions of anticapitalism that refer to Moses and the Scriptures and specific German-Jewish traditions of liberalism and socialism.[26]

Some of the children of these returnees became communists themselves and, since the 1970s or 1980s, have begun pondering the Jewish legacy of their families.[27] Some even saw Jewish traditions in family life, antifascist activities, or participation in the democratic changes as a natural and sufficient combination of the private and the public sphere: "To be Jewish in the context of my family," recalled one of this group, "always meant for me resistance, never religion or tradition."[28] Vincent von Wroblewsky, founder of a group of children of Jewish families in the period of German unification, considers the problematic identification with ideologies of emancipation as one of the main illusions of the Jewish return to East Germany.[29] Indeed, in retrospect it seems that for many GDR citizens of Jewish origin, antifascism became a common denominator that included many non-Jewish Germans; but this was a consensus that, for the Jewish side, tacitly included their own Jewishness.

In recent times, the media and some scholarly publications have referred to the reemergence of Jewish life in Germany.[30] On the one hand, this phenomenon is related to the developments described above; on the other hand, it is a very specific phenomenon almost exclusively found in East Berlin. In light of the downfall of communism, this phenomenon can also be seen in numerous East European urban centers.

Interviews with members of this generation show that in many families where the parents were active as party members, explicit acknowledgment of Jewish origin was very often taboo.[31] Children felt an immense pressure to be like other children, to belong, to accept the ideological truth even where it contradicted everyday

experience. "This whole construction GDR," recalls an inter-
viewee, "to me it was in a very specific way a unity of parents and
state."[32] Some, like the writer Chaim Noll, revolted against this
pressure by asserting negative responses to family and the GDR
authorities. Some children, on the other hand, recall that their
friends were usually from families with a similar background—
"Jewish kids, of course, and emigrants who had been in the West,"
mostly Mexico and England, which created a common bond.[33]
When the final crisis of the GDR began, and particularly after the
Wall came down, many members of these families returned to
their German-Jewish origins, as fragmented as this tradition may
have been.

Hence, what is reported in the media as a new emergence of
Jewish life in Germany is actually the return of this small group
of intellectuals and some other individuals to their Jewish roots
and traditions. It is the search for a Jewish identity in the midst
of a cultural crisis at the end of which history dissolved or dismissed all communist-based identities. But because of German
attitudes toward Jews, these individuals still considered a national
German identity as highly problematic. To put it differently, the
revival of Jewishness can be seen as the return of Jewish memory
across the East German cordon sanitaire. At the same time, however, it is also the rejection of a pure national German identity by
this generation. In general, their families had lived in the GDR for
political reasons and not due to a national identity. Against the
backdrop of the fading GDR and the rise of xenophobia and anti-
Semitism, questions of cultural identity became more relevant than
in the 1970s.

The fact that most of these persons of Jewish origin are intellectuals, however, contributes to their enjoying a relatively high public profile. One has to be careful, however, not to see the complicated process of redefining a cultural and intellectual identity by
a small group of Jewish Berliners as indicative of something much
larger, such as a new German-Jewish spring or the reemergence of
a real Jewish culture. On the one hand, we have here a small group
trying to create the façade of a Jewish milieu for the 1990s, echoing

the culturally rich Jewish life of Berlin before Nazism. On the other hand, their activities and publications address an almost exclusively German audience, for there is no vital or truly substantial Jewish social life to address. In the end, therefore, we confront here a highly illusionary phenomenon, the shadow of a shadow. By way of summary, I cite the words of a young Jewish scholar who recently returned from a short visit to Berlin and described his experience with the advocates of a new Jewish culture in these terms: "I had to show them how to make Matzebrei."[34]

Conclusion: Disremembering as a Form of Forgetting

One can clearly see today how the cordon sanitaire that was created in the Third Reich became an integral part of German culture after 1945. It was a forceful yellow-brown cord encircling German memory in both German states, keeping disturbing Jewish voices and recollections at a stark distance, letting them in only for short periods whenever it was morally unavoidable or whenever the international image of Germany was questioned. Public remembrance overlapped with periods of forgetting.

In this process, however, certain aspects of the Jewish memory of the Holocaust became relativized as they were integrated into German historical consciousness. Lately, and as a consequence of the important American movie *Schindler's List,* some topics, such as individual help by Germans for persecuted Jews, have been transformed into contemporary icons of German memory of the Third Reich. This again illustrates that the memory of the Holocaust is not static but is marked by changing forms, focus, textures, and narratives, all of which become implicated in the transfer of knowledge and feelings of memory itself to younger generations. This complex process, in turn, is not limited to scholarly debates but—in Germany and elsewhere—takes the form of emotional and intellectual battles being fought out across popular culture about the place of the Jews and the Holocaust in popular consciousness. Looking at German cinema and television, the media, museums, and monuments as the most influential forms of shaping and creating memory through historical representations,[35] it seems that today's specific modes of remembering increasingly become convenient forms of forgetting.[36] Even those aesthetic representations that try to counter contemporary forms of forgetting, as outstanding as they may be, often fail to cross the cordon sanitaire between German and Jewish recollections. And this is by no means only a question of knowledge, for there cannot be any doubt about the existence in Germany of widespread knowledge about the Holocaust. The complicated question is whether those who know really want to remember?

Obviously, the student of German and Jewish history has to ask self-critical questions about the temporality of the cordon sanitaire of memory. Almost everywhere it has become the fashion to dwell on memory, and when talking about memory the Western mind, these days, refers to World War II and to the Holocaust. Fifty years later, however, in all our scholarly discussions, are we not dealing more with the cultural ambiguities of disremembering than with human memory?

NOTES

1. Primo Levi, *The Drowned and the Saved* (London: Abacus Penguin Group, 1988) 17–18.

2. For a more general introduction to Jewish life in postwar Germany, see Erica Gurgauer, *Zwischen Erinnerung und Verdrängung-Juden in Deutschland nach 1945* (Reinbek bei Hamburg: Rowohlt Taschenbuch Verlag, 1993); Micha Brumlik, Doron Kiesel, Cilly Kugelmann, Julius Schoeps, eds., *Jüdisches Leben in Deutschland seit 1945* (Frankfurt am Main: Jüdischer Verlag, 1986); Frank Stern, *The Whitewashing of the Yellow Badge. Antisemitism and Philosemitism in Postwar Germany* (Oxford: Pergamon Press, 1992); see also Dagmar C. G. Lorenz and Gabriele Weinberger, eds., *Insiders and Outsiders. Jewish and Gentile Culture in Germany and Austria* (Detroit: Wayne State University Press, 1994).

3. See Meyer Levin, *In Search, an Autobiography* (New York: Horizon Press, 1950) 228–29.

4. Charlotte Holzer, *Erinnerungen* [unpub. ms] (Berlin 1966) archive of the author.

5. Office of Military Government, United States (OMGUS), report on Conditions of Jews in Berlin (15 September 1945), National Archives, Washington, D.C., Register Number 260, 44–45/6/9.

6. I owe this term to Elisabeth Domansky, Indiana University.

7. See Rivka Elkin, "The Survival of the Jewish Hospital in Berlin, 1938–1945," *Leo Baeck Yearbook* 38 (1993): 157–92; and Rivka Elkin, *"Das Jüdische Krankenhaus muß erhalten bleiben!" Das Jüdische Krankenhaus in Berlin zwischen 1938–1945* (Berlin: Freunde des Jüdischen Krankenhauses, 1993); on the deportation and survival of the children, see Rivka Elkin, "Kinder zur Aufbewahrung im Jüdischen Krankenhaus zu Berlin in den Jahren 1943–1945," *Tel Aviver Jahrbuch für deutsche Geschichte* 23 (1994): 247–73.

8. Levin, *In Search* 232.

9. Martin Riesenburger, *Das Licht verlöschte nicht. Ein Zeugnis aus der Nacht des Faschismus Predigten* (Berlin: Union-Verlag, 1984) 53–54.

10. Wolfgang Hildesheimer, *"Ich werde nun schweigen": Gespräch mit Hans Helmut Hillricks in der Reihe "Zeugen des Jahrhunderts,"* ed. Ingo Hermann (Göttingen: Lamuv Verlag, 1993) 51.

11. Hannah Arendt, Karl Jaspers, *Correspondence 1926–1969,* Complete Edition, ed. Lotte Köhler and Hans Sauer (New York: Harcourt Brace Jovanovich, 1992) 31–32.

12. Helmut Eschwege, "Die jüdische Bevölkerung der Jahre nach der Kapitulation Hitlerdeutschlands auf dem Gebiet der DDR bis zum Jahre 1953," in Siegfried Theodor Arndt, Helmut Eschwege, Peter Honigmann, Lothar Mertens, *Juden in der DDR. Geschichte, Probleme, Perspektiven* (Frankfurt: E. J. Brill, 1988) 65.

13. See Vincent von Wroblewsky, ed., *Zwischen Thora und Trabant. Juden in der DDR* (Berlin: Aufbau Taschenbuch Verlag, 1993) 11.

14. See Susann Heenen-Wolff, *Im Haus des Henkers. Gespräche in Deutschland* (Frankfurt am Main: Dvorah Verlag, 1992).

15. Hans Mayer, *Ein Deutscher auf Widerruf. Erinnerungen,* vol. 1 (Frankfurt am Main: Suhrkamp Verlag, 1982) 324.

16. See OMGUS, Judah Nadich, Report on Conditions of Jews in Berlin (15 September 1945), National Archives Register Number 260, and Nadich's book *Eisenhower and the Jews* (New York: 1953).

17. See the reports by Judah Nadich (note 16), 16–17.

18. See Eschwege, "Die jüdische Bevölkerung" 63–64.

19. See Angelika Königseder, Juliane Wetzel, *Lebensmut im Wartesaal. Die jüdischen DPs (Displaced Persons) im Nachkriegsdeutschland* (Frankfurt am Main: Fischer Taschenbuch Verlag, 1994).

20. Cited in Leonard Dinnerstein, *America and the Survivors of the Holocaust* (New York: Columbia University Press, 1982) 187.

21. Samuel Gringauz, "Our New German Policy and the DP's. Why Immediate Resettlement Is Imperative," *Commentary* 5 (1948): 509.

22. Julius Posner, *In Deutschland 1945-1946* (Jerusalem: n.p., 1947) 115-16.

23. Posner, *In Deutschland* 45-46.

24. Konrad Adenauer an Hertha Kraus (4/10/1945) in Gerhard Hirschfeld, Irina Renz, eds., *Besiegt und Befreit. Stimmen vom Kriegsende 1945* (Gerlingen: Bleicher Verlag, 1995) 72.

25. See Peter Maser, "Juden und Jüdische Gemeinden in der DDR bis in das Jahr 1988," *Tel Aviver Jahrbuch für deutsche Geschichte* 21 (1991): 393-426.

26. Wroblewsky, ed., *Zwischen Thora und Trabant* 45 (interview with Jochanaan Christoph Trilse-Finkelstein, born 1933).

27. In addition to the interviews cited, see Salomea Genin, "Wie ich in den Schoß der Familie zurückkehrte," in *Erinnerungen deutsch-jüdischer Frauen 1900-1990*, ed. Andreas Lixl-Purcell (Leipzig: Reclam Verlag, 1992) 423-24; and Wolfgang Herzberg, *Überleben heißt Erinnern. Lebensgeschichten deutscher Juden* (Berlin: Aufbau Verlag, 1990).

28. Wroblewsky, *Zwischen Thora und Trabant* 101 (interview with Sonja Beckmann, born 1952).

29. Wroblewsky, *Zwischen Thora and Trabant* 58.

30. See Sander L. Gilman and Karen Remmler, eds., *Reemerging Jewish Culture in Germany. Life and Literature Since 1989* (New York, London: New York University Press, 1994); Sander Gilman, *Jews in Today's German Culture* (Bloomington: Indiana University Press, 1995); introduction in Elena Lappin, ed., *Jewish Voices, German Words. Growing up Jewish in Postwar Germany and Austria* (North Haven: Catbird Press, 1995).

31. Wroblewsky, *Zwischen Thora und Trabant* 87 (interview with Irene Selle, born 1947).

32. Wroblewsky, *Zwischen Thora und Trabant* 133 (interview with Anetta Kahane, born 1954).

33. Wroblewsky, *Zwischen Thora und Trabant* 90 (interview with Irene Selle).

34. I owe this information to Jonathan Skolnik, Columbia University.

35. See James E. Young, *The Texture of Memory: Holocaust Memorials and Meaning* (New Haven: Yale University Press, 1993).

36. See Andreas Huyssen, *Twilight Memories: Marking Time in a Culture of Amnesia* (New York: Routledge, 1995).

TEN

A Lost War

World War II in Postwar German Memory

ELISABETH DOMANSKY

Stored and Re-stored Memories[1]

IN 1994, ONE YEAR BEFORE Germany was engulfed by the tidal wave of commemorations celebrating the fiftieth anniversary of the conclusion of World War II, Wülfrath, a small town in North Rhine-Westphalia, revisited its own "Zero Hour" (*Stunde Null*). The local historical museum organized an exhibition on the immediate postwar years based on the theme *Zeichen der Not* (Times of misery).[2] In preparation for the exhibition, articles in the local newspapers encouraged Wülfrath's citizens to contribute to the exhibition their own memorabilia of the years 1945 to 1948, which are commonly called the "postwar years" (*Nachkriegsjahre*).[3] The response was overwhelming. People brought to the museum photos, letters, clothes, and household items retrieved from drawers, boxes, and shelves in their basements and attics. Above all, they brought their memories.

These memories, which reemerged from storage places of their own, by far outnumbered the cultural artifacts of the postwar years.[4] Consequently, the eyewitnesses of those years, women and men who were children or young adults in 1945, were invited to attend two meetings where they could exchange their memories of the transition from the war to the postwar years. The first meeting was dominated by rather familiar anecdotes about occupation, the black market, and denazification. Everyone had a story to contribute about seeing, for the first time in one's life, black (American) soldiers, about wedding gowns made of parachute silk, about steel helmets that metamorphosed into stockpots. There were also many stories about the "denazification from below": Nazi paraphernalia were either burned, thrown away, buried in backyards, or hidden in the limestone quarries of the area. Ironically, many of those items were retrieved soon thereafter, to be given to American or British soldiers in exchange for badly needed cigarettes, *the* currency of the black market. While all the participants in the meeting agreed that times had been very hard—for some harder even than the war years—the leitmotif of all these stories was not so much suffering as pride in having endured and, finally, overcome hardship.[5]

From the perspective of a generation that experienced the so-called economic miracle in former West Germany, and that now lives rather comfortably on retirement payments, the immediate postwar years can be individually remembered as the beginning of one's own success story. The general outline of this success story was drawn by mainstream German politics in the 1950s and 1960s. Terms such as "Zero Hour," "Economic Miracle" and the famous slogan, "We have made it again!" (*Wir sind wieder wer!*) were key elements of the "master narrative" that was created in order to rally a majority of German society behind the effort of reconstructing West Germany, an effort that required substantial economic sacrifices from large parts of German society.[6] Since this effort was—all in all—a successful one, for individual Germans as well as for West German society in general, public, collective, and individual memories regarding the postwar years could easily converge. This official grand narrative was clearly recognizable in the way in which the participants in the discussion groups "restored" their own memories of "times of misery" by applying a finishing gloss to them—the gloss of a mythical new beginning that, through hard work, led to one's achievements as an individual and as a society.[7] A light mood prevailed during the first meeting.

The second meeting took a completely different turn. Prompted by questions about the difference between the postwar years and the war years, people—hesitatingly—began to remember and to relate stories of air raids, of low-level attacks, of expulsion and flight from the East and, less frequently, of front experiences.[8] Almost immediately it became clear that unlike the memories of the postwar years, these war memories were less encoded in safe narratives that would allow one to maintain the distanced perspective of the observer while relating them. People spoke with pauses, groping for words, trying not to be overwhelmed by feelings; some could not finish their stories. Several women broke down in tears when they began to talk about separated families and the loss of family members and friends—losses they thought they had long "come to terms" with. Old wounds were rediscovered under the scar tissue that had grown over them. It almost seemed as if the war was less "over" than the postwar years.[9]

The members of this second meeting also discovered or, in some cases, rediscovered that relating their war memories to each other was difficult not just because of their resurgent emotions but also because the war had left behind much more diverse and fragmented memories than the postwar years. Evidently, the war had been a much less unifying experience than the years immediately thereafter. Soldiers at the front seemed to have been in a very different war from the one that civilians experienced in cities that were subjected to air raids; soldiers who had been shipped early in the war to prisoner of war (POW) camps in the United States could not imagine what life in a Soviet POW camp had been like; evacuated citizens of big cities had seen a different war than inhabitants of the countryside to which evacuees were sent; to those who had lost their houses and homelands, the war meant something very different than it did to those who had been spared such losses. Above all, the war had been very different for those who had lost family members and friends than for those who had not.[10]

If the postwar memories of the members of these discussion groups could be described as a tapestry, a multipatterned but coherent narrative, then their war memories were much more like a puzzle, a puzzle, moreover, from which so many pieces were missing that the overall picture was no longer recognizable. There was not much evidence of a "master narrative" that would have allowed individual people to weave their own memories into a coherent, collective fabric; rather, the many different and fragmented war memories revealed traces of willed or "organized oblivion."[11] The word "repression" was used frequently during that second meeting. Some participants in the discussion group expressed their surprise at discovering that they obviously and unknowingly had "repressed" feelings of loss and pain. Others spoke about "repression" as a conscious strategy to keep pain at bay.

Ms. A.,[12] who had been seven years old in 1945, spoke about her reactions when she first read about the planned exhibition in the local newspapers. Those articles, she said, had reminded her of a cardboard box in her basement. The contents of that box, papers and photographs, had been collected by a nephew of hers who was close to her in age and who had passed the box on to her several years earlier. When Ms. A. remembered the box, she decided that she would bring it from the basement to her apartment so that she could "work all of that through." "And then," she said, "I started taking out just a few things at a time. But I could not work all of that through. The box was in our living room for three months. My husband used to sit on the couch and ask: 'What are you doing there?' And I continued to think, 'I'll work that through now, for myself.' But I just couldn't do it. The other day I took the box and carried it back into the basement. There it is now, in one of the farthest corners. You know," she said, "I know more or less what is in that box: letters from and photos of a brother who burned to death in Russia when he was nineteen years old; photos of another brother who died years later from the wounds he had received in the war; of the house in Pomerania that we lost. But I just could not bring myself to look at those things." And without pausing she continued: "I know that I am repressing something. But I want to. I am too afraid that if I don't, I might drown in a sea of sadness."[13]

This story of a woman who is torn between her desire to remember and her need to forget is not a uniquely "German" story. It has its counterparts in other countries. Haruko and Theodore Cook relate the story of an old man living in a small village in post–World War II Japan. This man keeps a box containing documents about his fallen brother's participation in what in Japan is still often called "the China Incident."[14] And although this old man does look at the box's contents, he "sees" and does not "see" them at the same time. He "sees" his brother as a war hero, but he does not "see" him as a soldier committing racist atrocities in Manchuria.[15]

There is hardly any image more indicative of what I would like to call the memory crisis[16] that resulted from the catastrophe of World War II than these boxes, of which there must be millions in all the former belligerent nations. While these boxes preserve mementos of lives and places that were loved, they also contain the evidence of their irretrievable loss. These boxes are not shrines at which one could mourn, however, as both of these stories aptly illustrate. Rather, they seem to be postwar reproductions of Pandora's box, the opening of which might unleash unspeakable horror or unbearable sadness. The keepers of these boxes know only too well what is also preserved in them: the unasked and unanswered question of why the lives and places that used to be present in their lives are no longer there.[17]

I would like to argue in this essay that, more than anything else, it is this huge void, this silence that engulfs World War II, that was repeatedly restored and re-stored in those boxes in the long aftermath of the war. Since these boxes were closed time and again and returned to the farthest and darkest corners of basements or attics, their contents could not and cannot be "worked through."[18] To this day the taboo of remembering and mourning the catastrophe of World War II—World War II as an event that cannot be separated from either "Auschwitz" or "Hiroshima" but that cannot be reduced to what those names have come to signify, either—is firmly in place, and not just in Germany.[19] The need for mourning still exists, however, and thus those boxes containing the remains of loved ones cannot be thrown away. They stay with their keepers as their own private memorials of World War II: black boxes of memory filled with mementos wrapped in silence.[20]

But does this silence really exist as I claim? If one scans the body of memoirs, diaries, oral histories, documentaries, exhibitions, and scholarly books on World War II and the Holocaust, which has been growing rapidly since the late 1970s, the answer would have to be negative, at least at first. The manufacture of these "histories" and "memories" seems to have been progressing in quantum leaps; the approach of every remotely "memorable" anniversary sets yet another frenzied production cycle of the new memory industry into motion. The production of memory, history—and of historians, as Jane Kramer has recently remarked—is clearly booming in Germany, and perhaps more so than elsewhere in Europe.[21] This production and—seemingly—instant consumption of the products of this memory industry have led many observers inside and outside Germany to conclude that by now Germany has done more to confront its recent past than any other nation involved in World War II.[22]

Such conclusions, however, usually confuse "knowing" with "remembering," conflate "memory" and "historical consciousness" and, moreover, rarely distinguish between public, collective, and individual memory and remembrance. Opinion polls, oral history projects, historical studies of memory and psychoanalytic explorations of remembrance conclusively show, however, that what people "know" is not necessarily what they "remember." And people who attend public commemorations or visit museum exhibits may go there for cathartic or nostalgic experiences rather than for the purpose of remembering.[23] Moreover, what individuals remember in certain contexts or at certain periods of time can differ quite considerably from what they remember under other circumstances. Their ability to remember is inextricably linked to "milieus of memory," which are formed in families, classes, neighborhoods and nations and which either support, suppress, distort or even destroy the potential of other collectives and of individuals to remember.[24] It is the public and collective memories of World War II that were offered to and created by German society after the war and their limiting and/or liberating potential for individual memories with which I am concerned in this essay. I will start my exploration of the succession and competition of various post–World War II memory milieus by comparing the remembrance of the Second World War in Germany to that of the First. Through this, I hope to make audible the silence about World War II, which looms behind all the noise that has been produced about this war in recent years.

A Remembered and a Forgotten War

World War II was not only the second war of global proportion for which Germany was responsible in this century; it was also the second world war that Germany lost. The outcome of World War II, however, was fundamentally different from that of World War I. While Germany had emerged from the bloodbath of World War I defeated but with its national boundaries and its national sovereignty virtually intact, it ceased to exist as a sovereign nation state at the end of World War II. Although the period of foreign occupation lasted only for a few years, the German "nation state" remained dismantled — "temporarily," as revisionist German politicians liked to emphasize, or "forever," as some former victims of German aggression wanted to believe. Germany emerged from the ruins of World War II not as one but as two separate German states. Moreover, these two German states, which would eventually regain full national sovereignty, were firmly integrated into and contained by the ideologically antagonistic power blocs that confronted each other in the ever-escalating, (not so) Cold War.

The radically different outcomes of this century's two World Wars engendered radically different conditions for remembering these two wars in Germany. While German society could create its own "sovereign" memories of the war despite its defeat, the politics of memory after World War II were, first and foremost, the politics of the victorious powers.[25] Reeducation strategies in East and West Germany were very different, but they pursued a common goal: the thorough denazification of German society. This included by necessity the destruction of the Third Reich's politics of memory and their replacement by radically new ways of making sense of and remembering World War II. As a result of this reeducation in both Germanys, the majority of post–World War II German society accepted Germany's responsibility for the outbreak of the war as well as for Germany's military defeat. There was no resurrection of any variation of the "stab-in-the-back" legend.[26]

While this difference in "coming to terms" with a lost war does not seem to be very surprising in light of the different outcomes of the two wars, another difference cannot be explained so easily. After World War I the remembrance of the war played a crucial, although ambiguous, role in the postwar construction of a new German national identity. For the reconstruction of Germany's national identity after 1945 and for the integration of the two German states into their respective alliance systems, World War II seems to have been insignificant. Post–World War I German society—very much like the societies of the other former belligerent nations—defined itself as a post-*war* society, a society fundamentally altered, shaped, and marked by the war. Post–World War II German society—and the same is true for other countries—defined itself as a *post*-war society, a society fundamentally altered, shaped, and marked not by the war but by its aftermath.[27] In both cases, this is true for the defeated as well as for the victorious nations. To be sure, for the Soviet Union and for the United States, it was the Second, not the First, World War that was a defining moment of their national identity in the twentieth century. For both, however, this had profound consequences on the domestic, but not on the foreign political stage. Once the war was over, both states treated their former enemies not as foes but as friends.[28] Consequently, for the first two decades after the foundation of the two German states and the division of the world into two power blocs, domestic politics in Europe and international politics in the world at large focused exclusively on the "results" of the war: the necessity of Germany's and Europe's political, social, and economic reconstruction, the consequences of Germany's separation into two states and, above all, the fighting of the Cold War.

This political preoccupation of the defeated and the victorious powers with the immediate postwar necessities can perhaps be explained by referring to the material and ideological conditions at the end of the war which required a concentration on the present rather than on the past. Another factor, however, does not allow for so simple a conclusion. Except for the brief period of the immediate postwar years, World War II produced no body of literature, artwork, or film in Germany that came close, either in depth or scope, to the outpouring of artistic and popular imagination that had been fueled by World War I.[29] It is true, the often quoted "Clear-Cutting Literature" (*Kahlschlagliteratur*), "Rubble Literature" (*Trümmerliteratur*), and "Rubble Film" (*Trümmerfilm*) were important German attempts to expose and explore Germany's catastrophic experiment at creating an Aryan racist, supremacist global order. However, these literary and visual explorations could thrive only in the regulated but, at the same time, protected climate of Allied-controlled cultural politics in the immediate postwar years. After the foundation of the two German states in 1949, critical films, short stories, plays, and novels could no longer compete with the literary and visual products of the entertainment industry in West Germany.[30]

Moreover, most artists working in the aftermath of World War II were inspired by this war in a very different way than those artists writing, painting, or creating films after the First World War. For many writers after World War I, the war had been the defining moment that caused them to begin their writing careers, whereas many of those writers dealing with World War II in the immediate postwar years and in the Federal Republic, such as Heinrich Böll or Günter Grass, had already been writers before the war or had intended to become writers independently of the war.[31] In addition, in post–World War II literature, film, and painting, attempts to come to terms with the war were, more often than not, over-shadowed by attempts to understand Nazism. Günter Grass's *The Tin Drum*, to name but one example, addresses, albeit in its own way, the problem of war in the context of National Socialism.[32] And Anselm Kiefer's paintings, although they explore the theme of scorched earth and devastation, are concerned with the uses and abuses of myth *by* human beings in history and politics.[33] Otto Dix's and George Grosz's paintings of war cripples and dead bodies, on the other hand, explore the brutality and destructive potential of the material conditions of war and their effects *on* human be-ings.[34] And even a film like *Die Brücke* (The bridge), one of the few box-office successes of post–World War II antiwar films in Germany, is as much a film about German male youth's indoctri-nation into Nazism as it is a film about the senselessness of war.[35] After the Second World War, there did not seem to be much left to say about war itself that had not already been said after the First. Consequently, to this day *the* antiwar novel and film every child in Germany knows is Erich Maria Remarque's *All Quiet on the Western Front*. His equally remarkable novel about World War II, *A Time to Live, a Time to Die*, is virtually unknown, as is Douglas Sirk's film version of 1958.[36] Moreover, the few early postwar at-tempts to produce antiwar films remained isolated and could not draw huge crowds. Audiences wanted to be entertained, not edu-cated, and flocked instead to the rather shallow box-office hits of the 1950s and 1960s. Quite openly and frankly, people expressed their desire to forget, a desire that almost assumed the status of a new "civil right."[37]

Even war monuments speak a different language after World War II than they did after World War I. While there are still quite a number of such monuments erected every year, they tend to commemorate the dead of both wars, thus conflating the two wars into one gigantic catastrophe. Moreover, in most cases, as at *Die Neue Wache* in Berlin, war victims and persecutors are indiscrim-inately remembered together, as if united in death.[38] In other cases, the names of those who died in World War II are simply added to World War I memorials, as if World War II had somehow been an afterthought to that first world war.[39] The way in which the dead were treated may well constitute the most telling difference in the remembrance of the two World Wars. While a substantial portion, if not the majority, of post–World War I German society lived with the constant presence of the "army of the dead," post–World War II German society lived and lives radically segregated from its war dead—soldiers and so-called civilian dead alike.[40] Fallen soldiers were not invited to come and dwell among the living. There did not seem to be any way of constructing post–World War II German society as a society indebted to the legacy of these dead. On the contrary, the legacy of the dead, forever tainted by the stain of National Socialism, had to be forgotten.[41] Consequently, even the so-called civilian dead were hastily burnt and buried in mass graves. The ruins of bombed buildings, which effectively constituted mass graves for many people, were quickly dismantled and replaced. In fact, West German—but not only West German—architecture and city planning in the 1950s and 1960s can be regarded as major contributions to forgetting the war. It was quite literally buried under the asphalt and concrete of the "modern" German cities of the fifties and sixties.[42]

This exclusion of the dead from post–World War II German society and the radical focus on the living indicate an almost desperate attempt to lose the war a second time, not militarily, but from one's memory and history. This desire certainly reflects the persistence of the "inability to mourn" that Alexander and Margarete Mitscherlich analyzed so poignantly almost thirty years ago.[43] The similarities in the post–World War II politics of memory among former opponents suggest, however, that the "inability to mourn" is not solely a German post–World War II deficiency. While feelings of guilt and the denial of German society's implication in the National Socialist regime certainly contribute to explaining German postwar politics of memory, they cannot explain them sufficiently, as the existence of similar strategies of forgetting in other countries demonstrates. What is it that unites the victors and losers of World War II in their politics of memory even after a war of such dimensions and such destruction? I shall try to answer this question by exploring some of the continuities and discontinuities in the "milieus of memory" that were formed in Germany, but not solely by Germany, in the five decades after the war.

Milieus of Memory and Oblivion

The Displacement of World War II by the Cold War

The remembrance of World War II began, of course, not with its end, but with its beginning. War memories glorifying Germany's heroic battles were produced almost instantly, as were books outside of Germany written by German refugees and writers in other countries, that either celebrated or attacked German politics.[44] However, one of the earliest strategies for remembering World War II was implemented in Germany as early as 1934. In that year, the National Socialist government declared the fifth Sunday before Easter to be *the* national day of commemorating the dead of World War I. The choice of this day followed numerous, yet ultimately unsuccessful, attempts by private organizations and public institutions during the Weimar Republic to create a single "National Day of Mourning" (*Volkstrauertag*) that would be celebrated throughout Germany. The intended meaning of such a day was changed quite radically, however, when it was finally implemented by the National Socialist government, which named this day "Heroes' Commemoration Day" (*Heldengedenktag*).[45] Mourning, which had been the main emphasis of the many Weimar initiatives in favor of a day for commemorating the dead of World War I, was now to be replaced by pride in Germany's heroes, whose example young people were encouraged and expected to follow. Moreover, those heroes no longer consisted only of the dead of World War I, who were retroactively incorporated into the ranks of fighters for National Socialism, but they now also included the dead who had gladly sacrificed their lives after the war in order to ensure the victory of National Socialism over its enemies. In 1940, "Heroes' Commemoration Day" was officially expanded to include the dead of World War II. In its own way these politics of memory incorporated World War I into the history of the Third Reich and, thus, created a connection between that war during which the National Socialist Movement was born, and the next war, which it fought in order to fulfill its historical—and historic—mission.[46]

With the complete failure of this mission in 1945 and Germany's subsequent occupation by the Allied powers, such remembrance strategies also came to an end. Ironically, the very chaos and uncertainty over Germany's future initially allowed for a plurality of public collective memory strategies that would not be achieved again until more than two decades after the foundation of the two German states. As most political groups—including the reconstituted parties and trade unions—reconsidered and rewrote their party platforms and political strategies in the immediate postwar years with the intention of preventing a recurrence of National Socialism, they were equally devoted to preventing another war from ever originating in Germany again. There can be no doubt that among the members of political organizations and also in the population at large, their diverse but very fresh memories of the war resulted in a strong, albeit often merely affective, pacifist and antimilitarist orientation.[47]

To be sure, there were also tendencies in the German population toward refusing responsibility for "Hitler's" war and for National Socialism in general.[48] But it was Allied occupational politics—in all of the occupation zones—that strengthened and favored these "politics of denial" at the expense of more conscious and conscientious politics. As far as the Soviet Zone was concerned, Stalinist doctrine, which differentiated between "Hitler" and the German population, shaped the memory of World War II. In addition, war was seen as an inherent element of capitalism, and thus the only lesson to be learned from any particular war was that of the destructive nature of the system in which it had originated. The creation of a socialist German state consequently seemed to preclude the resurgence of National Socialism and the initiation of another war by that state. World War II was "remembered" later on in East Germany, but as a different war from the one that had actually taken place. It was seen as the war that brought about the final triumph of socialism in East Germany. The celebration of International Labor Day, May 1, with military parades signified this connection most clearly.[49]

The earliest reeducation efforts of the Western Allies reveal similar patterns of thought about the nature of World War II and of the Nazi regime. The Nuremberg trials as well as the many local and regional attempts of Allied authorities to confront the German population with the regime's atrocities were all implicitly based on the assumption that "the Nazis" and the German population had not been identical and that World War II had been "Hitler's" war.[50] The course of denazification politics aided such messages, if only unintentionally. This was not only a result of denazification's quick conclusion, as has often been observed, but of denazification strategies themselves. The chosen classification, which was based on differentiated levels of implication in the regime and the assumed existence of non-Nazis, realistic though it was, encouraged those parts of German society that wanted to draw a sharp line between the "Nazis" and the "Germans," with the result that an ever-increasing number of "Germans" was included on one side and an ever-decreasing number of "Nazis" on the other.[51] Moreover, by singling out the Holocaust as Nazism's worst crime and later forcing West Germany to accept Germany's responsibility for the Holocaust, which resulted in West German "restitution" payments to Israel, the West, and most notably the United States, contributed to the separation of the Holocaust from the history of World War II and to World War II's displacement in memory by the Holocaust, as I will argue later in this essay.

Since the new political order that was implemented by the Allies in the western part of Germany could not, as in the East, be constructed as the final triumph of democratic traditions in German history but was seen as a gift brought to Germany from the outside after the war, the war had even less room in the memory of West Germany than it had in East Germany. The West German state did not commemorate the war's end on any official holiday. Moreover, instead of facing the catastrophic legacies of World War II by creating a new national commemoration day, "Heroes' Commemoration Day" was "denazified" into "National Day of Mourning" (*Volkstrauertag*). In 1950 and 1951 it was still celebrated on the fifth Sunday before Easter, but in order to break with the day's National Socialist tradition more thoroughly, it was moved in 1952 to the second Sunday before the first Sunday of Advent. This day was now devoted to the remembrance of the dead of World War I, World War II, and the victims of Nazi politics.[52] The return to a commemoration practice of the Weimar Republic contributed to blurring not only the distinction between those two very different wars but also to that between the victims and perpetrators of World War II.

While the Allied politics of memory in East and West were certainly informed by a profound lack of understanding as to the fundamentally different nature of World War I and World War II, the willingness not to "understand" the second war better was further exacerbated by several other factors.[53] The most immediately accessible of these factors is, clearly, the Cold War. The quickly escalating ideological conflict provided a powerful rationale for both superpowers to turn their spheres of influence into allies. It was not so much Germany's unconditional surrender in 1945 that ended its history as a fascist and belligerent nation as the foundation, in 1949, of the two German states. Firmly integrated into their respective alliance systems, those separate Germanys retroactively became members of the former antifascist coalition, even though this coalition now existed in two antagonistic blocs.

With the help of the Soviet Union, East Germany reconstructed itself as the state that finally represented all of the democratic traditions of German history, traditions that had always been opposed to Nazism and that had been temporarily defeated in the

Third Reich. East Germany and the Soviet Union could therefore safely reject any responsibility of East Germany for World War II, as they could, for the same reasons, reject any responsibility of East Germany for the Holocaust. Both World War II and the Holocaust belonged to the prehistory of West Germany and could, therefore, be forgotten in the East.[54] West Germany, on the other hand, by joining the anticommunist alliance of the West, retroactively also became a member of the former antifascist alliance. This was a result of the broad acceptance by Western policymakers of the doctrine of totalitarianism, according to which communism and fascism were but two faces of the same type of totalitarian dictatorship. For West Germany, consequently, the state of East Germany was the true heir of the Germany that had been responsible for the war and for the Holocaust. And while West Germany, under pressure from its Western allies, especially the United States, nevertheless had to shoulder the burden of the Holocaust's legacy, this seemed to be an unfair, but unavoidable, price to pay for West Germany's deliverance from its responsibility for its role in World War II.[55] In their different and yet very similar ways, both German states and both Cold War alliance systems burdened the respective "other" German state and its allies with the responsibility for World War II while forgetting "their" Germany's part in it. Germany's destruction in 1945 notwithstanding, the swiftness and smoothness with which both German states and both ideological power blocs turned away from the past and toward the present cannot be understood without taking the Cold War into consideration. This war is the main reason why the "Postwar" was the birthplace and the new location of the two Germanys.

While the East's politics of memory regarding World War II allowed individuals, at least those who identified with the new system, to make sense of their own individual losses in World War II as contributions to the victory of socialism, a similar strategy could not be pursued in West Germany. Memories of the war and the need for individual and collective mourning existed there, too, however. Publicly, they were expressed most clearly in persistent and widespread pacifist attitudes that outlasted the political decisions in favor of West Germany's membership in the European Defense Community in 1952 and in NATO in 1954. The endurance of these pacifist attitudes is all the more remarkable, when one considers the fact that Allied and West German politics, both of which were characterized by rigid anticommunism, early on tried to discredit pacifism by identifying it with communism. Even in 1958, for example, despite massive government propaganda, 52 percent of the West German population were in favor of strikes as means of preventing the Bundeswehr's equipment with tactical nuclear weapons.[56] Such attitudes were an embarrassment to the German government headed by Chancellor Konrad Adenauer; its firm commitment to the politics of "Western Integration" (*Westintegration*) was, by necessity, linked to strategies of forgetting West Germany's role in World War II. However, these officially pursued politics of "organized oblivion" could neither completely suppress individual and collective memories of World War II and the resulting pacifist attitudes, nor could they eliminate the need for mourning. Instead, remembering and mourning were transferred onto the Cold War. Not long after the conclusion of World War II, Germany's "unjust" and "unjustified" separation and loss of territories came to be seen in West Germany, as well as by some of its Western Allies, as results not of World War II but of the Cold War. Even the last POWs to return from the Soviet Union in 1955 were welcomed home more as prisoners released from POW camps of that still raging war than from those of World War II.[57]

In West Germany, the transference and displacement of memory from World War II to the Cold War became most obvious in the German government's choice of an official national holiday and of the commemoration practices attached to that day. The question of finding a meaningful day for mourning the dead of World War II was never officially addressed and, thus, German society simply returned to Weimar commemoration practices for the dead of World War I. In 1953, however, the West German government declared June 17, the day of the failed workers' revolt in East Germany of that same year, to be West Germany's official national holiday. This day was supposed to be one of public, collective, and individual remembering and mourning. There were ceremonies and speeches in parliament, conventions of refugee and expellee organizations, and commemorations in every school. Citizens of major German cities participated in silent marches (*Schweige-märsche*), torchlight processions, and lit, especially at the border between East and West Berlin, memorial fires (*Mahnfeuer*). Certainly, it was Cold War revisionism that provided the impetus and framework for the choice of this national holiday. Its celebration, however, bore a striking resemblance to memorial services.[58]

Those who were to be commemorated and mourned were the ones who had lost their lives in 1953 trying to fight (communist) dictatorship. "Our brothers and sisters" in the "Soviet Zone of Occupation," who, though still alive, nevertheless saw their lives waning away under the yoke of political oppression, were also to be included in one's thoughts. In addition, among West Germans, one needed to remember all those who had lost their homelands to which they longed to return. It is not difficult to discover beneath this veneer the picture of German society during the Third Reich, a picture that German politicians, historians, writers, and journalists collectively painted during the 1950s and 1960s. It was the image of a nation that, conquered and occupied by invading National Socialists, had found its life ruthlessly consumed by this brutal "alien" dictatorial regime while longing to have its homeland, the "true Germany," back. Such fantasies were most clearly expressed in the concept of "inner emigration" (*innere Emigration*), in which so many Germans claimed to have lived during the Third Reich.[59]

The mood at the commemorative events on June 17 was always a somber one. Speeches emphasized loss and suffering, and the musical pieces of choice were written in minor keys. Even more evocative of commemorations of the dead, however, was a practice recommended for remembering the "brothers and sisters" in the East on another occasion, on Christmas Eve. Three days before Christmas Eve of 1952, in his annual speech on this occasion, the mayor of West Berlin, Ernst Reuter, appealed to all of the city's citizens to display a lit candle in one of their windows on Christmas Eve. This candle was meant to express the remembrance of the "POWs who had not yet returned and of all those between the Elbe and the Oder who were being held prisoner by an inhuman regime in its KZ's (concentration camps [sic!]) and prisons."[60] In 1959, this practice was extended to all of West Germany.[61] This lighting of candles is strikingly reminiscent of the Catholic custom of celebrating All Saints Day. On this day, votive candles are lit on the graves of deceased family members and friends.[62] In the 1950s and 1960s, West German society replaced the image of Germans in the Third Reich in public commemorative ceremonies and practices with the image of East Germans in a state that was considered to be a gigantic concentration camp and prison, and substituted its own losses — of actual lives, of years in the lives of those who survived the war and of "home"—with the losses of East Germans and the loss of East Germany. By so doing, West German society engaged in an act of displacing and displaced memory and mourning.

The Displacement of World War II by the Holocaust and the Third World War

At the end of the 1960s, West German society began to experience a stability that brought some semblance of "normality" to the lives of people who had not known "normal" lives for almost three decades. Most refugees and expellees had settled into West German society, and more and more people began to reap the fruits of what has become known as the "economic miracle."[63] Not coincidentally, it was at this moment in time when a younger generation became dissatisfied with German society's exclusive focus on the present and, consequently, turned back toward the past in order to discover the roots of its present disenchantment. The protest of the so-called generation of 1968 has often been linked to the political, economic, and social stability that, by comparison with its parents and grandparents, this generation was privileged to experience. What contemporaries and historians of the cultural revolution of 1968 tend to overlook, however, is the fact that it was precisely this protest generation that had experienced the terror of war and the turmoil of the immediate postwar years as young children. While this generation consciously sought to explore its parents' (National Socialist) past, it simultaneously, although mostly subconsciously, tried to come to terms with its own traumatic experiences of war-related loss and death.[64] The formative role that the Vietnam war played for this generation's political socialization cannot simply be explained by an assumed general anti-Americanism of the New Left but should be seen in the context of the traumatic memories that this widely publicized war must have evoked among many members of this peer group.[65] The ensuing cultural revolution of 1968 had a profound influence on West German society's political structure, its value system, and its self-perception. It also radically changed the memory milieu in West Germany by questioning not only the dominant consensus about the Nazi past but, consequently, also the consensus about the international order of the Cold War.

The critical inquiry—the famous "Hinterfragen"—into the existing domestic and global order, an inquiry shared by the younger generation of other nations—led to two fundamental reorientations in the German politics of memory. First, the goals of West German foreign policy changed and, second, subsequently and consequently, the Cold War was replaced as the locus of displaced memories of World War II by the Holocaust and by the Third World War. The "New Policy toward the East" (Neue Ostpolitik) that was pursued by the Social Democratic/Liberal coalition governments, which, beginning in 1969, ended the long era of Christian Democratic/Liberal rule in West Germany, strove to end the period of revisionist foreign policy and to acknowledge the existing postwar order. This foreign policy complemented the previous politics of "Western Integration" in a more logical way than was acknowledged at the time by conservative politicians. It was also an expression of the growing willingness of a majority in German society to confront its National Socialist past more honestly and to accept Germany's division and loss of territories as the result of

Nazi Germany's aggression in World War II rather than as a consequence of the Cold War.[66] This new orientation toward renouncing revisionist foreign policy claims sharpened the focus of German politics on the postwar era and the results of the war even more, however. With the official recognition of Poland's western border and of the existence of East Germany as a sovereign state, the chapter of World War II in the book of German history seemed to have found its final version.

It is not surprising that the demise of Cold War concepts as guiding principles of West Germany's foreign policy also rendered obsolete the Cold War as the locus of displaced memories and displaced mourning for all those who supported overcoming Cold War attitudes. The resulting pluralism in West German politics of memory did not make collective and individual remembering and mourning easier, however; it simply imposed a different set of restrictions on them. As a result of the cultural revolution of 1968 and the subsequent changes in the Federal Republic's political climate, West German society became more politicized and polarized than it had been in the 1950s and 1960s. This came to bear directly on German politics of memory. The remembrance of World War II was increasingly used as one of the major weapons in the ideological battles of the 1970s and 1980s. Conservatives styled themselves guardians of the memory of Germany's loss of territories and loss of lives during the period of flight and expulsion from Eastern and Central Europe, a memory that had to be protected against all those who were willing to "sell out" Germany. To those on the Left, anyone who insisted on remembering and mourning this particular part of the history of World War II was a Cold Warrior unable to learn the true lessons of the past.[67] In both camps, there was little room for and little understanding of the human need to remember and to mourn, a need that transcends the realm of politics of memory. Thus, as Margarete Mitscherlich has recently argued, the "inability to mourn" was not overcome.[68] Instead, the Cold War was replaced as the locus of displaced memory and mourning by two new, complementary, yet separate loci of memory and mourning.

While originally West Germany's first government under Chancellor Konrad Adenauer had admitted Germany's responsibility for the Holocaust only under much foreign pressure, at the end of the 1970s, a growing segment of West German society gradually began to accept Germany's responsibility for the Holocaust on its own. This new openness toward remembering the Holocaust had two major sources. On the one hand, it was firmly rooted in the younger generation's rejection of mainstream politics of memory regarding the period of the Third Reich. The broad acceptance that these new and initially controversial politics of memory ultimately found in German society stemmed, on the other hand, from West Germany's realization that it would enhance its international reputation as a reliable member of the Western alliance system by embracing them. However, while the long overdue acknowledgment of Germany's responsibility for the Holocaust marked a decisive departure from older strategies of denial, it also constituted a new one. The main focus of the many books, documentary films, local history projects, and museum exhibits that explored the fate of the Jews under National Socialism was the lost "Jewish contributions to German culture." Remembered and mourned was not the loss of German, let alone European, Jewry, but the destruction of what came to be seen as a central part of *German* culture by National Socialism.[69] Thus, in the post–Cold War climate of the 1970s and 1980s, Jews and Jewish culture replaced East Germans and East Germany as metaphors for remembering and mourning the suffering and death inflicted upon Germany by National Socialism. The "war against the Jews" came to stand for National Socialism's "war against Germany."[70] It is not coincidental, in my opinion, that commemoration ceremonies for the Holocaust became increasingly more frequent in West Germany at precisely that moment when the number of commemoration ceremonies on the occasion of June 17 decreased and when more and more West Germans began to view this day as just another holiday. Moreover, the practices used for commemorations of "Kristallnacht" and other occasions—speeches, musical recitals, minutes of silence, wakes with candles—were very similar to those used for June 17 in the 1950s and 1960s.[71] The Holocaust had clearly replaced the Cold War as the locus for displaced memory and mourning.

It did not do so alone, however. The simultaneous development of a second locus of displaced memory and mourning resulted from the fact that the Holocaust and World War II, while not identical, were nevertheless inextricably linked with one another. The "war against the Jews" had, after all, been waged by Germans not *against* but *for* Germany, and it had been part of a larger war that aimed at establishing a new racist and supremacist global order. In order to ensure that the Holocaust could indeed serve as the new locus of displaced memory and mourning instead of evoking uncomfortable questions of responsibility and agency, it had to be separated from the history of World War II. The German insistence on the "uniqueness" and "inexplicability" of the Holocaust,[72] which thereby removes it from the context of the Third Reich as well as that of the Second World War, serves, more often than not, precisely this purpose.

This artificial separation of the Holocaust and the war in turn allowed the memories of World War II to be functionalized for alternative politics. The nuclear protest movements of the 1970s and 1980s, which were directed against the civilian use of nuclear energy as well as against the stationing, in Germany, of short-range nuclear weapons—the famous Pershing Missiles—rediscovered the remembrance of World War II as a useful political tool. Members and supporters of these movements realized that "mobilized" memories of the war against the "civilian" population in Germany were powerful allies in their fight to prevent "the" Third World War from happening.[73] The Third World War, consequently, became the second locus of displaced memories and mourning. The powerful images of the Third World War's scope of destruction and its impact on civilian societies allowed many Germans of the older and younger generations to remember and to speak about the trauma of World War II openly and publicly, while seeming to speak about a future war's "remembered" destructive impact on Germany and the world at large. Thus, for the first time in postwar German politics, there was an opportunity to create a strand of

public and collective memories of World War II that enabled individuals to integrate their own memories into a *grand* narrative.
This connection between the Third and the Second World Wars
enabled West German society to enter that stage of the mourning
process where action is once again possible. It also explains the
mass support that the antinuclear energy and peace movements
found among Germans of different generations and different political opinions.

Because of this mass mobilization of war memories, the number
of publications of memoirs, oral histories, and local studies of the
war years has mushroomed since the 1980s.[74] Many of these publications openly connect the need—and the urgency—to remember World War II with the political and moral obligation to prevent
the Third World War.[75] This reinterpretation of World War II is
reminiscent of post–World War I strategies for mourning the dead,
whereby individual and collective death was seen as a
(self)sacrifice that would ensure the future of the living.[76] Precisely
because of the interrelatedness of World War II and the Holocaust,
however, this attempt to remember World War II as the war that
endowed Germany with the specific and special mission of preventing a "nuclear Holocaust" can only be successful if the legitimacy of such claims is not challenged by questions about German
responsibility and agency during the war.[77] Consequently, most
memories of the "World War III–World War II" complex depict
German society at war as a community of suffering and not as a
society that inflicted war and suffering on others. Therefore, memories of everyday life on the homefront by far outnumber those of
the front.[78] There can be no doubt that the displacement of memories of World War II by the Holocaust and the Third World War
constitutes a strategy of selective remembering and forgetting in
the context of each of these displaced memory complexes. This is
not the whole picture, however. The very gap between them not
only separates these two events, it links them at the same time.
Nothing demonstrates this more clearly than the events of the year
1985 in West Germany.

In the 1980s the so-called "Wende," that is, the return to power of a Christian Democratic/Liberal coalition government in West Germany in 1982, began to challenge the new memory milieu. The politics of memory that were pursued in particular by Chancellor Helmut Kohl and a growing number of neoconservative intellectuals aimed, in my opinion, at reinstituting the displacement of World War II by the Cold War, albeit by a much more refined Cold War. There can be no doubt that the two events that have come to be identified with 1985, the *Historikerstreit* (Historians' Debate) and "Bitburg," both constitute attempts to once again eliminate the Holocaust from remembrance. The Historikerstreit revolved around and resulted from the efforts of a group of ultraconservative historians to remove the Holocaust from the context of the Third Reich and, thus, World War II. The Holocaust, or so they argued, was not part of German history but of an international history of violence in the nineteenth and twentieth centuries, which, an entity unto itself, developed separately from the context of the societies in which this violence occurred.[79]

The same strategy, although pursued in a less explicit way, informed the ceremony at the military cemetery at Bitburg where German soldiers who fell during World War II are buried. During this ceremony, President Reagan and Chancellor Helmut Kohl held hands as a gesture of reconciliation between former opponents.[80] Their joint attempt to solidify the myth of the "ordinary" Wehrmacht soldier who had had nothing to do with National Socialist politics of annihilation during World War II, and who had been an honorable opponent of the American soldiers fighting in the war, was also rooted in an attempt to eliminate the Holocaust from the history of that war. The effort at the Bitburg ceremony, as well as by ultraconservative historians in the Historikerstreit, to redraw the lines of German history without the Holocaust failed, however. The heated public debate that was sparked by both of these events showed that this return to 1950s' strategies of remembering would meet with fierce resistance. This resistance can only be explained by the fact that displacing the memory of World War II onto both the Holocaust *and* the Third World War preserves the memory of the connection between World War II and the Holocaust. It is true, as argued above, that both events are remembered *separately*. It is also true, however, that thereby *both* of them are remembered. Thus, the dominant politics of memory of the 1980s prevented the memory of responsibility and agency from sinking into complete oblivion.

The collapse of the Eastern Bloc and Germany's reunification have created a new configuration for German and international politics of memory in the 1990s. The memory of World War II is changing and being changed in countries such as Russia, Japan, France, and the United States. In Germany, there are groups who advocate the reconstruction of Dresden's Frauenkirche as a symbol of German suffering in World War II. There are also groups, however, who instigate public debate on the Wehrmacht's atrocities during World War II or who participate in initiatives to establish a Holocaust memorial in Germany.[81] It is obvious that, in some instances, the desire to create memorial sites or monuments constitutes an effort to deposit—and, thus, abandon—objectified memories at locations that are not so much sites of memory and mourning as they are waste sites of memory.[82] There are also honest attempts to remember, however.[83] It is not easy to predict the outcome of the many battles that are currently being fought in Germany, as well as in other former belligerent nations, over the memory of World War II. All of them demonstrate, however, that the "postwar" may be over, as some people claim.[84] The war most definitely is not.

NOTES

1. I would like to thank Gulie Arad, Ira Katznelson, and Jay Winter for their helpful comments on this essay. I feel most indebted to Jutta de Jong and Walter Tasche, who helped obtain material and information that was not easily accessible in the United States.

2. My translation does not quite capture the manifold meanings of the exhibition's theme. The German word *Zeichen* can be translated as "sign," "mark," and also as "signal." *Not* can be translated as "lack," "misery," or "suffering." The theme of the exhibition evokes all of these meanings for both words.

3. The exhibition took place at Niederbergisches Museum Wülfrath from 24 April to 19 June 1994. Several of the items on display had originally been collected for a similar exhibition that had taken place at the Westfälisches Freilichtmuseum Detmold in 1989, whereas others were given to the museum by citizens of Wülfrath. There is no catalogue of Wülfrath's exhibition, but there is one of the earlier exhibition in Detmold; see Ernst Helmut Segschneider, ed., *Zeichen der Not. Als der Stahlhelm zum Kochtopf wurde* (Detmold: Landschaftsverband Westfalen-Lippe and Westfälisches Freilichtmuseum, 1989). The so-called postwar years are usually considered to have begun with Germany's unconditional surrender in 1945 and to have ended with the currency reform in 1948.

4. This is a result of the very nature of these "signs of misery." Many items on display had been used before 1945, were then converted into something different, and continued to be used until they were worn out. To give a few examples: flour and sugar sacks were turned into clothes, uniform coats into winter coats, and swastika flags into carnival costumes. See the photographs in Segschneider, *Zeichen der Not*.

5. Excerpts from the discussions at these two meetings and from twenty individual interviews which I conducted subsequently with members of the discussion groups are currently being prepared for publication in Elisabeth Domansky and Jutta de Jong, *"Und dann ging alles den Bach 'runter." Wülfrather erinnern sich an die Nachkriegsjahre* (projected publication date, 1997). On the history of Germany during the immediate postwar years, see Christoph Kleßmann, *Die doppelte Staatsgründung: Deutsche Geschichte 1945-1955*, 5th ed. (Göttingen: Vandenhoeck & Ruprecht, 1991); Hermann Glaser, *The Rubble Years: The Cultural Roots of Postwar Germany, 1945-1948* (New York: Paragon House, 1986). On Wülfrath's history, see Ulrich Bauckhage, *Zum Beispiel Wülfrath: Der Weg einer deutschen Kleinstadt durch den Nationalsozialismus* (Essen: Frohn Verlag, 1988).

6. It is often overlooked that the famous "economic miracle" was a dream rather than an actual reality for the vast majority of all Germans during the 1950s and 1960s. See, for example, Kleßmann, *Die doppelte Staatsgründung*, esp. 223-26; see also Christoph Kleßmann, "Zwei Staaten, eine Nation: Deutsche Geschichte 1955-1970," in *Schriftenreihe der Bundeszentrale für politische Bildung*, vol. 265 (Bonn: Bundeszentrale für politische Bildung, 1988), esp. 39-44; Glaser, *Rubble Years*. See also Hermann Glaser, *Kulturgeschichte der Bundesrepublik Deutschland*, 3 vols. (Munich: Hanser, 1985-1989), esp. vol. 2: *Zwischen Grundgesetz und großer Koalition, 1949-1967*; Angela Delille and Andrea Grohn, *Blick zurück aufs Glück: Frauenleben und Familienpolitik in den 50er Jahren* (Berlin: Elefanten-Press, 1985); *Perlon-Zeit. Wie die Frauen ihr Wirtschaftswunder erlebten* (Berlin: Elefanten-Press, 1985); Lutz Niethammer, ed., *"Hinterher merkt man, daß es richtig ist, daß es*

schiefgegangen ist": Nachkriegs-Erfahrungen im Ruhr-Gebiet (Berlin and Bonn: Verlag J. H. W. Dietz Nachf., 1983); Wolfgang J. Mommsen, "'Wir sind wieder wer': Wandlungen im politischen Selbstverständnis der Deutschen," in Jürgen Habermas, ed., *Stichworte zur 'Geistigen Situation der Zeit,'* 2 vols. (Frankfurt/M.: Suhrkamp Verlag, 1979), vol. 1: *Nation und Republik* 185–209.

7. This narrative of a heroic new beginning by no means reflects an actual reality. To be sure, the cessation of armed conflict—and especially of aerial bombing—was greeted with great relief by most Germans. The immediate postwar years were, however, for many Germans years of worse suffering, hardship, and chaos than the war years had been. See Terry Chapman, *The German Front 1939–1945* (London: Barne & Jenkins, 1989); Kleßmann, *Die doppelte Staatsgründung* 39–41, 42, 44–53, 354–57; G. C. Paikert, *The German Exodus: A Selective Study on the Post-World War II Expulsion of German Populations and Its Effect* (The Hague: Martinus Nijhoff, 1962) 1–3; Hilde Kammer and Elisabeth Bartsch, eds., *Nationalsozialismus: Begriffe aus der Zeit der Gewaltherrschaft* (Hamburg: Rowohlt, 1992) 28; S. P. McKenzie, "The Treatment of Prisoners of War in World War II," *Journal of Modern History* 66 (September 1994): 487–520; Martin K. Sorge, *The Other Price of Hitler's War: German Military and Civilian Losses Resulting from World War II* (New York: Greenwood Press, 1986); Gregory Schroeder, *The Long Road Home: Evacuees, Postwar Victim Identities, and Social Policy in the Federal Republic* (Ph.D. diss.: Indiana University, forthcoming [1997]).

8. The lack of memories of front experiences results from the fact that more women than men attended the two meetings of eyewitnesses and, later on, participated in individual interviews. This reflects, on the one hand, the current demographic gender structure of this age group and, on the other hand, the demographic gender structure of the German population in the immediate postwar years. According to the 1946 census, for example, the population of all four occupation zones consisted of 44 percent women, 23 percent children, and 33 percent old men and war invalids. See Delille and Grohn, *Blick zurück aufs Glück* 13. It is estimated that seven million German women were either widowed or never married as a result of the demographic consequences of World War II. See Sibylle Meyer and Eva Schulze, "Von Wirtschaftswunder keine Spur: Die ökonomische und soziale Situation alleinstehender Frauen," in *Perlon-Zeit* 92–98. See also Kleßmann, *Die doppelte Staatsgründung* 42.

9. On the impact of traumatic experiences—in this case air raids—on remembering World War II in Germany, see Annemarie Tröger's excellent case study, "German Women's Memories of World War II," in Margaret Randolph Higonnet, Jane Jenson, Sonya Michel, and Margaret Collins Weitz, eds., *Behind the Lines: Gender and the Two World Wars* (New Haven: Yale University Press, 1987) 285–99. See also Martin Bergmann and Milton E.

Jucovy, eds., *Generations of the Holocaust* (New York: Basic Books, 1982); Barbara Heimannsberg and Christoph J. Schmidt, eds., *The Collective Silence: German Identity and the Legacy of Shame* (San Francisco: Jossey-Bass, 1993); Judith Lewis Herman, *Trauma and Recovery: The Aftermath of Violence—From Domestic Abuse to Political Terror* (New York: Basic Books, 1992); Bessel A. van der Kolk, "The Body Keeps the Score: Memory and the Evolving Psychobiology of Posttraumatic Stress," *Harvard Review of Psychiatry* 1.5 (January–February 1994): 253–65; Bessel A. van der Kolk, "The Intrusive Past: the Flexibility of Memory and the Engraving of Trauma," *American Imago* 48.4 (1991): 425–54; Jonathan Shay, *Achilles in Vietnam: Combat Trauma and the Undoing of Character* (New York: Maxwell Macmillan, 1994).

10. The results of these meetings and the subsequent interviews as well as the results of other oral history projects on World War II in Germany show how simplistic and reductionist attempts are to capture the war memories of different groups by terms such as "antagonistic memories," as Frank Stern does in his juxtaposition of war memories of "the" Jews and "the" Germans. See Frank Stern, "Antagonistic Memories: The Post-War Survival and Alienation of Jews and Germans," *International Yearbook of Oral History and Life Stories*, vol. 1: *Memory and Totalitarianism*, ed. by Luisa Passerini (New York: Oxford University Press, 1992) 21–43. On the diversity of war memories see Meyer and Schulze, *Von Liebe sprach damals keiner*; Lutz Niethammer, ed., *"Die Jahre weiß man nicht, wo man die heute hinsetzen soll": Faschismus-Erfahrungen im Ruhr-Gebiet* (Berlin: Verlag J. H. W. Dietz, 1983); Alison Owings, *Frauen: German Women Recall the Third Reich* (New Brunswick, NJ: Rutgers University Press, 1993); Ulla Roberts, *Starke Mütter-ferne Väter: Töchter reflektieren ihre Kindheit im Nationalsozialismus und in der Nachkriegszeit* (Frankfurt/M.: Fischer Taschenbuch Verlag, 1994); Gabriele Rosenthal, ed., *Die Hitlerjugend-Generation: Biographische Thematisierung als Vergangenheitsbewältigung* (Esser: Die blaue Eule, 1986); Tröger, "German Women's Memories," in Higonnet et al., eds., *Behind the Lines*; Ernst Helmut Segschneider, *Jahre im Abseits: Erinnerungen an die Kriegsgefangenschaft* (Bramsche: Rasch-Verlag, 1991).

11. This is Vaclav Havel's term for the politics of memory in totalitarian states. Quoted from Claudia Koonz's brilliant essay "Between Memory and Oblivion: Concentration Camps in German Memory," in John Gillis, ed., *Commemorations: The Politics of National Identity* (Princeton: Princton University Press, 1994), 258.

12. All initials of names were changed in order to secure the privacy of the interviewees.

13. Interviews with Ms. A., 27 April and 13 June 1994.

14. See Haruko Taya Cook and Theodore F. Cook, *Japan at War: An Oral History* (New York: New Press, 1992), 4.

15. Cook and Cook, *Japan at War,* 3–6.

16. This is the term that Richard Terdiman uses to characterize the ways in which European societies after the French Revolution of 1789 perceived the relationship between the past, the present, and the future; see Richard Terdiman, *Present Past: Modernity and the Memory Crisis* (Ithaca: Cornell University Press, 1993) 4.

17. In this interpretation I differ from Haruko Cook and Theodore Cook, who see the old Japanese man's box as a symbol of Japan's difficulties in confronting war guilt; see Cook and Cook, *Japan at War* 6. While I think that theirs is an important argument, I nevertheless think that forgetting the war cannot be reduced to the aspects of shame or guilt. The strategies of forgetting and the waves of remembering have been too similar in countries for which this question posed itself in radically different ways. See the literature cited in note 19.

18. On the concept of "working through," see Saul Friedlander, "Trauma, Transference and 'Working Through' in Writing the History of the Shoah," *History & Memory* 4.1 (Spring/Summer 1992): 39–59.

19. As most of the recent literature shows, the war was forgotten in many similar ways in countries with vastly different war experiences. See, for example, R. J. B. Bosworth, *Explaining Auschwitz and Hiroshima: History Writing and the Second World War, 1945-1990* (New York: Routledge, 1993). See also Nina Tumarkin, *The Living and the Dead: The Rise and Fall of the Cult of World War II in Russia* (New York: Basic Books, 1994); Cook and Cook, *Japan at War,* and Ian Buruma, *The Wages of Guilt: Memories of War in Germany and Japan* (New York: Farrar, Straus and Giroux, 1994); Henry Rousso, *The Vichy Syndrome: History and Memory in France since 1944* (Cambridge: Harvard University Press, 1994); Studs Terkel, *The Good War: An Oral History of World War II* (New York: Ballantine Books, 1984); and Louis Fairchild, *They Called It the War Effort: Oral Histories from World War II Orange, Texas* (Austin, TX: Eakin Press, 1993); John Bodnar, *Remaking America: Public Memory, Commemoration and Patriotism in the Twentieth Century* (Princeton: Princeton University Press, 1992), and John Bodnar's recent remarks in "The Enola Gay and the Problem of Remembering World War II in America" (Keynote address, National Parks and Conservation Association Conference, Jimmy Carter Library, Atlanta, Georgia, 9 March 1995 [unpublished manuscript]).

20. It is not always clear what makes people suddenly go to their basements and look for those boxes. Historical exhibitions, shifts in public politics of memory, and the occurrence of political events such as the Gulf War, the war in the former Yugoslavia, or outbreaks of domestic violence that trigger not so much cognitive as sensory memories may all contribute to such impulses. Reaching a certain age at which one examines one's life is

another factor. All of these aspects were mentioned, for example, during the interviews in Wülfrath. See Domansky and de Jong, *"Und dann ging alles den Bach 'runter."* A good survey of neurobiological, psychological, and psycho-analytical research on memory construction, storage, and retrieval is provided in Alan Baddeley, *Your Memory: A User's Guide* (London: Prion, 1993).

21. Jane Kramer, "Letter from Germany: The Politics of Memory," *New Yorker,* 14 August 1995: 48–65, 48.

22. See for example Buruma, *Wages of Guilt.* The idea of Germany's leading role in confronting its past also informed many articles in the American press on the occasion of the fiftieth anniversary of World War II's end in 1995. See, for example, Stephen Kinzer, "Germans More Willing to Confront Nazi Crimes," *New York Times,* 1 May 1995, 1. However, an obsession with the past does not necessarily indicate confrontation of the past. See Saul Friedlander's classic essay *Reflections of Nazism: An Essay on Kitsch and Death* (New York: Harper & Row, 1986).

23. There is certainly a distinct difference between cultural constructions of memory and the neurobiological processes occurring in the brain when events are processed into memories. However, much of the current historical literature on memory would definitely not be hurt by taking more note of contemporary scientific research on memory. This is most clearly demonstrated by Alice M. Hoffman and Howard S. Hoffman, *Archives of Memory: A Soldier Recalls World War II* (Louisville: University Press of Kentucky, 1990). The introduction to this fascinating case study provides a very good survey of current neurobiological, psychological, and psychoanalytical theories of memory, of the difference between knowing and remembering, between short-and long-term memory, sensory memory, retrieval, repression, and also the construction of false memories. See also Baddeley, *Your Memory.*

24. The classic study is Maurice Halbwachs, *On Collective Memory;* see the edition by Lewis A. Coser (Chicago: University of Chicago Press, 1992). See also Jan Assmann and Tonio Hölscher, eds., *Kultur und Gedächtnis* (Frankfurt/M.: Suhrkamp, 1988) which contains several contributions that try to think with Halbwachs beyond Halbwachs. An equally interesting engagement of Halbwachs is Mihran Dabag, "Gedächtnis und Identität," in *Armenien: Wiederentdeckung einer alten Kulturlandschaft* (Tübingen: Wasmuth Verlag, 1995 [Exhibition Catalogue]) 19–25. See also Paul Connerton, *How Societies Remember* (New York: Cambridge University Press, 1989).

25. After World War II, Germany could not, for example, begin the construction of war memorials before receiving the Allies' permission in 1952. See George Mosse, *Fallen Soldiers: Reshaping the Memory of the Two World Wars* (New York: Oxford University Press, 1990) 212. On Allied attempts to defeat the Third Reich's politics of memory by leveling some of its memori-

als, see Meinhold Lurz, *Kriegerdenkmäler in Deutschland*, vol. 6: *Die Bundesrepublik* (Heidelberg: Esprint-Verlag, 1987), esp. 123–27.

26. On the differences in remembering the two world wars in Germany see—in addition to Winter, *Sites of Memory*—especially James M. Diehl, "Germany in Defeat, 1918 and 1945: Some Comparisons and Contrasts," *History Teacher* 22.4 (August 1989): 398–409; and Gottfried Niedhart and Dieter Riesenberger, eds., *Lernen aus dem Krieg?: Deutsche Nachkriegszeiten 1918 und 1945* (Munich: Verlag C. H. Beck, 1992). On Western and Eastern reeducation strategies, see Kleßmann, *Die doppelte Staatsgründung* 87–99.

27. On the obsession with remembering, mourning, and explaining World War I in post–World War I France, Britain, and Germany—to name only the European examples—see Winter, *Sites of Memory*. See also Michael Jeismann and Rolf Westheider, "Wofür stirbt der Bürger? Nationaler Totenkult und Staatsbürgertum in Deutschland und Frankreich seit der französischen Revolution," in Reinhart Koselleck and Michael Jeismann, eds., *Der politische Totenkult: Kriegerdenkmäler in der Moderne* (Munich: Wilhelm Fink Verlag, 1994) 23–50, esp. 28–50.

28. On the use of war memories for the construction of national identity and social unity in the United States and the Soviet Union, see the studies cited in note 19.

29. Ulrich Barton and Hans-Harald Müller, "Die Weltkriege im Roman der Nachkriegszeiten," in Niedhart and Riesenberger, eds., *Lernen aus dem Krieg?* 300–18.

30. Kleßmann, *Die doppelte Staatsgründung* 157–71.

31. Barton and Müller, "Die Weltkriege im Roman der Nachkriegszeiten," in Niedhart and Riesenberger, eds., *Lernen aus dem Krieg?* 300–18. On World War I's importance for the development of English literature, see Paul Fussell's classic study *The Great War and Modern Memory* (London: Oxford University Press, 1975).

32. Günter Grass, *The Tin Drum* (New York: Pantheon, 1962; original title: *Die Blechtrommel,* 1959). See also Peter Beicken, "German Prose after 1945," in Charles Burdick, Hans-Adolf Jacobsen, and Winfried Kudszus, eds., *Contemporary Germany: Politics and Culture* (Boulder, CO: Westview Press, 1984), 319–39.

33. On Anselm Kiefer, see Mark Rosenthal's introduction to the catalogue *Anselm Kiefer,* ed. Mark Rosenthal (Munich: Prestel Verlag, 1987) 10–36; Andreas Huyssen, "Anselm Kiefer: The Terror of History, the Temptation of Myth," *October* 48 (Spring 1989): 25–45.

34. See Winter, *Sites of Memory* 159–64.

35. This very successful film that was directed by Bernhard Wicki and released in 1959, did not address the causes of war; see Manfred K. Wolfram, "Film in the Federal Republic of Germany," in Burdick, Jacobsen, and

Kudszus, eds., *Contemporary Germany*, 371–94. See also Irmgard Wilharm, "Krieg in deutschen Nachkriegsspielfilmen," in Niedhart and Riesenberger, eds., *Lernen aus dem Krieg?* 281–99.

36. Erich Maria Remarque, *All Quiet on the Western Front* (Boston: Little Brown, 1929); Erich Maria Remarque, *A Time to Love and a Time to Die* (New York: Harcourt, Brace, 1954). The German original is entitled *Zeit zu Leben* (to live, not to love [!]) *und Zeit zu Sterben* (Cologne: Kiepenheuer & Witsch, 1954).

37. Manfred Wolfram emphasizes the need to distinguish between films by committed film directors who wanted to challenge the shallowness of the dominant film production in Germany after 1945 and audiences who much preferred "Homeland Films" (*Heimatfilme*) to "Rubble Films" (*Trümmerfilme*) or critical films that were produced in later years. Wolfram, "Film in the Federal Republic," in Burdick, Jacobsen, and Kudszus, eds., *Contemporary Germany*, esp. 372–76. See also Anton Kaes, *From Hitler to Heimat: The Return of History as Film* (Cambridge: Harvard University Press, 1989).

38. See the critical analysis by Reinhart Koselleck, "Bilderverbot: Welches Totengedenken?" in *Frankfurter Allgemeine Zeitung*, 8 April 1993.

39. On war monuments, see Winter, *Sites of Memory* 78–116; George Mosse, *Fallen Soldiers*, esp. 99–106 and 212–15; Meinhold Lurz, *Kriegerdenkmäler in Deutschland*, vols. 3: *1. Weltkrieg*; 4: *Weimarer Republik*; and 5: *Drittes Reich* (Heidelberg: Esprint Verlag: 1985–1986); Sabine Behrenbeck, "Heldenkult oder Friedensmahnung?: Kriegerdenkmale nach beiden Weltkriegen," in Niedhart and Riesenberger, eds., *Lernen aus dem Krieg?* 344–64; Jeismann and Westheider, "Wofür stirbt der Bürger?" in Koselleck and Jeismann, eds., *Nationaler Totenkult*, 49–50.

40. On the image of "the army of the dead" see Winter, *Sites of Memory* 15–28. See also Ulrich Linse, "'Saatfrüchte sollen nicht vermahlen werden!': Zur Resymbolisierung des Soldatentods," in Klaus Vondung, ed., *Kriegserlebnis: Der Erste Weltkrieg in der literarischen Gestaltung und symbolischen Deutung der Nationen* (Göttingen: Vandenhoeck & Ruprecht, 1980), 262–74; George Mosse, *Fallen Soldiers*, esp. 78–80. Mosse sees the "cult of the fallen soldier" after World War I as one of the major differences between the remembrance of World War I and World War II. Ibid. 70–106 and 211–20.

41. This has recently been demonstrated again by the silence with which German society reacted to an Austrian initiative to bury the dead of Stalingrad, whose skeletons keep surfacing in the fields where they died. The German "People's League for the Maintenance of War Graves" (*Volksbund für Kriegsgräberfürsorge*) has been engaged since the early 1990s in a project of burying these dead rather quietly. See Timothy W. Ryback's excellent essay "Stalingrad: Letters from the Dead," *New Yorker*, 1 February 1993, 57–71.

42. On German postwar architecture, see Werner Durth and Niels Gut-schow, eds., *Träume in Trümmern: Planungen zum Wiederaufbau zerstörter Städte im Westen Deutschlands 1940-1950* (Braunschweig and Wiesbaden: Vieweg und Sohn, 1988); Jeffrey Diefendorf, *In the Wake of the War: The Reconstruction of German Cities after World War II* (New York: Oxford University Press, 1993); Rudy Koshar, "Building Pasts: Historic Preservation and Identity in Twentieth-Century Germany," in Gillis, ed., *Commemorations* 215-38, esp. 226-30.

43. Alexander and Margarete Mitscherlich, *The Inability to Mourn: Principles of Collective Behavior* (New York: Grove Press, 1975); German original: *Die Unfähigkeit zu trauern: Grundlagen kollektiven Verhaltens* (Munich: R. Piper & Co., 1967).

44. Two randomly chosen examples of books glorifying World War II are *1939 gegen England: Berichte und Bilder*, ed. Oberkommando der Wehrmacht (Berlin: Zeitgeschichte-Verlag Wilhelm Andermann, 1940), and *Das Zweite Kriegsjahr: Mit dem siegreichen deutschen Heer an der Kanalfront, durch Rumänien, Bulgarien, Serbien, Griechenland und Nordafrika*, ed. Berichterstaffel des O. K. H (Berlin: Wilhelm Limpert Verlag, 1943). An example of a book by a German political refugee who analyzed wartime life in Germany while living in exile in Sweden is Max Seydewitz, *Civil Life in Wartime Germany: The Story of the Home Front* (New York: Viking Press, 1945). Seydewitz joined the government of Saxony after the war.

45. On the attempts to establish one day on which all Germans would commemorate the dead of World War I during the Weimar Republic, see Lurz, *Kriegerdenkmäler*, vol. 4: *Weimarer Republik*, 413-26. One of the most active groups in pursuit of an official national day of mourning was the "People's League for the Maintenance of War Graves" (*Volksbund für Kriegsgräberfürsorge*). It was a new initiative of this group in 1934 that resulted in the National Socialist government's decision for such a day. See Lurz, ibid. 421. The fifth Sunday before Easter is called *Reminiscere* (remembering).

46. On the history of "Heroes' Commemoration Day" during the Third Reich see Lurz, *Kriegerdenkmäler*, vol. 5: *Drittes Reich*, 383-88.

47. This pacifist orientation remained "affective" insofar as it consisted of an emotional antimilitarism that did not translate into political action or specific electoral choices. See Guido Grünewald and Dieter Riesenberger, "Die Friedensbewegung nach den Weltkriegen," in Niedhart and Riesenberger, eds., *Lernen aus dem Krieg?* 96-120; Kleßmann, *Die doppelte Staatsgründung* 121-55; James M. Diehl, *The Thanks of the Fatherland: German Veterans after the Second World War* (Chapel Hill: University of Carolina Press, 1993). See also Lurz, *Kriegerdenkmäler*, vol. 6: *Bundesrepublik* 447-48.

48. According to opinion polls that were commissioned by the American

military authorities between 1946 and 1949, many Germans were convinced that "National Socialism had been a good, but badly realized idea." And a growing number of Germans would have preferred life in a National Socialist state to that in a Communist one (Kleßmann, *Die doppelte Staatsgründung,* 56). See also Diehl, "Germany in Defeat," *History Teacher* 398–400; Barbara Marshall, "German Reactions to Military Defeat, 1945–1947: The British View," in Volker Berghahn and Martin Kitchen, eds., *Germany in the Age of Total War* (London: Croom Helm, 1981). See also Gottfried Niedhart, "'So viel Anfang war nie' oder: 'Das Leben und nichts anderes': deutsche Nachkriegszeiten im Vergleich," in Niedhart and Riesenberger, eds., *Lernen aus dem Krieg?* 11–38, esp. 15–18 and 23–28.

49. George Mosse arrived at the conclusion that the "German Democratic Republic had faced the problem of honoring the fallen and had *displaced* (my italics) it onto the victims of National Socialism." Mosse, *Fallen Soldiers* 214. On remembering in East Germany, see Andreas Dorpalen, *German History in Marxist Perspective: The East German Approach* (Detroit: Wayne State University Press, 1985); Eve Rosenhaft, "The Uses of Remembrance: The Legacy of Communist Resistance in the German Democratic Republic," in Francis R. Nicosia and Lawrence D. Stokes, eds., *Germans against Nazism: Nonconformity, Opposition, and Resistance in the Third Reich. Essays in Honour of Peter Hoffmann* (New York: St. Martin's Press, 1990), 369–88.

50. On the agreement between Germany and the victors that the war had been "Hitler's war," see Diehl, "Germany in Defeat," *History Teacher* 398. A recent example of the persistence of this shared myth is Johannes Steinhoff, Peter Pechel, and Dennis Showalter, eds., *Voices from the Third Reich. An Oral History,* 2nd ed. (New York: DaCapo Press, 1994; 1st ed.: Washington, D.C., 1989).

51. On reeducation and denazification, see Karl-Ernst Bungenstab, *Umerziehung zur Demokratie?* (Bertelsmann Universitätsverlag: Düsseldorf, 1970); Kleßmann, *Die doppelte Staatsgrundung* 87–99; Lutz Niethammer, *Entnazifizierung in Bayern: Säuberung und Rehabilitierung unter amerikanischer Besatzung* (Frankfurt/M.: S. Fischer, 1972); Jutta-B. Lange Quassowski, *Neuordnung oder Restauration? Das Demokratiekonzept der amerikanischen Besatzungsmacht und die politische Sozialisation der Westdeutschen: Wirtschaftsordnung, Schulstruktur, politische Bildung* (Opladen: Leske und Budrich, 1979); Ekkehart Krippendorf, ed., *The Role of the United States in the Reconstruction of Italy and West Germany 1943–1949* (Berlin: John F. Kennedy Institute für Nordamerikastudien, Freie Universität Berlin, 1981); James F. Tent, *Mission on the Rhine: Reeducation and Denazification in American-Occupied Germany* (Chicago: University of Chicago Press, 1982).

52. This was expressed in characteristically vague terms in a decree by the

Federal Republic's Minister of the Interior that was issued on 3 March 1952. See Lurz, *Kriegerdenkmäler,* vol. 6: *Bundesrepublik* 510. On the history of the "National Day of Mourning" in the Federal Republic, see ibid. 509-27.

53. By World War II's fundamentally different nature, I mean its character as a racist war of extermination. See, for example, Michael Geyer, "Krieg als Gesellschaftspolitik: Anmerkungen zu neueren Arbeiten über das Dritte Reich im Zweiten Weltkrieg," *Archiv für Sozialgeschichte* 26 (1986): 557-601.

54. In addition to the literature quoted in note 49, see Elisabeth Domansky, "'Kristallnacht,' the Holocaust and German Unity: The Meaning of November 9 as an Anniversary in Germany," *History & Memory* 4.1 (Spring/Summer 1992): 60-94; Elisabeth Domansky, "Die gespaltene Erinnerung," in Manuel Köppen, ed., *Kunst und Literatur nach Auschwitz* (Berlin: Erich Schmidt Verlag, 1993): 178-96. East Germany had to forget not only its involvement in World War II but also many of its experiences under Soviet occupation. See Norman Naimark, *The Russians in Germany. A History of the Soviet Zone of Occupation, 1945-1949* (Cambridge: Belknap Press of Harvard University Press, 1995).

55. See Buruma, *Wages of Guilt;* Domansky, "'Kristallnacht,' The Holocaust and German Unity;" Domansky, "Die gespaltene Erinnerung." On "Wiedergutmachung," see Axel Frohn, "Holocaust and Shilumin: The Policy of 'Wiedergutmachung' in the Early 1950s," in *German Historical Institute. Occasional Papers,* no. 2 (Washington, D.C., 1991); Gotthard Jasper, "Wiedergutmachung und Westintegration: Die halbherzige justizielle Aufarbeitung der NS-Vergangenheit in der frühen Bundesrepublik," in Ludolf Herbst, ed., *Westdeutschland 1945-1955: Unterwerfung, Kontrolle, Integration* (Munich: R. Oldenbourg Verlag, 1986) 183-202; see also Ulrich Herbert, "Nicht entschädigungsfähig? Die Wiedergutmachungsansprüche der Ausländer," in Ludolf Herbst and Constantin Göschler, eds., *Wiedergutmachung in der Bundesrepublik Deutschland* (Munich: R. Oldenbourg Verlag, 1989) 273-302.

56. Kleßmann, *Zwei Staaten, eine Nation* 159.

57. On Germany's politics of "Western Integration" and on its revisionist politics and rhetoric regarding the East see Kleßmann, *Die doppelte Staatsgründung* 177-221. See also Kleßmann, "Zwei Staaten, eine Nation" 68-98; Paul Noack, "Die Ära Adenauer," in Franz Schneider, ed., *Der Weg der Bundesrepublik: Von 1945 bis zur Gegenwart* (Munich: C. H. Beck, 1985) 35-56, esp. 39-49; Anselm Doering-Manteuffel, ed., *Adenauerzeit: Stand, Perspektiven und methodische Aufgaben der Zeitgeschichtsforschung 1945-1967* (Bonn: Bouvier, 1993).

58. On the the history of the "17th of June" in the Federal Republic, see Lurz, *Kriegerdenkmäler,* vol. 6: *Bundesrepublik,* 528-33. Interestingly, Lurz argues that "elements of the former Heroes' Commemoration Day entered

the "Day of German Unity," albeit in a somewhat changed way." He also sees references to 20 July 1944, the day of the failed aristrocatic/military coup against Hitler (ibid, 528). The other national holiday that was commemorated in both German states was the 1st of May (Labor Day). The history of that day, however, belongs in a different context. See also Lurz, ibid. 533–35.

59. A good survey of historical interpretations of Nazism is Ian Kershaw, *The Nazi Dictatorship: Problems and Perspectives of Interpretation*, 2nd ed. (London: Edward Arnold, 1989). A particularly poignant example of an attempt to interpret National Socialism as an *alien* force occupying Germany is Friedrich Meinecke, *The German Catastrophe: Reflections and Recollections* (Cambridge: Harvard University Press, 1950; German original: *Die deutsche Katastrophe: Betrachtungen und Erinnerungen* (Wiesbaden: E. Brockhaus, 1946). On "inner emigration" (*innere Emigration*), a form of existence that was particularly claimed by German intellectuals, see Beicken, "German Prose after 1945," in Burdick, Jacobsen, and Kudszus, eds., *Contemporary Germany*, esp. 320; Glaser, *Rubble Years* 17–24.

60. Quoted from "Kerzen für die Sowjetzone," in *Kölner Stadt-Anzeiger*, 22 December 1959.

61. Ibid.

62. I have not found any evidence yet for the origins of Ernst Reuter's suggestion and for the reasons of its acceptance, first, in Berlin and, then, in West Germany.

63. See Kleßmann, *Die doppelte Staatsgründung* 223–26; see also Kleßmann, "Zwei Staaten, eine Nation" 39–44.

64. Rudi Dutschke, for example, was born in 1940. Most books on the student movement of 1968 stress the solidly middle-class background of the leaders and members of the students' revolt but fail to notice this generation's experience of war. See, for example, the dust jacket to Uwe Bergmann, Rudi Dutschke, Wolfgang Lefèvre, and Bernd Rabehl, *Rebellion der Studenten oder: Die neue Opposition* (Reinbek/Hamburg: Rowohlt, 1968). See also Daniel Cohn-Bendit, *Wir haben sie so geliebt, die Revolution* (Frankfurt/M.: Athenäum, 1987). A good introduction to the many protest movements that joined ranks in 1968 or were initiated by '1968' is Roland Roth and Dieter Hecht, eds., "Neue soziale Bewegungen in der Bundesrepublik Deutschland," in *Schriftenreihe der Bundeszentrale für politische Bildung*, vol. 252 (Bonn: Bundeszentrale für politische Bildung, 1987); informative is also Charlene Spretnack and Fritjof Capra, *Green Politics: The Global Promise* (Santa Fe: Bear & Company, 1986). Discussions on "second-generation" trauma with regard to Germany usually deal with the trauma of the Nazi past, not of World War II. See Heimannsberg and Schmidt, eds., *Collective Silence*.

65. On the assumed anti-Americanism of the generation of 1968, see, for

example, Emil-Peter Müller, *Antiamerikanismus in Deutschland: Zwischen Care-Paket und Cruise Missile* (Cologne: Deutscher Instituts-Verlag, 1986), and, recently, Dan Diner, *Verkehrte Welten: Antiamerikanismus in Deutschland* (Frankfurt/M.: Eichborn, 1993). But see also Albrecht Goeschel, *Die Ungleichzeitigkeit in der Kultur* (Stuttgart: W. Kohlhammer, 1991).

66. On the "New Policy toward the East" (*Neue Ostpolitik*), see Kleßmann, "Zwei Staaten, eine Nation," esp. 228–35. See also Michael Wolffsohn, "Die sozial-liberale Koalition: Von der Deutschland- zur Außenpolitik," in Schneider, ed., *Der Weg der Bundesrepublik*, 102–31.

67. See Domansky, "'Kristallnacht'"; Dirk Moses, "Revolution and History: Neo-Conservative Intellectuals," Response to Vergangenheitsbewältigung from 1968 to 1983" (Paper, presented at the 19th Annual Conference of the German Studies Association, Chicago, Illinois, 22 September 1995 [unpublished]).

68. In contrast to the original "inability to mourn," or so Margarete Mitscherlich argued, now must be added the lack of "mourning for the missed work of mourning" (*Trauer über die versäumte Trauerarbeit*); quoted from Niedhart, "'So viel Anfang war nie,'" in Niedhart and Riesenberger, eds., *Lernen aus dem Krieg?* 35.

69. See, for example, Domansky, "'Kristallnacht.'" On the history of "Wiedergutmachung," see the literature quoted in note 55.

70. This quote refers to the book by Lucy S. Dawidowicz, *The War Against the Jews 1933-1945* (New York: Holt, Rinehart and Winston, 1975).

71. There is neither a comprehensive study on Holocaust commemorations in Germany nor on the celebration of the 17th of June.

72. The insistence on the Holocaust's "uniqueness" or "inexplicability" can mean different things in different political, religious, or national contexts. In Germany, the Holocaust's "uniqueness" is very often emphasized in order to see it as ultimately detached from German history; see Domansky, "'Kristallnacht,'" esp. 78–80.

73. In its very Eurocentric way, the peace movement always imagined "the" Third World War as a nuclear war, between the United States and the Soviet Union, ravaging Europe. An author who uses the concept of the Third World War most engagingly is Bosworth, *Explaining Auschwitz and Hiroshima*.

74. To give just a few examples: Andreas C. Bimmer et al., *Alltagsleben im Krieg: Marburgerinnen erinnern sich an den Zweiten Weltkrieg* (Marburg: Presseamt der Stadt, 1985); Ulrich Borsdorf and Mathilde Jamin, eds., *Über Leben im Krieg: Kriegserfahrungen einer Industrieregion 1939–1945* (Reinbek/Hamburg: Rowohlt Taschenbuch Verlag, 1989); Ingeborg Bruns, *Als Vater aus dem Krieg heimkehrte: Töchter erinnern sich* (Frankfurt/M.: Fischer Taschenbuch, 1991); Alois Stadtmüller, *Aschaffenburg im Zweiten Weltkrieg: Bombenangriffe - Belagerung - Übergabe* (Aschaffenburg: Paul

Pattloch Verlag, 1970); Ulla Roberts, *Starke Mütter, ferne Väter;* Susanne Zur Nieden, *Alltag im Ausnahmezustand: Frauentagebücher im zerstörten Deutschland, 1943-1945* (Berlin: Orlanda Frauen-Verlag, 1993).

75. See, as just one example, Lilo Klug, ed., *Surviving the Fire: Mother Courage and World War II* (Seattle: Open Hand Publishing, 1989).

76. See Winter, *Sites of Memory;* Mosse, *Fallen Soldiers.*

77. For example, during his speech in the German parliament on the occasion of the fiftieth anniversary of "Kristallnacht," the speaker of the House, Philipp Jenninger, spoke of German society's "special ethical responsibility for the future" (*Ethik der Zukunftsverantwortung*); see Domansky, "'Kristallnacht'" 78. There are numerous other examples, however, expressing the same attitude.

78. See the literature quoted in notes 73 and 74.

79. On the "Historikerstreit," see Geoff Eley, "Nazism, Politics and the Image of the Past: Thoughts on the West German *Historikerstreit, 1986-1987,*" *Past and Present* 12 (November 1988): 171-208; Charles S. Maier, *The Unmasterable Past: History, Holocaust, and German National Identity* (Cambridge: Harvard University Press, 1988); Richard J. Evans, *In Hitler's Shadow: West German Historians and the Attempt to Escape from the Past* (New York: Pantheon Books, 1989). On attempts in the 1980s to change the representation of the Holocaust, see Saul Friedlander, "Historical Writing and the Memory of the Holocaust," in Berel Lang, ed., *Writing and the Holocaust* (New York: Holmes & Meier, 1988) 66-80.

80. On Bitburg, see Geoffrey H. Hartmann, ed., *Bitburg in Moral and Political Perspective* (Bloomington: Indiana University Press, 1986).

81. On German responses to the bombing of Dresden, see Andrew John Spencer, *Of Literature and Legend: German Writers and the Bombing of Dresden* (Ph.D. diss., Ohio State University, 1992 [microfiche]). See also Klaus Naumann, "Dresdener Pieta: Eine Fallstudie zum 'Gedenkjahr 1995,'" *Mittelweg 36.*4 (1995): 67-81. One of the most active institutions that pursue alternative politics of memory is the "Hamburg Institute for Social Research" (*Hamburger Institut für Sozialforschung*). In 1995 it organized an exhibition on the German Wehrmacht's involvement in genocidal atrocities during World War II. See the exhibition catalogue, Hannes Heer, ed., *Vernichtungskrieg: Verbrechen der Wehrmacht 1941-1944: Ausstel-lungs-katalog* (Hamburg: Hamburger Edition 1996). As further contributions to alternative politics of memory by employees or collaborators of the Hamburg Institute on "ordinary" German soldiers' knowledge of and involvement in genocidal politics, see Hannes Heer and Klaus Naumann, eds., *Vernichtungskrieg: Verbrechen der Wehrmacht 1941-1944* (Hamburg: Hamburger Edition, 1995); Hannes Heer, ed., *Stets zu erschießen sind Frauen, die in der Roten Armee dienen: Geständnisse deutscher Kriegsgefangener über*

ihren Einsatz an der Ostfront (Hamburg: Hamburger Edition, 1995); Walter Manoschek, ed., *"Es gibt nur eines für das Judentum: Vernichtung:" Das Judenbild in deutschen Soldatenbriefen 1939-1944* (Hamburg: Hamburger Edition, 1995). On attempts to create a Holocaust memorial in Germany, see Jane Kramer's informative and very thoughtful essay "Letter from Germany: The Politics of Memory," *New Yorker,* 14 August 1995: 48-65.

82. A striking expression of this possibility is the fact that while there are large sums of money available in West Germany for the construction of a Holocaust memorial, the actual concentration camp sites are crumbling for want of money to maintain them. See Kramer, "Letter from Germany." See also Timothy W. Ryback, "Report from Dachau," *New Yorker,* 3 August 1992, 43-61. Anton Kaes, in *From Hitler to Heimat,* expresses similar concerns to those of these authors, but with regard to films as a means of representing the past (see esp. 196-98).

83. Among the best examples are the annual competitions among German students at the primary and high school level for the "Award of the President of the Federal Republic for Researching Germany's Past" (*Schülerwettbewerb Deutsche Geschichte*). See, for example, the excellent publication of one year's results: Dieter Galinski and Wolf Schmidt, eds., *Die Kriegsjahre in Deutschland 1939-1945: Ergebnisse und Anregungen aus dem Schülerwettbewerb Deutsche Geschichte um den Preis des Bundespräsidenten 1982/83* (Hamburg: Verlag Erziehung und Wissenschaft, 1985).

84. Such ideas were widely circulated after the collapse of the Eastern Bloc. In 1995 they even informed panels at the American Historical Association's annual convention.

ELEVEN

Deportation and Memory

Official History and the Rewriting of World War II

ANNETTE WIEVIORKA

FRANCE IS UNIQUE. It is the only country in the world where World War II is remembered on three different occasions: 8 May is a bank holiday dedicated to the celebration of the capitulation of the Third Reich and the victory of the Allied forces; on National Deportation Day, the last Sunday in April, the liberation of the Nazi concentration camps is celebrated; and on 16 July, if it falls on a Sunday, the anniversary of the Vel d'Hiv round-up is marked to commemorate the "racist and antisemitic persecutions that took place under the *de facto* authority known as the 'Government of the French State' (L'Etat français) 1940–1944"; if the sixteenth is a weekday, the celebration is held on the following Sunday. For each of these dates and each of these celebrations there is a long history rich with controversial arguments.[1]

Law No. 54–415 was passed on 14 April 1954. It specified the last Sunday in April for the commemoration of deportation. The text of the law is very short, consisting of only two articles, and it deserves to be quoted in its entirety:

ARTICLE 1. The French Republic honors once a year, on the last Sunday in April, the memory of the heroes and victims deported to the Nazi camps during the course of the 1939–1945 war.

ARTICLE 2. The last Sunday in April becomes "National remembrance day for the victims and heroes of the Deportation." Official ceremonies will be held in remembrance of the sufferings and the tortures endured by the deportees in the concentration camps and to honor the courage and the heroism of the victims, both men and women.

In other words, in 1954, ten years after the liberation of Paris, the state insisted upon the necessity to devote one day to the specific remembrance of deportation. Such was not always the case, as we can see if we consider the grandiose ceremony organized on 11 November 1945 by General De Gaulle before he left power. De Gaulle and Henri Frenay, then his Minister of Prisoners, Deportees, and Refugees, wished to honor the dead of World War II in the same way the dead of World War I had been honored with the decision to bury the Unknown Soldier at the Arc de Triomphe and the cult that ensued. The complexity of the French situation during World War II, the various ways in which the French had fought—the battles of 1940 and 1944–1945, the resistance, the numerous battlefields—made it impossible to choose one sole figure to represent all those who had given their lives for France. The very first time he visited Mont Valérien,[2] on 1 November 1944, General De Gaulle was undoubtedly overwhelmed by the beauty of this highly evocative site; he went along with Henri Frenay's idea to transform the site into a World War II memorial where bodies would be buried to represent all those who had been killed in action. "I see the final monument," Henri Frenay wrote, "as a sort of lighthouse; it would be built on the highest point of Mont Valérien, where so many résistants were shot dead by the enemy. The bodies would be buried in a crypt, and so that Paris and future generations would never forget, the lighthouse would beam the 'V' of victory every night upon the city."[3] While waiting for the erection of what was to be the final grave, a huge ceremony was held on 11 November 1945, during which a temporary funeral was celebrated. Fifteen bodies that had been kept at the Arc de Triomphe, next to the grave of the Unknown Soldier were transferred to the Mont Valérien crypt. These bodies, possessing the highest symbolic significance, were to represent the various dead of the various battles: those of the Battle of France, those of the Free French Forces in Africa, the *résistants* and the freedom fighters on French soil between 1941 and 1945, and the armies that participated in the Libération in 1944–1945. Among these fifteen fighters, eleven had been killed "facing the enemy," and four represented the martyrs of France. Among these was Renée Levy, a "political deportee" who had been decapitated in Cologne in August 1943.

Renée Levy was not chosen at random. As we can see in the minutes of the meeting of the Consistoire of Paris, "At Mr. Adolphe Caen's insistence, one of the bodies representing the war victims was chosen among the Jews. It was the body of Renée Levy, the granddaughter of Chief Rabbi Albert Levy." The Jews understood the ceremony of 11 November 1945 as a symbol that showed they belonged to the nation and had been accepted back into the bosom of the *République*. Their exclusion had been symbolically marked, right after the defeat and well before any anti-Jewish measures were on the agenda. It became apparent when the Chief Rabbi of France, Isaïe Schwartz, was pushed aside. Like Reverend Boegner, the highest Protestant authority at the time, he had followed the government to Bordeaux and then to Vichy. At the end of July 1940, Reverend Boegner came upon him in Vichy as he was strolling through the park with his wife; he was "a highly respectable man, an ardent patriot who has been very deeply wounded. He is here because this is where the government is, but he never asks to be received for fear of a refusal. He had asked to be allowed to speak on the radio in Bordeaux knowing I had been allowed to do it. His request was never answered."[4] On 14 July 1940, nobody was there to represent the French armed forces or the government at the ceremonies held in the Vichy synagogue. Such days belonged to the past. On 1 January 1945, De Gaulle resumed old habits and granted "a private interview" to chief Rabbi Julien Weill.[5]

The many celebrations of the immediate postwar period, the harshness of the inscriptions on the plaques, the steles, or the monuments built by the various religious groups never stress the specificity of the sufferings of the Jews, nor do they mention the responsibility of Vichy in the genocide. The great majority of the Jews of France wished for a return to a normal situation, which meant to their condition before the war. They advocated a return to the republican assimiliationist model as it had been defined by Maurice Liber: the Jews of France are French citizens of the Hebrew faith, and the immigrants who wish to settle in France should also become French citizens of the Hebrew faith. These Jews generally use the word "assimilation" which, at the time, carried no derogatory connotations and did not imply that Jews should dissolve into the nation. The definition given by Maurice Liber, himself a Jew of Polish origin, in 1920 was therefore still valid: "Judaism exists on principles that can be thus defined: the Jews have become citizens like any others—it is what we call emancipation—and they must naturally be similar to their fellow citizens—this is what we call assimilation—in everything that is not their religion, for Judaism is in essence a religion and should be kept as such."[6]

Inaugurated in 1949, the memorial at the synagogue on the Rue de la Victoire is quite representative of this vision of Judaism. The idea of a monument to the World War II dead that would respect the tradition of the World War I monuments was circulating within the Jewish community. In 1948, the Paris Consistoire began to raise money "for the erection of the memorial of the Paris Jewish Community." On this monument, one can read:

> 1939–1945
> To the memory
> of our brothers
> who fought
> in the war
> and in the Résistance
> To those who perished in the
> deportation camps
> who were executed tortured

burnt and to the
innumerable victims
of German barbarism

There was already, within the grounds of the synagogue, a monument dedicated to the 1914–1918 war, a large plaque that still remains invisible from the street since it is set in the yard that separates the synagogue from the offices of the Consistoire. The names of the Israelites from the Paris Community who gave their lives for France were engraved upon it. The number of the World War II dead was so high that it was unthinkable to list all their names. The monument to the 1939–1945 dead is an homage to ALL the victims of the war, both French and foreign. These victims are enumerated in a certain order: those who fought in the war and the liberation, followed by the fighters of the resistance, who are in turn followed by the deportees, who come last. Beyond the Jews, the people who initiated the project also wished to honor "all the French, regardless of their religion or the group they belonged to, who gave their lives for their country and for the ideal of liberty it represents."

On 27 February 1949, at 11 A.M., the French president, Vincent Auriol, came up to the gate of the temple where he was met by the president of the the Paris Consistoire, George Wormser, and the president of the central Consistoire, Leon Meiss, who was accompanied by the rabbinate.[7]

The temple was shrouded in black and illuminated from all sides; the crowd was enormous. It was the second time that a president of the République had appeared officially inside any synagogue. Indeed, on 26 May 1916, President Raymond Poincarré attended the service held in honor of the lawyers who had died for their country. For the officers of the Consistoire, the presence of the highest authority of the state is of the utmost importance:

Vincent Auriol had come to the temple to accomplish acts of highest significance: surrounded by the members of the government in their most official attire, he had come to wipe away the blemish that the Nazi occupiers, along with a few French citizens who had gone astray, tried to cast upon our religious gathering places; in a way, he was going to symbolically consecrate the full and unrestricted reinstatement of French Jews within the bosom of a nation from which they had been temporarily excluded and restore them in their equality; it is, however, to be noted that this full reinstatement of the Jews had already been symbolically and unanimously accomplished by the people of France as early as the first hour of the liberation; lastly, he was going to express his good feelings toward Judaism throughout the world.

It was, therefore, the ultimate act of reconciliation between the Jews and France, five years after the liberation of Paris.

Leading the prayer, Rabbi Kaplan, the chief rabbi of Paris, did something that had never been done since the establishment of the ceremony: he distinguished between those who had died fighting for France as soldiers or as members of the resistance and the deportees: "Deep is the pain of the survivors who saw the ashes of their beloved ones darkened, dispersed, and mingled with other ashes in the camps where they had suffered and where they were exterminated." They were buried without proper religious care, and for them, the community returned to the tradition of the "Memory Books." A metal box, made of bronze, was sealed at the foot of the monument to receive the book inscribed with the names of the dead. This Memory Book also marked a return to the *Memorbuch* of the Middle Ages. When a man died, murdered as a Jew who had refused apostasy, the Kiddush Hashem, the Blessing of the Name, was said over him and he was never to be forgotten. As the chief rabbi very clearly stressed, the Memory Book was there to mark the difference between those who had given their lives for France and the deportees who joined the long line of martyrs who had died for the "Blessing of the Name." The names of the deportees were never sealed in the box. The Jews were not in a hurry to have the names of their dead written into the book; also, nobody even thought about publishing the names of the deportees. This was probably so because no mourning had occurred. Given the aura of uncertainty surrounding their death, and also given the fact that there were no corpses and the place where they had died was far away—in distant Poland, which is nowhere, as Jarry used to say—all these factors probably induced more than one to think that their beloved were not really dead, that they might return some day. To write their names into a memory book or upon a stele meant accepting the reality of their death in unthinkable circumstances.

On this inaugural day, after the traditional prayers, the ritual moved away from Judaism in the direction of another cult, which Antoine Prost calls the "Republican cult of the dead,"[8] a ritual that is performed every 11 November in front of each of the 30,000 monuments to the dead of World War I. A trumpet sounds "Sonnerie Aux Morts" (Last post), a musical score composed by the leader of the Garde Républicaine and officially adopted in 1932. It "spread progressively but rapidly to become, just before World War II, specifically reserved for all the celebrations held in front of the monuments to the dead; it is the tune . . . that is always sounded on those occasions." A minute of silence is observed; it too belongs to that same ritual of the Republic. Then, the assembly returns to the Jewish ritual with the prayer for the dead, recited by the chief rabbi, which is followed by El Mole Rahamim and the recitation of the Kaddish by the whole audience. The Sacred Scrolls are taken out of the Holy Ark, and the Rabbi of Paris says, as is customary during the Saturday morning service, the prayer for France. "La Marseillaise" gushes out of the organ. The Torah is then put away. The Président de la République, followed by all the officials in attendance, proceeds under the peristyle of the temple. Orphaned children, sons of deportees, unveil the monument.

This monument, as well as the ceremony surrounding its inauguration, shows that we have returned to the Republican model. In the end, its theme is Gallic. The Occupation and Vichy are nothing but a parenthesis that does not cut into the course of a history that began with the emancipation of the Jews.

When the law of 1954 mentioned deportation to the Nazi camps, it did not mention the deportation of the Jews, even though Jews constituted the largest group of deportees from France.[9] The fact that the law was voted in unanimously shows clearly that the question of the specificity of the genocide was not politically relevant at the time. The law wanted the French to celebrate and remember mostly the heroes or the resistance deportees. These views were in perfect harmony with the views of the Jewish world at the time. Indeed, since the Libération, the Jewish organizations, and particularly the immigrant organizations among them, celebrated the heroes of the Warsaw Ghetto who had, according to the set phrase, "saved the honor of the Jews"; the victims of the Shoah at large were rarely referred to. The Warsaw Ghetto uprising had given the Jews a place among those who had actively taken up arms in the war and, therefore, they had been acknowledged as members of humankind who had fought a war against Nazism. Israel also celebrated these heroes, among them Mordekhai Anieliewicz. On 9 August 1953, in reaction against the setting of the first stone of the Tombeau du martyr juif inconnu (the grave of the unknown Jewish martyr)[10] in Paris, the Knesset passed a law on the Shoah and *gevurah* (heroism). The date chosen, Nissan 27, links the celebration of memory to heroism since it was one week after the celebration of the Warsaw Ghetto. Until the 1970s, the memory of the fighters and of the rebellion came first, in accordance with the traditional Zionist ideal.

It would be wrong, however, to say that there was no memory of the Shoah. Numerous memorials were built in the Jewish sections of the cemeteries of Bagneux and Pantin near Paris, and the names of those who had been, in the usual words, "the victims of the Nazi barbarians" were carved on the headstones of graves by the *Landsmanshaften*. These associations of *landsleit* also created transnational committees to publish the memorial books of the communities that had disappeared.[11] But this memory remained private and restricted to the circles of families and friends of the victims. It did not make any attempt to become public. Isaac Schneersohn was the first to demand a public celebration of memory.[12] He had the idea of creating *the* memorial for all the victims of the genocide. While France was still occupied, Isaac Schneersohn created, in the town of Grenoble, the Centre de documentation juive, the CDJC (Jewish documentation center), which published a considerable amount of documentation after the liberation. However, it seems that Isaac Schneersohn felt, as Yerushalmi explains, that: "Rituals are more important than chronicles in the process of transmission of a collective memory."[13] Schneersohn thinks that, with the material it has published, the Jewish documentation center has built "a spiritual monument to the Jewish communities that were victims of the Nazis. But the material published interests only a few individuals, experts on politics, history, law, or sociology. As important as these fields and these people may be, the CDJC feels that its task, which is summed up in its motto 'Do not forget,' will not be complete if it fails to have a direct and powerful effect on the imagination of the masses."[14] Isaac Schneersohn's assistant, Jacques Sabille, further clarifies the name that was retained for the memorial, "Grave for an unknown Jewish martyr": "Those who created, after World War I, the Republican and nonreligious cult of the 'Unknown Soldier' paved the way. Their initiative was perfectly consistent with the new line defined at the beginning of the new century."[15]

The idea of such a monument provoked violent reactions within the Jewish community, in particular among immigrants: "To build monuments in relation to spiritual principles, whether to God, to the soul, or to the dead, is in contradiction to the spirit of Judaism. . . . Such a monument is nothing but a replica of the memorial to the 'Unknown Jewish Soldier.' It is far from representing anything related to Jewish genius."[16]

Indeed, the only link between the memorial and the Jewish tradition is the room devoted to the Memory Book. However, contrary to the Memory Book of the Synagogue de La Victoire, this Memory Book was to hold the names of all the victims who perished in the catastrophe and who never received proper burial; and these names were to be kept forever. Two copies of this book were to be made and one given to the State of Israel. Thus, the "Grave for an unknown Jewish martyr," which was to become "The Memorial" in 1974, was built for the whole world. It gathers all the dead for the purpose of memory.

The first stone was laid on 17 May 1953 in the neighborhood of the *Pletzl* on property given by the City of Paris.[17] The ceremony was grandiose; it was also quite similar to the commemorating ceremonies held every 11 November in front of every memorial to the dead of the Great War. Delegates of the various groups to which the victims of Nazi terror belonged stood alongside veterans surrounding the stele, their flags forming a vast crown of blue, white, and red French flags around it. The bugle opened the ceremony with "Aux Champs," followed by "La Marseillaise." At the end, the bugle played "Sonnerie Aux Morts." Rabbis were present, in lieu of the Catholic clergy. The only specifically Jewish features of the ceremony were an orphan saying Kaddish and the choir of the synagogue de La Victoire singing the "Chant des Partisans Juifs" (Song of the Jewish partisans). Imitating the roles of other schoolchildren, the orphans filed past the monument, leaving flowers behind them.

The monument was inaugurated in October 1956. It is really the memorial to the dead of the Shoah. Set a few feet away from the street, it is made of a huge cylinder that bears the names of the places where Jews were killed: Belzec, Treblinka, Maidanek, Auschwitz, Sobibor, Buchenwald, and the Warsaw Ghetto. Further, above the the entrance to the crypt, a wall bears a star of David and is inscribed both in Hebrew and in French:

> In front of the unknown Jewish martyr show your respect and your
> piety for all martyrs let your thoughts wander along with them
> theirs is a path of pain, and walking it, you will reach the highest
> peaks of justice and truth.

In 1957, an urn containing ashes from one of the Birkenau crematoria was transferred to the crypt.[18] Whereas the monument inaugurated in 1949 in front of the synagogue on the Rue des Victoire in Paris gives a place to the Jews of France among all the dead of the war, the *Mémorial* on Rue Geoffroy Lasnier gives a place to all the Jews of Europe who were victims of the genocide. After 1957, a ceremony at the *Mémorial* was included in the celebration of National Deportation Day. "Brief and dignified," according to the administrative terminology, it is usually held in front of the *Mémorial*: flowers, lighting the flame, a minute of silence, "Last Post."

Between the end of the 1950s and the beginning of the 1960s, a specific memory of the Shoah slowly emerged and dissociated itself from the memory of the deportation. First, there were a few major literary achievements that met with immense success, for instance, André Schwartz-Bart's *The Last of the Just* and Anna Langfus's *Les bagages de sable*. There was also Adolf Eichmann's abduction—this "Nuremberg of the Jewish people," as Ben-Gurion later wrote. The decision to kidnap Eichmann and bring him to trial was obviously a political decision, and we may therefore wonder about the motivations behind it. Was it, as Ben-Gurion wrote, "To remind public opinion throughout the world of who is behind those who are working toward the destruction of the State of Israel and of who their accomplices are, consciously or unconsciously?"[19] Was it to extol the heroism of the Israelis, in contrast to the supposed passivity of the European Jews? Was it to shame the world for having abandoned the Jews and to urge the superpowers to support Israel more strongly? Or was it to fill a few internal gaps and reinforce the social cohesion of the young country: "The gap between the new urban middle-class and the old rural elite of the kibbutz movement . . . the gap between the European-raised generation—with their sabra children—and the oriental immigrants . . . , the gap between generations."

Abba Eban, the Israeli minister of education and culture at the time of the Eichmann trial, said more precisely, "Yet, shared memories often reminded the Israelis that history had treated the whole Jewish people in such a way that, in the end, they also shared a common fate. One of the highest moments of truth regarding unification came with the abduction of Adolf Eichmann and his trial."[20]

With the law instituting Yad Vashem, Israel positioned itself, for the first time, as the world center of the memory and the history of the genocide. This position of centrality became even clearer as the trial of Adolf Eichmann reached well beyond the boundaries of Israel itself. As Gideon Hausner wrote, "By trying Eichmann according to Israeli law, the State of Israel has extended its protective arm over the whole Jewish people."[21]

Following the Eichmann trial, many legal procedures were launched in Germany; several led to trials: in Düsseldorf, the trial, between September and October 1964, of the ten torturers of Treblinka; in Frankfurt in 1964, the trial of twenty-two members of the Auschwitz staff; in Munich in 1966–1967, the trial of the officers in charge of the Final Solution in the Netherlands. In 1966–1967, Robert Kempner, the former American prosecutor at the Nuremberg trials, acted as lawyer for the families of Anne Frank and Edith Stein.

The year 1964 was the first after the twenty-year limitation period on war crimes. After this date, it would be impossible to bring anybody to trial. Some people were worried: What if Hitler himself were still alive? What if Bormann was arrested? Or Mengele? They would have been beyond the reach of the law. These and other reasons persuaded the French representatives to vote unanimously in parliament for a law excluding crimes against mankind from the statute of limitations. At that time, nobody even thought of Barbie, Touvier, Papon, or Bousquet. From then on, if there was to be a trial, it would have to be for crimes against mankind. According to the definition given in Nuremberg, that meant genocide.

All these signs show that the Jewish memory of the Shoah was being constituted when the 1967–1968 multifaceted crisis broke out concerning the site of Auschwitz. It emerged during the inauguration of the International Memorial on 16 April 1967. Upon his return, Georges Wellers, one of 250 French delegates, explained his views in the journal of the CDJC, Le Monde Juif. The keynote address, given by Prime Minister Cyrankiewicz, himself a former inmate at Auschwitz, did not mention Jews even once. According to his speech, the gas chambers were meant for "the extermination of the Polish nation." A large portion of the very moving speech given by Robert Waiz, president since 1962 of the Auschwitz International Committee (CIA), was devoted to the

Jews. However, his speech was delivered in French and was not translated. Wellers had very little to say about the third speech, given by the Soviet general in command of the Red Army avant-garde that liberated Auschwitz, "Except perhaps that we heard as much about Auschwitz as about Vietnam, and as much about the Nazis as about the Americans."[22]

As for Robert Waiz, he made his letter of resignation public on 6 May 1968. He resigned as president because the members of the general secretariat of the CIA, all from Warsaw, were all linked to the Zbowid, an organization of Polish veterans. He emphasized the protest, coming from all over the world, that followed the inauguration of the international monument: nowhere could the word Jew be found on the Auschwitz plaques. Above all, his resignation took place after the Six Day War and the violent anti-Semitic demonstrations that followed and that convinced the last Jews remaining in Poland to leave the country. Robert Waiz wrote, "At the beginning of June 1967, when Israel was being menaced from all sides, when the Jews of Israel were under the threat of total annihilation, I asked the Secretary General of the CIA to call a meeting of the ruling committee. Indeed, millions of survivors live in Israel; they are represented in three organizations, two of which are affiliated with the CIA. For three months, my requests were repeatedly answered by official refusals." And he concluded:

> Over the past few weeks, and particularly during the celebration of the Warsaw Ghetto uprising and during the inauguration of the Jewish block at the Auschwitz museum, several Polish leaders never ceased to oppose Jews and Zionists in order to justify their attitude against Israel and the measures they were taking against the Jews of Poland.
>
> These leaders, and among them, Vice-minister Rusinek, the secretary general of Zwobid, are against anti-Semitism when they talk of the millions of victims of Nazi racism. But they are against Israel, where a few thousand Auschwitz survivors have taken refuge. They use the dead against the living.
>
> I cannot personally dissociate the two; under the present condi-

tions, I cannot accept the fact that the general secretariat of the CIA is very closely linked to Zwobid.[23]

In addition to the aftermath of the Eichmann trial, the Six Day War marked a rupture, revealing new forms of behavior among the Jews of France. First, they feared that Israel would be destroyed, a reminder of other destructions. This anxiety was expressed in a very moving article written by Raymond Aron on 4 June 1967, the day before Israel's preemptive attack against Egypt, and published in the 12 June issue of *Le Figaro Littéraire* under the title "Facing a Tragedy." Aron writes:

> An irresistible feeling of solidarity rises in us. Where it comes from does not matter. If the great powers of the world, according to the cold calculation of their interests, allow the small State of Israel to be destroyed, it would be a crime; this crime against a state that is not my own, a crime so small when considered on the scale of the world, would deprive me of the strength to live, and I believe that millions and millions of men would be ashamed of the human race.

Raymond Aron called this possible destruction a "staticide." Also, and this is where the consequences of the Six Day War are particular to the French situation, it put an end to the belief that total assimilation would ever be possible for the Jews of France. This understanding stemmed, of course, from the French policy toward the Jewish State and from the famous statement issued by General De Gaulle during a press conference in November 1967, when he referred to the Jews as "an elite people, sure of themselves and domineering." For Raymond Aron, "De Gaulle has deliberately and willfully opened a new era in Jewish history and perhaps a new age of anti-Semitism. Again, everything becomes possible, and everything starts all over. Of course, we do not refer to persecutions, only to 'malevolence and spite.' This is not a time of contempt, only a time of suspicion."

The opening of this "time of suspicion" prompted Raymond Aron and many others to become conscious of the existence of a residual Jewish identity, a notion that is hard to define but one that came in conflict with their French identity. This violent feeling, experienced by a great many French Jews during the Six Day War, awakened their interest in a fact that had voluntarily been put aside in the aftermath of the Second World War: the Jews had been excluded from the French national community by the Vichy regime. The last element that emerged during those years was the constitution of groups of militants for memory.

The fight of these groups was a fight against the reemergence of the Vichy past, and it became the root of a new Jewish identity as it became evident upon the occurrence of several "cases" after 1978.[24] In 1978 the weekly L'Express published an interview with the Vichy former commissioner for Jewish affairs, Darquier de Pellepoix, who explained that only lice had been gassed in Auschwitz; Robert Faurisson first publicly challenged the facts of history with his revisionist denial thesis; the French public was overcome with emotion when the Holocaust television series was broadcast and, for the first time, French citizens were accused of crimes against mankind. From then on, the battle of the Jews of France for memory could be reduced to the exposure of "Nazi cruelty." The Jews of France were now focused on the responsibility of Vichy. Naional Deportation Day was contested. On 5 May 1986, the Jewish Telegraphic Agency (a Jewish news service) published the following statement of protest:

> Mrs Eliane Klein, Chairwoman of the Orléans branch of the CRIF (Representative council of the Jewish institutions of France), and Mr. Jean Kahn, Chairman of the Alsatian branch of the CRIF, feel outraged by the fact that on 27 April, in the course of the ceremonies held for National Deportation Day in their respective cities, and also most probably in other cities of France, under the tutelage of the highest military and political authorities, a national statement was read that had been written by the National Federation of Deportees and Prisoners, résistants, and patriots (FNDRIRP). This statement, which never once mentions the word "Jew" tends, in fact, to obliterate the specificity of the martyrdom of the Jews by failing to mention that the Jewish victims were not deported as

political opponents or as *résistants* but as Jews. When the statement establishes a parallel between deportation and famine in the Sahel region of Africa, it contributes to the banalization of the Shoah and thus follows the same trend as other attempts in this direction today. Protest must be voiced at the national level to prevent the renewal of such practices.[25]

The celebration of National Deportation Day takes into account the demand of the Jewish community to stress the specificity of the deportation of the Jews. Thus, ceremonies are held in Drancy, a camp in the suburbs of Paris from which the majority of the Jews were sent from France to Auschwitz. More important still, two similar ceremonies were organized, one at the memorial to the unknown Jewish martyr, the other at the Ile de la Cité memorial, where the deportation of the *résistants* is commemorated.

This change in the official policy of celebration was, however, not deemed to be sufficient. Following Serge Klarsfeld's actions, new and very active groups appeared that relied heavily on the media for the defense of memory. First, there was the Fils et filles des déportés juifs de France (Sons and daughters of Jewish deportees from France). This organization was created in 1979, precisely "to support the action of Serge and Beate Klarsfeld whose aim was to put an end to the impunity of those, both German and French, who were responsible for the deportation of the Jews of France between 1940 and 1944." On the eve of the 1992 commemoration, a Vel d'Hiv Committee was created, composed mostly of former communists and former extreme leftists. Because 1992 was the fiftieth anniversary of the first deportations from France, it was marked by several public celebrations and controversies. The year 1992 is without any doubt an important date in the construction of the memory of the genocide in France. A major concession occurred in the weeks preceding the fiftieth anniversary of the 16 and 17 July 1942 massive arrests, known to all as the Rafle du Vel d'Hiv (the Vel d'Hiv round-up), in which 13,000 Jews, including a large number of children, were arrested: For the first time in French history, a petition was addressed to the *president* asking him to make a symbolic gesture that would acknowledge the responsibility of the French in the genocide. The French press compared such an act to Willy Brandt kneeling in Warsaw before the monument to the Ghetto uprising, and to Juan Carlos begging forgiveness for the deportation of the Jews from Spain centuries ago. On 14 July Mitterrand declared that it was out of the question to ask the *République* to justify itself:

> Throughout its history, the French *République* has always had a very open attitude, it has always considered that citizen rights were to be granted to anyone who had been recognized as a citizen, and particularly to the Jews of France. Please, do not hold this *République* accountable! It has done its duty. For the past two centuries, a period during which the *Républiques* followed one another, it was the *République* that, for all purposes, decided upon all the measures taken toward equality and citizenship. . . . *La République* was always the one to extend its hand in order to avoid racial segregation. Please, do not hold *La République* accountable! But in 1940, there existed a 'French State'; it was the Vichy regime; it was not *La République*. And this 'French State' must be held accountable; this I accept, naturally, how could I not accept it? I wholly share the emotion of those who come to me, but to be precise, the *Résistance,* and, after it, De Gaulle's government, and then the fourth *République* as well as the next one, were founded as rejections of that 'French State'; this must be made clear.[26]

Serge Klarsfeld's answer reopened the discussion when he questioned the responsibility of the Chief of State himself: "François Mitterrand is true to himself," he said, "inasmuch as he joined Vichy in April 1942 before joining the *Résistance*." He also underlined the fact that every year the French president had flowers deposited on the grave of the former Maréchal Philippe Pétain.[27]

After 1945, the anniversary of the 16 July round-up had always been celebrated where the Vel d'Hiv used to stand, on the very spot where a large number of the Jews arrested on that day had been held prisoners. The intense media attention that preceded the celebration of the fiftieth anniversary and the violent verbal attacks on the highest authority of the country account for the massive crowds that attended the celebration in 1992. The Comité Vel d'Hiv 1942 (Vel d'Hiv committee 1942) demanded again that the highest magistrate of France "should issue a solemn statement, on 16 July, on the very grounds of the Vel D'Hiv round-up." There was nothing new in the course of the 1992 ceremony, and it unfolded according to the protocol the memory committee of the CRIF had decided upon. There were speeches (whereas during the ceremonies of National Deportation Day there are no speeches), flowers, songs by the Yiddish singer Talila, and the recitation of the Kaddish memorial prayer. The one new fact was the presence of a chief of state at these ceremonies. Indeed, François Mitterrand had come and was greeted as soon as he stepped out of his limousine by much whistling and little applause. A few catcalls were then heard: *"Mitterrand à Vichy"* (Mitterrand, go back to Vichy). Robert Badinter, himself the son of deportees and the Chairman of the Conseil constitutionel (highest court of law in France), was designated to quiet the whistles and the catcalls, which he did with anger in his voice before proceeding to deliver his own speech.

The presence of the Président de la République was not enough to satisfy Serge Klarsfeld, nor was it enough for the organizers of the Comité Vel d'Hiv 1942. If Serge Klarsfeld demanded a public statement on 26 August for the anniversary of the southern zone round-ups, the Comité Vel d'Hiv 1942 went even further. The newspaper *Le Monde* published a press release in which they wished to address "all national representatives and invite every one of them to start working on a bill that would transform 16 July into a national day for the commemoration of the persecutions and crimes perpetrated by the French State of Vichy." Though nobody knows why, Serge Klarsfeld abandoned his own proposal. But he did not cease to fight: on 21 July, he announced that the president had decided he would stop sending flowers to the grave of former Maréchal Pétain on 11 November. It would later appear, and the truth was disclosed by Serge Klarsfeld's own son Arno, that this was pure invention; Klarsfeld had tried to force Mitterrand's hand. Indeed, on 11 November 1992, the *Préfet* of

Vendée (the representative of the central administration in that part of the country) brought flowers to the grave of former Maréchal Pétain. Protest came from all sides, from associations of former *résistants* and former deportees, and from Jewish organizations. It was abundantly commented upon in the media.

At the same time, and with relative discretion, Jean Le Garrec, a socialist representative and the chairman of the finance committee in the *Assemblée Nationale* (parliament), proposed a bill whose objective was to make 16 July into a national commemoration day. On 22 December, in an interview on Radio J, a Jewish radio station, Mitterrand said:

> I do not want the misunderstanding to grow any deeper. . . . If the nation had been engaged in this sorry adventure that the Vichy government represents, pardon would be called for. It is what Willy Brandt did in the name of Germany. . . . But France as a whole was never engaged in these doings, and neither was the République, it was a different regime, a temporary regime.

Yet, on the eve of his departure for Israel, Mitterrand said he was "ready to make some sort of solemn gesture."

The gesture he made was to pass a decree, on 3 February 1993, instituting 16 July as the official day for the commemoration of "the racist and anti-Semitic persecutions committed under the de facto authority known as the 'Government of the French State 1940–1944.'" For the first time in the history of the French République, a national day of commemoration was established by a decree issued by the president and not after a law had been passed in parliament. In the order of commemoration, the deportation and the genocide are two distinct notions since "racist and anti-Semitic crimes" applies in fact to the destruction of the Jews.

The law, therefore, provided an official day for the commemoration, on 16 July if it falls on a Sunday, or on the following Sunday in case it falls on a weekday. A "National Committee for the defense of the memory of racist and anti-Semitic persecutions perpetrated under the de facto authority known as the 'Government of the French State'" was formed. It was supposed to design a monument and to supervise its construction on the site of the former Vel d'Hiv in Paris. It was also supposed to design and build two steles, one on one of the sites where the Jews had been held, and the other on the grounds of *La Maison d'Izieu* (The House in Izieu), whose memorial museum was in great part financed by the state and which was inaugurated by François Mitterrand himself on 24 April 1994. The committee also decided on the text that was to be inscribed on the stele of the monument; finally, a commemorative plaque was to be affixed in each and every département of France.

On 17 July 1994, the Vel d'Hiv monument, which is to be the physical symbol of the commemoration, was inaugurated by the president of the republic, François Mitterrand, the prime minister, Edouard Balladur, and the mayor of Paris, Jacques Chirac. It is a figurative monument: seven statues cast in bronze stand witness to the persecutions. They belong to various age groups: a grown-up couple with a baby, a younger man with his pregnant wife, an old lady, a child. They are, according to the sculptor W. Spizer,

> sitting or lying down along a large curve, they are lost, distraught . . . the curve could be the curved track of the velodrome. . . . It can also be interpreted otherwise: it could be a perfect, timeless orb symbolizing hope as opposed to the misery of these wretched people. . . . It could also represent a raft caught in a storm. . . . More practically, the curve, which both links the group to, and excludes it from, the surrounding urban context, constitutes a path leading to meditation.

The inscription that was then unveiled can now be found in every département of France: "The French République honors the victims of the racist and anti-Semitic persecutions together with the victims of the crimes against mankind perpetrated under the de facto authority known as the 'Government of the French State' (1940–1944). We shall never forget." In France, it was the first, and so far the only, time the State had a direct involvement in a campaign for the erection of steles and monuments.[28] The last episode of this story takes place when Jacques Chirac, who was elected president two months before, delivered his speech on the occasion of the fifty-third anniversary of the round-up. For this speech, the historical research was done carefully, thoroughly, and with great competence; the speech itself was finely wrought, and each word was carefully weighed. It began with a strong moral judgment: "These dark hours forever sully our history; they are an insult to our past and our traditions." The new French president went even further: "Yes, the criminal folly of the occupiers was seconded by the French, by the French state." The opening "Yes" of this last sentence shows that the speech was definitely taking a stand, choosing a side in the debate; it was an answer to the question of the responsibility of the state, a question Jacques Chirac asked to himself, but a question that has never ceased to be at the core of the controversy. The president then described the round-up in very precise terms: the 4,500 policemen and *gendarmes* "under the authority of their superiors were answering a request made by the nazis" when, at dawn, they arrested men, women, and children. "France, the homeland of the Enlightenment and of the Rights of Man, a land of welcome and asylum, France, on that day, committed the irreparable." President Chirac also pointed out that the Beaune-la-Rolande and Pithiviers transit camps, where some of the people who were arrested on 16 July 1942 remained for a brief period before they were sent to Drancy and then deported to Auschwitz, had been opened by the Vichy government. The anniversary of the Vel d'Hiv round-up allowed Jacques Chirac to mention the deportation of all the Jews, the 76,000 Jews from France who never returned. "We have an eternal debt toward these people," he remarked. He then urged France to cast an uncompromising eye upon its past: "To acknowledge the errors of the past and the errors committed by the state, not to conceal the dark hours of our history, is the very simple way in which we can fight for our idea of man, of his freedom and of his dignity. It is to fight against dark forces."

Actually, if we read this speech closely, Chirac does not accept what Mitterrand had refused to do: neither one agrees to hold *La République* accountable for the crimes committed by the Vichy regime. When he speaks of "The Other France" Chirac uses exactly the same tone as General De Gaulle when he referred to "the France that was never at Vichy" and that was "always correct, generous, faithful to its traditions and to its spirit." The leaders of the Jewish community, the chief rabbi of France Leon Sitruk, or the newly elected president of the CRIF, Henri Hajdenberg, expressed their deepest satisfaction. Indeed, Chirac's speech did not start a new controversy, excepting Jean Marie Le Pen's remark when he said that the president had "sullied the nation." A poll conducted by IFOP, in conjunction with the weekly L'Evènement du Jeudi, showed that 72 percent of the French approved of Jacques Chirac's speech. However, this speech raises two questions. First, there is the problem of the collective guilt of the French. During the debates that preceded the trial of the Nazi criminals in Nuremberg, the legal profession, as a whole, rejected the idea of collective guilt for the German people. Is it possible, then, to make "France" guilty of the crimes committed by Vichy? The second problem that the historians and the politicians have never ceased to discuss is the question of the continuity of the state. For Marie France Garaud and Pierre Juillet, Vichy was not "France": "The Republic is free or it is not the Republic. An enslaved state is no longer a state. And this is not a feeling or an interpretation, but a fact; it is the political and the institutional reality." For there is, beyond Chirac's speech, an even deeper problem: what is the state? As far as the bureaus of the administration, justice, and the police are concerned, the continuity is obvious between Vichy and the regimes that preceded and followed it. But when a country was occupied and when institutions like the parliament no longer existed, can we still say that no rupture has taken place?

Over fifty years, the perception of the events in France linked to Nazism has undergone fundamental changes. The official memory, the memory upon which the state passes laws, and, more generally, the memory policy of the state has largely been turned into the memory of the genocide. It is interesting to note the insistence on the responsibility of Vichy in the genocide. This insistence is a new fact, one that originates with the children born during or after the war. For their elders, the return to the institutions of the *République* and the disappearance of the anti-Semitic German or Vichy laws marked a return to Republican normalcy and allowed the Jews to come back to live in France. The attitude of world Jewry was totally different regarding Germany. For all the Jewish organizations, Germany was to blame for the catastrophe and the country was put off-limits. In 1950, the Jewish Agency closed its offices in Munich, which had been kept open to facilitate the departure of displaced persons; it also urged the Jews to leave the country within the next six weeks. The following year, the Jewish World Congress broke its ties with the established West German Jewish communities. Nothing of this sort happened with France. Except for a very few, the Jews of France remained in their country, which also became a sanctuary for others, for nearly 30,000 Jewish survivors from Poland came to live in France right after the war. Later, the French Jews from Algeria, where the Vichy laws had been far harsher than in France itself (though Algeria was never occupied), would choose to come to France rather than emigrate to Israel.

Why did the Jews change the way they regarded France? What happened between the decades that followed the war and today? Why is Vichy put on the same level as Nazi Germany? These questions can only be understood within the larger French context of the double crisis of the republican model and of national identity. Also, one must take into account the international context with its new models of Jewish identity. The emancipation of French Jews has been celebrated as the paradigm of the blessings of the French revolution. In France, the Jew is a Frenchman and a patriot; he is true to the *République* but also belongs to the Jewish faith in the privacy of his home. The République granted the Jews integration and advancement. Today, a new model is being developed whose roots plunge into the historical references of the 1940s. The Jews of France have now reached the end of a one-hundred-and-fifty-year-old-process marked by their assimilation and their integration into the French nation. Their demand for a particular memory brings to the fore their exclusion from the national community as it was created by the Vichy counter-revolution. There is a glaring contrast between, on one hand, a memory that separates and excludes—as if permanent remembrance could revive the period of Vichy and German occupation—and, on the other, the perfect integration of those very people who are actually fighting this fight: lawyers, teachers, and others. This integration is also visible in the rise of the number of exogamic marriages, a rise that is characteristic of the diaspora at large, and of France in particular.

However, beyond the particular case of the French, the demand for the constitution of a Jewish memory of persecution is, in the last analysis, the expression of a claim to an identity for the non-religious Jews, be they in France, the United States, or Israel. The models that were in place at the beginning of the century are no longer operational: How can you be a Bundist, after all, when Jewish "masses" or a Jewish "proletariat" no longer exist and when Yiddish has ceased to be a language of communication? How can one believe that the communist or the extreme leftist utopias could ever open onto a brighter future? In the years following the war, the memory activists were mainly communists, and those born after the war were extreme leftists. The war operates as the myth from which their Jewishness springs, and the various ways in which this memory is expressed—the commemorative Day of the Shoah, the building of memorials, the pilgrimages to Auschwitz, the march of the living—these are beginning to constitute a new secular religion. And the Jews of France have demanded, not without some success, the recognition of this new secular religion and its integration into the affairs of the state. They have also demanded the necessary means that would help it grow and develop.

NOTES

1. We shall leave aside the history of 8 May, which bears no direct relationship to the theme discussed here. See, among others, Henry Rousso's *The Vichy Syndrome. History and Memory in France since 1944,* trans. Arthur Goldhammer (Cambridge: Harvard University Press, 1991; 2nd ed. 1994). We shall, however, make mention of the recent argument opposing François

Bayrou, Minister of National Education, and the History and Geography Teachers' Association. In the new history curriculum for primary schools, 8 May appears as "Armistice of World War II." In its 23 March 1995 press release, the Teachers' Association voices its indignation: "The minister conducts a revision of history when he presents, as part of the official curriculum to be taught in all the schools of the République, the unconditional capitulation of Germany as an armistice. The Association is baffled by this outrageous position and notes that even the most dangerous revisionists would not dare to make public such a contention without awakening the most unanimous indignation."

2. Mont Valérien in Suresnes was the main site of the Nazi repression in the Paris area. One thousand hostages and résistants were shot there.

3. Henri Frenay, *La nuit finira. Mémoires de résistance. 1940-1945* (Paris: Robert Laffont, 1973) 549. About Mont Valérien, see Serge Barcellini and Annette Wieviorka, *Passant souviens-toi. Lieux du souvenir de la Seconde Guerre mondiale en France* (Paris: Plon, 1995) 156-74. About the ceremony itself, see Gérard Namer, *Batailles pour la mémoire. La commémoration en France de 1945 à nos jours* (Paris: Papyrus, 1983). Nothing was done at Mont Valerien after the 11 November 1945 celebration and the burial of the bodies. In 1958, when General De Gaulle came back to power, he decided to reactivate the project of a memorial dedicated to the French fighters. Sixteen high-relief plaques were then sculpted, each an illustration of a different aspect of the fighting that had taken place. Henri Lagriffoul did the sculpture symbolizing deportation; it shows two hands trying, in a last and desperate effort, to rip away the barbed wire that cuts into a tortured heart. This representation excludes the deportation of the Jews.

4. *Carnets du pasteur Boegner. 1940-1945*, introduction and notes by Philippe Boegner (Paris: Fayard, 1992) 43-44.

5. Records of the ACIP.

6. This important statement by Maurice Liber was published in 1920 in *Foi et réveil*. It is quoted in full by Robert Somer, "La doctrine politique et l'action religieuse du grand Rabbin Maurice Liber," *Revue des études juives. Historia Judaica* 125.1-3 (January–September 1966): 15-17.

7. What follows is based on the detailed report of the inauguration ceremony as recorded in the 48-page brochure *Compte-rendu détaillé des assemblées générales ordinaires et extraordinaires du 12 Juin 1949 et de l'inauguration du monument aux Morts par M. le Président de la République* (Record of the ordinary and extraordinary general meetings of 12 June 1949 and of the inauguration of the memorial to the dead by the president of the republic) (ACIP, 1949).

8. Antoine Prost, "Le monument aux morts," in *Les lieux de mémoire*, vol. 1: *La République* (Paris: Gallimard, 1984) 209ff.

9. Indeed, of the 140,000 deportees from France, about 75,000 were Jews. There are 2,500 Jews among the 40,000 survivors from France.

10. Regarding the conflict between French Jews and Israel, let us say simply that the Israelis managed to impose Yad Vashem as the only international memorial with the exclusive right to keep registries of the names of the victims and to give authorizations for the building of memorials throughout the world. The function of the memorial on Rue Geoffroy Lasnier is, therefore, solely national—contrary to the ambition of its instigator. In 1995, after the creation of the Holocaust Memorial Museum in Washington and with the systematic collection of the testimonies of survivors initiated by Steven Spielberg, the period of strong affirmation of Israel's centrality in terms of conserving memory of the genocide seems to belong to the prehistory of memory.

11. See Jack Kugelmass and Jonathan Boyarin, *From a Ruined Garden. The Memorial Books of Polish Jewry* (New York: Schocken Books, 1983). This book contains the bibliography established in 1980 by Zacharie Baker, Annette Wieviorka, and Itzhok Niborski, *Les livres du souvenir. Mémoriaux juifs de Pologne* (Paris: Archives-Gallimard, 1983).

12. See Annette Wieviorka, "Un lieu de mémoire et d'histoire: Le mémorial du martyr juif inconnu," *Revue de l'Université de Bruxelles* (1987): 107–32. A shortened version was published earlier as "The French Struggle for Memory," *Dimensions* 3.2 (1987).

13. Josef Hayim Yerushalmi, *Zakhor. Histoire juive et mémoire* (Paris: La Découverte, 1984) 30.

14. Isaac Schneersohn, "Rapport moral," in *Le Monde juif* (January 1958): 47.

15. Jacques Sabille, "La création du mémorial," in *Le Monde juif* (July–December 1963).

16. Open letter from Dr. Engelson to Isaac Schneersohn, Maccabi, no. 7.

17. What follows is based on a description given in a brochure published by the CDJC (undated): "Comment s'est déroulée la cérémonie."

18. For the first time, an urn containing ashes was buried at the Père Lachaise cemetery upon the initiative of the Amicale d'Auschwitz (Auschwitz society), on 30 June 1946, in the location of the memorial to the Auschwitz dead. At that time, the Consistoire Central asked the Auschwitz society how they had managed to gather the ashes and then offered similar urns to the various Jewish communities throughout the country; these urns were to be included in the various memorials to the victims of the Shoah. Concerning this, see Annette Wieviorka, *Déportation et génocide entre la mémoire et l'oubli* (Paris: Plon, 1992).

19. This letter was made public on 20 May 1960 and was published by *Le Monde* on May 28 of that same year.

20. Abba Eban, *L'épopée d'Israël moderne* (Paris: Buchet Chastel, 1975) 181.

21. Gideon Hausner, *Justice à Jérusalem. Eichmann devant ses juges,* translation from English (Paris: Flammarion, 1966) 536.

22. Georges Wellers, "Quelques impressions du pèlerinage à Auschwitz," *Le Monde juif* 46 (1967).

23. Robert Waiz's letter was published in 1969 in *Le Monde juif.* Since the fall of communism, the question of the site of Auschwitz has remained highly controversial.

24. See Rousso, *Vichy Syndrome,* as well as Eric Conan and Henry Rousso, *Vichy, un passé qui ne passe pas* (Paris: Fayard, 1994).

25. Quoted in Serge Barcellini, "Sur deux journées nationales commémorant la déportation et les persécutions des années noires," *Vingtième siècle: Revue d'histoire* 45 (January–March 1995): 87.

26. *Le Monde* (16 July 1992).

27. This aspect of François Mitterrand's life is the subject of Pierre Péan's book, *Une jeunesse française: François Mitterrand 1934–1947* (Paris: Fayard, 1994). In the fall of 1994, the book reawakened the controversy about François Mitterrand's past association with Vichy.

28. Concerning these questions and for further descriptions of various monuments, see Serge Barcellini and Annette Wieviorka, *Passant, souviens-toi!*

TWELVE

The Jews and the Spirit of Europe

A Morphological Approach

SHMUEL TRIGANO

The Appearance of the Forgotten People[1]

THE SECOND WORLD WAR caught the Jews of Europe by surprise, so much so that they could not understand what had happened to them. The nature of the event was, indeed, unimaginable to a modern consciousness. In order to understand it, one must have an idea of the symbolic and political dimensions of the agreement by which the Jews lived in the lands that Napoleon, the heir of the Revolution, had conquered. On the basis of this compact, the Jews were to be considered as individual citizens in the modern nation-states of Western Europe.[2] Accordingly, they had to give up the historical bonds they had formed over many centuries and become abstract individuals whose Jewishness was no more than a private affair. This arrangement appeared to most Jews to hold the best promise for human progress, and so they agreed to sacrifice their now meaningless specificity on the altar of the political universal. This is the structural principle of Jewish modernity, in its institutional dimension as well as in its ideology. The modern Jew can hardly think outside of this mental framework, and modern consciousness can approach the Jews only in this specific light.

Yet in Auschwitz, this whole arrangement was radically called into question. The Nazis gathered the Jews in the concentration camps with no regard for either their individual citizenship or their respective nationalities. Even if they were hunted down and arrested as individuals, or even if they were conscious that they were individuals before they were generic Jews, at Auschwitz the Jews once again collectively faced their existence as a people. Moreover, they did so under the pressure of necessity and not as a matter of ideological choice or commitment, as in the cases of Bundism and Zionism, two prominent examples of collective Jewish experience in modern times.

Auschwitz reactivated an archaic concept that modern consciousness did not know how to handle.[3] It showed the latent weakness of modernity in recognizing the Jews as a people. From the start, indeed, Jewish modern existence has been a cause of trouble, an anxious source of strangeness in the process of European nation-state building. In Auschwitz, when Jewish individuals were persecuted as members of a despised people, they once again took on definition, if only in the negative, as a people. Jewish peoplehood reappeared, then, as a by-product of massive persecution.

Such a disaster, which concerns the Jews directly, also concerns modern Europe, though on the less evident side: not that of human rights but that of the nation. Indeed, if it was difficult for modern Europe to conceive of a possible existence for the Jews as a people, it was also difficult for Europe to make the existence of the nation as clear as the ideal of human rights. In theories of the social contract, there was always a difficulty in laying the foundations of social bonds. In Benedict Spinoza's *Treatise on Religious and Political Philosophy*[4] as well as in Rousseau's *Social Contract,* we find a paradoxical appeal to religion and myth in order to establish the authority of the law. The "nations" always erupted violently. Nationalism, as a process of converting a society of citizens into one of masses that wiped out individuals, is an absolutely modern phenomenon and must be taken into account when speaking about modernity. It cannot be set apart, as if it were an exception to modernity. Political modernity developed, indeed, against the background of an antithesis between citizenship and nation, and the divorce of these two was part of the origin of the tragedy of modernity. The Jews increasingly came to personify this disaster, as faithful citizens who nonetheless were suspected of being a separate and secret nation.

That is why Auschwitz calls modernity into question and especially challenges the foundations of the national identities of the European states. It shakes the roots of democracy, confronts the nature of the democratic social link, the status of the particular within the political Universal (the State). Indeed, it calls for a complete rethinking of the idea of the nation. Thus, while Jewish fate became a collective one in the Shoah, this collective fate has to be regarded for what it was—an unthinkable taboo for modern consciousness.

The Shoah therefore also remained a mystery for the European mind. The same process of globalization occurred for Europe at large. From this viewpoint, a united Europe was already forming in the camps through the mixing of the different European nationalities, as if it was forming around the void that Jewish fate conveyed symbolically inside Europe. Is it a coincidence that the concept of "crimes against mankind" (that is to say, the basis of a concept of justice that is supposed to transcend that of states and nations) developed in Europe in order to judge the Nazi war criminals? We have here one of the first attempts in Europe's search for an identity, an attempt to overcome its own failures. And yet for the reasons described above, this new global entity—"Europe"—was obliterated for the European nations. The building of Europe was and still is merely an economic and bureaucratic issue.

The Jewish Sign in the Symbolic System of Europe

Because of the obliteration of the Jew within Europe, the Shoah is a turning point in the history of European self-understanding. Europe is, indeed, a unique example of a civilization whose center is outside itself. From its own viewpoint, Europe is a secondary identity, the "new Israel" drawing its essence from "ancient Israel," just as much as Europe draws its essence from Athens and Rome.[5] In its relationship to Israel, Christianity repeats what the Romans did in their relationship to Hellenism.

From the earliest period of its emergence, Christian Europe drew its own truth from what it regarded to be the decline of "ancient Israel," the "Israel according to the flesh." The latter was the Jews' Israel, the circumcised one, which is opposed to the "Israel according to the spirit," the Christians' Israel.[6] This spirit based itself on the negation of the flesh or the letter, the Jewish letter which henceforth was to carry a Christian meaning. Christianity is thus Judeocentric, even if the Jew is absent. Herein lies the origin of the spirit of Europe and of the fabulous historical dynamics of twenty centuries of history, which drew its energy from the dialectics of the Heavens and the Earth, the spirit and the body (modernity is the swing from the Heavens to the Earth, from the spirit to the body).[7]

Indeed, this dialectics explains the enduring creativity of Europe. All Christian "heresies" (including Protestantism), for example, opposed the "Old Testament" to the "New Testament" in order to prove their legitimacy. The materialistic revolution of modernity can also be understood as a reversal of the value of the spiritual pole and its subjugation by the material one. Thus, the status of the "spirit" changed: it was dismissed and the "flesh" was regarded as primary.

Throughout the medieval period, when Europe defined itself by the spirit, it excluded the Jews of the flesh. When Europe was "catholic" (the original signification of "catholicity" is "universality"), it regarded the Jews as a separated people, a global and alien entity, to be confined to ghettos. In becoming "modern," Europe "Judaized" (i.e., entered the "flesh"), and the Jews were excluded once again. When Europe's catholicity split up into many particular nation-states, the Jews were no longer viewed as a historical people. They became merely a "denomination," a religion, and were then regarded as the very image of an invalidated spirituality or, in the worst case, as the image of transnational cosmopolitan-ism. As such, they were once again looked upon as suspect among the peoples enclosed in their narcissistic nation-states (the "Jewish plot" was one of the major images of the modern Jew).[8] In moder-nity's repression of the Jew, modernity created a question for itself that was not faced by Christianity in the idealistic age. Jewishness in Europe is a "non-place": the advent of (a spiritual) Israel through the negation of (a material) Israel, and Europe, defining itself in the non-place of Jewishness, cannot truly enjoy a place for itself. The Jews stand always as a figure for the Other, the metaphysical and historical Other, according to whom one defines oneself and assumes an identity. That is why the Jew became the symbolic point of mediation between the two faces of Europe, playing a referential role in all major European movements (ide-alism and materialism, tradition and modernity). In every attempt to renew European civilization, the "Jewish question" arose anew, in the Christian era as well as in the modern era.

After the Second World War, a new development of this sym-bolic morphology occurred. The physical destruction of the Jews amounted to the elimination of one of the main elements in the fabric of Europe and the end of the play between the "letter" and the "spirit." Without the destroyed Jewish "letter" (body), Europe lost the symbolic reference of its own definition and, thus, the symbolic space to insure its continuation. Christianity kept the Jews enclosed in the "letter" while it identified itself with the "spirit." Modernity identified the Jews with the "spirit" while it identified itself with the old "letter" (the "matter," the "flesh," and the "body"). In the Shoah, the "letter" as such was destroyed and, with it, the foundations of modernity itself.

This can explain why in the 1960s and 1970s there developed (first of all in France) a literary myth of the Jewish "letter," of Jewishness as a writing experience. Jabès and the literary move-ment "Change" (with Jean Pierre Faye as its leader) attempted to again "Judaize" the "letter," to find in the "letter," now defined as Jewish, a new source of creativity.[9] But, then, the letter referred not to the "spirit," but only to itself. The everlasting exile of the Jewish letter was one of the key notions of this theory. Jean Pierre

Faye himself developed a famous criticism of the use of the Jewish sign in Nazi discourse.[10] Following him and others, the meaning of the "letter" became more literary than Jewish.

From Universalism to Particularity: The Internal Contradictions of Jewish Modernity

This dialectics of the "letter" and the "spirit" had a counterpart in the processes of Jewish self-definition. If, in the first stage of the emancipation era, the Jews renounced their "particularity," at the end of the nineteenth century there began a second stage, which was marked by the return of a corporate or collective dimension of Jewish identity, this partly a by-product of anti-Semitism and partly an internal Jewish development. This development simultaneously opposed and continued the categories of Jewish modernity.

Three versions of this renewed identity can be recognized. In its *humanitarian version*, we have a pragmatic reassertion of a global, transnational Jewish identity. This is a paradoxical phenomenon, for it seems to be at variance with the processes of Jewish integration (the obliteration of a separate "Jewish people") as a result of citizenship but is, in fact, only possible thanks to the gaining of citizenship. This phenomenon can be identified with the appearance of world Jewish institutions, the aims of which were to take action in aid of Jews (of a "Jewish people") everywhere in the world and to negotiate with the states of the world. Examples of such institutions are the Alliance Israelite Universelle, founded in 1860, the Anglo-Jewish Association (1871), or the Hilfsverein der Deutschen Juden (1901). In the *anarchistic and cosmopolitan version* of Jewish identity, world revolution is the ultimate value, the aim of which is the critical revisitation of the values of citizenship and of the democratic nation-state (Marx's "Jewish question" is the prominent example). On this model, there is a negation of the emancipation but also of Jewish particularity (this even if the massive commitment to the social revolution on the part of an important segment of European Jewry may be considered a form of [infra-Jewish] collective identity). The third version was a *national one,* according to two models. Jewish nationalism, along the lines of the Polish Bund, aimed at establishing Jewish autonomy within Polish politics, while political Zionism, which was born in the heart of Europe, based itself on Jewish national specificity yet was not at odds with humanitarian logic.

Political Zionism is very significant. Theodor Herzl's analysis is clear: the bestowal of European citizenship on the Jews would not integrate the Jews as individuals. They have to become a modern nation, a state like others which would grant its own citizenship. But this national Jewish citizenship would involve only the failed Jews of the European emancipation. Herzl imagined a sort of exchange between the European nations and the future Jewish state,[11] an exchange by which the European states would exchange their unsuccessful Jews for the acceptance of the new Jewish state in the array of the European states. In short, Herzlian Zionism is a way of being part of Europe while leaving it geographically: a geographical way out of Europe which is at the same time a symbolic entrance to Europe. Political Zionism is one of the major indicators that the Jewish people could not find its place in modern Europe.

Thus, Jewish modernity displays the extreme poles of the modern spectrum: the individual experience and the mass or collective experience. And, as we have noted with respect to the national phenomenon in Europe, this dialectical situation (and especially the geosymbolic wandering of the Jewish sign in Zionism) reveals how much the "Jewish people" remained unfamiliar to modern Jewish consciousness and came back only obscurely as a return of the repressed, to reach its highest (dis)appearance in the Shoah.

Postwar European Judaism

The most significant shock brought on by the Shoah concerned Jewish citizenship and the ideology of emancipation. An interesting example is the French Jewish case. After the war, Judaism significantly came back to life in Europe only in France, and France is today the main center of Jewish life in Europe. This revival was possible in France because 80 percent of French Jewry had been saved and also because De Gaulle represented a spirited resistance to the Vichy Regime and Nazism.

For the leading intellectual circles of French Judaism, this renewal was not supposed to be a reaffirmation of the old denominational model but was meant to revive the European Jewish ambition to achieve the philosophical universal. From a Jewish viewpoint, France might assume, after the war, the philosophical and spiritual role that Germany had played before and for which it was discredited after Nazism. This project developed more precisely in what is today called the "Ecole d'Orsay." This school of thought was born during the resistance, in the Jewish scout movement (Eclaireurs Israélites de France) under the impetus of Robert Gamzon (1950–1961) and Jacob Gordin (1896–1947). It was planned as a school for Jewish lay leaders, who would revive French Judaism after the war. Its original name was Gilbert Bloch's School (after the name of a Jewish resistance fighter killed by the Nazis), and it was established in Orsay, near Paris. Jacob Gordin and then Léon Askenazi were its spiritual and intellectual leaders. This school, where Jewish students were housed while studying at the university, played an important role in the reconstruction of Jewish life in France and was active between 1946 and 1970. With the "Colloque des Intellectuels Juifs de Langue française," it was the main intellectual institution of French Jewry until the mid-1970s. Such thinkers as André Neher, Emmanuel Lévinas, Léon Askenazi, Eliane Amado-Levy Valensi, and others were closely linked to it.

The Orsay School tried to combine a faithfulness to the basic tenets of religious Judaism with a dialogue with European and modern culture. It affirmed the global relevance of the Judaic message at the end of the twentieth century. "In the ruins of the present," Edmond Fleg asked, "what can the tradition and hope of Israel as seen by today's eyes supply for the spiritual reconstruction of Israel and of the world?"[12] An implicit assumption was that the Shoah made it a requirement of the Jews to feel responsible for all mankind. The genocide hurt the Jewish people especially, but by its very character it required modern man and especially Jews to produce, from their Hebraic and biblical roots, answers to the failures of modernity. It called not for a radical condemnation but a "tikkun," a repairing. As André Neher said: "The desire to redo the emancipation while, this time, remaining faithful to a clear and undamaged Judaism, has no parallel elsewhere."[13] What was at stake was not the obliteration of the specificity of Jewish martyrdom but its position at the center of human fate. Levinas wrote: "The martyrdom of this people becomes a palpable example, the concrete projection of Calvary and of all human suffering, a concrete symbol of a humanity which learns to recognize itself, and a providential prefiguration of a future messianic humanity."[14] Jewish particularism was assumed, but it now had a different meaning: no longer a confinement in the "letter," the myth, but resistance to murder and death. Eliane Amado-Lévy Valensi explained: "Just as the Christ 'takes upon himself' men's sins, Israel is suffering from men's evil. The illusion of individuation is broken in his sensitivity, which puts him at the nerve center of human suffering and makes him the echo of the world's distress."[15] The Holocaust is defined as the ultimate effect of the "refusal of nations to recognize in the Jewish condition their very humanity, divided and painful."[16] This Jewish condition embodies, therefore, the failure of human unity and the hope of its future unification. Levinas also wrote: "Israel (is the) . . . hostage of men. . . . This one, hostage of all the others, is necessary to them, for without him morality will not take shape anywhere."[17] Therefore, if the failure of modernity called for a return to Judaism, this return could only be achieved through a general reorientation of the European mind toward the specific intelligence of the people that transcended the abyss of misfortune and carries messianic hope.

On the intellectual plane, the Jews had to go back to the texts of Judaism, to their tradition re-shaped as a genuine system of thought, that is, endowed with a capacity to ask questions. The Orsay intellectuals raised again the eternal philosophical questions but did so in a totally new perspective, a Jewish one.

The Birth of the "Jewish Community"

The Orsay School was not only an intellectual movement but also a school to train lay leaders for French Jewry. It had a very strong concern for the collective future of the Jews, defined as a "Jewish community," a new political category for French Jewry and for Western European democracy. The Jews as members of a "community" were citizens but no longer to be regarded merely as individuals. There was now a new feeling of belonging to a Jewish people. This drastic development emphatically expressed the consequence of the mass exclusion of the Jews from the entitlements of French citizenship by the Vichy Regime. The foundation of a representative Council of the French Jews (CRIF) during the Résistance was the clearest indication of the beginning of this new era, for the CRIF, the president of which was (until 1981) also the president of the Consistoire central (the main religious institution), sought to represent the Jews globally on the national scene.[18]

One should not understand the notion of a Jewish community in its medieval sense of *kahal*, a fully contained society with its own self-government (even if it depended, then, on a stronger power). The Jewish community within the framework of European democracy (and especially in France) is a symbolic one; that is not to say it is less real, but it is essentially founded on the reality of symbols. It is a voluntary association, which does not include all the Jews but only a part of them, and not always the same part. This community might achieve a state of permanence, if only a psychological and symbolic one. It will sponsor permanent Jewish institutions, but they do not involve all the Jews. The Jews come together only on specific occasions, and only at such moments can one speak of them as a "community," and these moments are not of long duration. Jewish community life, therefore, has two faces: that of the institutional community and also that of the emotional community. In such a condition, the Jewish community in the European democracies can be defined as a network of Jewish self-recognition, through which the Jews interact for mutual help,

solidarity, collective action, and memory. This network is connected with all the networks of the global society, of which the
Jews as citizens are members. The community is, therefore, not a
form of withdrawal from the condition of general citizenship but
an addition to it. Nevertheless, this new political category of a
citizen-community shattered the classical consensus of the norms
of Jewish citizenship in modern Europe, and especially in France,
with its strong tradition of Jacobinic centralism.

Because the community is dispersed through the larger society
(and this is a paradox), it does not have specifically religious
boundaries but more secular ones, and it needs a secular point of
reference. This point of reference was found in Zionism during the
Six Day War, when Jews went into the streets of France and made
public demonstrations of their identification with Israel. It was a
powerful, climactic moment, and Jewish community life in France
for many years drew from this event its legitimacy, authority, and
collective enthusiasm. Paradoxically, Zionism, a strong symbol of
the "Jewish nation," helped rebuild Jewish life in Europe,
wounded as it was by the Shoah, and thereby a European Jewish
identity. From a Jewish viewpoint, there was no contradiction in
maintaining Jewish citizenship in a democracy and in identifying
with the State of Israel, because that state was supposed to amend
the democratic idea in all its crises during the twentieth century.
Therefore, Israel symbolically strengthened Jewish continuity in
terms of democratic citizenship, which had failed to protect the
Jews from destruction.

But there was nevertheless a price to pay: the symbolic and
spiritual absence of the Jews in Europe. For Judaism was most
present in Europe only when its spirit was occupied with Israel.
For the Jews, is this strong attachment to Israel a real loss of
Europe? It is, in fact, the basic agreement on which political Zionism was built. Taking the Jews outside Europe geographically,
it became the European Jews' way to have a link with Europe,
which had rejected them. Identifying with a distant state, the Jews
asserted their presence in Europe. Nevertheless, the powerful
identification of contemporary European Jewry with the contem-

porary Jewish nation calls into question the historical consistency of European Judaism after the war.

This switch from a negative identity (the "people" revealed in the camps), which stemmed from the Shoah, to a positive one, which derived from Zionism (the "people" revealed in an independent state) was, in fact, in crisis at the end of the 1960s: continuity between Zionism and citizenship, the Shoah and Europe was broken. The break was part of a generational phenomenon. The baby-boomers' relationship to the Shoah played the most decisive role. This generation was now entering adulthood and discovering its own connection to the Shoah. Also, an unexpected encounter occurred between the new generation of North African Jews now in France and the native Ashkenazic generation. For the Sefardic Jews, the amazing discovery of the Shoah became a strong basis for their identification as Jews. It shattered the idealistic relation with European culture they had in North Africa and gave shape to their sense of trouble. This discovery (a generational phenomenon more than an ethnic one) coincided, indeed, with their coming to France and helped them rationalize their feelings of alienation as newcomers. From a sociological viewpoint, we can note that it was through such an identification that they could defend the weakened identity of their uprooted community as well as their collective identity. This Jewish identity was indeed original: it developed far from the home country in a multi-ethnic land, and it had a collective dimension. A majority of North African Jews were French citizens (especially the Algerian Jews, after 1870) or culturally French. They were newcomers but not typical "immigrants," and their condition was such that they felt alienated "at home." At the same time, in the 1960s, they were joined by their Ashkenazic counterparts, who engaged in revolutionary leftist militantism that was clearly motivated by the memory of the Shoah and a will to change human life for the better.

That spelled the end of the Orsay spirit. Three dates, all very close to one another, were decisive: 1962, which saw the huge immigration of North African Jews to France; 1967, the period of the Six Day War; 1968, the time of the student uprising. In practical terms, this period marked the beginning of the end of the "Colloque des Intellectuels Juifs," for many leading intellectuals (except Levinas) emigrated to Israel. And symbolically, the Six Day War demolished Orsay's basic assumptions about the dialectics of the universal and the particular. From now on, when the Jews sought to have the Jewish specificity of the Shoah be broadly "recognized," and when they argued that the State of Israel—that is to say, the revival of the Jewish nation—was the product of the Shoah, they aimed, in fact, to legitimize and justify their collective identity no longer on the basis of the universal but on that of the particular. On the other hand, when some sectors of Jewish opinion fought, later, against this discourse and insisted on the universal significance of the Jewish genocide, they were trying to retrieve their Jewish status as individuals, to define their identity as if Auschwitz had not occurred as a defining part of Jewish fate.

This evolution can also be explained by the general (morphological) evolution within Europe itself. Its process of unification generated a weakening of the states. Consequently, intermediate identities, like regional identities, were revived. We have here a notably paradoxical evolution: a European political universal is in the process of being constituted, but this process generates fragmentation and particularization. The "nations" are coming back very powerfully while the states are declining.

Against this background one can understand a new strategy of Jewish identity, the "memory strategy," which developed in the 1980s. On the one hand, this strategy tried to undertake a new globalization of Jewish fate at the European level, but on the other hand, it defined it as a particularistic, nonrational entity.

The 1980s: A Turning Point for European Judaism

The evolution of French and European Judaism during the 1980s shows a dissociation of the universal and the particular, Zionism and democracy, community and state—all of which the thought of the Orsay School attempted to keep together. We find herein a sure sign that the postwar period and its dialectical project have reached their endpoint.

During this period, the memory of the Shoah took another turn and with it the meaning of the community changed. The Shoah became progressively the center of Jewish and even public debate, but no longer according to Orsay's philosophical principles. Rather, a process of sacralization occurred, and rational perspectives fell back. As Karl Mannheim explains in his analysis of the process of symbolic transformation: the symbol became an emblem, a flag.[19] The taboo became a totem.

The Jews sought for the European recognition of the Jewish specificity of Auschwitz. They no longer felt morally obligated by the Shoah. Europe now had to be. This change of attitude might explain why the victimization of the Jews became for the Jews the new way to the universal, a lachrymose universal. The belated recognition of Jewish suffering by the gentiles became for many Jews more important than their own positive existence, which the elevation of Auschwitz to a place of centrality obliterated.

The "Carmel convent affair" (1984–1985) exemplifies this evolution. The eruption of this affair occurred in the only Jewish secular community in Europe, the Centre Communautaire Laïc Juif of Brussels and its journal *Regards*.[20] The center took the lead in shaping a European Jewish movement of public opinion. It is interesting to note that the representatives of religious Judaism felt touched by this affair only in a very distant way, except for ex-Great Rabbi of France Sirat's participation in the Jewish delegation that met with a European Episcopal delegation in Geneva.

The symbolism and emotions evoked by such an affair are rich in signification. Polish Christianity planned to mark the Auschwitz camp area with its own religious symbols and to create there a Carmel convent. The Jews passionately opposed this plan and demanded that in Auschwitz only silence was to reign. The conflict was clearly a symbolic one. Catholic Poles and Jews were fighting for the "ownership" of the memory of the Shoah, of a place which stands as the paradigm of the destruction of the Jews, of their rejection by enlightened Europe, the blind spot of the European consciousness. Moreover, Auschwitz represents a place in Eastern Europe where the Jewish condition was always a collective, non-individual one. The sacralization of this space by secular Jews is most interesting. Their claim that this area will be dedicated to silence (i.e., the unthinkable) generates a sort of transcendence, a sense of sacredness. And, indeed, the memory of the Jewish martyrdom is apprehended here as a form of transcendence. It becomes a cause of repeated invocation, of ritual and ceremony, rather than of historical thinking. This transcendence, interpreted in a particularistic way, takes the Shoah (grasped as a coerced withdrawal from the modern condition of Jewish individualism and as a paradigm of Jewish collective fate) out of history and sacralizes it, this even as a Jewish collective identity remains unthinkable in modern Europe.

The paradox is that this sacredness became the basis for a new Jewish secular identity. From the time of the rise of the Israeli political right, the identification with Israel and Zionism of this sizable circle of people became vexed, so much so that it attenuated its Zionist "civil religion." The "memory of the Shoah," specific to secular Judaism, is a sort of return to (a secular) religion and to a new collective identity. This memory became the criterion for the differentiation and distinctiveness of the Jews in Europe. In this respect, we should note the European dimension of the "Carmel convent affair" confrontation: Belgian and French Jews pitted themselves against Catholic Poles and the Vatican, culminating in a meeting in Geneva. In this affair there clearly appears a Jewish collective identification with its symbolic source in the Shoah. The Jewish need to maintain the sacredness of Auschwitz (and its signification as a place and not merely as a symbol) embodies the new dimension of this Jewish identity: the Shoah is no longer to be regarded as an opportunity for the development of new thinking for a universal mission of the Jews but as a source of silence, mystery, a nonrational thrust outside of history, and as something far away from the religious character and norms of Judaism.

As part of this strategy of memory, one finds an attempt to develop a kind of universalization of the Shoah: a "human rights Jewish strategy of memory." This strategy assumes that, inherited from the Shoah, there is a special Jewish claim to morality, which authorizes the Jews to intervene in universal world affairs, such as in Yugoslavia, Rwanda, and so on. This ambition is very problematic, for any morality stemming from the Shoah cannot be an automatic part of ethnic inheritance, if we are to speak truly of morality.

Parallel to the separation of the universal and the particular, the ethnic, historical dimension of Jewishness (the "Jewish people") was separated from its religious, Judaic dimension. Their integration was the very basis for postwar French Jewish renewal. Now, in the 1980s, the two were set apart. Understandably, the "Jewish community" entered a crisis. Because it is far from sure that there always is in France a Jewish identity based on communal definition, the 1980s will perhaps be regarded in the future as marking the end of the Jewish community. There is, indeed, observable today a process of fragmentation, which can be understood as a conflict of two opposite sources of sacredness.

In addition to a secular Jewish identity based on a strategy of memory, we also find a new turn to religious affirmation, which can be defined as a "neo-Judaic strategy of Jewish identity." This development is part of a general development in the Jewish world, involving a return (hazara biteshuva) to Judaism, very much influenced by the ultra-orthodox stream of Judaism (no longer consistorial). It can be called neo-Judaic because this version of Judaism is very different from postwar Judaism. It consists of critics of modernity, whose reassertion of Judaism no longer opens on to the outside world and to new forms of intellectual creativity but stresses instead a sealing off of the Jewish community. One no longer finds here an impetus to generate a renewal of Jewish thinking, to seek philosophical ways to embrace the universal, or to feel responsible for mankind in general. This neoreligious affirmation shows no interest in Europe. Nor is it devoted especially to Israel, or, needless to say, to a broader sense of the Jewish community.

Rather, these neo-Judaists create sectarian communities that wish to live apart from a global Jewish community. As such, they are more and more peripheral to the broader life of the Jews.

In conclusion, it appears that the European process tends to produce consequences for the Jews that resemble those of medieval Catholicism. The Jewish "letter" might now be seen as the Jewish suffering "body," with Auschwitz the critical ingredient in a recomposition of European identity and the object of a newly emergent global discourse. The unthinkability of Auschwitz (which is no longer "Auschwitz" but the "Shoah," a Hebrew word that insists on the mystery of the event and removes it from thought and reason) is interpreted within the larger problematics that this essay tries to develop. Two strategies emerge within this general framework: the memory strategy, which demands silence with respect to Auschwitz, and the strategy of neo-Judaism, which takes no interest in Auschwitz. Both will result in a narrowly ethnic, closed definition of Jewish existence if they do not lift their sights to the level of the universal. They will lead to a minority-oriented Jewishness, a sort of neo-Bundist identity, but one without Yiddish and without territory, or a neoyeshivic Judaism lacking in intellectual genius, in which Jews will not be able to enjoy the rights stemming from a new (and still vague) European power.

This development of newly emergent Jewish strategies of identity can be interpreted against the larger background of efforts at European unification. The latter might indeed prompt a radical change for the Jews and be a turning point in their more than one-hundred-year-old struggle for identification. There will be structural and morphological consequences to such a process, which will suspend the political and imaginary institution of the frontier and will produce a decompartmentalization of modern national identities. Parallel to this trend toward a mass identity of Europe, a mass approach to Jewish identity occurs with respect to the strategy of memory and the neo-Judaic strategy. Both contribute to a redefinition of Jewish identity at a European level.

In the light of European evolution and its consequences, we might ask ourselves if Europe is forging anew its "catholicity," its universality. If so, it would appear that this catholicity is consciously being asserted in religious terms. These terms are not part of the central discourse of efforts to forge a united Europe, but nonetheless they are among the most powerful discourses to be heard today. Pope John Paul II explicitly defines his policy as a new evangelization of Europe. This project draws its authority from his policy regarding Eastern Europe, where especially in Poland the Church is regarded as a very important cause of the collapse of the communist regimes. If Europe is indeed rebuilding its catholicity, its imperial universality, will the Jews once again be regarded by Europeans as a particularist, closed, and alien entity? The Vatican's recent strong interest in the Jews and in the Shoah, as well as the public debates in some European states on these themes, are interesting indications of possible developments ahead, which could see the conjunction of a Jewish and a European evolution.

NOTES

1. I shall follow the Durkheimian approach of social morphology and, therefore, I shall try to analyze the existence of the social group on the basis of its formal, political, as well as demographic substrata and of its correlations with the structures of imagination.

2. See Shmuel Trigano, *La république et les Juifs* (Paris: Presses d'Aujourd'hui, 1982); idem, "The French Revolution and the Jews," *Modern Judaism* (October 1990); idem, "From Individual to Collectivity: the Rebirth of the 'Jewish Nation' in France," in *The Jews in Modern France,* ed. F. Malino and B. Wasserstein (Hanover, NH: University Press of New England, 1985).

3. See Shmuel Trigano, "Les Juifs comme peuple à l'épreuve de la Shoa" in *Penser Auschwitz,* special issue of *Pardès* 9–10 (1989), ed. Shmuel Trigano.

4. Published in 1670, see Part 5.

5. See Rémy Brague, *Europe, la voie romaine* (Paris: Centurion, 1992).

6. Saint Paul (Rom. 2:29): "This is the Jew . . . according to the spirit and not the letter"; (Rom. 9:8): "The children according to the flesh are not God's children." This problematic was in fact the invention of the first Jewish philosopher, Philo of Alexandria (1st century), and gave conceptual structure to the Paulinian discourse and to the Church Fathers' theology. This discourse helped distinguish the new European entity from the Greco-Roman world.

7. See Shmuel Trigano, "L'apostasie du Messie, le paradoxe de l'Emancipation," *Esprit* 5 (May 1979).

8. The appearance of the nation-state had serious repercussions for the morphological conditions of Jewish life. During the Ancien Regime, the Jews were considered strangers in all the European states, as one people scattered everywhere and transcending the different kingdoms, who enjoyed an administrative semi-autonomy and constituted for itself a quasi-complete society, even if, in the global outside system, the "Jewish nation" was counted among the guilds (corporate bodies). With the French revolution and the rise of the nation-state, this entity became an impossible one because of the new order of citizenship and also because as many national Judaisms as European states began to appear. The Jews, then, had to renounce their trans-state identity in order to fit into the framework of national identity, which gave them their citizenship. That is why the advent of the nation-state indicates the end of a European Judaism as a global entity. This is especially the case in Western Europe. In the East, it was more difficult to build the nation-state, owing to the demographic divisions of the peoples. The Jews produced in Eastern Europe an identity of their own and retained their attributes as a people within states in which they always had difficulty finding a recognized and secure place. The Polish case is a good example.

9. See "L'imprononçable, l'écriture nomade," *Change,* 22 (February 1975).

10. See Jean Pierre Faye, *Migrations du récit sur le peuple juif* (Paris: Belfond, 1974).

11. See Theodor Herzl, *The State of the Jews,* introduction.

12. See Edmond Fleg, *Le chant nouveau* (Paris: Ed. des E.I.F., 1945; 2nd ed. Albin Michel, 1972).

13. See André Neher, *L'existence juive, solitude et affrontement* (Paris: Seuil, 1962) 259.

14. See Emmanuel Levinas, *Difficile liberté* (Paris: Albin Michel, 1963) 223.

15. See Eliane Amado Lévy-Valensi, *Les niveaux de l'être. La connaissance et le mal* (Paris: P.U.F.) 595.

16. See Ioav Tiar, "Crise de la diaspora française," *Esprit* 9 M 1667 (September 1980): 65.

17. See Emmanuel Lévinas, "Vieux comme le monde," in *Quatre lectures talmudiques* (Paris: Ed. de Minuit, 1968) 181–86.

18. See Shmuel Trigano, "Le concept de communauté comme catégorie de définition du judaisme français," *Archives Européennes de Sociologie* 1 (1994), partial English translation in J. Webber, ed., *Jewish Identities in the New Europe* (London: Littman Library of Jewish Civilization, 1994).

19. See Karl Mannheim, *Ideology and Utopia* (New York: HBJ Books, 1985).

20. See "Dossiers Juifs et chrétiens après Auschwitz," *Regards* (17 October–12 November 1986).

CONTRIBUTORS

Gulie Ne'eman Arad teaches history at Tel Aviv University and is coeditor of the journal *History & Memory*. Her forthcoming book on the response of the American Jewish leadership to the Nazi regime will be published by Indiana University Press.

Ilan Avisar teaches film studies at Tel Aviv University. He is the author of *Screening the Holocaust; Film Art* (in Hebrew); and *Visions of Israel* (forthcoming), among other works.

Michael André Bernstein teaches English and Comparative Literature at the University of California, Berkeley. His recent books include *Bitter Carnival: Ressentiment and the Abject Hero* and *Foregone Conclusions: Against Apocalyptic History*. He is currently completing a novel entitled *Progressive Lenses*.

Elisabeth Domansky teaches modern German history at Indiana University, Bloomington. She is currently completing a book entitled *Class Struggle, Science, and Modernity: The German Metalworkers' Union and the Formation of Bourgeois Society in Germany, 1891–1914*. Her work-in-progress includes the study (coauthored with Jutta de Jong), *"Und dann ging alles den Bach 'runter": Wülfrather erinnern sich an die Kriegs- und Nachkriegsjahre* ["And then everything went down the drain": Citizens of Wülfrath remember the war and postwar years].

Saul Friedlander is Professor of History at Tel Aviv University and at the University of California, Los Angeles. He is the author of numerous books, including *When Memory Comes; Reflections of Nazism: An Essay on Kitsch and Death*; and *Memory, History, and the Extermination of the Jews of Europe*. He edited *Probing the Limits of Representation: Nazism and the "Final Solution"* and is senior editor of the journal *History & Memory*. His most recent book is *Nazi Germany and the Jews*, vol. 1: *The Years of Persecution, 1933–1939*.

Evyatar Friesel serves currently as Israel State Archivist. He is Professor Emeritus of Jewish History at the Hebrew University of Jerusalem. Among his publications are *Atlas of Modern Jewish History* and *The Days and the Seasons: Memoirs*.

Michael L. Morgan is Professor of Philosophy and Jewish Studies at Indiana University. He is the editor of *The Jewish Thought of Emil Fackenheim* and of *Jewish Philosophers and Jewish Philosophy*; and he is the author of *Dilemmas in Modern Jewish Thought* and *To Seize Memory: Post-Holocaust Jewish Thought in Its Historical Context* (forthcoming).

Jehuda Reinharz, President of Brandeis University and Richard Koret Professor of Modern Jewish History, is the author, coauthor, or editor of twenty books, including the definitive biography of Chaim Weizmann, of which two volumes have been published by Oxford University Press. In 1990, he was the first recipient of the President of Israel Prize, awarded annually by the Israeli Knesset for outstanding scholarly work in the field of Zionism.

Alvin H. Rosenfeld is Professor of English and Director of the Robert A. and Sandra S. Borns Jewish Studies Program at Indiana University. He is the author and editor of numerous books, including *Confronting the Holocaust: The Impact of Elie Wiesel*; *A Double Dying: Reflections on Holocaust Literature*; and *Imagining Hitler*.

Anita Shapira, Ruben Merenfeld Professor for the Study of Zionism at Tel Aviv University, has published numerous books and articles on the history of Zionism and the Jewish community in Palestine. Her most notable publications in English are *Berl: The Biography of a Socialist Zionist, Berl Katznelson, 1887-1944*, and *Land and Power: The Zionist Resort to Force, 1881-1948*.

Frank Stern teaches German history at Ben-Gurion University of the Negev in Beer-Sheva. His publications include books and articles on German postwar history, problems of anti-Semitism, German-Jewish topics, and German cinema. His book *Jews in the Minds of Germans: The Ambiguous Shadow of the Past in Film and Literature* will be published by Indiana University Press.

Shmuel Trigano is Professor of Sociology at the University of Paris–Nanterre; he is founding director of the *Collège des Etudes Juives* at the *Alliance Israélite Universelle* and co-founding director of *Pardès*, a journal of Jewish studies. He is the author of numerous books on Jewish thought, history, and the sociology of Judaism, including *La demeure oubliée, Philosophie de la Loi*. He edited the four-volume *La société juive à travers les âges*.

Annette Wieviorka is a research director at the Centre National de la Recherche Scientifique and editor of the journal *Archives Juives*. She has published several books and articles on the Second World War, on the Holocaust, and on how they are remembered in French culture, including *Les livres du souvenir, mémoriaux juifs de Pologne*; *Déportation et génocide entre la mémoire et l'oubli*; *Passant souviens-toi, les lieux du souvenir de la Seconde Guerre mondiale en France*; and *Le procès de Nuremberg*.

INDEX